From With Babies and Banners: Story of the Women's Emergency Brigade. Courtesy The Archives of Labor and Urban Affairs, Wayne State University.

AMERICAN FAMILY LIFE FILMS

Judith Trojan

The Scarecrow Press, Inc.
Metuchen, N.J., & London
1981

HQ10
.T73

Library of Congress Cataloging in Publication Data

Trojan, Judith.
    American family life films.

    Bibliography: p.
    Includes indexes.
    1. Family life education--Film catalogs.
2. Family--United States--Film catalogs. I. Title.
HQ10.T73   016.3068'0973   80-14748
ISBN 0-8108-1313-0

For my grandparents,

Hattie and Paul Brockel

ACKNOWLEDGMENTS

My very special thanks go to Eleanor Trojan for her editing skill and her patience and support as a mother and a friend.

I am especially grateful to Brian Dana Camp for his memory and editorial assist. Thanks also to Maryann Chach, and to Carol A. Emmens for her advice.

Finally, I am indebted to my longtime employer, the Educational Film Library Association, whose resources have been of enormous help in the preparation of this book; and to the numerous filmmakers, producers, and distributors listed herein for their time, photographs, and, of course, their films.

TABLE OF CONTENTS

ABOUT THIS BOOK

In the course of my film evaluation and reference work at the Educational Film Library Association (EFLA) over these past several years, as well as my free-lance writing career, I have noted a decided increase in the production of and demand for 16mm films on various aspects of American family life. The recent production trend has mirrored the concerns of American society, evolving from cinema vérité childbirth films to those on funky alternative life-styles and serious ethnic concerns. Currently, need is great for films on the effects of separation and divorce, as well as films on family counseling, problem and teen pregnancies, breastfeeding, parent effectiveness training, single parenting and stepparenting, fatherhood, runaways, and crime (i.e., wife beating and child abuse). Other important areas of concern to families continue to be: health and child care, nutrition, home and money management, mental illness, death and dying, women's studies, and all aspects of aging and child development. And young filmmakers will eternally focus on their grandparents in an effort to explore their roots and reexamine their ethnic heritage.

My goal in this book is to provide a single, comprehensive resource of easily accessible 16mm films that cover the broad spectrum of family dynamics in America, past and present. My target audience encompasses social workers, family and guidance counselors and therapists, medical personnel, community programmers, librarians, and teachers on the primary through college and adult school levels. The book is, in other words, for all those whose job it is to deal effectively with the family condition.

On the whole, I have limited my entries to films produced within the United States and claiming an American point of view and setting. Although a few specially selected Canadian and internationally produced films are included--because they touch on universal themes in an extraordinary way, e.g., Caroline Leaf's THE STREET and Jan Kadar's LIES MY FATHER TOLD ME--this book is, first and foremost, a book about American sensibilities.

Entries are restricted to those available on 16mm, with one

exception. At this writing, AN AMERICAN FAMILY is available
exclusively on videotape. This series is of such monumental importance that its omission would be inexcusable. Many of the major
distributors whose films are annotated in this book will, however,
supply 16mm-to-video transfers. Finally, all films are sound, unless otherwise noted (sil.).

Annotations were culled from my own extensive screenings or
from producers' and distributors' notes or catalog descriptions. My
research covered films released through late 1978. If secondary resources (distributors' catalogs) were used to determine a content
synopsis for a film, all laudatory comments were excised, leaving
only a concise and hopefully clear feeling for the general theme of
the film. Annotations are, therefore, non-evaluative.

I divided my film listings into two sections. The major por-
tion of the book encompasses Shorts and Documentaries, i.e., all
short dramatic films, plus short animations and experimental and
educational films. Short and feature-length documentaries are a
prime focus, as well. The second division, Selected Dramatic Features, contains only those dramatic films of feature length (general-
ly over 59 minutes) originally produced for screening in motion picture theaters or on TV as dramatic specials. Various helpful indexes complete the book and are discussed below.

Subject Index

The Subject Index should be one of a programmer's most valuable tools. All shorts and documentaries are indexed here; most
films are noted under two or more subject headings.

Shorts and Documentaries

These films are listed alphabetically by title. Each film entry carries full bibliographic information--title, running time, color
or black-and-white, production and/or release year, name of director and/or producer, name of primary distributor (sales and/or
rental source), and age level (as recommended by producer or distributor). Omission of age level simply means it is unknown and
indeterminable. Where applicable, annotations also contain a cast
list, series title, some film-festival awards, and whether the entry
is a training film, documentary, animation, dramatic film, etc.
Due to the enormous number of shorts and documentaries annotated,
a festival award search for each of these titles would have been impossible. Festival awards are, therefore, incomplete; they were
pulled from producers' and distributors' promotional material and
catalogs, as well as American Film Festival files to which I, as a
staff member, had access.

Major Series Titles are also cross-indexed in this section,
since many series are often more widely known than individual film
titles, e.g., ABC Afterschool Specials.

Selected Dramatic Features

Films are listed alphabetically by title, with a very brief descriptive annotation and a programming note categorizing the broad subject focus of each film (Dra=Drama, Bio=Biography, Com=Comedy). See the Abbreviations Key below for further subjects.

Bibliographic material covers: title, running time, color or black-and-white, year, director, cast list, and one or more rental sources. I refrained from including films from the Silent period, with the exception of THE JAZZ SINGER (1927), which straddles both the Silent and Sound periods. Silent family life films could easily fill another whole book.

Selected Resources

Since this text is not a print resource, I have kept my bibliography short and current. It should be sufficient for background material on the genre and enable you to plan a viable program. For your further convenience, I have annotated all entries and divided them into: Articles (about shorts, documentaries, dramatic features, and TV); Books & Pamphlets (supplemental filmographies, screenplays, cinema histories, some outstanding study guides); Media Distributors & Publishers (a handful of established firms that offer reliable service and quality family life products); and Periodicals.

Distributor Address List

This is an address index to sales and/or rental sources for all films listed in the book. Most sales sources also rent prints. If not, they usually can direct you to the nearest rental library.

Due to the relatively low sales/rental volume in the 16mm business, companies frequently, and without much notice, move; drop titles; revise old titles; and, of course, add new titles to their collections. If you are unable to reach a distributor at an address listed herein, the company or individual may have moved, gone out of business, merged with another, or undergone a name change. Many large public libraries have extensive, contemporary film collections; if you're lucky, they may have a print of the film you require for the "price" of your library card. In addition, large universities have low-cost rental collections (some for sale, too). See the Educational Film Locator, published in 1978 by R. R. Bowker Company, for a comprehensive guide to university and college rental collections.

ABBREVIATIONS USED IN THIS BOOK

p.	production year	Com	Comedy
r.	release year	Dra	Drama
n. d.	no date	Doc-Dra	Docu-Drama
Vt	videotape	Fan	Fantasy
b&w	black and white	His	History/Historical
min.	minutes	Hor	Horror
sec.	seconds	Mus	Musical
sil.	silent	Mys	Mystery
sou.	sound	Sat	Satire
Bio	Biography	Wes	Western

AUDIENCE LEVEL KEY

PS	Preschool, ages 3-4
K	Kindergarten, ages 4-5
E	Elementary, grades 1-3, ages 6-8
I	Intermediate, grades 4-6, ages 9-11
J	Junior High, grades 7-9, ages 12-14
S	Senior High, grades 10-12, ages 15-18
C	College
A	General Adult
Prof	Professional Adult Audiences, e. g. , teachers, psychologists, social workers, medical personnel, law enforcement personnel, etc.

SAMPLE ENTRY

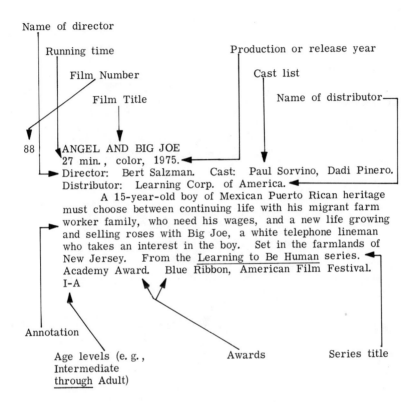

Name of director

Running time

Film Number

Film Title

Production or release year

Cast list

Name of distributor—

88 ANGEL AND BIG JOE
27 min., color, 1975.
Director: Bert Salzman. Cast: Paul Sorvino, Dadi Pinero.
Distributor: Learning Corp. of America.
A 15-year-old boy of Mexican Puerto Rican heritage
must choose between continuing life with his migrant farm
worker family, who need his wages, and a new life growing
and selling roses with Big Joe, a white telephone lineman
who takes an interest in the boy. Set in the farmlands of
New Jersey. From the Learning to Be Human series.
Academy Award. Blue Ribbon, American Film Festival.
I-A

Annotation

Age levels (e. g.,
Intermediate
through Adult)

Awards

Series title

INTRODUCTION

TV DAZE   I loved Lucy. Unlike Mama, Harriet Nelson, and
            Margaret Anderson, wife to the father who always
knew best, Lucy Ricardo never tied her apron strings. As a
housewife, she was rarely content or a success in the traditional sense of the term. She did try. But her efficient, happy-
homemaker schemes tested husband Ricky's Latin patience. I
prefer to think of her 6-foot-long loaf of home-baked bread as
an over-achievement rather than a colossal misuse of yeast.

        Lucy's marriage to Ricky was constantly put to the test.
Her "part-time jobs" and unceasing quest for her own show-business
career drove a wedge between the couple. Her tight friendship with
dowdy housewife Ethel Mertz was possible only because Ethel was a
closet vaudevillian, who also had nerve to burn.

        Though I never doubted Lucy's love for Ricky, Little Ricky,
and her surrogate family--Ethel and Fred Mertz--I knew that Lucy
would never rest till she tried (and she tried everything) to break
out of her housewife/mother role for at least a few minutes a day.
It's interesting to note, in retrospect, that Lucy never felt secure
vicariously sharing Ricky's show-business limelight. She wanted
some of that spotlight on her own head.

        Not so for Harriet, Margaret, and Mama; they were wives
and mothers, first and last. Nurturing, selfless images who were
always there to fulfill others' dreams and needs, they wielded power
from their kitchens. Margaret, Mama, and Harriet were pristine,
comforting characters who rarely, if ever, rocked the boat. More
often than not, it was their unassuming good sense that kept the ship
afloat. I Remember Mama (1949-57), The Adventures of Ozzie and
Harriet (1952-66), and Father Knows Best (1954-62) were all popular shows in TV's seminal years. They were the first of their
kind--and therefore immeasurably influential. They must have been
a hard act for real-life wives, husbands, and parents to follow.
As for me--a kid born in 1947 and growing up with TV--I only
wanted to emulate Lucy. She had dreams.

Following TV's first crop of nuclear-family fantasies came the single-parent syndrome--a wave of successful and equally unreal family shows dealing with life in one-parent and blended families, e. g. , Bachelor Father (1957-62), The Andy Griffith Show (1960-68), My Three Sons (1960-72), Family Affair (1966-71), The Courtship of Eddie's Father (1969-72), The Brady Bunch (1969-74), The Partridge Family (1970-74), and Westerns like The Rifleman (1958-63), Bonanza (1959-73), and The Big Valley (1965-69). Even Owen Marshall: Counselor at Law (1971-74) was a widower with a daughter.

The Seventies managed to rise above this sea of dross thanks to the contributions of two men, with two quite different talents. The first--writer/producer/director Norman Lear--brought the "issue-oriented" sit-com into American living rooms. And the second--writer Alex Haley--brought his Roots.

In the controversial series All in the Family (prem. 1971), two of its spinoffs--Maude (prem. 1972) and The Jeffersons (prem. 1975)--and the syndicated late-night soap spoof, Mary Hartman, Mary Hartman (prem. 1976), Lear and his team covered a wide range of topics previously untouched and untouchable on network TV, e. g. , racial prejudice, miscegenation, mental illness, the Vietnam War, aging, death and dying, pregnancy, abortion, childbirth, rape, women's rights, menopause, impotence, sexuality, adultery, divorce, alcoholism, and retirement. To present these issues in a humorous way was even more of a risk. The Bunkers, especially, grew as the years wore on to be much more than a blue-collar family with a red-neck at the helm and a dingbat in the kitchen. The dizzy wife blossomed into a sensitive, honest, aware woman. And the rigid husband was forced to swallow his pride on more than one occasion and consider a more liberal view. This was progress, no matter how heavy-handed the humor. Today, Archie and Edith Bunker's favorite chairs sit enshrined in the Smithsonian Institution in Washton, D. C.

With this progress, however, came a regressive, highly rated group of TV series devoted to less-complicated eras. Happy Days (prem. 1974) celebrated family life of the Fifties, without the complications of McCarthy and the Cold War. Main concerns centered around dating, buddies, burgers, and The Fonz. The phenomenal success of The Waltons (prem. 1972) and Little House on the Prairie (prem. 1974) proved that people were still comforted by sentimental notions of the past.

One dramatic series--Family, which was produced by Aaron Spelling and Leonard Goldberg and premiered in 1976--did attempt to satisfy real-life concerns. The Lawrences, an upper-middle-class family, seemed to have everything: looks, brains, goals, and money. But unlike the Andersons of old, the Lawrences had to do a lot of "homework" to sustain their tranquil California existence. Psychological crises arose at every turn for the Lawrences: Family segments usually revolved around two family members' concurrent and not-necessarily-related personal "changes. "

Most segments were open-ended. Happy, happy endings were rare; but even the adolescent Lawrences possessed an unusual sensitivity to the needs of others. Often, the youngsters displayed a therapeutic savvy that real-life adults take many years of psychotherapy to acquire. In fact, all of the Lawrences seemed to come by this psychoanalytic talent naturally.

While the Lawrences, like the Andersons, still made most American families look bleak in comparison, their interpersonal caring and sharing was worth emulating, and their personal and family crises, although contrived, were especially contemporary and identifiable. A sophisticated soap? Yes. Positive role models for white, middle-class American families? Yes; and why not?

Black and other minority families were not so lucky. They could, however, feel pride in Alex Haley's autobiographical miniseries Roots, based directly on his best-selling book and viewed by an unprecedented 130,000,000 viewers in January 1977. Roots and its fine sequel, Roots: The Next Generations, telecast in February 1979, presented an enormously moving picture of many generations of one Afro-American family and their struggle to sustain memory of their African heritage as well as gain acceptance as respected members of the American middle-class community.

Although the original Roots highlighted sensational aspects of the fight up from slavery, Roots II focused more directly on the familial triumphs--the courtships, marriages, births, and deaths that distinguished and, at the same time, universalized the Haley clan. Showcasing a company of brilliantly talented young actors, Roots II underscored the moral courage that led to the family's success in business, higher education, and life in general. So dignified a picture of black family life could and should lay the groundwork and create the demand for more of the same.

While too numerous to mention here, made-for-TV dramatic specials have in many cases been kind to family life. Many are now available on 16mm and can be found listed in the Selected Dramatic Features section of this book. But there are a handful that should be singled out for special mention. ABC-TV's anthology of daytime dramas--Afterschool Specials--were the first to handle such themes as separation and divorce, alcoholic parents, adoption, emotional problems, handicapped peers, etc. Geared for adolescent audiences, these values dramas were special because they dealt seriously with adolescent life crises.

Five made-for-TV dramatic features come to mind, among a long list, as ones that dealt sensitively with complex family issues: That Certain Summer (1972)--father-son relationship/homosexual father; Sybil (1976)--child abuse/mental illness; The Gathering (1977) --dying parent/husband-wife and father-son estrangement; A Question of Love (1978)--child custody/Lesbian mothers; and Friendly Fire (1979)--wartime death of son/parental grief and political activism. Unfortunately, these five films are not yet available on 16mm.

The best and worst examples of TV's documentary coverage of the American family are for the most part available on 16mm. Sources for these can be found in the <u>Shorts and Documentaries</u> section of this book.   Two documentary achievements are worth noting here.   The 1973 PBS cinema vérité portrait of <u>An American Family</u> --the Louds of California--did much to question the ethics of such "live-in" exposé profiles, while revealing an upper-middle-class family's bankrupt value system.   Twelve hours with this family were aired over a three-month period.   The notoriety brought about by this documentary wrought many changes in the Loud household--one of which was divorce.

In contrast, in January 1979 a standard-format, three-hour NBC marathon documentary--<u>The American Family: An Endangered Species?</u>--visited with traditional, alternative, and troubled American families to examine the present and predict the future of the American family unit.   Comments by various "experts" slowed the pace a bit, but the profile vignettes opened up the pain and the pleasures of family and alternative group living in America today.

All-in-all, it seems like a forward-looking time to be a family in videoland.   The seeds sown in the Seventies will have to be watered in the Eighties by new Lears and Haleys if a fresh crop of innovative family life programs are to grow.

HOLLYWOOD HEARTHS   As the lengthy list of <u>Selected Dramatic Features</u> near the back of this book reveals, family life has always been a big ticket at the box office. Even Public Enemy No. 1 had a sweet-faced mom who believed in her sonny boy till the last shootout.   Every decade has had its share of landmark films, and many of these landmarks focused in major ways on family life.   The Thirties opened with THE CHAMP (1931) and closed with GONE WITH THE WIND (1939), but not before giving us such highly regarded family films as OUR DAILY BREAD (1934), IMITATION OF LIFE (1934), and ALICE ADAMS (1935).

The Forties were packed with important family life films, from the mighty--THE BEST YEARS OF OUR LIVES (1946), THE GRAPES OF WRATH (1940), and THE MAGNIFICENT AMBERSONS (1942)--to the endearing MEET ME IN ST. LOUIS (1944), A TREE GROWS IN BROOKLYN (1945), and I REMEMBER MAMA (1948). Bette Davis won the family fortune in THE LITTLE FOXES (1941); Tracy won Hepburn in WOMAN OF THE YEAR (1942); and Joan Crawford won an Academy Award for MILDRED PIERCE (1945), as an abused mother.

Heavyweight dramatic and literary adaptations filled the Fifties--A STREETCAR NAMED DESIRE (1951), THE COUNTRY GIRL (1954), EAST OF EDEN (1955), GIANT (1956), and CAT ON A HOT TIN ROOF (1958).   There were some fine Westerns-- SHANE (1953) and THE SEARCHERS (1956); a pro-union labor drama --SALT OF THE EARTH (1954); and the Academy Award-winning Bronx drama--MARTY (1955).

The Sixties flirted with controversial racial issues--A RAISIN IN THE SUN (1961); TO KILL A MOCKINGBIRD (1963); ONE PO- TATO, TWO POTATO (1964); NOTHING BUT A MAN (1964); GUESS WHO'S COMING TO DINNER? (1967), and with "open marriage" [sic]--BOB & CAROL & TED & ALICE (1969) and WHO'S AFRAID OF VIRGINIA WOOLF? (1966).   Paul Newman directed his wife, actress Joanne Woodward, in a noteworthy study of a suffocating mother/daughter relationship, RACHEL, RACHEL (1968).   And actor Paul Newman had problems of his own with his celluloid father in HUD (1963).

The Seventies gave serious space to much that ails American family life, beginning in 1970 with such effective but dissimilar "men's films" as: JOE, HUSBANDS, and I NEVER SANG FOR MY FATHER.   There were top-notch ethnic studies--THE EMIGRANTS (1972), THE NEW LAND (1973), THE GODFATHER (1972, 1974), HESTER STREET (1975), and BLOODBROTHERS (1978).   A new and welcome group of films examined women's pain and conflicts--ALICE DOESN'T LIVE HERE ANYMORE (1974), A WOMAN UNDER THE IN- FLUENCE (1974), THE TURNING POINT (1977), and AN UNMAR- RIED WOMAN (1978).   COMING HOME (1978) chronicled the effects of the Vietnam War on a marriage.   And Robert Altman's epic A WEDDING (1978) and Woody Allen's unsmiling INTERIORS (1978) closed the decade with some food for thought.

I have tried in this introduction to highlight just a few of the many dramatic images of American family life parlayed by TV and feature films throughout the years.   It's important to realize how far we've come.   It's more important to recognize how far we've still got to go in order for art not merely to reflect but truly en- hance American family life by its example.

Judith Trojan
May 1979

All Shorts and Documentaries are indexed here. The number following each film title is the entry number, not the page number.

ABORTION

ADOLESCENCE

(see also COURTSHIP AND ENGAGEMENT; JUVENILE DE-
    LINQUENCY; PARENT-CHILD; SEX EDUCATION)

ADOLESCENCE, cont.

ADOPTION AND FOSTER CARE

ALCOHOLISM AND DRUG DEPENDENCE

THE AMISH

ARTISTS AND ARTISANS

AUTHORS

AUTISM

BABYSITTING

BATTERED SPOUSES

BLACK STUDIES

BREASTFEEDING

BREASTFEEDING, cont.

CAJUNS

CHILD ABUSE AND NEGLECT

CHILD CARE

(see also   ADOPTION AND FOSTER CARE; BABYSITTING;
  BREASTFEEDING; CHILD ABUSE AND NEGLECT; PARENT-
  CHILD; SINGLE-PARENT FAMILIES; STEPPARENTING)

CHILD DEVELOPMENT

  (see also ADOLESCENCE; AUTISM; CHILDBIRTH; CHILDHOOD;
    THE HANDICAPPED; PARENT-CHILD; PSYCHOLOGY AND
    PSYCHIATRY; SEX EDUCATION)

CHILD DEVELOPMENT, cont.

CHILDBIRTH

(see also   PREGNANCY)

CHILDHOOD

(see also   CHILD DEVELOPMENT)

CHINESE AMERICANS

COMMUNITY AND SOCIAL SERVICES

(see also   SOCIAL ISSUES)

CONSUMER EDUCATION

COURTSHIP AND ENGAGEMENT

(see also MARRIAGE)

CROSS CULTURAL STUDIES

DEATH AND DYING

EDUCATION

(see also TEACHER EDUCATION)

EDUCATION, cont.

ESKIMOS

ETHNIC STUDIES

(see also   THE AMISH; BLACK STUDIES; CAJUNS; CHINESE
AMERICANS; ESKIMOS; GREEK AMERICANS; HAWAIIANS;
HUNGARIAN AMERICANS; IRISH AMERICANS; ITALIAN AMERI-
CANS; JAPANESE AMERICANS; JEWISH AMERICANS; KOREAN
AMERICANS; LITHUANIAN AMERICANS; MEXICAN AMERI-
CANS; NATIVE INDIAN AMERICANS; POLISH AMERICANS;
PUERTO RICANS; SERBIAN AMERICANS; SWEDISH AMERI-
CANS; VIETNAMESE AMERICANS)

FAMILY ADVENTURES

FILM CLASSICS

GRANDPARENTS

GRANDPARENTS, cont.

GREEK AMERICANS

THE HANDICAPPED

(see also   AUTISM)

HAWAIIANS

HEALTH AND MEDICINE

(see also ABORTION; ALCOHOLISM AND DRUG DEPENDENCE;
CHILDBIRTH; DEATH AND DYING; THE HANDICAPPED; NU-
TRITION; PREGNANCY; PSYCHOLOGY AND PSYCHIATRY)

HEALTH AND MEDICINE, cont.

HISTORY, U.S.

(see also ETHNIC STUDIES)

HISTORY, U.S., cont.

HOME ECONOMICS

(see also BABYSITTING; CHILD CARE; CONSUMER EDUCATION;
    NUTRITION)

HOUSING

HUMOR AND SATIRE

HUNGARIAN AMERICANS

1 American Family Life Films

IRISH AMERICANS

ITALIAN AMERICANS

JAPANESE AMERICANS

JEWISH AMERICANS

JUVENILE DELINQUENCY

LITERATURE, cont.

LITHUANIAN AMERICANS

MARRIAGE

(see also BATTERED SPOUSES; CHILDBIRTH; COURTSHIP AND
  ENGAGEMENT; SEPARATION AND DIVORCE; SEX ROLES)

MEN'S STUDIES

(see also CHILDBIRTH; SEX ROLES)

MEXICAN AMERICANS

NATIVE INDIAN AMERICANS

NUTRITION

(see also   BREASTFEEDING)

PARENT-CHILD

PERFORMING ARTS

PETS

Animal Partners   91
Baby Rabbit   114
Big Henry and the Polka Dot Kid   150
The Case of the Elevator Duck   226
The Escape of a One-Ton Pet   427
The Family Chooses a Pet   463
Herbert's Babies   642
Horses--To Care Is to Love   666
I Don't Want to Sell Babe   688
J. T.   758
Lost Puppy   853
Love and Duty: Which Comes First?   856
My Turtle Died Today   995
One Special Dog   1063

PHYSICAL FITNESS

(see also SPORTS)

Be Fit and Live   132
Big Town   151
Nine Months in Motion   1022
Superjock   1339

POLICE AND LAW ENFORCEMENT

(see also JUVENILE DELINQUENCY; PRISONS)

A Call for Help   208
Child Abuse   244
Child Molesters: Facts and Fiction   251
Cops   317
Corpus Delicti--Homicide   318
Crime and the Criminal   323
Death Notification   350
Domestic Disturbance Calls   387
Domestic Disturbances   388
Gaucho   559
The Georges of New York City   563
Investigating Cases of Child Abuse and Neglect   741
The Medical Witness   912
Mrs. Cop   939
My Dad's a Cop   981
The New Police--Family Crisis Intervention   1015
Police Marriage Film I: Husband/Wife Personal Issues   1126
Police Marriage Film II: The Policeman's Family   1127
Police Marriage Film III: Social Issues; The Family in the Com-
    munity   1128
Presenting the Case   1141

PROFILES, cont.

PSYCHOLOGY AND PSYCHIATRY

(see also ALCOHOLISM AND DRUG DEPENDENCE; BATTERED
   SPOUSES; CHILD ABUSE AND NEGLECT; CHILD DEVELOP-
   MENT; DEATH AND DYING; JUVENILE DELINQUENCY;
   SEPARATION AND DIVORCE)

PUERTO RICANS

RELIGION

(see also   VALUES)

SAFETY

(see also   BABYSITTING)

SEPARATION AND DIVORCE

SERBIAN AMERICANS

SEX EDUCATION

(see also ABORTION; CHILDBIRTH; PREGNANCY; SEX ROLES)

SEX ROLES

(see also MEN'S STUDIES; WOMEN'S STUDIES)

SEX ROLES, cont.

SIBLINGS

SINGLE-PARENT FAMILIES

SOCIAL STUDIES

(see also CROSS CULTURAL STUDIES; ETHNIC STUDIES; HIS-
TORY, U.S.)

SPORTS

SPORTS, cont.

STEPPARENTING

SWEDISH AMERICANS

TEACHER EDUCATION

(see also   EDUCATION)

VALUES, cont.

VIETNAMESE AMERICANS

VOCATIONAL GUIDANCE

VOCATIONAL GUIDANCE, cont.
  Working with My Dad 1550
  Your Career: Your Decision? 1570

WAR AND PEACE

  American Revolution: The Cause of Liberty 69
  American Revolution: The Impossible War 70
  And Another Family for Peace 80
  Dawn of the American Revolution: A Lexington Family 340
  Dr. Spock and His Babies 383
  Guilty by Reason of Race 605
  In Dark Places: Remembering the Holocaust 708
  Individual and Family Actions on Warning 719
  Letter from a Mother 820
  My Country, Right or Wrong? 980
  Sam 1228
  1776: American Revolution on the Frontier 1258
  Soldier's Home 1299
  Subversion? 1332
  You Don't Have to Buy This War, Mrs. Smith 1564

WOMEN'S STUDIES

  (see also ABORTION; BATTERED SPOUSES; BREASTFEEDING;
     CHILDBIRTH; PREGNANCY; SEX ROLES)

  Ain't Nobody's Business 27
  Album 32
  All That I Marry 51
  Am I Wife, Mother ... or Me? 60
  ...And Everything Nice 82
  Animated Women Series 92
  Anonymous Was a Woman 96
  Anything You Want to Be 99
  Back to School, Back to Work 118
  Being a Prisoner 140
  By Themselves 202
  The Cabinet 205
  Careers and Babies 220
  Catherine 227
  Chris and Bernie 274
  Chris Begins Again 275
  Clorae and Albie 283
  Do I Really Want a Child? 381
  Does Anybody Need Me Anymore? 385
  Elizabeth Swados: The Girl with the Incredible Feeling 415
  The Female Line 498
  Fog Pumas 522
  Girls at 12 574
  Growing Up Female: As Six Become One 599

SHORTS AND DOCUMENTARIES

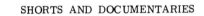

1   A TO B
       35 min., color, 1973.
       Director: Nell Cox. Distributor: Time-Life Multimedia.
             Teenage girl rebels against parental authority and
       family custom to mix with a new, hippie crowd.
       Red Ribbon, American Film Festival.   J-A

2   ABC AFTERSCHOOL SPECIALS see
          THE BRIDGE OF ADAM RUSH 195
          FOLLOW THE NORTH STAR 523
          FRANCESCA, BABY 540
          GAUCHO 559
          MAKE-BELIEVE MARRIAGE 875
          ME AND DAD'S NEW WIFE 907
          MIGHTY MOOSE AND THE QUARTERBACK KID 926
          MOM AND DAD CAN'T HEAR ME 944
          MY MOM'S HAVING A BABY 992
          ONE OF A KIND 1062
          P.J. AND THE PRESIDENT'S SON 1075
          THE PINBALLS 1110
          ROOKIE OF THE YEAR 1213
          SARA'S SUMMER OF THE SWANS 1233
          THE SECRET LIFE OF T. K. DEARING 1246
          THE SKATING RINK 1286
          VERY GOOD FRIENDS 1446

3   ABC CHILDREN'S NOVEL FOR TELEVISION SERIES see
          THE ESCAPE OF A ONE-TON PET 427

4   THE ABC OF BABYSITTING see
          BABYSITTERS' GUIDE 116

5   ABC WEEKEND SPECIALS SERIES see
          MY DEAR UNCLE SHERLOCK 982
          THE SEVEN WISHES OF JOANNA PEABODY 1256
          THE WINGED COLT 1528

                               3

6   ABBY'S FIRST TWO YEARS: A BACKWARD LOOK
        30 min. , b&w, 1960.
        Director: L. Joseph Stone for the Child Study Dept. , Vassar
        College. Distributor: New York University.
              Abby's development from two months to two years
        (in flashback), showing her relationships with adults and
        children, self-awareness, play patterns, routines, locomo-
        tion, etc. From the Vassar Studies of Normal Personality
        Development series. C, Prof

7   ABNORMAL PSYCHOLOGY SERIES   see
            DEPENDENCE: A NEW DEFINITION 358
            DEPRESSION: A STUDY IN ABNORMAL BEHAVIOR   359

8   ABORTION: PUBLIC ISSUE OR PRIVATE MATTER?
        25 min. , color, 1971.
        Director: Bill Leonard for WRC-TV. Distributor: Films
        Inc.
              Both pro- and anti-abortion activists (doctors, reli-
        gious leaders, patients, birthright groups, feminists) in the
        Washington, D.C. , area speak out. Questions whether
        women as individuals--separate from family, church, state--
        have a right to decide whether or not to abort. S-A

9   ABOUT PEOPLE SERIES   see
            EMOTIONAL ILLNESS 420
            MARRIAGE PROBLEMS 890
            WHAT IS NORMAL? 1497

10   ABUSIVE PARENTS
        30 min. , color, 1977.
        Producer: National Center on Child Abuse and Neglect, HEW.
        Distributor: National Audiovisual Center.
              Presents a panel of women incarcerated for child
        abuse, who now belong to a prison chapter of Parents Anony-
        mous.   A social worker comments on the dynamics of child
        abuse.   Originally a videotape.   From the We Can Help
        series.   Training film.   C-A, Prof

11   ACCESS
        23 min. , color, 1977.
        Director: Miriam Weinstein. Distributor: Polymorph Films.
              Visits with two handicapped adults, who discuss how
        they and their families more or less came to terms with
        their handicaps.   One is a wife and mother of three grown
        children.   She contracted polio while still a young mother.
        The second individual is a man afflicted only recently with
        a crippling nerve disease.   1st Prize, International Rehabili-
        tation Film Festival.   C-A

12   ACQUIRING LIFE SCRIPTS see
        LEARNING TO LIVE SERIES 810

13   ACT TWO--LINDSEY
        17 min. , color, 1973.
        Producer: National Institute of Mental Health. Distributor:
        National Audiovisual Center.
                Focuses on a student's home and classroom environ-
        ment. Stresses that family and peer pressures, unmet
        emotional needs, and teachers all play important roles in
        influencing Lindsey's behavior. From the One To Grow On
        series. C-A

14   ADAM'S BIRTH see
        MY LIFE IN ART 990

15   ADAPTING TO PARENTHOOD
        20 min. , color, 1975.
        Director: Alvin Fiering. Distributor: Polymorph Films.
                New parents discuss how their first babies changed
        their married life-styles, attitudes, and relationships with
        partners. Home life is observed. S-A

16   ADOLESCENCE: CRISIS OR OPPORTUNITY
        $12\frac{1}{2}$ min. , color, 1973.
        Director: Norman Siegel. Distributor: FilmFair Com-
        munications.
                Highlights the confusion and depression adolescents
        experience in their move toward a sense of individuality
        and independence from parents. The experiences and
        thoughts of one girl, in particular; with comments from a
        psychiatrist. J-S

17   ADOLESCENCE: THE WINDS OF CHANGE
        30 min. , color, 1975.
        Directors: Glen Howard & Carolyn Ferris. Distributor:
        Harper & Row Media.
                Explores not only the changes (physical, sexual,
        cognitive), but also the effects of parental attitudes on an
        adolescent's development. From the Development of the
        Child series. C-A

18   ADOLESCENT RESPONSIBILITIES: CRAIG AND MARK
        28 min. , color, 1973.
        Producer: Gregory Heimer. Distributor: Encyclopaedia
        Britannica Educational Corp.
                A Southern California family tries to decide whether
        to leave the city for rural life in Colorado. They con-
        sider work, money, responsibilities, and privileges, as
        their oldest sons--teenagers Craig and Mark--struggle for

independence.   Cinema vérité.   See also   PARENTAL
ROLES: DON AND MAE   (1083).   From the Getting
Together series.   J-S, A

19   THE ADULT YEARS
        12 min., color, 1976.
        Producer: National Medical Audiovisual Center with the
        Emory University School of Nursing.   Distributor: Na-
        tional Audiovisual Center.
               Highlights multiplicity of roles, productivity, rais-
        ing children, physical and emotional changes, and self-
        esteem.   From the Behaviorally Speaking series.   C-A

20   THE ADVOCATES: ON ABORTION AT WILL IN THE
        FIRST TWELVE WEEKS
        57 min., b&w, 1969.
        Producers: WGBH-TV, Boston & KCET-TV, Los Angeles.
        Distributor: Indiana University, Audio-Visual Center.
               Advocates and opponents of legalized abortion argue
        whether a woman has the right to determine if she should
        have an abortion during the first three months of pregnancy.
        Notes that most abortions are sought by married women
        and that unwanted children run the risk of being socially
        maladjusted or mentally ill.   S-A

21   AFTER OUR BABY DIED
        20 min., color, 1975.
        Director: Grania Gurievitch.   Distributor: National Audio-
        visual Center.
               American parents, whose babies were victims of
        Sudden Infant Death Syndrome, discuss the heartbreak and
        psychological aftereffects of losing their babies to SIDS.
        From the Sudden Infant Death Syndrome series.   Blue
        Ribbon, American Film Festival.   A, Prof

22   AFTER THE EAGLE
        18 min., color, p. 1976, r. 1977.
        Director: Greg Goldman.   Distributor: University of
        Southern California.
               A young Indian learns the importance of his heritage.

23   AFTER THE FIRST
        14 min., color, 1971.
        Director: Nicholas Frangakis.   Distributor: TeleKETICS.
               A boy is initially excited about his birthday gift--
        his first hunting rifle--until he sees the cruelty and final-
        ity of death the gift implies.   J-A

24   THE AGED
        17 min., color, p. 1972, r. 1973.
        Producer: WNET/13.   Distributor: Carousel Films.

A young Vietnam veteran returns home to find his aged, infirm parents destitute in New York City. He tries to get help for them, but, in the process, loses his money (to a nursing home), his job, and his wife. He finally learns about a helpful neighborhood geriatric project. From the 51st State TV series. S-A

25   AGGRESSION-ASSERTION
      8 min. , color, 1972.
      Director: Graham Parker for Moreland-Latchford Productions. Distributor: Paramount Communications.
          Open-ended drama about a boy who, as a result of family hostilities, takes his anger to the playground and then has various choices about how to direct this anger. From the Moral Decision Making series.   I-J

From Ahynung America: Two Korean Families.   Courtesy Macmillan Films.

26   AHYNUNG AMERICA: TWO KOREAN FAMILIES
      59 min. , color, 1978.
      Director: Patricia Lewis Jaffe. Distributor: Macmillan Films.
          The experiences of two Korean families in America --one newly arrived family who operate a grocery store in Manhattan; the other, a family of established, talented musicians. I-A

27   AIN'T NOBODY'S BUSINESS
      52 min. , color, p. 1976, r. 1977.
      Director: Sally Barrett-Page. Distributor: Mountain Moving Picture Company.
          Explores the issue of prostitution with six prostitutes; a male member of the Vice Squad; Margo St. James;

footage from the First World Meeting of Prostitutes held
in 1976; and footage in the prostitutes' homes, with parents
and children present.   S-A

28   AIR CONDITIONED COMFORT
        6 min. , color, p. 1974, r. 1977.
        Director: Roc Caivano.   Distributor: Phoenix Films.
            The tables are turned on a coarse, sloppy family
        who are traveling through the National Parks of western
        America in a camper loaded with all the comforts of
        home.   They disregard the natural beauty around them,
        deface it, and head for the closest rest rooms and burger
        stands.   S-A

29   AIR FORCE FAMILY HOUSING
        14 min. , color, 1960.
        Producer: Dept. of the Air Force.   Distributor: National
        Audiovisual Center.
            The Air Force aims to provide comfortable, eco-
        nomical, and convenient housing for U.S. -based Air Force
        families.   A

30   AIRPLANE TRIP (4th Edition)
        15 min. , color, 1972.
        Producer: Greg Heimer.   Distributor: Encyclopaedia
        Britannica Educational Corp.
            Peter and his father take a flight on a DC-10
        from Los Angeles to Miami.   E-I

31   ALBERT ELLIS: A DEMONSTRATION WITH A YOUNG
        DIVORCED WOMAN
        30 min. , color, 1972.
        Producer: Dr. John M. Whiteley.   Distributor: American
        Personnel and Guidance Association.
            Ellis shows this young woman, divorced at 29 and
        guilty about future relationships with men, how her illogi-
        cal and irrational beliefs cause emotional problems.
        C-A, Prof

32   ALBUM
        5 min. , color, 1976.
        Director: Linda Heller.   Distributor: Serious Business
        Company.
            A female child grows from childhood to sexual
        awareness in the family milieu.   Animated.

33   ALCOHOL AND INSIGHT
        29 min. , color, 1974.
        Producer: NBC-TV for the Social and Rehabilitation Ser-
        vice, Dept. of Health, Education & Welfare.   Distributor:
        National Audiovisual Center.

The work of the U.S. Social and Rehabilitation Service Program at the Research and Training Center of George Washington University, which studies alcoholism as a family disease. From the Alcohol series. C-A

34   ALCOHOL AND THE CLINIC
29 min. , color, 1974.
Producer: NBC-TV for the Social and Rehabilitation Service, Dept. of Health, Education & Welfare. Distributor: National Audiovisual Center.
Shows how a clinic can support the alcoholic and his or her family in acute care, early rehabilitation, and during a lifetime program. Set in the Washington (D.C.) Hospital Center's Counseling Center for Alcohol Abuse. From the Alcohol series. C-A

35   ALCOHOL AND THE FAMILY
29 min. , color, 1974.
Producer: NBC-TV for the Social and Rehabilitation Service, Dept. of Health, Education & Welfare. Distributor: National Audiovisual Center.
Discusses the quarterway house for alcoholic women, the halfway house for men, or the interim family as a solution for many alcoholics in the period after release from a hospital. These alternatives are found in the Washington, D.C. , area. From the Alcohol series. C-A

36   ALCOHOL AND THE TEENAGER
29 min. , color, 1974.
Producer: NBC-TV for the Social and Rehabilitation Service, Dept. of Health, Education & Welfare. Distributor: National Audiovisual Center.
Covers a boy whose parents are alcoholics, a teenage girl's alcoholism, and the rehabilitation possibilities of Alcoholics Anonymous. From the Alcohol series. S-A

37   ALCOHOL AND THE WOMAN
29 min. , color, 1974.
Producer: NBC-TV for the Social and Rehabilitation Service, Dept. of Health, Education & Welfare. Distributor: National Audiovisual Center.
Problems of identifying and rehabilitating the female alcoholic. Two recovered alcoholics discuss danger signals and rehabilitation. From the Alcohol series. C-A

38   ALCOHOL AND THERAPY
29 min. , color, 1974.
Producer: NBC-TV for the Social and Rehabilitation Service, Dept. of Health, Education & Welfare. Distributor: National Audiovisual Center.

Two rehabilitation facilities that provide psychiatric family counseling. From the <u>Alcohol</u> series. C-A

39   ALCOHOL: CRISIS FOR THE UNBORN
16 min. , color, 1977.
Director: Edward A. Franck for the National Foundation-March of Dimes. Distributor: Association Films.
The tragic results of drinking during pregnancy, i. e. , Fetal Alcohol Syndrome. S-A

40   ALCOHOL, PILLS & RECOVERY
27 min. , color, 1978.
Director: Paul Kleiter. Distributor: FMS Productions.
Joseph A. Pursch, M. D. , psychiatrist and Chief of the Naval Alcohol Rehabilitation Service, Naval Regional Medical Center, Long Beach, Calif. , is involved in alcoholic rehabilitation. He notes the newly recognized danger of sedativism, in which more and more people are combining alcohol and pills with resulting cross-addiction. He introduces an average American couple who are victims of sedativism. S-A

41   ALCOHOL SERIES   see
ALCOHOL AND INSIGHT   33
ALCOHOL AND THE CLINIC   34
ALCOHOL AND THE FAMILY   35
ALCOHOL AND THE TEENAGER   36
ALCOHOL AND THE WOMAN   37
ALCOHOL AND THERAPY   38

42   ALCOHOLISM AND THE FAMILY
42 min. , color, 1978.
Director: Rick Miner. Distributor: FMS Productions.
Father Joseph C. Martin (a Roman Catholic priest of the Archdiocese of Baltimore who has worked extensively in the treatment of alcoholism) explores the effects of alcoholism on the family before and after sobriety.
He advocates treatment for the whole family because he believes that the family of an alcoholic has severe problems and must "get well" just like the recovering alcoholic. From the <u>Father Martin Lecture</u> series. S-A

43   ALCOHOLISM: I WAS GOIN' TO SCHOOL DRUNK
26 min. , color, 1976.
Producer: Philip S. Hobel. Distributor: Document Associates.
Deals with teenage drinking and teens whose parents are alcoholics. Includes discussion of the double standard. From the <u>Youth Under the Influence</u> series. S-A

44   ALCOHOLISM: OUT OF THE SHADOWS
     30 min. , color, 1971.
     Director: David Tapper for ABC-TV News.   Distributor:
     Xerox Films.
          Three married couples talk about how alcoholism
     affected their marriages.   Each couple includes one or
     two non-drinking alcoholics.   S-A

45   ALCOHOLISM: WHO GETS HURT?
     13 min. , color, 1975.
     Director: Norman Tokar.   Cast: Fred MacMurray, Kurt
     Russell.   Distributor: Walt Disney Educational Media
     Company.
          A boy reacts in various ways to his father's alco-
     holism.   He isolates himself; then he joins a Boy Scout
     troop.   Edited from the feature film FOLLOW ME, BOYS!
     From the Questions!!! Answers??   Set 1 series.
     I-J

46   ALEX HALEY: THE SEARCH FOR ROOTS
     18 min. , color, 1977.
     Producer: Tony Brown for WNET/13.   Distributor: Films
     for the Humanities.
          How and why Haley came to write Roots.   Also de-
     scribes his journey aboard a Liberian freighter to relive
     the journey of his ancestor Kunta Kinte.   From the Black
     Journal TV series.   I-A

47   ALL ABOUT FIRE
     10 min. , color, 1976.
     Director: Fred Calvert for Farmhouse Films, in coopera-
     tion with the National Safety Council.   Distributor: Pyra-
     mid Films.
          Fire hazards in a home are pointed out by a family
     cat and by a fire captain who visits the house on three
     calls.   The family ignores the warnings and suffers the
     consequences.   Animated.   K-A

48   ALL BOTTLED UP
     11 min. , color, 1975.
     Producer: Charles Cahill and Associates.   Distributor:
     AIMS Instructional Media Services.
          How a child perceives alcoholic parents and how
     s/he shouldn't personalize the abuse, keep feelings inside,
     or overreact.   Produced with the AL-ANON Family Group
     and ALA-TEENS of the So. California Alcoholism Council
     of Greater Los Angeles.   J-A

49   ALL KINDS OF BABIES
     $9\frac{1}{2}$ min. , color, 1969.
     Director: Joe Clair.   Distributor: Carousel Films.

Notes that all living things come into this world as babies (animals, humans, plants) and grow into the same kinds of living things as their parents. Framed by two urban families of different ethnic backgrounds. <u>See also</u> IT TAKES A LOT OF GROWING (747).   PS-E

50   ALL OUT
27 min., color or b&w, 1975.
Director: Paul Stanley for Paulist Productions. Cast: Bob Hastings, Nan Martin, Phil Abbott. Distributor: The Media Guild.

Four game-show contestants are asked to do increasingly degrading things for money. Each contestant drops out, until one man is left. For $100,000, he must decide whether to ask his wife to play Russian Roulette. She consents to play, if he insists, but loses all respect for him. From the <u>Insight</u> series.   S-A

51   ALL THAT I MARRY
22 min., color, p. 1978, r. 1979.
Director: Carol Coren. Distributor: Temple University.

Six women of various ages describe experiences in and expectations from marriage.   S-A

52   ALLEGORY
8 min., b&w, 1972.
Director: Seth Winston. Distributor: University of Southern California.

An old man on his deathbed refuses to see the son he has rejected.

53   THE ALLELUIA KID
25 min., color, 1977.
Director: Jay Sandrich. Cast: Philip Michael Thomas, Helen Martin. Distributor: Paulist Productions.

A black, all-American quarterback is on the verge of a spectacular career. He's ashamed of his humble, religious upbringing, and clashes with his grandmother who feels that all talent comes from God. The young man's career is subsequently cut short by illness, and he goes through some positive changes. From the <u>Insight</u> series. S-A

54   THE ALLEN CASE
25 min. & 75 min., b&w, 197?.
Producer: Instrux, Inc., for Social and Rehabilitation Service, Dept. of Health, Education & Welfare. Distributor: National Audiovisual Center.

A mother receives aid for her dependent children. Demonstrates how she is helped to cope with her problem,

and how social workers can increase their skill in treat-
ment-oriented interviewing. Training Film. C,
Prof

55 ALL'S FAIR
    14 min., color, 1976.
    Producer: Paramount Television. Distributor: Para-
    mount Communications.
        The Brady kids question their ethics when they
    allow the quarterback of the opposing school football team
    to steal a phony play book. Specially edited vignette from
    the Brady Bunch TV series, and a part of the Brady
    Bunch Values and Guidance series. E-I

56 ALMOS' A MAN
    39 min., color, 1977.
    Director: Stan Lathan. Cast: LeVar Burton. Story:
    Richard Wright. Distributor: Perspective Films.
        A black teenager is a farm worker with his parents
    in the Deep South of the late Thirties. He persuades his
    mother to give him an advance on his earnings to buy a
    used handgun. He accidently kills a mule with the gun,
    and, as a result, his father demeans him in front of the
    landowner. The son hops a passing freighter, to search
    for independence from his family. From the American
    Short Story series. J-A

57 ALONE IN MY LOBSTER BOAT
    16 min., color, 1972.
    Producer: John H. Secondari Productions. Distributor:
    Xerox Films.
        The 12-year-old son of a Maine lobsterman is now
    ready to go out lobstering on his own, after having worked
    on his dad's boat for two years. From the Come Over
    to My House series. E-I

58 ALONE IN THE FAMILY
    13 min., color, 1975.
    Producer: WGBH-TV, Boston. Distributor: Films Inc.
        Two short portraits of real-life American kids;
    vignettes include: BEING BY MYSELF--Lori Morris
    comes from a big family, works as a waitress in the
    family's seafood restaurant, and talks about growing up.
    MY BIG BROTHER--Dexter Maxwell lives in Harlem and
    talks about being an only child with a single parent. He
    misses a father, but he does have a "Big Brother." From
    the Best of Zoom series. E-I

59 ALTERNATIVE EDUCATION SERIES see
    MORE THAN A SCHOOL 952

60   AM I WIFE, MOTHER ... OR ME?
          31 min. , color, 1975.
          Director: Sam O'Steen. Cast: Hope Lange, Earl Holli-
          man. Distributor: Learning Corp. of America.
                A wife and mother in her mid-thirties leaves home
          to find her identity. She begins a satisfying new life with
          a job and her own apartment, but her husband continually
          begs her to return to their home. Open-ended. Edited
          from the dramatic TV film I LOVE YOU ... GOODBYE
          (1789), and part of the Being a Woman series. J-A

61   AMERICA: EVERYTHING YOU'VE EVER DREAMED OF
          25 min. , color, 1973.
          Directors: Tony Ganz & Rhoden Streeter. Distributor:
          Films Inc.
                Short, satiric vignettes highlighting various aspects
          of modern culture. Some titles are: HONEYMOON HOTEL
          --A honeymoon resort that promotes "plastic" romance:
          heart-shaped bathtubs, red velvet walls, champagne, etc.
          THE BEST OF YOUR LIFE--A visit to a retirement com-
          munity in Sun City, Ariz. S-A

62   AMERICA: MY COUNTRY
          10 min. , color, 1971.
          Producer: Coronet Films. Distributor: Coronet Films.
                As a little boy and his family drive across America,
          the child realizes what makes America so great: its
          natural beauty, huge cities, and people. E-I

63   THE AMERICAN ALCOHOLIC
          55 min. , color, 1968.
          Producer: NBC-TV News. Distributor: McGraw-Hill
          Films.
                Study of average, middle-class American alcoholics--
          family people who live in the suburban house next door.
          Some men and women discuss their difficult drinking prob-
          lems and how they try to stop. S-A

64   AN AMERICAN FAMILY SERIES (12 Programs)
          60 min. each, color, 1972-73. Avail. video only.
          Producer/Director: Craig Gilbert. Camera: Alan Ray-
          mond & John Terry. Sound: Susan Raymond. Distribu-
          tor: WNET/Thirteen Media Services.
                Controversial cinema vérité profile of the Loud
          family of California. C-A

65   AMERICAN GOTHIC
          44 min. , color, 1976.
          Director: Fred Kelleher, Jr. Distributor: Diocese of
          Buffalo, Office of Communications.
                A young couple move into an eerie, old apartment

building. The wife becomes interested in a strange woman
and her young son who live on the floor above. The wife
soon fears that the child is being abused. Questions how
difficult it is for people to report abuse before tragedy
results. From the I and Thou series. Dramatic film. A

66   AMERICAN HERITAGE SERIES   see
      AMERICAN REVOLUTION: THE CAUSE OF LIBERTY
      69
      AMERICAN REVOLUTION: THE IMPOSSIBLE WAR   70

67   THE AMERICAN INDIAN IN TRANSITION
      22 min. , color, 1974.
      Director: J. Michael Hagopian. Distributor: Atlantis
      Productions.
            Three generations of one North American Indian
      family, as seen through the eyes of the grandmother.
      She reflects on the stress of living on a reservation in a
      white man's world. S-A

68   THE AMERICAN PARADE: THE 34TH STAR
      34 min. , color, 1975.
      Producer: CBS-TV News. Distributor: BFA Educational
      Media.
            Through the 20-year story and perspective of the
      Simpson family--who settled in the Kansas Territory--
      larger political, economic, and social land-related issues
      of the day are shown. Underscores the family unit as the
      backbone of U.S. expansion. J-A

69   AMERICAN REVOLUTION: THE CAUSE OF LIBERTY
      24 min. , color, 1972.
      Director: William Francisco for Robert Saudek Associates.
      Cast: Michael Douglas, Keene Curtis. Distributor:
      Learning Corp. of America.
            Drama based on Revolutionary War correspondence
      between idealistic young John Laurens and his father
      Henry, elected President of the First Continental Congress.
      Since he is studying in England, John is full of conflicting
      emotion over who is right--the colonies or England. See
      also AMERICAN REVOLUTION: THE IMPOSSIBLE WAR
      (70). From the American Heritage series. Freedoms
      Foundation Award. J-A

70   AMERICAN REVOLUTION: THE IMPOSSIBLE WAR
      25 min. , color, 1972.
      Director: William Francisco for Robert Saudek Associates.
      Cast: Michael Douglas, Keene Curtis. Distributor: Learn-
      ing Corp. of America.
            Continues the true story of John and Henry Laurens,
      begun in AMERICAN REVOLUTION: THE CAUSE OF LIB-

ERTY (69).   Here, son John becomes actively and tragically involved in the Revolutionary War, as his father
struggles in the political arena.   Father and son are
supportive of each other throughout their individual struggles.   From the American Heritage series.   J-A

71   AMERICAN SCENE SERIES   see
        SWEDES IN AMERICA   1341

72   THE AMERICAN SHORT STORY SERIES   see
        ALMOS' A MAN   56
        BERNICE BOBS HER HAIR   145
        THE DISPLACED PERSON   378
        SOLDIER'S HOME   1299

73   THE AMERICAN WEST: A DYING BREED
        23 min. , b&w, 1976.
        Director: Martin Ritt.   Cast: Paul Newman, Melvyn
        Douglas, Brandon de Wilde.   Distributor: Films Inc.
              Conflict between a rancher with high ethical
        standards and his opportunistic son.   Excerpt from the
        1962 film HUD (1784).   S-A

74   THE AMERICANS: BORICUAS
        19 min. , color, 1978.
        Producer: Tom Spain.   Distributor: Human Resources
        Development Trust.
              Reveals aspects of contemporary Puerto Rican
        family life, cultural attitudes, and health care.   Filmed
        in a large urban hospital.   Training film.   C-A, Prof

75   THE AMISH: A PEOPLE OF PRESERVATION
        28 min. & 52 min. , color, p. 1975, r. 1976.
        Director: John L. Ruth.   Distributor: Encyclopaedia
        Britannica Educational Corp.
              Examines their life-style, history, attitudes of
        their young, and relationship to neighboring community.
        Filmed in Lancaster, Pa.   S-A

76   ANATOMY OF A TEEN-AGE COURTSHIP
        $26\frac{1}{2}$ min. , color, 1969.
        Producer: Nett-Link Productions.   Distributor: Coronet
        Films.
              A high-school couple face indecision about their
        relationship, parental problems, and fears about the future
        as they move toward engagement.   Second edition of ARE
        YOU READY FOR MARRIAGE?   See also   ANATOMY OF
        A TEEN-AGE ENGAGEMENT (77).   S-C

77   ANATOMY OF A TEEN-AGE ENGAGEMENT
        26 min. , color, 1969.

Producer: Nett-Link Productions.   Distributor: Coronet
Films.
        A young couple point out problems and doubts that
are common during teenage engagements.   They begin to
have second thoughts.   Second edition of THE MEANING
OF ENGAGEMENT.   See also ANATOMY OF A TEEN-
AGE COURTSHIP (76) and ANATOMY OF A TEEN-AGE
MARRIAGE (78).   S-C

78   ANATOMY OF A TEEN-AGE MARRIAGE
       24 min. , color, 1972.
       Producer: Cine-Image Productions, Ltd.   Distributor:
       Coronet Films.
               After five months of marriage, a teenaged couple
       face unexpected problems and responsibilities; both must
       make some changes if their marriage is to survive.
       Second edition of MARRIAGE IS A PARTNERSHIP.   See
       also ANATOMY OF A TEEN-AGE COURTSHIP (76) and
       ANATOMY OF A TEEN-AGE ENGAGEMENT (77).   S-C

79   THE ANATOMY OF TERRORISM SERIES   see
           EXECUTIVE DECISION   437
           PERSONAL AND FAMILY SECURITY   1102

80   AND ANOTHER FAMILY FOR PEACE
       32 min. , b&w, 1971.
       Director: Donald MacDonald for Another Mother for Peace.
       Distributors: Films Inc. ; Kit Parker Films (rental only).
               Documentary portrait of five bitter families who
       were directly affected by U. S. intervention in Vietnam.
       Their sons or husbands were killed, crippled, or were
       POWs at the time of filming.   S-A

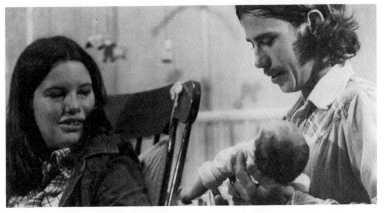

From And Baby Makes Two.   Courtesy Films Inc.

81   AND BABY MAKES TWO
          27 min., color, 1978.
          Director: Nancy Littlefield for KNBC-TV.   Distributor:
          Films Inc.
               Examines the epidemic of teen pregnancies by
          visiting a special school for pregnant teenagers. Here,
          and at an alternative school, girls and boys talk about
          their sexual ignorance, the affect on their families, and
          their squashed dreams. Host: Valerie Bertinelli.   S-A

82   ...AND EVERYTHING NICE
          20 min., color, 1974.
          Director: Norma Adams.   Distributor: BFA Educational
          Media.
               How women's attitudes toward themselves and their
          roles have changed as a result of consciousness-raising
          groups. Includes an actual group, with focus on a married
          woman in her mid-thirties. With Gloria Steinem.   S-A

83   ...AND I WANT TIME
          28 min., color, 1977.
          Director: Arthur Hiller.   Cast: Ali MacGraw, Ryan
          O'Neal. Distributor: Paramount Communications.
               Traces a young couple's relationship from marriage
          through the untimely death of the wife.   Excerpt from the
          1970 film LOVE STORY (1846).   J-A

84   ...AND THEN ICE CREAM
          11 min., b&w, 1951.
          Director: L. Joseph Stone for the Child Study Dept.,
          Vassar College. Distributor: New York University.
               Questions whether a child's appetite should deter-
          mine his or her diet or whether grown-ups should be re-
          sponsible for selection of the child's balanced meals.
          From the Vassar Studies of Normal Personality Develop-
          ment series.   C, Prof

85   AND THEN WHAT HAPPENED? STARRING DONNA,
          ALICE AND YOU
          10 min., color, 1972.
          Director: Stelios Roccos.   Distributor: Paramount Com-
          munications.
               Donna visits some friends, but her little sister
          Alice disappears.   Donna finds the child in the middle of
          the pond in a boat.   Film ends here, allowing the viewer
          to create a rescue.   From the Read On! series.   E

86   AND WHO SHALL FEED THIS WORLD?
          47 min., color, 1974.
          Director: Darold Murray for NBC-TV.   Distributor:
          Films Inc.

Contrasts the lives of two farm families--one in
North Dakota, the other in India--to reflect on aspects of
the world food shortage.   Blue Ribbon, American Film
Festival.   S-A

87   ANDY
         60 min. , color, 1977.
         Director: Mary Elaine Evans.   Distributor: Mary Elaine
         Evans.
              At $2\frac{1}{2}$, Andy Detwiler lost both arms in a farming
         accident.   Here, at $7\frac{1}{2}$, he functions as a normal little
         boy in rural West Liberty, Ohio, using his feet as hands.
         His strong character, family, and community ties make
         his life a happy one.   E-A

88   ANGEL AND BIG JOE
         27 min. , color, 1975.
         Director: Bert Salzman.   Cast: Paul Sorvino, Dadi
         Pinero.   Distributor: Learning Corp. of America.
              A 15-year-old boy of Mexican-Puerto Rican heritage
         must choose between continuing life with his migrant farm
         worker family, who need his wages, and a new life grow-
         ing and selling roses with Big Joe, a white telephone line-
         man who takes an interest in the boy.   Set in the farm-
         lands of New Jersey.   From the Learning to Be Human
         series.   Academy Award.   Blue Ribbon, American Film
         Festival.   I-A

89   ANGELA'S ISLAND
         23 min. , color, 1978.
         Director: Marc Brugnoni for NBC-TV.   Distributor: Films
         Inc.
              At Goldwater Hospital on Roosevelt Island (N. Y.),
         Angela's rehabilitation counselor, herself handicapped by
         polio, works with Angela to help her cope.   The 11-year-
         old's mother recalls her child's birth and the desertion
         of the father, who mistakenly thought Angela was mentally
         retarded.   Blue Ribbon, American Film Festival.   S-C

90   ANGRY BOY
         33 min. , b&w, 1951.
         Producer: Affiliated Film Producers.   Distributor: Inter-
         national Film Bureau.
              An emotionally disturbed 10-year-old boy is caught
         stealing.   A psychiatric team traces his emotional problem
         back to its source--unhealthy family relationships.   C,
         Prof

91   ANIMAL PARTNERS
         13 min. , color, 1975.
         Producer: WGBH-TV, Boston.   Distributor: Films Inc.

Two short portraits of real-life American kids;
vignettes include: SLED DOGS--Sally Heckman and her
family raise and race Siberian huskies. TRICK RIDERS--
Donna Warvel and Sonja Copeland are trick horseback
riders in a Wild West show. From the <u>Best of Zoom</u>
series. E-I

92   ANIMATED WOMEN SERIES
15 min., color, p. 1977, r. 1978.
Directors: See below. Distributor: Texture Films.
Animated series of vignettes that satirize male/fe-
male relationships and female aspirations. Titles that ap-
ply here are: MADE FOR EACH OTHER, by Barbara
Bottner--A Woman faces the impossibility of being everything to her man. THE BALLAD OF LUCY JORDAN, by
Ian Moo Young--Tale of a 37-year-old housewife whose
life is on the brink of despair. S-A

93   ANNA AND POPPY
13 min., color, 1976.
Director: Mike Rhodes for Paulist Productions. Distributor: The Media Guild.
The death of her beloved grandfather causes a
child great sorrow until she comes to terms with her loss
and realizes that her grandfather will live on in her memory. From the <u>Bloomin' Human</u> series. Dramatic film.
J-A

94   ANNA N: LIFE HISTORY FROM BIRTH TO FIFTEEN
YEARS; THE DEVELOPMENT OF EMOTIONAL PROBLEMS
IN A CHILD REARED IN A NEUROTIC ENVIRONMENT
60 min., b&w, sil., 1952.
Producers: Margaret E. Fries, M.D., & Paul J. Woolf,
M.S. Distributor: New York University.
Looks at a child (from birth to 15 years) of superior
intelligence whose hereditary endowment and neurotic parents, grandparents, and sister result in a personality difficult to categorize. Predictions are based on interaction
with her neurotic family and her inhibited, depressed
mother. From the <u>Studies on Integrated Development:</u>
<u>Interaction Between Child and Environment</u> series. Train-
ing film. C, Prof

95   ANNIE AND THE OLD ONE
$14\frac{1}{2}$ min., color, 1976.
Producer: Greenhouse Films. Book: Miska Miles. Distributor: BFA Educational Media.
A Navajo girl tries to prevent her grandmother from
finishing work on a loomed rug because the old woman has
predicted her own death upon completion of the rug. The
grandmother helps the child understand the inevitable cycle
of life. E-J

96   ANONYMOUS WAS A WOMAN
          28 min., color, 1977.
          Director: Mirra Bank for WNET/13. Distributor: Films Inc.
               Shows that so-called anonymous 18th- and 19th-century American folk art, e.g., samplers, paintings, quilts, rugs, and needlework, were in actuality the end products of "feminine education" of the day. Women produced them as decorative items for the home during time off from exhausting household chores. From the Originals: Women in Art series. S-A

97   ANOTHER DAY IN THE GAS STATION   see
          FOR LOVE OR MONEY 530

98   ANXIETY: ITS PHENOMENOLOGY IN THE FIRST YEAR OF LIFE
          20 min., b&w, sil., 1953.
          Producer: René A. Spitz, M.D. Distributor: New York University.
               The phenomenology of anxiety, from birth to the end of the first year, with behavioristic observations of its manifestations. From the Film Studies of the Psychoanalytic Research Project on Problems in Infancy series. Training film. C, Prof

99   ANYTHING YOU WANT TO BE
          8 min., b&w, 1971.
          Director: Liane Brandon. Distributor: New Day Films.
               Classic film satirizing the traditional roles (housewife, mother, secretary) that young women continue to be pressured into, by parents, teachers, and society. Blue Ribbon, American Film Festival. J-A

100   APPALACHIA: RICH LAND, POOR PEOPLE
          59 min., b&w, p. 1968, r. 1969.
          Director: Jack Willis for WNET/13. Distributor: Indiana University, Audio-Visual Center.
               In eastern Kentucky, the people are prisoners of the land. Due to lack of education and other vocational skills, they are tied to the mines, where mechanization is beginning to replace people. The result--lives that begin and end in poverty. A local family is interviewed. S-A

101   APPALACHIAN FIDDLER see
          FOOT-STOMPIN' MUSIC 528

102   APPRECIATING OUR PARENTS see
          PARENTS--WHO NEEDS THEM? 1093

103   ARE YOU READY FOR MARRIAGE? see
          ANATOMY OF A TEEN-AGE COURTSHIP 76

104   ARE YOU READY FOR THE POSTPARTUM EXPERIENCE?
       17 min. , color, 1975.
       Director: Philip Courter. Distributor: Parenting Pictures.
            Covers day and nighttime care, breastfeeding,
       father's first solo with baby, and community postpartum
       classes. New mothers share feeding, scheduling, and child-
       care experiences, emotional and physical feelings. A cou-
       ple adjusts to a new life as a family. A

105   ARE YOU THE ONE?
       24 min. , color, 1969.
       Director: Wetzel O. Whitaker. Distributor: Brigham
       Young University.
            Designed to make young people aware of differences
       in people that lead to incompatible marriages. Also factors
       to be considered before selecting a mate. From the Prep-
       aration for Marriage series. S-A

106   AROUND THE WAY WITH KAREEMA
       18 min. , color, p. 1974, r. 1975.
       Directors: Mark Harris & John Friedman. Distributor:
       Education Development Center.
            The weekend activities of a 4-year-old, middle child
       in a large, urban black family. Shows that even when she is
       responsible for caring for the younger siblings. From the
       Exploring Childhood: Family and Society series. J-A

107   ARTHUR AND LILLIE
       30 min. , color, 1975.
       Directors: Jon Else, Kristine Samuelson, & Steven Kovacs.
       Distributor: Pyramid Films.
            Profile of onetime Hollywood film distributor and
       exhibitor, Arthur Mayer, age 87, and his wife Lillie. He
       is now a university professor. CINE Golden Eagle. Golden
       Gate Award, San Francisco International Film Festival.
       J-A

108   ASSESSMENT OF THE FAMILY AS A SYSTEM
       40 min. , color, 1973.
       Producer: National Medical Audiovisual Center. Distribu-
       tor: National Audiovisual Center.
            Demonstrates the process of gathering data about
       the family as an open system, which can provide a frame-
       work for evaluating families on a functional-dysfunctional
       continuum. Notes areas of family behavior that the nurse
       should explore. Training film. C, Prof

109   AT THE DOCTOR'S
       10 min. , b&w, p. 1972, r. 1975.
       Directors: Henry Felt & John Friedman. Distributor:
       Education Development Center.

A 6-year-old girl and her 10-year-old brother go to the doctor and must deal as best they can with the experience. From the Exploring Childhood: Family and Society series. J-A

110   AT YOUR AGE
10 min., color, 1972.
Producer: Yehuda Tarmu. Distributor: FilmFair Communications.
Elementary-age children discuss aging, death, parents, and older brothers and sisters. E

111   AUCTIONEERS   see
FAST-TALKING JOBS   488

112   BABY BLUE
8 min., b&w, 1966.
Producer: USC, Dept. of Cinema. Distributor: University of Southern California.
A young American wife suffers emotional conflict due to her infidelity while her husband is off fighting in Vietnam.

113   A BABY IS BORN (Revised)
23 min., color, 1977.
Producers: Sheri Gillette Espar & Henry Mayer, M.D. Distributor: Perennial Education.
A young couple deliver their first child. A doctor explains the procedure, as the supportive husband observes and comforts his wife. With an Epilogue on proper postnatal care and birth control for the future. CINE Golden Eagle. Chris Award, Columbus Film Festival. Red Ribbon, American Film Festival. First Prize, National Educational Film Festival. Avail. in Spanish. J-A

114   BABY RABBIT
11 min., color, 1971.
Producer: Larry Klingman. Distributor: Churchill Films.
Three city children raise a family of rabbits and observe that, like themselves (brother, sister, baby brother), the rabbit family needs food, sleep, and a warm shelter in order to live and grow. From the Reading Readiness series. E

115   BABY-SITTING BASICS
12 min., color, 1974.
Producer: Charles Cahill & Associates. Distributor: AIMS Instructional Media Services.
Do's, don't's, and duties of babysitters--e.g., meeting the family before the job, medical background, phone messages, safety, discipline, etc. J-S

116   BABYSITTERS' GUIDE
        10 min. , color, 1975.
        Producer: Sid Davis Productions, with the West Covina
        (Calif.) Police Dept. Distributor: Sid Davis Productions.
                Safety tips. Revised edition of THE ABC OF BABY-
        SITTING. J-A

117   BABYSITTING
        27 min. , color, p. 1974, r. 1976.
        Director: Ian Stuart for Summerhill Productions. Distribu-
        tor: Paramount Communications.
                Responsibilities of babysitters and parents. Qualifi-
        cations of prospective babysitters. From the Community
        Protection and Crime Prevention series. I-A

118   BACK TO SCHOOL, BACK TO WORK
        20 min. , color, 1973.
        Director: Joan Pearlman. Distributor: American Person-
        nel and Guidance Association.
                Ten vignettes that focus on problems (self-doubts,
        negative family reactions) that crop up when a housewife
        returns to work or school and juggles home/job or home/
        school responsibilities. Family Life Film Award, National
        Council on Family Relations. A

119   BACKGROUND
        19 min. , color, 1975-77.
        Director: Carmen D'Avino. Distributor: Grove Press
        Film Division.
                Combines live action and animation, photographs and
        paper cutouts, sculpture and paintings, to tell the life story
        of painter/sculptor/filmmaker Carmen D'Avino. C-A

120   BACKTRACK
        14 min. , color, 1977.
        Director: Ron Ellis. Distributor: Phoenix Films.
                A lonely drifter returns home after 16 years to
        settle the affairs of his deceased mother. He finds that he
        has a 15-year-old daughter. He tries to meet her, but must
        confront her mother first. J-A

121   BAIT, BITE AND SWITCH see
            THE CONSUMER FRAUD SERIES 312

122   THE BALLAD OF LUCY JORDAN see
            ANIMATED WOMEN SERIES 92

123   BARB: BREAKING THE CYCLE OF CHILD ABUSE
        $28\frac{1}{2}$ min. , color, 1977.
        Producer: Cavalcade Productions. Distributor: MTI Tele-
        programs.

Barbara was a neglected child, and now has trouble
coping with her own little daughter.   After neighbors report
her to the police, she makes an effort to understand her
behavior and cope.   Notes how courts and social agencies
can provide a supportive network for abusive parents.
Training film.   C-A, Prof

124   BATHING BABIES IN THREE CULTURES (Revised Edition)
9 min. , b&w, 1954.
Producers: Gregory Bateson & Margaret Mead.   Distributor: New York University.
Shows the interplay between mother and child in
three different locations: bathing in the Sepik River of New
Guinea; in an American bathroom; and in a mountain village
of Bali, Indonesia.   From the Character Formation in Different Cultures series.   C, Prof

125   BATHING YOUR BABY ... A TOUCH OF LOVE
19 min. , color, 1977.
Director: Mel London for Johnson & Johnson Baby Products
Co.   Distributor: Association Films.
How to bathe a newborn.   Notes bonding between
mother and child that occurs during this time.   S-A

126   BATTERED CHILD
58 min. , b&w, 1969.
Director: Bob Kaiser for WTTW-TV.   Distributor: Indiana University, Audio-Visual Center.
Documentary on child abuse, based on the book The
Battered Child, by Dr. C. Henry Kempe and Roy E. Helfer.
Actual casework by a team of psychiatrists, pediatricians,
and social workers is shown.   Stresses that parents need
psychiatric help rather than penal action.   S-A

127   THE BATTERED CHILD, PARTS 1 & 2
27 min. (Part 1), 26 min. (Part 2), b&w, 1970.
Producer: National Medical Audiovisual Center, with Dr.
Norman Ende, Prof. of Pathology, Emory Univ. School of
Medicine.   Distributor: National Audiovisual Center.
Discusses the autopsy findings of death resulting
from child abuse.   Covers patterns of battered child in-
juries (internal and external) and interpretation.   Kinescope.
From the Clinical Pathology--Forensic Medicine Outlines
series.   Training film.   C, Prof

128   BATTERED SPOUSES
27 min. , color, 1978.
Director: David Ferron.   Distributor: Harper & Row
Media.
Alternatives open to battered persons.   C-A, Prof

129   BATTERED WIVES
        45 min., color, 1979.
        Director: Peter Werner. Cast: Karen Grassle, Mike
        Farrell, Chip Fields, LeVar Burton. Distributor: Learning
        Corp. of America.
            Two marriages are torn apart by abusive husbands.   S-A

130   BATTERED WIVES: A LEGACY OF VIOLENCE
        $28\frac{1}{2}$ min., color, 1978.
        Producer: Woman's Eye. Distributor: Woman's Eye.
            Historical, social, psychological, and legal aspects
        of wife abuse. With three victims and professional view-
        points.   C-A

131   BATTERED WOMEN: VIOLENCE BEHIND CLOSED DOORS
        21 min., color, 1977.
        Director: Christina Crowley for the J. Gary Mitchell Film
        Co. Distributor: MTI Teleprograms.
            Group discussions and interviews with men and women
        explore wife beating: why it happens, why it continues, and
        why it is tolerated as an integral part of some marriages.
        Silver Medal, New York International Film & Television
        Festival. Special Jury Award, San Francisco International
        Film Festival.   C-A

132   BE FIT AND LIVE
        18 min., color, 1974.
        Director: Ralph Luce. Distributor: Pyramid Films.
            A stay-at-home, physically sluggish family learns
        how to get into a regular, life-lengthening exercise program.
        I-A

133   BEGIN WITH THE END IN MIND
        29 min., color, 1972.
        Director: Keith Atkinson. Distributor: Brigham Young
        University.
            A young man disagrees with his father and is forced
        to leave home. Their minister asks the father to teach a
        class of young men his son's age. As a result, the man
        learns how to deal more effectively with young people and
        is reconciled with his son.   J-A

134   THE BEGINNING OF LIFE
        30 min., color, 1969.
        Photography: Lennart Nilsson. Producer: Swedish Broad-
        casting Corp. Distributor: Benchmark Films.
            A human embryo's development from fertilized ovum
        to birth. Blue Ribbon, American Film Festival.   J-A

135   THE BEGINNING OF PREGNANCY
        30 min., b&w, 1956.

Producer: WQED-TV, Pittsburgh. Distributors: Association Films (rental only); Indiana University, Audio-Visual
Center (rental only).
    Describes what happens to mother and baby during
the early months of pregnancy. Explains how characteristics are inherited and twins are conceived. From the
Months Before Birth series. S-C

136   BEHAVIOR MODIFICATION SERIES see
        REWARD AND PUNISHMENT 1200

137   BEHAVIOR MODIFICATION SPECIAL EDUCATION SERIES
    see
        CHILDHOOD AGGRESSION: A SOCIAL LEARNING AP-
           PROACH TO FAMILY THERAPY 258
        JAMIE 763
        PEER CONDUCTED BEHAVIOR MODIFICATION 1098
        SIBLINGS AS BEHAVIOR MODIFIERS 1273

138   BEHAVIORAL INTERVIEWING WITH COUPLES
    14 min. , color, 1976.
    Directors: Phil Stockton & Dr. John Gottman. Distribu-
    tors: Behavioral Images; Research Press.
        Demonstrates one method of behaviorally interviewing
couples during early counseling sessions. Six stages of the
method are explicated, and the behavior of a couple and
therapist are observed for analysis. Training film. C,
Prof

139   BEHAVIORALLY SPEAKING SERIES see
        THE ADULT YEARS 19

140   BEING A PRISONER
    28 min. , color, 1975.
    Director: Suzanne Jasper. Distributor: Women Make
    Movies.
        The effects of separating mothers and their children
due to the incarceration of the women (even in minimum-
security facilities) come through the stories of various female prisoners. Gold Plaque, Chicago International Film
Festival. Jury Award, Grenoble Film Festival. C-A,
Prof

141   BEING A WOMAN SERIES see
        AM I WIFE, MOTHER ... OR ME? 60
        DO I REALLY WANT A CHILD? 381
        DOES ANYBODY NEED ME ANYMORE? 385

142   BEING BY MYSELF see
        ALONE IN THE FAMILY 58

143   BEING REAL
        11 min., color, 1973.
        Director: Mike Rhodes for Paulist Productions. Distribu-
        tor: The Media Guild.
             Dramatic vignettes question what makes individuals
        special; relates this to marital relationships, etc. From
        the Vignette series. J-A

144   BEN FRANKLIN--PORTRAIT OF A FAMILY
        25 min., color, 1976.
        Producer: Division of Audiovisual Arts, National Park Ser-
        vice. Distributor: National Audiovisual Center.
             His relationship with wife and family during the years
        before and after the Revolutionary War.

145   BERNICE BOBS HER HAIR
        $47\frac{1}{2}$ min., color, 1977.
        Director: Joan Micklin Silver. Cast: Shelley Duvall, Bud
        Cort. Story: F. Scott Fitzgerald. Distributor: Perspec-
        tive Films.
             Bernice is transformed from an ugly duckling into a
        vampish coquette by her cousin, and ends up attracting all
        her cousin's suitors. Her cousin tricks her into bobbing
        her hair, but Bernice gets her revenge. From the Ameri-
        can Short Story series. Red Ribbon, American Film Festi-
        val. CINE Golden Eagle. J-A

146   THE BEST OF YOUR LIFE see
             AMERICA: EVERYTHING YOU'VE EVER DREAMED OF
             61

147   THE BEST OF ZOOM SERIES see
             ALONE IN THE FAMILY 58
             ANIMAL PARTNERS 91
             COUNTRY FAMILIES 320
             FAST-TALKING JOBS 488
             FIRST IT SEEMED KINDA STRANGE 513
             FOOT-STOMPIN' MUSIC 528
             FOR LOVE OR MONEY 530
             FROM GENERATION TO GENERATION 546
             HELPING MY PARENTS 639
             IN BUSINESS FOR MYSELF 707
             IT'S HARDER FOR PATRICK 750
             MY FAMILY BUSINESS 983
             ROOTED IN THE PAST 1214
             WORKING WITH MY DAD 1550

148   BEYOND LSD: A FILM FOR CONCERNED ADULTS AND
        TEENAGERS
        25 min., color, 1968.
        Producer: Paul Burnford. Distributor: BFA Educational
        Media.

A group of parents try to understand what went
wrong in their relationships with their teenagers who use
drugs. S-A

149   THE BIG DINNER TABLE
       11 min. , color, 1968.
       Producer: Wexler Film Productions. Distributor: Peren-
       nial Education.
            Shows indigenous family mealtimes in 34 worldwide
       locations. The need for four basic food groups is explained.
       Avail. in Spanish. From the Nutrition Education series. E

150   BIG HENRY AND THE POLKA DOT KID
       33 min. , color, 1977.
       Director: Richard Marquand. Cast: Ned Beatty, Estelle
       Parsons, Chris Barnes. Distributor: Learning Corp. of
       America.
            A young boy loses both his parents and comes to
       live on his uncle's farm. The boy tries to establish a re-
       lationship with his new family, while convincing his uncle
       to allow a blind old dog to live. From the Learning to Be
       Human series and the Special Treat TV series. Emmy
       Award. Christopher Award. ACT Achievement in Children's
       Television Award. E-A

151   BIG TOWN
       25 min. , color, 1973.
       Directors: Eliot Noyes, Jr. & Claudia Weill. Distributor:
       Texture Films.
            Includes five satiric views of life in the big city and
       environs. Those vignettes applicable to family life are:
       MARRIAGE--A quick look at a city marriage bureau, those
       who get married and those who marry the couples. COM-
       MUTERS--Suburban, city-bound husbands and urban, sub-
       urban-bound maids. YOGA--Bored suburban housewives
       taking daily classes. I-A

152   BILINGUAL FILM SERIES, MODULE I: LET'S GET READY!
       see
       OUR FAMILY ALBUM/NUESTRO ALBUM DE LA FAMI-
           LIA! 1069

153   BILL AND SUZI: NEW PARENTS
       13 min. , b&w, 1975.
       Director: Henry Felt. Distributor: Education Development
       Center.
            Examines how becoming a parent for the first time
       affects a couple's life together--e.g. , jealousy of father be-
       fore and after the birth, adjustment in life-style, pleasures
       and difficulties of the child. With noted pediatrician Dr. T.
       Berry Brazelton of Harvard. From the Exploring Childhood:
       Seeing Development series. S-A, Prof

154   THE BILL OF RIGHTS IN ACTION: FREEDOM OF RELI-
        GION
        21 min. , color, 1969.
        Director: Bernard Wilets.   Distributor : BFA Educational
        Media.
                Real-life lawyers argue the constitutional issues in-
        volved in the case of a pregnant woman injured in a car
        accident, who, due to religious beliefs, refuses a lifesaving
        blood transfusion.   Questions whether the judge should or-
        der the transfusion that would save the life of the woman
        and unborn child over the objections of the woman and her
        husband.   I-A

155   THE BIRCH CANOE BUILDER
        23 min. , color, 1970.
        Director: Craig Hinde.   Distributor: Paramount Communi-
        cations.
                Seventy-ish Bill Hafeman and his wife live in the
        wilds of northern Minnesota.   They've lived in the wilder-
        ness for 50 years; this film shows why and how, as well
        as Bill's expertise as a canoe craftsman.   From the Yes-
        terday and Today series.   Gold Medal, Atlanta Film Festi-
        val.   Red Ribbon, American Film Festival.   First Prize,
        Information Film Producers of America.   I-A

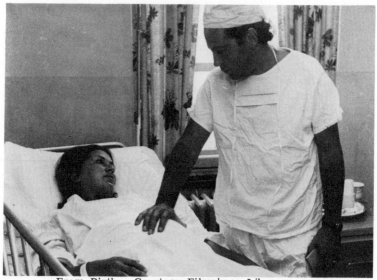

From Birth.   Courtesy Filmakers Library.

156   BIRTH
        40 min & 76 min. , b&w, 1969.

Directors: Arthur Barron & Evelyn Barron. Distributor:
Filmakers Library.
　　　　Cinema vérité study of the last three months of a
pregnancy and the birth of the child of artist Bruce North
and his wife Debbie. Daily life of couple--learning the
Lamaze method, talking with other parents, sharing feelings.
C-A

157　　BIRTH
　　　　57 min., color, p. 1976, r. 1977.
　　　　Director: Sam Pillsbury. Distributor: Films Inc.
　　　　　Psychiatrist R. D. Laing questions the immediate
and long-term effects of many of the detached, routine
childbirth procedures practiced in Western society. First
Prize, Melbourne Film Festival. C-A

158　　BIRTH AND THE FIRST FIFTEEN MINUTES OF LIFE
　　　　10 min., b&w, sil., 1948.
　　　　Producer: René A. Spitz, M.D. Distributor: New York
University.
　　　　　Shows the birth of a baby and its reactions to stim-
uli presented within 15 minutes after birth, as well as
during the first feeding 24 hours later. Also contrasts a
second baby's reactions to the same stimuli. From the
Film Studies of the Psychoanalytic Research Project on
Problems in Infancy series. C, Prof

159　　BIRTH DAY--THROUGH THE EYES OF THE MOTHER
　　　　29 min., color, 1970.
　　　　Director: Lawrence A. Williams. Distributor: Lawren
Productions.
　　　　　A subjective view of labor and delivery, from the
mother's point of view. From examination and prep through
delivery. Young mother is unwed. Chris Statuette, Columbus Film Festival. CINE Golden Eagle. S-A

160　　THE BIRTH FILM
　　　　35 min., color, 1973.
　　　　Director: Susan Kleckner. Distributor: New Yorker Films.
　　　　　Kris Glen, lawyer, feminist, and mother of a 2-year-
old, decides to have her second child at home, with a doc-
tor standing by. Her child and husband also participate.
Post-recorded narration explains birth to her young child.
S-A

161　　BIRTH OF A FAMILY
　　　　24 min., color, 1975.
　　　　Producer: Catfish Productions, Inc. Distributor: Peren-
nial Education.
　　　　　Demonstrates advantages of preparing for childbirth.
Intercuts couple's attendance at childbirth prep class with

scenes of actual birth.   Stresses importance of knowing beforehand what is likely to happen during all phases of labor and delivery.   Lamaze method.   S-A

162   THE BIRTH OF THE BABY
29 min. , b&w, 1956.
Producer: WQED, Pittsburgh.   Distributors: Association Films (rental only); Indiana University, Audio-Visual Center (rental only).
From onset of labor pains and hospital admittance, through stages of labor and delivery.   From the Months Before Birth series.   S-A

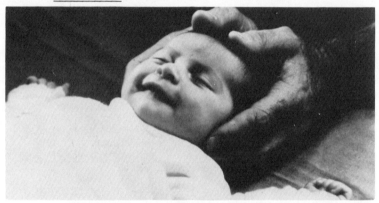

From Birth Without Violence.   Courtesy New Yorker Films.

163   BIRTH WITHOUT VIOLENCE
21 min. , b&w, 1975.
Directors: Dr. Frederick Leboyer & Pierre Marie Goulet.
Distributor: New Yorker Films.
Documents Dr. Leboyer's method of child delivery, as discussed in his book of the same name (Knopf, 1975). Method aims to minimize birth trauma, with a quiet, low-lighted delivery room, laying of infant on mother's stomach with umbilical cord unsevered, and massaging of child for 4-5 minutes.   Then, cord is cut, baby is bathed and stroked and set down to rest.   No slapping, crying, bright lights, or brusque movements.   Non-narrated.   Red Ribbon, American Film Festival.   S-A, Prof

164   BIRTHDAY
28 min. , color, p. 1976, r. 1978.
Director: Nancy Porter for WGBH-TV.   Distributor: Education Development Center.
Dr. Lonny Higgins, obstetrician/gynecologist/wife/ mother, attempts to integrate the Leboyer method of child-

birth into her hospital.   Here, she traces her professional
development, counsels a young couple in the Leboyer
method, cares for her son, and balances demands of career and family.   S-A

165   BITTER WIND
         30 min. , color, 1963.
         Director: Scott Whitaker.   Distributor: Brigham Young
         University.
                 Billy's early life on the reservation was happy, but
         now both parents have begun to drink.   His family breaks
         up over their alcoholism, but he and two young missionaries
         manage to bring the family back together and help his par-
         ents fight their drinking problem.   Navajo soundtrack.   I-A

166   BLACK JOURNAL TV SERIES   see
         ALEX HALEY: THE SEARCH FOR ROOTS   46

167   BLOOMIN' HUMAN SERIES   see
         ANNA AND POPPY   93
         DESERT TREK   360
         MY MAIN MAN   991
         THE PROMISE   1150
         THINGS ARE DIFFERENT NOW   1369

168   BLOSSOM IN VIRGO
         13 min. , color, p. 1977, r. 1978.
         Director: Michael Day.   Distributor: Phoenix Films.
                 A celebration of a natural childbirth.   C-A

169   BOBBY
         12 min. , color and b&w, p. 1976, r. 1977.
         Director: Robin Armstrong.   Distributor: New York State
         Society for Autistic Children (rental only).
                 Young Bobby is autistic.   Shows the struggle of his
         day-to-day existence, as well as his interaction with par-
         ents and brother.   Notes how autism affects families.   J-A

170   THE BODY HUMAN: THE MIRACLE MONTHS
         50 min. , color, 1977.
         Director: Alfred R. Kelman for Tomorrow Entertainment /
         Medcom.   Distributor: Trainex Corporation.
                 Extraordinary footage traces human development from
         ovulation, development of embryo and fetus in mother's
         womb.   With focus on the resolution of three dangerous
         pregnancies.   Shows the latest medical advances in pre-
         natal care which have enabled such women to give birth to
         healthy babies.   C-A

171   THE BOND OF BREASTFEEDING
         20 min. , color, 1978.

Director: Julian Aston. Distributor: Perennial Education.
Advantages of the method; aims to answer common
questions and relate experiences of breastfeeding mothers.
C-A, Prof

172   THE BONDI STORY
12 min. , color, 1976.
Director: Griff Ruggles. Distributor: Film Communicators.
Jay and Carol Bondi lost their two children and the
entire neighboring family in a fire that occurred next door
to them. Jay demonstrates home fire detectors (thermal,
gas, smoke) and explains their use, installation, and the
merits of each. A

173   THE BONDING BIRTH EXPERIENCE
21 min. , color, 1976.
Director: Gay Courter. Distributor: Parenting Pictures.
Follows an expectant family from early labor at
home, through hospital labor and delivery, initial stages
of family attachment, postpartum in the hospital, breastfeeding, and home adjustment. Focuses on emotions during
these events, not specific techniques. This is a third
child. C-A

174   BOOKS ALIVE: A RAISIN IN THE SUN
6 min. , color, 1969.
Producer: Turnley Walker. Distributor: BFA Educational
Media.
Son assumes responsibility as head of black family
in face of prejudice and poverty, and tries to better him-
self and his family. From the play by Lorraine Hansberry.
S-A

175   BORN WITH A HABIT
30 min. , color, 1977.
Director: Edward A. Mason, M.D. Distributor: Documentaries for Learning.
Experiences of several women who gave birth to
babies addicted to heroin or methadone. Medical and social
work professionals examine and discuss two babies, in particular, and note the symptoms of neonatal withdrawal.
Honorable Mention, American Film Festival. Obstetrics
Award, John Muir Medical Film Festival. C-A, Prof

176   BOSS TOAD
26 min. , b&w, 1964.
Director: John Furia. Cast: Brian Keith, Ann Sothern
Richard Eyer. Distributor: Paulist Productions.
A teenager is pulled between the well-meaning re-
strictions placed on him by his parents and the selfish

demands of his girlfriend, whose parents don't believe in
discipline. The boy accepts and defends his parents' restrictions as coming from love. From the Insight series. J

177   BOURBON IN SUBURBIA
       27 min. , color, 1970.
       Director: John M. Lucas for Paulist Productions. Cast:
       Anne Francis, Marie Windsor. Distributor: The Media
       Guild.
             A suburban housewife falls deeper and deeper into
       alcoholism. After degrading behavior and the loss of her
       kids' respect, she decides to face the fact that she's an
       alcoholic. Covers the first three points of the Alcoholics
       Anonymous program. From the Insight series. S-A

178   A BOX FOR MR. LIPTON
       28 min. , color, 1972.
       Director: Marc Daniels for Paulist Productions. Cast:
       Kenneth Mars, Anne Seymour, Pat Barry, Robert Harris.
       Distributor: The Media Guild.
             A man allows everyone to manipulate him, and as
       a result he loses touch with himself and can't relate to his
       teenage children. From the Insight series. J-S

179   A BOY NAMED TERRY EGAN
       53 min. , color or b&w, 1973.
       Director: Isaac Kleinerman for CBS-TV News. Distribu-
       tor: Carousel Films.
             CBS-TV News spent a year with the Egan family,
       observing their 9-year-old autistic child at home and at
       Loyola University's Child Guidance Center, a school for
       autistic and emotionally disturbed children. Documents
       his gains during this one year, while his parents talk
       about their doubts, confusion, and self-blame. S-A

180   BOY OF THE NAVAJOS (Revised Edition)
       $10\frac{1}{2}$ min. , color, 1975.
       Producer: Coronet Films. Distributor: Coronet Films.
             A Navajo boy herds sheep in the Arizona desert,
       spends evenings with his parents and sister in the hogan,
       and joins them on a family trip to the trading post. E-I

181   BOY OF THE SEMINOLES (INDIANS OF THE EVERGLADES)
       $10\frac{1}{2}$ min. , color, 1956.
       Producer: Coronet Films. Distributor: Coronet Films.
             Life among the Seminole Indians of the Everglades--
       experiences a child's life-style and that of his family. E-I

182   BOYHOOD OF ABRAHAM LINCOLN
       $10\frac{1}{2}$ min. , color, 1967.
       Producer: Coronet Films. Distributor: Coronet Films.

Filmed at his reconstructed boyhood home in Rock-
port, Ind.   Points out that he survived a childhood spent
in poverty and that the encouragement of his stepmother in-
stilled a desire for learning.   From the Boyhood series.
Freedoms Foundation Award.   E-I

183   BOYHOOD OF GEORGE WASHINGTON (Revised Edition)
8 min. , color, 1975.
Producer: Coronet Films.   Distributor: Coronet Films.
        As a Virginia farmer at Mount Vernon, George Wash-
ington looks back over his earliest years--growing up on
his half-brother's Mount Vernon estate, etc.   From the
Boyhood series.   E-I

184   BOYHOOD OF GEORGE WASHINGTON CARVER
$12\frac{1}{2}$ min. , color, 1973.
Director: Robert Flaxman.   Distributor: Coronet Films.
        His early life in Missouri.   From the Boyhood
series.   Chris Award, Columbus Film Festival.   Honorable
Mention, Birmingham Educational Film Festival.   E-J

185   BOYHOOD OF THOMAS EDISON (Revised Edition)
$13\frac{1}{2}$ min. , color, 1978.
Producer: Jay Tannenbaum.   Distributor: Coronet Films.
        Filmed at Edison's boyhood home in Milan, Ohio.
Shows that even as a boy, Edison had great curiosity, per-
sistence, and ingenuity.   From the Boyhood series.   E-I

186   BOYHOOD SERIES   see
        BOYHOOD OF ABRAHAM LINCOLN   182
        BOYHOOD OF GEORGE WASHINGTON   183
        BOYHOOD OF GEORGE WASHINGTON CARVER   184
        BOYHOOD OF THOMAS EDISON   185

187   A BOY'S MAN
60 sec. , color, 1967.
Producer: St. Francis Productions.   Distributor: Tele-
KETICS.
        A boy's relationship with his father.   Portrays the
dignity of fatherhood.   A vignette especially for Father's
Day.   From the TeleSPOTS series.   E-A

188   THE BRADY BUNCH VALUES AND GUIDANCE SERIES   see
        ALL'S FAIR   55
        I AM ME   686
        MY BROTHER'S KEEPER   978
        WHAT PRICE HONESTY?   1500

189   BREAD & BUTTERFLIES SERIES   see
        ME, MYSELF & MAYBE   908
        OUR OWN TWO HANDS   1072

TAKING CARE OF BUSINESS 1344
THINGS, IDEAS, PEOPLE 1370
THE WAY WE LIVE 1465

190 BREAKUP
$14\frac{1}{2}$ min. , color, 1973.
Producer: KETC-TV. Distributor: Agency for Instructional
TV.
Becky's parents are separated; she imagines the re-
sults if they divorce. Captioned version avail. From the
Inside/Out series. I

191 BREASTFEEDING: A SPECIAL CLOSENESS
23 min. , color, 1977.
Directors: Daniel Bailes & Robert Silverthorne. Distributor: Motion, Inc.
Introduction to infant care and nurturing. Features
various ethnic and economic groups in an exploration of
the questions and fears raised by breastfeeding. Parents
discuss fitting breastfeeding into their family life and work.
J-A

192 THE BREASTFEEDING EXPERIENCE
23 min. , color, 1978.
Director: Gay Courter. Distributor: Parenting Pictures.
Experiences and feelings of 21 nursing mothers.
How to manage nursing for the first time, nursing for those
who work, nursing twins, etc. A, Prof

193 BRIAN AT SEVENTEEN
30 min. , b&w, 1971.
Exec. Producer: Gary Schlosser for the National Institute
of Mental Health. Distributor: National Audiovisual Center.
An adolescent's view of how school is both fulfilling
and not fulfilling his educational needs. Gives perspective
on his educational experience, his parents, and his life in
general. From the Social Seminar series. C-A

194 THE BRIDGE
10 min. , color, 1978.
Producer: Visual Transit Authority. Distributor: Brigham
Young University.
A man must choose whether to save his young son's
life or a train full of passengers. S-A

195 THE BRIDGE OF ADAM RUSH
47 min. , color, 1975.
Producer: Daniel Wilson. Distributor: Time-Life Multimedia.
In the early 1800s, 12-year-old Adam leaves Phila-

delphia and joins his mother with her new husband on a
farm.   His stepfather makes what the boy feels to be un-
reasonable demands upon him.   When they are forced to
build a bridge together in record time, their relationship
is strengthened.   An ABC Afterschool Special.   From the
Teenage Years series.   Christopher Award.   CINE Golden
Eagle.   I-A

196   A BRIDGE TO ADOPTION
       27 min. , color, 1967.
       Director: Leo Trachtenberg.   Distributor: Harvest Films.
            The story of three adoptive children and how each
       finds a home.   Explains New York State adoptive processes
       on both public and private levels.   C-A

197   BROTHERS AND SISTERS
       14 min. , color, 1973.
       Producer: WNVT-TV.   Distributor: Agency for Instruc-
       tional TV.
            David fails to attend his sister's class play when he
       promised he would.   From the Inside/Out series.   I

198   BUBBLE, BUBBLE, TOYS, AND TROUBLE
       10 min. , color, 1975.
       Producer: Production House, Inc. , for the U.S. Consumer
       Product Safety Commission.   Distributor: National Audio-
       visual Center.
            Evaluation of good and bad children's toys and ele-
       ments of danger to watch out for.   A

199   THE BURKS OF GEORGIA
       56 min. , color, 1976.
       Directors: Albert Maysles, David Maysles, Ellen Hovde,
       Muffie Meyer for Westinghouse Broadcasting Corp.   Dis-
       tributor: Carousel Films.
            Profile of a poor, rural American family in which
       ten of 13 children survive and live with or within yards of
       their parents.   Under-educated and unskilled, they work
       for low wages in a local carpet factory and live on land
       cluttered with grandchildren, livestock, and junked cars.
       From the Six American Families series.   S-A

From <u>The Burks of Georgia</u>.   Courtesy Carousel Films.

200   BUT IS THIS PROGRESS?
         51 min., color, 1973.
         Director: Darold Murray for NBC-TV News.   Distributor:
         Films Inc.
              Studies the effects of 20th-century technology on
         three generations of Americans (a couple in their seventies;
         a wealthy, middle-aged couple who grew up during the De-
         pression; and a young woman), and questions the quality
         of life that technology creates.   J-A

201   ...BUT WHAT IF THE DREAM COMES TRUE
         52 min., b&w or color, 1971.
         Producer: Robert Markowitz for CBS-TV News.   Narra-
         tor: Charles Kuralt.   Distributor: Carousel Films.
              The Sam Greenawalt family of Birmingham, Mich.,
         has everything and wants more.   Sam and his wife are
         vaguely dissatisfied with their values and position in life;
         they move to a better home and neighborhood, but face
         trouble in paradise--the wife's discontent as a homemaker,
         racial problems in surrounding communities, and their
         children.   Blue Ribbon, American Film Festival.   J-A

202   BY THEMSELVES
         34 min. , b&w, 1977.
         Director: Marlene Booth.   Distributor: University of
         California, Extension Media Center.
                Three single, professional women--one divorced,
         one widowed, and one unmarried--discuss their lives.   C-A

203   CBS CHILDREN'S HOUR SERIES   see
            J. T.   758

204   C. I. A. CASE OFFICER
         30 min. , color, 1978.
         Director: Saul Landau.   Distributors: Institute for Policy
         Studies; Penny Bernstein.
                Profile of former C. I. A. officer John Stockwell and
         his family.   Stockwell served the C. I. A. for 12 years in
         Africa and Vietnam.   He served as Chief of the Angolan
         Task Force during 1975 and early 1976.   He discusses his
         disillusionment with the C. I. A. , and his family (ex-wife,
         two sons, mother, and father) reflect on Stockwell's entry
         into and exit from service.   The film reveals a man who
         quit for all the wrong reasons (stomach pains and disgust
         with sloppy tactics), and a wife who divorced him for all
         the right reasons.   C-A

205   THE CABINET
         14 min. , color, 1972.
         Director: Suzanne Bauman.   Distributor: Carousel Films.
                Wooden cabinet full of family memorabilia (dolls,
         old photos, puppets, and toys) comes alive to trace the
         inner life and thoughts of a young girl who grows up and
         old.   Animation and live action.   CINE Golden Eagle.   J-A

206   CABINETMAKING   see
            18TH CENTURY LIFE IN WILLIAMSBURG, VIRGINIA   411

207   THE CALIFORNIA REICH
         60 min. , color, p. 1975, r. 1976.
         Directors: Walter F. Parkes & Keith Critchlow.   Distribu-
         tor: Paramount Pictures Corp.
                A visit with some of the members of the Nationalist
         Socialist White People's Party in several California cities.
         The horror of this film is the revelation that blue-collar
         families living in suburban tract houses are avid members
         of the Party.   Parents are shown indoctrinating children.
         Children mouth racist slurs.   Families celebrate Hitler's
         birthday.   Red Ribbon, American Film Festival.   S-A

208   A CALL FOR HELP
         19 min. , color, 1976.
         Director: Vincent Scarza for the Bureau of Community

Health Services, Public Health Service. Distributor: National Audiovisual Center.

Designed to help police deal with Sudden Infant Death Syndrome deaths. Includes examples of proper interviewing techniques. Training film. From the Sudden Infant Death Syndrome series. C, Prof

209 CALL ME MAMA
14 min., color, 1977.
Director: Miriam Weinstein. Distributor: Polymorph Films.

Questions whether there is a right or best way to raise a child, with focus on the 30-year-old filmmaker and her 18-month-old son Eli. J-A

210 CAMPAIGN
20 min., color, 1973.
Director: Jim Kennedy. Distributor: Churchill Films.

Documents a young housewife/mother's race for a California State Senate seat. She wages a rousing campaign with the help of volunteers and comes within 1 percent of defeating her opponent. J-A

211 CAN A PARENT BE HUMAN?
$11\frac{1}{2}$ min., color, 1971.
Director: Kent Mackenzie. Distributor: Churchill Films.

Young people discuss parent/child contact, i.e., parents who frighten their children vs. those who manage successful contact. Open-ended. From the Searching Years: The Family series. J-A

212 CAN DO/CAN'T DO
15 min., color, 1973.
Producer: WVIZ-TV. Distributor: Agency for Instructional TV.

Dotty wishes she were her brother or sisters. Designed to help children deal with and accept stages of their own growth and development. From the Inside/Out series. I

213 CAN I TALK TO YOU, DAD?
60 sec., color, 1968.
Director: Bruce Baker. Distributor: TeleKETICS.

Dramatic vignette in which a teenager tries to get his father to listen to him, but the father remains absorbed in something else. From the TeleSPOTS series. J-A

214 CAN YOU HEAR ME?
26 min., color, 1968.
Producer: Lester Cooper for ABC-TV. Distributor: International Film Bureau.

A family attempts to make a normal home life for their deaf child. The mother and child must learn certain skills before they can communicate; they learn language at home and at the John Tracy Clinic in Los Angeles. They are encouraged to continue by associating with families who share common problems. C-A

215   CARE OF THE INFANT--ANIMAL AND HUMAN
       22 min. , color, 1976.
       Director: Ivan Tors. Distributor: Perennial Education.
             Filmed in the U.S. and Africa, this production compares and contrasts childbirth, postnatal care, and early infant development in animals of the African bush (elephants, giraffes, baboons, wildebeest) with humans. Similarities are emphasized, and points to areas that can lead to abuse, neglect, and future mental illness. S-A

216   CARE OF THE NEWBORN BABY--THE NURSE'S ROLE IN
       INSTRUCTING THE PARENTS
       31 min. , b&w, 1944.
       Producer: Office of Education, with the U.S. Public Health Dept. Distributor: National Audiovisual Center.
             How nurses can teach parents to care for their newborn babies--in the home, clinic, and hospital. Training film. From the Nursing series. C, Prof

217   CARE OF THE YOUNG RETARDED CHILD
       18 min. , color, 1965.
       Producer: Carl J. Ross. Distributor: International Film Bureau.
             Stresses importance of good care and management. Such children will follow some growth patterns, but some will be slower. A public health nurse works in family situations and child psychologists assess children in a hospital clinic. C-A, Prof

218   CARE THROUGH PARENTS: CREATING A NEW SPACE IN
       PEDIATRICS
       14 min. , color, 1974.
       Producer: Jonathan Flaccus/CORT Motion Pictures for Family Health Care Nursing, School of Nursing, University of California. Distributor: University of California, Extension Media Center.
             Ways in which parents can participate in the care of a hospitalized child and why this participation is essential to the child's well-being, thus avoiding the traumatic effects of separation. A

219   CAREER AWARENESS: THE ALTERNATIVE
       11 min. , color, 1971.
       Director: Skeets McGrew. Distributor: BFA Educational Media.

A young boy can't understand why his father would
quit a lucrative executive position for a job building boats.
I-J

220   CAREERS AND BABIES
        20 min. , color, 1976.
        Director: Georgia Morris.   Distributor: Polymorph Films.
             Four women--two have children, two do not--react
        to the question of having careers and babies.   S-A

221   CARL ROGERS ON MARRIAGE: AN INTERVIEW WITH BOB
        AND CAROL
        44 min. , color, 1973.
        Director: Dr. John M. Whiteley.   Distributor: American
        Personnel and Guidance Association.
             A dramatic change in the nature of a six-year mar-
        riage comes about because of the man's outside affairs.
        The couple have an open marriage now and discuss stresses
        and enrichment that resulted.   Dr. Rogers comments.
        Training film.   C, Prof

222   CARL ROGERS ON MARRIAGE: AN INTERVIEW WITH HAL
        AND JANE
        44 min. , color, 1973.
        Director: Dr. John M. Whiteley.   Distributor: American
        Personnel and Guidance Association.
             This couple have five children and have been mar-
        ried 15 years.   During this interview, their problems,
        pain, and sources of joy come through.   Hal suffers because
        Jane is training for a profession and eventually becomes in-
        dependent.   Dr. Rogers comments.   Training film.   C,
        Prof

223   CARL ROGERS ON MARRIAGE: AN INTERVIEW WITH
        JANE AND JERRY
        44 min. , color, 1973.
        Director: Dr. John M. Whiteley.   Distributor: American
        Personnel and Guidance Association.
             After 17 years of marriage and two children, the
        wife causes the family to return to a former home where
        she can accept a professional position for which she's
        trained.   This devastates her husband, but he finally agrees
        to change jobs and move.   They discuss children, sex, and
        money, too.   Dr. Rogers comments.   Training film.   C,
        Prof

224   CARL ROGERS ON MARRIAGE: AN INTERVIEW WITH
        NANCY AND JOHN
        42 min. , color, 1973.
        Director: Dr. John M. Whiteley.   Distributor: American
        Personnel and Guidance Association.

This couple lived together for one-and-a-half years before marriage. After being married for six months, they compare and contrast married life with living together without marriage. Dr. Rogers comments. Training film. C, Prof

225   CARL ROGERS ON MARRIAGE: PERSONS AS PARTNERS
28 min. , color, 1973.
Director: Dr. John M. Whiteley. Distributor: American Personnel and Guidance Association.
Dr. Rogers notes factors that distinguish satisfying male/female partnerships and those that cause unhappiness, separation, or divorce. Training film. C, Prof

226   THE CASE OF THE ELEVATOR DUCK
17 min. , color, 1974.
Director: Joan Micklin Silver. Distributor: Learning Corp. of America.
A black boy living in an urban housing project finds a duck in the elevator. The child aims to keep the pet until he can find its owners. His mother has her own ideas about the matter. Red Ribbon, American Film Festival. E-I

227   CATHERINE
22 min. , b&w, 1974.
Director: Amelia Anderson. Distributor: Creative Film Society.
A psychological drama comparing widely different life-styles of two sisters: one is single, the other is married and living in suburbia with mother, dog, kids. The sisters confront each other and examine their values. Gold Medal, Virgin Islands International Film Festival. C-A

228   CAVALCADE OF AMERICA SERIES   see
A MATTER OF HONOR: SAM HOUSTON   904
WHAT MIGHT HAVE BEEN: JEFFERSON DAVIS   1499
YOUNG ANDY JACKSON   1566

229   CECILY
7 min. , color, 1974.
Director: Pavla Reznickova for Short Film Prague. Distributor: Learning Corp. of America.
Animated tale of a homely little girl who loves to sing, but who is abused by her grandmother to such an extent that she literally takes off for Africa, forms an elephant orchestra and becomes world famous. E-I

230   CELEBRATING PASSOVER   see
FROM GENERATION TO GENERATION   546

231   CELEBRATION IN FRESH POWDER
        27 min. , color, 1973.
        Director: Paul Stanley for Paulist Productions. Cast: Can-
        dace Clark, Lynne Marta, Rick Kelman, Michael Shea.
        Distributor: The Media Guild.
                A pregnant teenager has a hard time facing an abor-
        tion. Her boyfriend finally owns up to his responsibility
        and proposes three choices: abortion, marriage, have the
        baby outside of marriage. She surprises her parents with
        her decision. From the Insight series. S-A

232   THE CESAREAN BIRTH EXPERIENCE
        25 min. , color, 1976.
        Director: Gay Courter. Distributor: Parenting Pictures.
                Cesarean-section mothers from urban and rural
        homes share their birth and recovery experiences. Emer-
        gency cesarean sections are also shown, from parents'
        point of view. C-A, Prof

233   A CHAIN TO BE BROKEN
        27 min. , color, 1978.
        Director: Jim Tartan. Distributor: FMS Productions.
                Individual and community solutions and alternatives
        to child abuse. Professionals and child abusers are heard.
        Community resources--Parents Anonymous, a crisis house,
        and a Trauma Council--are explored. Stresses the hered-
        itary nature of child abuse. Host: Arte Johnson. C-A

234   THE CHALLENGE
        12 min. , color, 1957
        Producer: USC, Dept. of Cinema. Distributor: University
        of Southern California.
                The problems and progress of first- and second-
        generation Japanese Americans. Documents reasons for
        the immigration of the first generation to America and
        their subsequent struggle for acceptance and retention of
        their cultural heritage for their children. S-A

235   CHANGES
        14½ min. , color, 1975.
        Producer: National Instructional TV. Distributor: Agency
        for Instructional TV.
                Twins David and Susanna mature at different rates
        and are uncomfortable with the social aspects of growing
        up. From the Self Incorporated series.   J

236   CHANGING LIFE SCRIPTS see
            LEARNING TO LIVE SERIES   810

237   THE CHANGING SCENE SERIES   see
            LINDA AND JIMMY   832
            ONE MORE YEAR ON THE FAMILY FARM?   1061

238   CHARACTER FORMATION IN DIFFERENT CULTURES
      SERIES see
         BATHING BABIES IN THREE CULTURES   124

239   A CHARACTER NEUROSIS WITH DEPRESSIVE AND COM-
      PULSIVE TRENDS IN THE MAKING: LIFE HISTORY OF
      MARY FROM BIRTH TO FIFTEEN YEARS
      40 min., b&w, sil., p. 1945, r. 1952.
      Producers: Margaret E. Fries, M.D., & Paul J. Woolf,
      M.S. Distributor: New York University.
         Shows interaction between Mary and her parents and
      the limiting effect of the familial situation on her personal-
      ity development. From the Studies on Integrated Develop-
      ment: Interaction Between Child and Environment series.
      Previous title--A PSYCHONEUROSIS WITH COMPULSIVE
      TRENDS IN THE MAKING. C, Prof

240   CHECK-IN TIME
      13 min., color, 1974.
      Director: Bernard Selling. Distributor: TeleKETICS.
         Dramatic episode in the life of a family with an
      alcoholic father. He breaks the bond of trust that he, his
      wife, and daughter once had. I-A

241   THE CHICAGO MATERNITY CENTER STORY
      60 min., b&w, p. 1976, r. 1977.
      Producer: Kartemquin Films, Ltd. Distributors: Hay-
      market Films; Women Make Movies.
         Documents the doomed efforts of black, Latin, and
      white mothers to save the Chicago Maternity Center, a
      78-year-old home-delivery service. Pushes to make health
      care more human and less institutional. Film available in
      two 30-min. parts from Women Make Movies: Part I,
      HEALTH CARE WORTH FIGHTING FOR; Part II, THE
      STRUGGLE FOR CONTROL. Silver Hugo, Chicago Inter-
      national Film Festival. S-A

242   CHICANO FROM THE SOUTHWEST
      15 min., color, 1970.
      Producer: Maclovia Rodriguez. Distributor: Encyclopaedia
      Britannica Educational Corp.
         Young Pancho is torn between the exotic lure of
      city life and more stable family traditions. From the
      Newcomers to the City series. I-J

243   CHICKEN SOUP
      14 min., b&w, p. 1970, r. 1973.
      Director: Ken Schneider. Distributor: Carousel Films.
         Willie and Anna Schecter celebrate the Jewish ritual
      of making some old-fashioned chicken soup in the Bronx.
      Also underscores their strong marital bond. Traces proc-
      ess from bird to bowl. Some commentary in Yiddish. I-A

244   CHILD ABUSE
29 min. , color and b&w, 1977.
Director: R. Durrell Robinson.   Distributor: AIMS
Instructional Media Services.
Battered-child syndrome, father/daughter incest,
and child neglect are dramatized to raise police conscious-
ness when investigating such cases.   Training film.   Red
Ribbon, American Film Festival.   C, Prof

245   CHILD ABUSE AND THE LAW
27 min. , color, 1977.
Producer: The Motion Picture Company, Inc.   Distributor:
Perennial Education.
What teachers can do to identify and legally help
abused and/or neglected school-age children.   Training
film.   C, Prof

246   CHILD ABUSE: CRADLE OF VIOLENCE
20 min. , color, p. 1975, r. 1976.
Director: J. Gary Mitchell.   Distributor: MTI Teleprograms.
Explores problem by documenting the stories of
former and currently abusing parents.   Outlets for violence
or abuse are given.   Underlines need for citizens to report suspected abuse.   S-A

247   CHILD ABUSE--DON'T HIDE THE HURT
12½ min. , color, 1978.
Producer: Charles Cahill & Associates.   Distributor:
AIMS Instructional Media Services.
Dramatizes a typical child-abuse case.   Covers the
child's sense of guilt and legal protection available to help
the parent.   Notes that abused children usually grow up to
be abusive parents, unless the pattern can be broken.   E-I

248   CHILD BEHAVIOR=YOU
15 min. , color, 1973.
Producer: Crawley Films Ltd. for the National Film
Board of Canada.   Distributor: Benchmark Films.
The role parents play in shaping a child's behavior,
and ways to identify and cope with various child behavior
problems during infancy, preschool, middle childhood, and
adolescence.   Stresses B. F. Skinner's theory of reinforc-
ing desired behavior.   S-A

249   CHILD LANGUAGE: LEARNING WITHOUT TEACHING
20 min. , color, 1974.
Producer: Davidson Films.   Distributor: Davidson Films.
Emphasizes the problems children face when learning
to communicate and that children need to be listened to--
to what they say and how they say it.   From the Early
Childhood Development series.   C-A

250   CHILD MOLESTATION: WHEN TO SAY NO
         $13\frac{1}{2}$ min. , color, 1978.
         Producer: Charles Cahill & Associates.   Distributor:
         AIMS Instructional Media Services.
                Teaches children how to deal with four approaches--
         a small boy approached on a playground, a young girl in-
         vited to a neighbor's apartment alone, an attempt by a
         close relative, and a young girl stopped on a public street.
         I-J

251   CHILD MOLESTERS: FACTS AND FICTION
         30 min. , color, p. 1972, r. 1974.
         Director: Ian Stuart for Summerhill Productions.   Distribu-
         tor: Paramount Communications.
                Parents and children discuss the issues, facts, and
         myths related to child molesters.   A penologist covers of-
         fenders and role of police and courts.   From the Commu-
         nity Protection and Crime Prevention series.   S-A

252   CHILD/PARENT RELATIONSHIPS
         $28\frac{1}{2}$ min. , color, 1976.
         Producer: WTTW/Chicago for the Par Leadership Training
         Foundation.   Distributors: Perennial Education; National
         Audiovisual Center (rental only).
                Discusses infant stimulation and image building with
         everyday activities for parents, grandparents, and preschool
         children.   A composite of vignettes from the first five
         films in the Look at Me! series.   A

253   THE CHILD: PART I, JAMIE, ETHAN AND MARLON,
         THE FIRST TWO MONTHS
         29 min. , color, p. 1973, r. 1975.
         Director: Robert Humble for the National Film Board of
         Canada.   Distributor: CRM/McGraw-Hill Films.
                Cinema vérité record of the growth and development
         of three infants from birth through two months of age.   No
         lecture; just observation of family life.   S-A

254   THE CHILD: PART II, JAMIE, ETHAN AND KEIR, 2-14
         MONTHS
         28 min. , color, p. 1973, r. 1975.
         Director: Robert Humble for the National Film Board of
         Canada.   Distributor: CRM/McGraw-Hill Films.
                Traces the development (discovery, basic skills,
         personality development, mood changes) of three children
         from two to 14 months.   Cinema vérité record of family
         and growth patterns.   S-A

255   THE CHILD: PART III, DEBBIE AND ROBERT, 12-24
         MONTHS
         29 min. , color, p. 1973, r. 1975.

Director: Robert Humble for the National Film Board of Canada.   Distributor: CRM/McGraw-Hill Films.

Cinema vérité study of family and growth patterns of two children from one to two years.   Shows that mastery of physical skills precedes mastery of language, development of active interest in household and family activities, and other-oriented form of imitation.   National Council on Family Relations Award.   S-A

256   CHILDBIRTH
17 min., color, 1972.
Director: Alvin Fiering.   Distributor: Polymorph Films.

The birth of a baby, plus interaction of parents through prep classes, labor and delivery, care of baby during rooming-in.   Short version of NOT ME ALONE (1034).   S-A

257   CHILDBIRTH AND PROBLEMS OF CHILD PATIENTS
59 min., color, 1974.
Producer: University of Kentucky for Rescue and Emergency Medical Services Division, National Highway Traffic Safety Administration.   Distributor: National Audiovisual Center.

Training film for emergency medical technicians. From the Medical-Legal Component series.   C-A, Prof

258   CHILDHOOD AGGRESSION: A SOCIAL LEARNING APPROACH TO FAMILY THERAPY
31 min., color, 1974.
Director: Steven D. McAdam.   Distributor: The Media Guild.

A boy's aggressive behavior makes his family miserable and affects his schoolwork.   He and his family go for treatment at the Oregon Research Institute Family Center, and changes are shown within the family as treatment progresses.   Reenacted case study by family involved. From the Behavior Modification Special Education series. Film formerly titled A SOCIAL LEARNING APPROACH TO FAMILY THERAPY.   CINE Golden Eagle.   National Council on Family Relations Award.   C-A, Prof

259   CHILDHOOD SEXUAL ABUSE: FOUR CASE STUDIES
50 min., color, 1977.
Producer: Cavalcade Productions.   Distributor: MTI Teleprograms.

Four female victims of childhood sexual abuse try to work through their painful memories during a weekend therapy group.   Training film.   Based on the same cases presented in THE LAST TABOO (802).   C, Prof

260   CHILDHOOD: THE ENCHANTED YEARS
52 min., color, 1970.

Director: Nicolas L. Noxon for MGM Documentary. Distributor: Films Inc.

Experiments and long-term studies by psychologists continually try to fathom the mystery of a child's rate of mental development. National Council on Family Relations Award. S-A

261   CHILDREN: A CASE OF NEGLECT
56 min. , color, 1974.
Producer: Pamela Hill for ABC-TV News. Distributor: Macmillan Films.

Examines low- and middle-income parents' inability to meet basic medical costs for their children's good health. S-A, Prof

262   CHILDREN IN PERIL
22 min. , color, 1972.
Producer: Marlene Sanders for ABC-TV News. Distributor: Xerox Films.

A tour of several agencies and hospitals throughout the U.S. where battered children are treated. Also visits parent therapy groups. News Women's Club of New York, Front Page Award. S-A

263   CHILDREN IN THE HOSPITAL
44 min. , b&w, 1962.
Director: Edward A. Mason, M.D. Distributors: Documentaries for Learning; International Film Bureau.

Documents the emotional responses of two young girls to the stress of being hospitalized for illness and separated from their parents. C-A, Prof

264   CHILDREN OF DIVORCE
37 min. , color, 1976.
Director: Mike Gavin for NBC-TV. Narrator: Barbara Walters. Distributor: Films Inc.

Studies show that the real victims of divorce are the children, and that as a result parents should keep their hostilities in check and allow free access to both parents. Covers child-support laws, Parents without Partners, and questions of custody. Christopher Award. S-A

265   CHILDREN OF DIVORCE--TRANSITIONAL ISSUES FOR ELEMENTARY SCHOOL AGE
12 min. , color, 1977.
Producer: Dr. John M. Whiteley. Distributor: American Personnel and Guidance Association.

Vignettes raise problems encountered by children whose parents are getting divorced or who are entering into new family relationships. Highlights anxiety reactions. A stimulus film. E

266   CHILDREN OF DIVORCE--TRANSITIONAL ISSUES FOR
      JUNIOR HIGH AND HIGH SCHOOL AGES
      12 min. , color, 1977.
      Producer: Dr. John M. Whiteley. Distributor: American
      Personnel and Guidance Association.
            Vignettes present anxiety-provoking situations for
      teens whose parents are divorcing or beginning new rela-
      tionships. J-S

267   CHILDREN OF THE FIELDS
      20 min. , color, 1973.
      Producer: Bobwin Associates, Inc. Distributor: Xerox
      Films.
            Focuses on the 10-year-old daughter of a Chicano
      migrant family who moves from Arizona to New Mexico to
      California. It's a tough life--continually moving with the
      crops--but her loving family makes her happy. From the
      Come Over to My House series. E-I

268   CHILDREN OF THE LONG-BEAKED BIRD
      29 min. , color, p. 1975, r. 1976.
      Producer: Peter Davis with Swedish Television. Distribu-
      tor: Bullfrog Films.
            A portrait of a native American family and especially
      of 12-year-old Dominic, who straddles the traditional ways
      of his forefathers and contemporary American culture. The
      family lives near the Little Big Horn battlefield; Dominic
      is the great-great-grandson of a Crow Indian scout who
      tried to warn Custer. I-J, A

269   CHILDREN'S AGGRESSION: ITS ORIGIN AND CONTROL
      17 min. , color, 1974.
      Producer: Davidson Films. Distributor: Davidson Films.
            Examines the basis for normal aggression in young
      children. Presents methods for effectively managing this
      behavior. From the Early Childhood Development series.
      C-A

270   CHILDREN'S CLOTHES--HOW TO CHOOSE THEM
      21 min. , color, 1967.
      Sponsor: Buster Brown Textiles. Distributor: Association
      Films.
            Covers quality, fabric, laundry tests, stitching,
      hems, snaps, elastic, labels. S-A

271   CHILD'S PLAY
      20 min. , color, 1978.
      Producer: McGraw-Hill Films & Coast Community College.
      Distributor: CRM/McGraw-Hill Films.
            Shows how mental, social, emotional, and physical
      growth are affected by a child's form of play. Notes par-

ents' role in introducing new playthings that offer learning
challenges.   From the Developmental Psychology series.
S-A

272   CHINESE RESTAURANT   see
          MY FAMILY BUSINESS 983

273   CHOICES
          28½ min. , color, 1977.
          Director: Gilbert Altschul for Gallaudet College.   Distribu-
          tor: Journal Films.
                    A deaf couple and their friends, who are not deaf,
          face similar decisions--whether to rent or buy a new house,
          to go back to work after the children return to school, etc.
          Decision making for deaf adults.   A

274   CHRIS AND BERNIE
          25 min. , color, 1974.
          Directors: Bonnie Friedman & Deborah Shaffer.
          Distributor: New Day Films.
                    Two single, divorced women live together and share
          child-rearing and housekeeping duties.   One is a nurse,
          the other is a carpenter.   Red Ribbon, American Film
          Festival.   S-A

275   CHRIS BEGINS AGAIN
          26 min. , color, 1975.
          Director: David Vogt.   Distributor: Education Development
          Center.
                    Traces the daily activities of a 30-year-old mother
          who contacted the Education Development Center's Career
          Education Project ("designed to meet the career-related
          needs of home-based adults") to make major life changes.
          S-A

276   CHRISTMAS IN APPALACHIA
          29 min. , b&w, 1965.
          Producer: Bernard Birnbaum for CBS-TV News.   Narrator:
          Charles Kuralt.   Distributor: Carousel Films.
                    The poverty of the abandoned coal mining community
          of Whitesburg, Ky. --discouraged adults, hopeless children,
          shacks for homes, poor education, a barren Christmas in
          a land of plenty.   Blue Ribbon, American Film Festival.
          J-A

277   CIDER MAKER
          18 min. , color, 1975.
          Director: Philip Courter.   Distributor: Paramount Com-
          munications.
                    A visit to a family-run cider mill in New Jersey.
          From the Yesterday and Today series.   I-A

278   CIPHER IN THE SNOW
      24 min. , color, 1973.
      Director: Keith Atkinson.   Distributor: Brigham Young
      University.
            A young boy withdraws from family, peers, and
      teachers and finally dies.   No one cared enough about him
      to predict this tragedy.   His parents' total unconcern set
      the pattern in motion.   Dramatic film.   Golden Delfan
      Award, Tehran International Film Festival.   I-A, Prof

279   THE CIRCLE OF LIFE SERIES   see
            TO BE A PARENT   1397
            TO BE GROWING OLDER   1398
            TO BE MARRIED   1399

280   CLAUDE
      3 min. , color, 1965.
      Director: Dan McLaughlin.   Distributor: Pyramid Films.
            A small boy with a football-shaped head lives in a
      posh house with a pair of conformist parents.   They con-
      tinually downgrade him, but Claude has better things to do.
      He ignores them.   Animation.   Silver Hugo, Chicago Inter-
      national Film Festival.   S-A

281   CLEROW WILSON'S GREAT ESCAPE
      25 min. , color, 1978.
      Producer: DePatie-Freleng Productions.   Distributor: Mac-
      millan Films.
            Animated saga of comedian "Flip" Wilson's ghetto
      childhood in Jersey City, N. J. , where he grew up with
      numerous brothers and sisters, who were farmed out to
      foster parents.   J-S

282   CLINICAL PATHOLOGY--FORENSIC MEDICINE OUTLINES
      SERIES   see
            THE BATTERED CHILD, PARTS 1 & 2   127

283   CLORAE AND ALBIE
      36 min. , color, 1975.
      Director: Joyce Chopra.   Distributor: Education Develop-
      ment Center.
            Profiles two black high-school friends who are now
      in their twenties.   Clorae got married.   Albie went to
      work.   They discuss how their present lives compare with
      the dreams they envisioned as adolescents.   One is divorced
      with three children and is going back to high school so that
      she can study to be a nurse.   The other is working her
      way through college.   From the Role of Women in American
      Society series.   Red Ribbon, American Film Festival.   S-A

284   CLOSEUP: INFLATION   see
            INFLATION--ONE COMPANY FIGHTS THE BATTLE   726

285   CLOWNS ARE FOR LAUGHING
        10 min. , color , 1972.
        Director: Arthur Gould.   Distributor: Pyramid Films.
            A wishful fantasy of a father and a son who are
        transformed into tramp clowns.   E

286   COCKABOODY
        9 min. , color, 1973.
        Directors: John Hubley & Faith Hubley.   Distributors: Pyr-
        amid Films; Films Inc.
            Animated tale of two sisters--aged three and five--
        who engage in some fantasy and play while Mom and Dad
        are out for the evening.   Examines their free-spirited
        banter as they explore their parents' things and experience
        sibling rivalry.   Voice-overs are the filmmakers' own
        daughters.   CINE Golden Eagle.   Golden Gate Award, San
        Francisco International Film Festival.   Silver Praxinoscope,
        New York International Animation Festival.   PS-I, A

287   COLLEGE CAN BE KILLING
        60 min. , color, 1978.
        Directors: Michael Hirsh & C. Richard Sato for WTTW.
        Distributor: Indiana University, Audio-Visual Center.
            Parents, students, deans, and advisors analyze the
        problem of student suicide.   S-A

288   COLONIAL LIVING
        15 min. , color, 1957.
        Director: Robert Longini.   Distributor: International Film
        Bureau.
            Life in an 18th-century Virginia town.   Household
        activities and the execution of crafts are shown.   Captioned
        version avail.   I-J

289   COME OVER TO MY HOUSE SERIES   see
            ALONE IN MY LOBSTER BOAT   57
            CHILDREN OF THE FIELDS   267
            I DON'T WANT TO SELL BABE   688
            NAVAJO GIRL   1005
            THEY'RE ATTACKING MY TREE FORT   1366
            TROUBLE ON MY PAPER ROUTE   1421
            WE'LL MAKE OUR OWN TEAM   1482

290   COMFORTS OF HOME
        40 min. , color, 1974.
        Director: Jerome Shore.   Story: Flannery O'Connor.
        Distributor: Phoenix Films.
            A mother and son have a seemingly good relationship
        until a young girl comes into the household and changes
        things.   S-A

291   COMING HOME
       27 min. , color, 1974.
       Director: Bill Thompson for WQED-TV. Distributor: The
       Stanfield House.
               Teenaged Charlotte leaves a state institution to live
       at Elm House, a residential home for the retarded, where
       she shares "a family life" with 11 other retarded young
       adults. Thoughts of neighbors about this residential facility--
       some for, some violently opposed--are noted. C-A

292   THE COMING OF THE CLONE
       28 min. , color, 1973.
       Director: Murray Golden for Paulist Productions. Cast:
       Barry Sullivan, Gary Collins, Brooke Bundy. Distributor:
       The Media Guild.
               A young, research scientist and his wife are ap-
       proached to become the first parents of a clone. The hus-
       band is all for it. The wife is opposed; she doesn't want
       to miss out on conventional motherhood. From the Insight
       series. S-A

293   COMMIT OR DESTRUCT
       30 min. , b&w, 1965.
       Producer: Lane Slate for NET. Distributor: Indiana
       University, Audio-Visual Center.
               The home life and work of a launch-control officer
       at the Western Test Range of Vandenburg Air Force Base.
       The officer and his wife and three children live in a Cali-
       fornia factory town that depends on the Air Force Base for
       its existence. Contrasts normal, middle-class family life
       with the nature of his job--to launch rockets that can de-
       stroy the world. From the Legacy series. J-A

294   COMMUNICATING FAMILY PLANNING--SPEAK, THEY ARE
       LISTENING
       27 min. , color, 1974.
       Producer: Airlie Productions for the Office of Population,
       Agency for International Development. Distributor: Na-
       tional Audiovisual Center.
               Demonstrates ways modern information, education,
       and mass media techniques can be used to bring people into
       a family planning program. From the International Popula-
       tion Programs series. A

295   COMMUNITY LIFE see
           18TH CENTURY LIFE IN WILLIAMSBURG, VIRGINIA 411

296   COMMUNITY LIFE: CARING ABOUT OUR COMMUNITY
       SERIES see
           TOO MANY PEOPLE 1410

297   A COMMUNITY NURSERY SCHOOL
         40 min. , b&w, 1966.
         Director: George Bouwman for the Horace Mann School,
         N. Y. Distributor: New York University.
               A cooperative nursery school in action, with children
         relating to each other, parents, and teachers. C-A

298   COMMUNITY PROTECTION AND CRIME PREVENTION
         SERIES see
             BABYSITTING 117
             CHILD MOLESTERS: FACTS AND FICTION 251

299   COMMUTERS see
             BIG TOWN 151

300   COMPARATIVE CULTURES AND GEOGRAPHY SERIES see
             TWO FAMILIES: AFRICAN AND AMERICAN 1426
             TWO FARMS: HUNGARY AND WISCONSIN 1427

301   CONCEPTION AND PREGNANCY
         28 min. , color, 1977.
         Producer: WXYZ-TV, Michigan. Distributor: McGraw-
         Hill Films.
               Physiology of conception: early indications, causes
         of difficulties, importance of good prenatal care. From
         the Inner Woman series. S-A

302   CONCEPTS IN TRANSACTIONAL ANALYSIS; BUILDING A
         NURTURING PARENT THERAPY IN A GROUP SETTING
         WITH MORRIS AND NATALIE HAIMOWITZ: PATSY
         18 min. , color, 1973.
         Director: Dr. John M. Whiteley. Distributor: American
         Personnel and Guidance Association.
               Morris and Natalie Haimowitz explore how to help a
         client learn to nurture him or herself, especially when the
         client's early parenting was non-supportive or mistreating.
         Training film. C, Prof

303   CONCEPTS IN TRANSACTIONAL ANALYSIS; THERAPY IN
         A GROUP SETTING WITH MORRIS AND NATALIE HAIMO-
         WITZ: BRUCE
         25 min. , color, 1973.
         Director: Dr. John M. Whiteley. Distributor: American
         Personnel and Guidance Association.
               Focuses on the parent-adult-child ego states that
         constitute the structure of personality in TA theory. Train-
         ing film. C, Prof

304   CONCEPTS IN TRANSACTIONAL ANALYSIS; THERAPY IN
         A GROUP SETTING WITH MORRIS AND NATALIE HAIMO-
         WITZ: MARY
         25 min. , color, 1973.

Director: Dr. John M. Whiteley. Distributor: American Personnel and Guidance Association.

Highlights the TA concept of scripts. Script decisions are usually formed early in childhood under parental pressure, and these decisions shape behavior. Training film. C, Prof

305 CONFLICT AND AWARENESS: A FILM SERIES ON HUMAN VALUES see
PARENT/CHILD RELATIONSHIPS: IT'S MY DECISION AS LONG AS IT'S WHAT YOU WANT 1079
SELF IDENTITY/SEX ROLES: I ONLY WANT YOU TO BE HAPPY 1250
SEPARATION/DIVORCE: IT HAS NOTHING TO DO WITH YOU 1255
YOUNG MARRIAGE: WHEN'S THE BIG DAY? 1567

306 CONQUEST TV SERIES see
MOTHER LOVE 960

307 CONSTRUCTIVE USE OF THE EMOTIONS
22 min., color, 1970.
Director: Charles G. Schelling. Distributor: University of California, Extension Media Center.

Sherman Kingsbury, researcher and consultant, reviews the classic methods parents use to isolate, inhibit, and disorient children. Anxiety, fighting, loving, and withdrawal are also discussed, as well as emotions. From the Management Development series. A, Prof

308 CONSUMER CON CAPERS
23 min., color, 1976.
Producer: Parthenon Pictures. Distributor: Pyramid Films.

A condensed version of the five films in the Consumer Fraud series (312), in which a family is educated to be good consumers. J-A

309 CONSUMER EDUCATION: BUDGETING
12 min., color, 1968.
Producer: Bailey-Film Associates. Distributor: BFA Educational Media.

Two sisters move into their own apartment. They overspend. Indicates the importance of sound budgeting. See also CONSUMER EDUCATION: INSTALLMENT BUYING (310) and CONSUMER EDUCATION: RETAIL CREDIT BUYING (311). J-C

310 CONSUMER EDUCATION: INSTALLMENT BUYING
13 min., color, 1968.
Producer: Bailey-Film Associates. Distributor: BFA Educational Media.

Two sisters learn about installment buying as they

go off to buy a car. See also CONSUMER EDUCATION: BUDGETING (309) and CONSUMER EDUCATION: RETAIL CREDIT BUYING (311).   J-C

311   CONSUMER EDUCATION: RETAIL CREDIT BUYING
       11 min. , color, 1968.
       Producer: Bailey-Film Associates.   Distributor: BFA Educational Media.
            A father shows his two daughters the right way to compute credit charges, the money paid in interest charges, and all other facets of buying on credit. See also CON-SUMER EDUCATION: BUDGETING (309) and CONSUMER EDUCATION: INSTALLMENT BUYING (310).   J-C

312   THE CONSUMER FRAUD SERIES (5 Films)
       10 min. each, color, 1976.
       Producer: Parthenon Pictures.   Distributor: Pyramid Films.
            Designed to educate consumers through comic dramatization involving members of the Gulley family.   In each film, family members can reverse their mistakes. Titles include: BAIT, BITE AND SWITCH--Teenager Gals-worthy Gulley visits a stereo store to buy an advertised special tape deck, which has been sold; he's sold an ex-pensive model instead.   HOME SWEET HOME IMPROVE-MENTS--The Gulley family is high-pressured into signing a contract for an outrageously high amount of money.   I'LL ONLY CHARGE YOU FOR THE PARTS--A man posing as a utility company inspector offers to do work, charging only for the materials.   He is paid and disappears.   THOSE MAIL ORDER MILLIONS--Grandma Gulley falls for a mail-order work-at-home scheme.   YOUR CREDIT IS GOOD UNFORTUNATELY--The young married Gulleys buy furni-ture and appliances on time and can't meet the payments, so everything is repossessed. See also CONSUMER CON CAPERS (308).   J-A

313   CONSUMER REPORTS SERIES see
          FOOD FOLLIES 526

314   CONSUMERS IN A CHANGING WORLD SERIES see
          PLAY THE SHOPPING GAME 1120

315   CONVERSATIONS IN VERMONT
       26 min. , b&w, 1970.
       Director: Robert Frank.   Distributor: New Yorker Films.
            The filmmaker examines the gap between himself and his children, as well as his own angst.   Montage of family-album photos detail themes of growing up.   C-A

316   COPING WITH PARENTS
       15 min. , color, 1973.

Director: Ben Norman. Distributor: FilmFair Communications.

Three common conflicts between teens and their parents are dramatized--a girl's mother nags her, a boy's father regularly seems to criticize and argue with him, and a third boy feels his mother ignores him. A narrator explains how the teens reinforce their parents' behavior. J-A

317 COPS
18 min. , b&w, 1971.
Producer: CBS-TV News. Distributor: Carousel Films.

Cops are also human beings, husbands, and fathers. Shows how they react to continual stress and handle anxiety and fear. From the 60 Minutes TV series. I-A

318 CORPUS DELICTI--HOMICIDE
17 min. , color, 1975.
Producer: Woroner Films, Inc. Distributor: MTI Teleprograms.

A jealous husband (victim) accuses his friend of having an affair with his wife. The friend (defendant) assumes that the jealous husband is reaching for a weapon, so he pulls out a gun and shoots him. A trial develops the concept of corpus delicti. From the National District Attorney's Association Evidence Training series. C, Prof

319 COUNSELING--A CRITICAL INCIDENT
8 min. , color, 1971.
Producer: National Institute of Mental Health. Distributor: National Audiovisual Center.

Pastor counsels a distraught mother who has discovered that her child smokes pot. Questions the counselor's position on this case and the relationship between the counselor's views on religion, popular opinion, public laws, and the treatment of others. From the Professional Drug Films series. C-A, Prof

320 COUNTRY FAMILIES
13 min. , color, 1975.
Producer: WGBH-TV, Boston. Distributor: Films Inc.

Two short portraits of real-life American kids; vignettes include: MOUNTAIN COUSINS--Chuck visits his cousin Steve in North Carolina. They do farm chores and have fun. FARM LIFE--Renae's family runs a corn farm in Nebraska. When Himiko comes from Japan to spend the summer, Renae gives her a tour of the farm. Then the family gathers for a hearty meal and goes social dancing. From the Best of Zoom series. E-I

321   THE COUPLE
15 min. , b&w, 1968.
Director: Michael Wadley.   Distributor: New York University.
    Dramatic look at the problems a young married couple have in relating and adjusting to each other.   C-A

322   CRAIG AT HOME
13 min. , b&w, 1974
Director: John Friedman.   Distributor: Education Development Center.
    Craig, at four, is the youngest of four children in a suburban, black family.   The father is a school principal. From the Exploring Childhood: Family and Society series. J-A

323   CRIME AND THE CRIMINAL
33 min. , b&w, 1973.
Director: Richard Brooks.   Book: Truman Capote.   Distributor: Learning Corp. of America.
    Explores a murderer's childhood background to give some insight into his senseless and brutal slaying (with an accomplice) of a Kansas farm family.   True story.   Excerpt from the feature film IN COLD BLOOD.   From the Great Themes of Literature series.   S-A

324   CRIME AT HOME--WHAT TO DO
21 min. , color, 1976.
Producer: Rick Pollack Productions.   Distributor: MTI Teleprograms.
    By showing how crimes in the home are initiated, aims to motivate viewers to make home protection a must. A

325   CRIME IN THE HOME
22 min. , color, 1973.
Producer: Macko Productions, with the Los Angeles County Sheriff's Dept.   Distributor: AIMS Instructional Media Services.
    Dramatic vignettes indicate how to protect yourself and your home.   Focuses on doors, windows, locks, guns, confrontation, property identification, empty houses, etc. With prevention tips.   J-A

326   CRIME, IT'S A MATTER OF TIME (RESIDENTIAL)
13 min. , color, 1974.
Producer: Woroner Films, Inc.   Distributor: MTI Teleprograms.
    Residential crime through the eyes of a fictional burglar.   Points out poor security and low-cost correction methods.   S-A

327   THE CRIME OF INNOCENCE
       27 min. , color or b&w, 1974.
       Director: Marc Daniels for Paulist Productions.   Cast:
       Martin Sheen, Lynn Carlin.   Distributor: The Media Guild.
              Homeowners, fearing lowered property values and
       harm to their children, fight for the eviction of a group of
       mentally retarded people who have rented a neighborhood
       house.   From the Insight series.   J-A

328   CRISIS IN LEVITTOWN, PA
       28 min. , b&w, 1958.
       Director: Lee R. Bobker for Dynamic Films.   Distributor:
       Kit Parker Films (rental only).
              Interviews with bigoted, unbigoted, and middle-of-the-
       road residents of a tract housing development about blacks
       living in their neighborhood.   A black man had purchased
       one of the tract houses in 1957 and caused a massive re-
       action from residents.   C-A

329   CRITICAL MOMENTS IN TEACHING SERIES   see
          WHAT DO I KNOW ABOUT BENNY?   1491

330   A CRY FOR HELP (PROTECTIVE SERVICES AND THE
       NEGLECTED CHILD)
       $19\frac{1}{2}$ min. , color, 1978.
       Producer: Charles Cahill & Associates, with the American
       Humane Association.   Distributor: AIMS Instructional Media
       Services.
              Three typical child-neglect cases are dramatized to
       show how a professional in child-protective services can
       help the child and parent.   Training film.   C, Prof

331   A CRY FOR THE CHILDREN
       11 min. , color, 1977.
       Director: James R. Burgess.   Distributor: Film Commu-
       nicators.
              The emotional impact on firefighters of children's
       deaths in home fires.   Presses for family home escape
       planning and installation of home fire (especially smoke)
       detectors.   S-A

332   A CRY OF PAIN
       15 min. , color, 1977.
       Director: John S. Allen.   Distributor: Mass Media Minis-
       tries.
              Explores the tragedy of child abuse in America, with
       suggestions for helping children and parents who live in
       destructive family relationships.   Includes interviews with
       abusive parents.   S-A

333   CUM LAUDE, COME LONELY
       27 min. , color, 1976.
       Director: John Meredyth Lucas for Paulist Productions.

Cast: John Megna, Gary Collins, Mariclare Costello.   Distributor: The Media Guild.

A shy, scholarly teenager is always at odds with his macho father and stutters because he is unable to confront him.   A classmate helps the boy assert himself; and after the father is taken ill, father and son reach an understanding.   From the Insight series.   S-A

334   THE CUMMINGTON STORY
40 min. , b&w, 1944.
Director: Helen Grayson.   Distributor: National Audiovisual Center.

The experiences of a refugee family who arrive in a New England town.   They at first face the problem of being "different" and then are accepted into community life.   Music by Aaron Copland.   C-A

335   DAD AND I
15 min. , color, 1970.
Producer: Northern Virginia Educational Telecommunications Association.   Distributor: Agency for Instructional TV.

Steve and his father enjoy an afternoon of fishing.   From the Ripples series.   E

336   DAD AND ME
11 min. , color, 1971.
Producer: King Screen Productions.   Distributor: BFA Educational Media.

Darrett, a black 7-year-old, aims to grow up to be just like his dad.   His dad has a good job, is a fine sportsman, a family man, and a loving parent.   Set in a mixed, low-income New York City apartment complex.   E-I

337   DANCING PROPHET
15 min. , color, 1971.
Director: Bruce Baker.   Distributor: TeleKETICS.

A black man, destined to be a minister by his father, goes into dance instead, using his talents to entertain the aged and infirm in his spare time.   Father and son struggle with their individual and conflicting interpretations of the ministry.   CINE Golden Eagle.   S-A

338   DANGER IN SPORTS: PAYING THE PRICE
56 min. , color, 1974.
Director: Phil Lewis for ABC-TV News.   Distributor: Macmillan Films.

Deflates the mystique of high-school football, noting the crippling injuries that often result.   Enlightening film for parents.   J-A

339   DAVID: OFF AND ON
42 min. , color, 1973.

Director: Martha Coolidge. Distributor: Films Inc.

By age 21, David Coolidge--brother of the filmmaker-- had been an alcoholic, heroin addict, a convict, and a mental patient. This film profile of a straightened-out dropout of the Sixties analyzes his troubled upper-middle-class family history, a sister who cares, and many of David's demons. John Grierson Award, American Film Festival. S-A

340 DAWN OF THE AMERICAN REVOLUTION: A LEXINGTON FAMILY
$15\frac{1}{2}$ min. , color, 1964.
Producer: Coronet Films. Distributor: Coronet Films.

The events that led to the outbreak of the American Revolution, with focus on the Miller family of Lexington and their visiting English uncle. Their young son becomes a drummer boy to help summon the Minutemen. Freedoms Foundation Award. I-S

341 DAY CARE TODAY
25 min. , color, 1973.
Director: Miriam Weinstein. Distributor: Polymorph Films.

Three day-care centers are viewed--a community-based center, a factory-related center for children of employees, and a university-related teacher training center that is open to the community. Studies comparative child care. C-A

342 THE DAY GRANDPA DIED
$11\frac{1}{2}$ min. , color, 1970.
Producer: King Screen Productions. Distributor: BFA Educational Media.

A young Jewish boy struggles to accept the death of his grandfather. E-I

343 A DAY IN THE FOREST
11 min. , color, 1976.
Producer: U.S. Forest Service. Distributor: National Audiovisual Center.

A family's carelessness in the forest is used to introduce forest-fire prevention. I-A

344 A DAY IN THE LIFE OF BONNIE CONSOLO
$16\frac{1}{2}$ min. , color, p. 1974, r. 1975.
Director: Barry Spinello. Distributor: Barr Films.

Bonnie Consolo, although born without arms, leads a productive life. Follows her through a typical day as she cares for her home and family and shares her thoughts about life. J-A

345 A DAY IN THE LIFE OF HARVEY MCNEILL
9 min. , color, 1976.

Producer: Ben Norman. Distributor: FilmFair Communications.

Harvey is a high-school student and a member of a solid, working-class family. The father has been laid off at the factory, but they survive because they utilize community resources that are for the most part free. J-A

346   THE DAY LIFE BEGINS
23 min. , b&w, 1963.
Producer: Jules Power for ABC-TV. Distributor: Carousel Films.

Traces the miracle of birth from the division of the one-celled amoeba to a complicated human birth. Actual animal births are included. Points out the difference between instinctive animal reproduction and the act of love between human parents. E-I

347   A DAY ON AN AMERICAN FARM
42 min. , color, 1963.
Producer: U.S. Dept. of Agriculture. Distributor: National Audiovisual Center.

With the use of modern equipment, long-range planning, and good management, the operation of a 300-acre dairy farm can be a successful family enterprise. Notes the role of the co-op and family participation in community life.

348   DEATH
43 min. , b&w, 1969.
Directors: Arthur Barron & Evelyn Barron. Distributor: Filmakers Library.

A portrait of a 52-year-old terminal cancer patient at Calvary Hospital, New York. Covers the responses of his family, hospital personnel, and other patients, and the problems of communicating to the dying person. C-A, Prof

349   DEATH: HOW CAN YOU LIVE WITH IT?
19 min. , color, 1976.
Director: Bernard McEveety. Cast: Will Geer, Johnny Whitaker. Distributor: Walt Disney Educational Media.

A boy must face the approaching death of his beloved grandfather. Excerpt from the feature film NAPOLEON AND SAMANTHA. From the Questions!!! Answers?? Set II series. I-J

350   DEATH NOTIFICATION
27 min. , color, p. 1976, r. 1977.
Director: D. Ferron. Distributor: Harper & Row Media.

How law officers should deal with reactions of survivors and their own emotional involvement when notifying survivors of a death in the family. Training film. C, Prof

351   DEATH OF A GANDY DANCER
        26 min. , color, p. 1976, r. 1977.
        Director: Arthur Barron.   Distributor: Learning Corp.
        of America.
              A young boy, his mother and father struggle with the
        terminal condition of the child's grandfather.   From the
        Learning to Be Human series.   Blue Ribbon, American
        Film Festival.   I-A

352   DECIDING
        14 min. , color, 1973.
        Producer: Centron Films.   Distributor: Centron Films.
              A brother and sister go out to buy a gift for their
        father.   Illustrates purchasing concepts.   From the Ele-
        mentary Consumer Education series.   E-J

353   THE DECISION
        $5\frac{1}{2}$ min. , color, 1975.
        Director: Rolf Brandis.   Distributor: Xerox Films.
              Questions whether a man should risk defying the
        Establishment or leave things alone.   His wife helps him
        make his historic decision.   Live action.   S-A

354   DECISIONS, DECISIONS
        29 min. , color, 1978.
        Director: Roger S. Olson.   Distributor: Brigham Young
        University.
              Debbie and Tom decide to marry, and as a result
        they are forced to make many other large and small de-
        cisions affecting themselves and their family and friends.
        S-A

355   DEGAS IN NEW ORLEANS
        14 min. , color, 1977.
        Director: Gary Goldman.   Distributor: Phoenix Films.
              In 1872, at age 38, Edgar Degas came to New Or-
        leans to visit his mother's family.   While there, he only
        painted family portraits.   His family urged him to marry;
        this only intensified his resolve to paint.   S-A

356   DELINQUENCY: THE PROCESS BEGINS
        28 min. , color, 1976.
        Producer: Joel Levitch for Jason Films.   Distributor:
        MTI Teleprograms.
              Profiles two 13-year-old boys from different ethnic
        and family backgrounds.   The influences on their lives are
        shown to include social forces as well as inherited patho-
        logical tendencies.   Parents, law officials, and educators
        discuss the juvenile justice system.   From the Issues in
        Juvenile Delinquency series.   J-A

357   DEMETRI ALEXANDROS' DIVE
        9 min. , color, 1977.

Producer: Lifestyle Productions. Distributor: Encyclopaedia Britannica Educational Corp.

The weekend of the Holy Cross service is an important holiday in the Greek-American community (men and boys dive for the cross). A young boy is sad because he won't have his father with him for the holiday. The boy wants to dive in memory of his father, but his mother refuses to allow him to dive because he is too young.   E-I

358   DEPENDENCE: A NEW DEFINITION
24 min. , color, 1972.
Producer: Tom Lazarus. Distributor: CRM/McGraw-Hill Films.

Examines human dependencies, e. g. , genetically inherited traits; drug dependency of unborn infants; pathological dependency of people with unmet oral needs in infancy; the role of family, marriage, church, nation, and job in molding dependent relationships. From the Abnormal Psychology series.   S-A

359   DEPRESSION: A STUDY IN ABNORMAL BEHAVIOR
27 min. , color, 1973.
Producer: Tom Lazarus. Distributor: CRM/McGraw-Hill Films.

Follows a young housewife/teacher during a period of depression--from her inability to functioning normally and her husband's attempt to ignore her erratic behavior, to his awareness that she is seriously disturbed and must be hospitalized. From the Abnormal Psychology series. Chris Bronze Plaque, Columbus Film Festival.   S-A

360   DESERT TREK
17 min. , color, 1976.
Producer: Mike Rhodes for Paulist Productions. Distributor: The Media Guild.

A boy, his uncle, and two of the boy's friends go into the desert to do a science project. All the children have been warned that the trek may prove dangerous, and the boy has been made aware of his uncle's diabetes. One boy turns out to be irresponsible, and a crisis results. Dramatic film. From the Bloomin' Human series.   I-J

361   THE DETACHED AMERICANS
33 min. , b&w, 1964.
Producer: WCAU-TV, Philadelphia. Narrator: Harry Reasoner. Distributor: Carousel Films.

Examines the problem of apathy. Points up reasons that stem, in most part, from the family.   I-A

362   DEVELOPMENT
33 min. , color, 1971.
Producer: Bruce Hart. Distributor: CRM/McGraw-Hill Films.

A sampling of human psychological development re-search. In one study, a mother and child are placed in a room alone with toys. As stressful factors are added, the child's physical contact with the mother increases and exploration decreases. From the Psychology Today series and the Developmental Psychology series. S-A

363 THE DEVELOPMENT OF FEELINGS IN CHILDREN
35 min. , color, p. 1974, r. 1975.
Director: Donald F. Connors, Jr. Distributor: Parents'
Magazine Films.
Shows how the caregiver can help a child develop and express his/her feelings. Includes events that may traumatize a child--first day at school, a stay in the hos-pital, a new baby, a death in the family. CINE Golden Eagle. S-A

364 THE DEVELOPMENT OF THE CHILD SERIES see
ADOLESCENCE: THE WINDS OF CHANGE 17
INFANCY 721

365 DEVELOPMENTAL CAREGIVING: DAY CARE CENTER
FOR INFANTS AND TODDLERS
28 min. , color, 1977.
Director: Josef Bohmer for Jewish Board of Guardians.
Distributor: New York University.
Notes the importance of sound day care for the first three years of life, the importance of individualized care-giver-child relationships, and the coordination of child care at the center with the care provided at home. C-A

366 DEVELOPMENTAL PSYCHOLOGY SERIES see
CHILD'S PLAY 271
DEVELOPMENT 362
HEREDITY AND ENVIRONMENT 644
INFANCY 722
MORAL JUDGMENT AND REASONING 950
PERSONALITY: EARLY CHILDHOOD 1103
PERSONALITY: MIDDLE CHILDHOOD 1104
PRENATAL DEVELOPMENT 1137
SEX ROLE DEVELOPMENT 1260

367 THE DEVIL'S WORK
28 min. , color, 1977.
Director: Don Fouser for WNET-TV. Distributor: Films
Inc.
Ten-year-old Joseph Jefferson tours Illinois in 1839 with a family theater troupe, often suffering through hard times. The family decides to build a theater in Springfield, Ill. , but the townspeople are opposed, so they levy a tax that the family can't pay. A lawyer saves the day for the family; his name is Abe Lincoln. From the Ourstory series. J-S

368   DEW DROP
      16 min. , color, 1978.
      Director: Gregg Schiffner. Distributor: Serious Business
      Company.
            The filmmaker's sense of loss as he comes to terms
      with his father's dying. Subjective camera--from the point
      of view of the dying man. Impressionistic use of home
      movies to convey a full range of father-son-family emotions.
      S-A

369   DIAL A-L-C-O-H-O-L SERIES   see
      IN THE BEGINNING   711
      THE LEGEND OF PAULIE GREEN   815

370   DIARIES, NOTES & SKETCHES   see
      LOST   LOST   LOST   851

371   THE DIARY OF A HARLEM FAMILY
      20 min. , b&w, 1968.
      Director: Joseph Filipowic. Distributor: Indiana Univer-
      sity, Audio-Visual Center.
            The photos of Gordon Parks explore the poverty-
      level existence of one black family in Harlem, N. Y. , e.g. ,
      lack of utilities and food, mother's despair, father's drink-
      ing. S-A

372   A DIFFERENT DRUM
      21 min. , color, 1974.
      Director: Scott Whitaker. Cast: Chief Dan George, Jay
      Silverheels. Distributor: Brigham Young University.
            A young Comanche boy is torn between his family's
      desire for him to attend college and his own desire and aptitude
      for a career as an auto mechanic. Cindy Award, Informa-
      tion Film Producers of America.   I-A

373   DIFFERENT FOLKS
      $14\frac{1}{2}$ min. , color, 1975.
      Director: Robert Gardner. Distributor: Agency for In-
      structional TV.
            A boy is uneasy and rebellious because his mother
      brings in most of the family income and he and his father
      and sister do the housework. From the Self Incorporated
      series. Red Ribbon, American Film Festival.   J, A

374   A DIFFERENT KIND OF HURT
      18 min. , color, p. 1976, r. 1977.
      Director: Anne Devaney for Children's Rehabilitation Unit,
      University of Kansas Medical Center. Distributor: Chil-
      dren's Rehabilitation Unit, University of Kansas Medical
      Center.
            The dynamics of child abuse and the important role
      of physicians in detecting signs of child abuse or neglect.
      Suggests action and possible results of that action for phy-
      sicians.   C, Prof

375   DIFFERENT WITH DIGNITY
      12 min. , color, 1973.
      Producer: Mike Rhodes for Paulist Productions. Distribu-
      tor: The Media Guild.
          Dramatic vignettes raise questions about male/female
      roles in contemporary society, especially in marriage.
      From the Vignette series.   J-A

376   THE DISAPPEARING HANDICAP
      29 min. , color, 1977.
      Director: Conrad Bentzen. Distributor: Special Purpose
      Films.
          A treatment program for disabled children and their
      families, emphasizing normal behavior of children as they
      learn to cope with disabilities.   C-A

377   DISAPPOINTMENT: A DAY THAT DIDN'T HAPPEN
      11 min. , color, 1973.
      Director: David Greene for Guidance Associates/Motion
      Media. Distributor: Xerox Films.
          Jennie and her parents enthusiastically prepare for
      a visit from her favorite uncle, who calls suddenly and
      cancels. Jennie is deeply disappointed.   I-J

378   THE DISPLACED PERSON
      $57\frac{1}{2}$ min. , color, 1977.
      Director: Glenn Jordan. Cast: John Houseman, Irene
      Worth. Story: Flannery O'Connor. Distributor: Perspec-
      tive Films.
          A Polish refugee arrives with his family at a Georgia
      farm in the 1940s. A priest who arranged their placement
      doesn't succeed in integrating them with people already liv-
      ing and working on the farm. Hostility builds, and tragedy
      results.   From the American Short Story series.   S-A

379   DIVORCE: FOR BETTER OR FOR WORSE
      49 min. , color, 1977.
      Director: James Benjamin for ABC-TV News. Distributor:
      CRM/McGraw-Hill Films.
          Such areas as: lawyers and the law, marriage and
      sex counseling, and displaced homemakers are covered,
      while actual case histories stress the need for legal reform,
      stricter regulation of counselors and therapists, greater
      public awareness of the financial and emotional problems
      facing divorced persons.   S-A

380   DIVORCE (PARTS I & II)
      20 min. each, color, 1975.
      Director: Ian Bernard. Distributor: American Personnel
      and Guidance Association.
          Two stimulus vignette films that aim to help define
      problems that occur in divorce situations. Part I focuses
      on fears, the stigma of divorce, emotional issues. Part II

focuses on relating to ex-spouse and problems of children.
Family Life Award, National Council of Family Relations.
C-A, Prof

381   DO I REALLY WANT A CHILD?
28 min. , color, 1975.
Director: Sam O'Steen.   Cast: Cloris Leachman, Martin
Balsam.   Distributor: Learning Corp. of America.
A 40-year-old woman with a fulfilling professional
career and a secure, childless marriage is pregnant; she
and her husband go through agony trying to decide whether
to have the child.   Edited from the TV film A BRAND
NEW LIFE (1632), and part of the Being a Woman series.
J-A

382   DR. BENJAMIN SPOCK--AN AMERICAN INSTITUTION
45 min. , color, p. 1977, r. 1978.
Director: Philip R. Blake.   Distributor: Phoenix Films.
Profile of the "baby doctor," including interviews
with his wife and children.   S-A

383   DR. SPOCK AND HIS BABIES
27 min. , b&w, 1970.
Director: Herman J. Engel.   Distributor: Texture Films.
The fellow who wrote the most famous book on child
care (1946) became one of the most outspoken leaders of
the peace movement of the Sixties.   A political profile.
Silver Dragon Award, Cracow Film Festival.   C-A

384   DOCTORS FOR PEOPLE
27 min. , color, 1977.
Sponsor: The American Academy of Family Physicians.
Distributor: Association Films.
The role of and need for the family physician, who
treats the whole family at all times, not just during a
crisis.   A

385   DOES ANYBODY NEED ME ANYMORE?
29 min. , color, 1975.
Director: Paul Bogart.   Cast: Maureen Stapleton, Paul
Sorvino.   Distributor: Learning Corp. of America.
A 46-year-old housewife painfully comes to terms
with her empty nest; she has to decide what to do with the
rest of her life.   Edited from the TV film TELL ME
WHERE IT HURTS (2036), and part of the Being a Woman
series.   J-A

386   DOLLEY AND THE "GREAT LITTLE MADISON"
28 min. , color, 1978.
Producer: Gaby Monet for Concepts Unlimited.   Cast: Lois
Nettleton.   Distributor: Modern Talking Picture Service.
A dramatization of the life of the Presidential couple--
James and Dolley Madison.   Spans 40 years of her life with
James and her return to Washington society as a widow.   I-A

387   DOMESTIC DISTURBANCE CALLS
       24 min. , color, 1972.
       Producer: Woroner Films, Inc. Distributor: MTI Tele-
       programs.
            Reenactments of common domestic disturbances take
       officers through important steps of interrogation while re-
       sponding to a complaint. Training film. C, Prof

388   DOMESTIC DISTURBANCES
       20 min. , color, 1978.
       Director: Paul Eide. Distributor: MTI Teleprograms.
            Shows police how to handle domestic disturbance
       calls, in this case, a violent quarrel between a husband
       and a wife, with the complaint phoned in by a neighbor.
       Training film. C, Prof

389   DONNIE
       25 min. , color, p. 1976, r. 1977.
       Director: Richard Shanahan. Distributor: Jerome L.
       Schulman, M. D. , Children's Memorial Hospital.
            Considers the personality development, impact on
       family, and social issues raised by hospitalization of a
       child who has spent two of his two-and-a-half years in an
       intensive care unit. C-A, Prof

390   DON'T GIVE UP ON ME
       $28\frac{1}{2}$ min. , color, 1975.
       Producer: Cavalcade Productions. Distributor: MTI
       Teleprograms.
            Barbara, the mother of two small children, has been
       accused of abusive behavior. Her baby may be taken away
       from her. A state-assigned caseworker tries to help Bar-
       bara deal with her problem. An adapted case history.
       Training film. Best of Category Award, National Council
       on Family Relations. C, Prof

391   THE DOONESBURY SPECIAL
       26 min. , color, 1977.
       Directors: John Hubley, Faith Hubley, Garry Trudeau. Dis-
       tributor: Pyramid Films.
            Based on Trudeau's comic strip "Doonesbury. "
       Young people live in a communal arrangement and must
       face personality quirks and changing viewpoints (Sixties vs.
       Seventies) of their housemates. Animation. Red Ribbon,
       American Film Festival. J-A

392   DOUBLE TROUBLE
       $14\frac{1}{2}$ min. , color, 1975.
       Director: Robert Gardner. Distributor: Agency for In-
       structional TV.
            Delia is upset about her mother's serious stroke,
       and her family doesn't help any by withholding information
       from her and not giving her any responsibility. From the
       Self-Incorporated series. J

393   DOUBLETALK
9 min. , color, 1975.
Director: Alan Beattie. Distributor: Learning Corp. of
America.
A young man comes to pick up a girl for a date.
Viewers hear not only what he, she, and her parents say,
but what they're thinking as well. Red Ribbon, American
Film Festival. S-A

394   A DREAM IS WHAT YOU WAKE UP FROM
50 min. , color, 1978.
Director: Larry Bullard. Distributors: Third World
Newsreel; California Newsreel.
Cinema vérité study of three black families' day-to-
day activities; focuses on how they survive stress in different ways. Contrasts objective/subjective perceptions
of the world around them. C-A

395   DRINK, DRANK, DRUNK
59 min. , color, 1974.
Producer: WQED, Pittsburgh. Distributor: Indiana University, Audio-Visual Center.
Offers advice to Americans with alcoholic spouses,
relatives, friends, and co-workers on how to recognize and
handle an alcoholic. Makes note of AL-ANON, for families
of alcoholics who refuse treatment. With Carol Burnett.
S-A

396   DRUGS AND MEDICINES: HELP FOR A FRIEND
14 min. , color, 1975.
Producer: Moreland-Latchford Productions. Distributor:
Coronet Films.
Twelve-year-old Ted visits a drug clinic and talks
with a social worker and psychiatrist about ways to help
his brother, who is misusing drugs. I-J

397   DRUGS AND MEDICINES: USING THEM SAFELY
10 min. , color, 1975.
Producer: Moreland-Latchford Productions. Distributor:
Coronet Films.
When Judy leaves her prescription medicine within
reach of her younger sister, a possible disaster is avoided
because the medicine is in a safety container. I-J

398   DYING
97 min. , color, 1976.
Director: Michael Roemer. Distributor: WGBH-TV Educational Foundation.
Documentary on the lives of those with terminal
cancer, i. e. , family reactions, relations, and expressions
of those facing death. Includes focus on three such individuals and their families. Each episode ends in death.
Also includes a young widow who talks of her husband's
death. Blue Ribbon, American Film Festival. J-A, Prof

399   AN EAMES CELEBRATION: SEVERAL WORLDS OF
      CHARLES AND RAY EAMES
      90 min. , color, 1975.
      Director: Perry Miller Adato.   Distributor: Indiana Uni-
      versity, Audio-Visual Center.
             Profile of the prolific married couple--Charles and
      Ray Eames--the noted designers, filmmakers, artists.
      Red Ribbon, American Film Festival.   S-A

400   EARLY ABORTION
      8 min. , color, 1973.
      Director: Alan Barker.   Distributor: Perennial Education.
             Description of atraumatic aspiration abortion pro-
      cedures.   Includes an actual abortion and a "q & a" ses-
      sion with a group of patients.   S-A

401   EARLY CHILDHOOD DEVELOPMENT SERIES   see
         CHILD LANGUAGE: LEARNING WITHOUT TEACHING
             249
         CHILDREN'S AGGRESSION: ITS ORIGIN AND CONTROL
             269
         EGO DEVELOPMENT: THE CORE OF A HEALTHY
             PERSONALITY 408
         TEACHERS, PARENTS AND CHILDREN 1352

402   EARLY MARRIAGE
      26 min. , color, 1961.
      Producer: Churchill-Wexler Film Productions.   Distributor:
      Perennial Education.
             Shows that society as a whole has an important stake
      in every marriage, which indicates that marriage should be
      taken seriously by its partners.   J-S

403   EAST SIDE/WEST SIDE TV SERIES   see
         NO HIDING PLACE 1025
         WHO DO YOU KILL? 1514

404   ECHOES
      11 min. , color, 1974.
      Director: William Hubbell for Guidance Associates/Motion
      Media.   Distributor: Xerox Films.
             Eleven-year-old Ellen walks with her grandfather in
      the family cemetery and discovers the grave of 11-year-old
      Mary, who died in 1883.   Ellen comes closer to Mary by
      looking through an old family album; Ellen discovers her
      roots.   CINE Golden Eagle.   Certificate of Merit, Chicago
      International Film Festival.   I-J

405   ECONOMICS FOR ELEMENTARY SERIES   see
         INTERDEPENDENCE 734

406   EDDIE
      27 min. , color, 1974.

Director: Paul Stanley for Paulist Productions. Cast: Don
Stroud, Ellen Geer. Distributor: The Media Guild.
A super-jock fathers a retarded child. The man is
enraged and decides to institutionalize the baby boy so that
no one will ever know about the child. His wife refuses.
He sees no other recourse than to kill the child himself.
While attending a meeting of the National Association for
Retarded Children, the couple realize that they share com-
mon problems with many other couples. From the Insight
series. S-A

407   EDNA ST. VINCENT MILLAY: MILLAY AT STEEPLETOP
25 min. , color, p. 1974, r. 1976.
Director: Kevin Brownlow. Distributor: Films for the
Humanities.
Visits the poet's home and farm, where her sister,
Norma Millay Ellis, reflects on Edna's life and reads her
poems. Edna lived at Steepletop from 1925 until her death
in 1950. S-A

408   EGO DEVELOPMENT: THE CORE OF A HEALTHY PER-
SONALITY
20 min. , color, p. 1973, r. 1974.
Producer: Davidson Films. Distributor: Davidson Films.
Aims to isolate different stages of ego development
by first demonstrating how genetic factors affect personality
development. Also touches on mothering, satisfaction or
frustration of a child's oral-sensory needs, determining a
sense of trust or mistrust, muscular maturation in toddlers,
and sense of independence or self-doubt. From the Early
Childhood Development series. C-A, Prof

409   EGO STATES   see
        LEARNING TO LIVE SERIES   810

410   EIGHT INFANTS: TENSION MANIFESTATIONS IN RE-
SPONSE TO PERCEPTUAL STIMULATION
42 min. , b&w, sil. , 1950.
Producers: Sibylle Escalona, Ph. D. , & Mary Leitch, M. D. ,
for the Menninger Foundation, Dept. of Research. Distributor: New York University.
Behavior of eight infants--18 to 25 weeks of age--is
examined before and after introduction of toys, vigorous
play with siblings, and visiting relatives, etc. From the
Infant Psychology series. C, Prof

411   18TH CENTURY LIFE IN WILLIAMSBURG, VIRGINIA (3
Films)
10-21 min. each, color, 1966.
Producer: Colonial Williamsburg & Eastman Kodak Co.
Distributor: McGraw-Hill Films.
A series of three films that follow a cabinetmaker
and his family through a typical day in Williamsburg, Va.

Titles include: HOME LIFE (21 min.)--Covers the morning
hours; family breakfast; master and son go to cabinet shop;
slaves keep house.   CABINETMAKING (10 min.)--Afternoon
in the cabinet shop; son is taught skills of craft.   COM-
MUNITY LIFE (13 min.)--Mid-afternoon and evening; social
life; quiet evening at home; children do homework; mother
weaves cloth.   E-I

412   ELEMENTARY CONSUMER EDUCATION SERIES   see
          DECIDING   352
      WISE AND RESPONSIBLE CONSUMERSHIP   1531

413   ELEPHANTS
      27 min., color with b&w, p. 1973, r. 1974.
      Director: Richard P. Rogers.   Distributor: Film Images.
          Autobiographical film.   Harvard-educated filmmaker
      combines old family photos with parent interviews in an at-
      tempt to reject their conservative values.   S-A

414   ELIZA
      27 min., color, 1977.
      Director: Don Fouser for WNET-TV.   Distributor: Films
      Inc.
          Drama about a 17-year-old girl who took over man-
      agement of a South Carolina plantation and her ailing mother
      when her father was recalled to military duty in Antigua
      (1738).   She experimented with indigo, followed it up on her
      husband's estates and soon exported more than 135,000
      pounds of it annually.   True story of Eliza Lucas Pinckney,
      who lived to be 80.   From the Ourstory series.   J-S

415   ELIZABETH SWADOS: THE GIRL WITH THE INCREDIBLE
      FEELING
      39 min., color, 1977.
      Director: Linda Feferman.   Distributor: Phoenix Films.
          Eclectic profile of the composer, performer, musi-
      cian, and writer.   Much on her early family life; with
      home movies, live action, and animation.   Red Ribbon,
      American Film Festival.   S-A

416   EMERGENCY CHILDBIRTH
      22 min., color, 1961.
      Producer: Dept. of the Navy.   Distributor: National
      Audiovisual Center.
          Prepares corpsmen to assist in an emergency child-
      birth; with procedures, precautions, and postpartum care.
      Training film.   A, Prof

417   EMERGENCY CHILDBIRTH
      28 min., color, 1965.
      Producer: Public Health Service.   Distributor: National
      Audiovisual Center.
          Designed to prepare lay persons to help during an

emergency delivery when it is impossible to get mother to
the hospital.   Also, care of mother and baby after delivery.
Training film.   From the Medical Self-Help series.   A

418   EMERGENCY CHILDBIRTH
25 min. , color, 1978.
Producer: Paul Burnford.   Distributor: Perennial Education.
        A primer for adults who may be called upon to
assist in a childbirth; preliminaries through actual birth
and after.   Training film.   A

419   EMOTIONAL ASPECTS OF PREGNANCY
20 min. , color, p. 1977, r. 1978.
Director: Sally Marschall.   Distributor: Perennial Education.
        Prepares expectant mothers and fathers for emo-
tional changes experienced by both partners during pregnancy.   Focuses on two expectant couples and a single,
expectant mother.   Best of Category Award, National Council on Family Relations.   S-A

420   EMOTIONAL ILLNESS
30 min. , b&w, 1964.
Producer: Lloyd Ellingwood for NET.   Host: Dr. Maria
Piers.   Distributor: Indiana University, Audio-Visual Center.
        A young man's wife is suddenly hospitalized due to
a nervous breakdown.   Dr. Piers discusses his reactions
of fear and guilt, explores myths about mental disturbances
and psychiatry, and answers common questions about mental illness and psychiatry.   From the About People series.
S-A

421   EMOTIONAL TIES IN INFANCY
12 min. , b&w, 1971.
Producer: Office of Child Development, Dept. of Health,
Education & Welfare.   Distributor: National Audiovisual
Center.
        Compares four 8-to-10-month-old infants: a home-
raised girl with strong attachment to her mother; an institutionalized child strongly attached to his nurse; another
institutionalized baby who is indiscriminate in his attachment to any adult; and an institutionalized baby who is
withdrawn and uninterested in his surroundings and has
formed no attachments.   Points to the importance of strong
emotional ties between infant and adult.   C, Prof

422   EMPIRE OF THE SUN
25 min. , color, 1973.
Directors: Fred Gebauer & Phyllis Gebauer.   Distributor:
University of California, Extension Media Center.
        The beliefs, attitudes, and life-style of young men

and women who live in a religious community near Santa
Barbara, Calif., called the Brotherhood of the Sun. They
work their land, pray and meditate, raise crops and live-
stock, and run a store that sells community-produced
goods. S-A

423   ENERGY MONSTERS: HOW TO STARVE THEM
       $12\frac{1}{2}$ min., color, 1978.
       Producer: William Boundey. Distributor: BFA Educational
       Media.
              Jan begins a campaign to eliminate her family's
       wasteful uses of energy. She and her brother make a
       solar oven that can cook a hot dog. E-J

424   ERIKSON ON ERIKSON: ON CHILD CARE
       14 min., color, 1978.
       Director: Thomas Sand. Distributor: Parents' Magazine
       Films.
              Erik Erikson, his wife, and students at the Erikson
       Institute exchange thoughts on Erikson's Eight Stages of Man.
       This film covers unrealistic, unattainable child-development
       goals. C-A, Prof

425   ERIKSON ON ERIKSON: ON DEVELOPMENTAL STAGES
       19 min., color, 1978.
       Director: Thomas Sand. Distributor: Parents' Magazine
       Films.
              Erik Erikson, his wife, and students at the Erikson
       Institute exchange thoughts on Erikson's Eight Stages of
       Man. This film deals with the stages from birth through
       old age--each with its positive gains and specific conflicts.
       C-A, Prof

426   ERIKSON ON ERIKSON: ON THE COMMUNITY
       17 min., color, 1978.
       Director: Thomas Sand. Distributor: Parents' Magazine
       Films.
              Erik Erikson, his wife and students at the Erikson
       Institute exchange thoughts on Erikson's Eight Stages of
       Man. This film explores the forms of community life best
       able to prepare a child for productive adulthood in the
       world of the future. C-A, Prof

427   THE ESCAPE OF A ONE-TON PET
       41 min., color, 1978.
       Director: Richard Bennett. Cast: Stacy Swor, James Calla-
       han, Richard Yniguez. Distributor: Time-Life Multimedia.
              Fourteen-year-old Pru is determined to become a
       veterinarian and rancher like her father. She runs away
       with her orphaned bull to save it from being sold to slaugh-
       ter by her debt-ridden father. Set in California's Napa
       Valley ranch region. From the ABC Children's Novel for
       Television series and the Teenage Years series. I-A

428   ESKIMO FAMILY
17 min. , color, 1959.
Producer: William Deneen.   Distributor: Encyclopaedia
Britannica Educational Corp.
A family's annual trek from winter camp to spring
hunting grounds.   Includes a hard journey, a hunt, a trip
to the trading post and to town to visit relatives.   Set in
Alaska.   I-S

429   ESSENTIAL ELEMENTS OF INTERVIEWING SERIES   see
EVERY STATE IS DIFFERENT--CHILD SUPPORT OFF
AND ON 432
I JUST WANT TO LIVE WITH MY KIDS LIKE I USED
TO 691
I'M SORRY, I NEED YOUR BROTHER'S ANSWER, SO
COULD YOU TRANSLATE?   703
IN SEARCH OF HELP--WELFARE OR SURVIVORS'
BENEFITS   710
MY HUSBAND LEFT OUT ON US   988
MY HUSBAND STOPPED SUPPORT PAYMENTS   989

430   EUGENIE
16 min. , color, 1977.
Director: Susan Sussman.   Distributor: Phoenix Films.
A 12-year-old girl lives with her divorced mother
and younger sister.   She is faced with emotional adjustment to common puberty problems and troubled by her
mother, who is more wrapped up in her beauty and boyfriend than her children.   Red Ribbon, American Film
Festival.   J-A

431   EVAN'S CORNER
23 min. , color, 1969.
Producer: Stephen Bosustow Productions.   Distributor:
BFA Educational Media.
Evan lives in an urban ghetto home, with seven
members of his black family in two rooms.   Evan wants a
private place for himself, but when his mother finds a corner for him, he realizes that being alone in a corner is not
an ideal way to live.   E-I

432   EVERY STATE IS DIFFERENT--CHILD SUPPORT OFF AND
ON
17 min. , color, 1975.
Producer: Blackside for Assistance Payments Administration, Dept. of Health, Education & Welfare.   Distributor:
National Audiovisual Center.
A divorced woman, who has been on welfare in
another state, applies for assistance.   Points out that inter-
viewers must be able to deal with hostility and suspicion
that information is being withheld.   Training film.   From
the Essential Elements of Interviewing series.   C, Prof

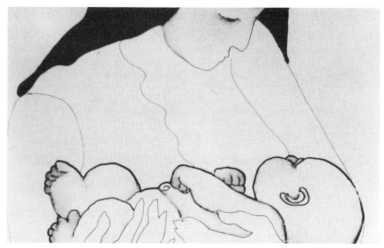

From Everybody Rides the Carousel.   Courtesy Pyramid
Films.

433   EVERYBODY RIDES THE CAROUSEL
       72 min., color, 1976.
       Directors: John Hubley & Faith Hubley.   Distributor: Pyr-
       amid Films.
              Animation illustrates Erik Erikson's Eight Stages of
       Man theory.   Vignettes trace personality development,
       emotional changes, and needs through the following stages:
       newborn, toddler, childhood, school age, adolescence,
       young adulthood, adulthood, old age.   Available in three
       24-minute parts.   CINE Golden Eagle.   Blue Ribbon, Ameri-
       can Film Festival.   S-A

434   EVERYDAY PARENTING
       $28\frac{1}{2}$ min., color, 1976.
       Producer: WTTW/Chicago for the Par Leadership Training
       Foundation.   Distributors: Perennial Education; National
       Audiovisual Center (rental only).
              How preschool parents can help their children grow
       up happier and smarter by sharing everyday activities; in-
       cludes activities and games.   From the Look at Me! series.
       A

435   AN EXAMPLE OF MENTAL HEALTH CONSULTATION
       44 min., b&w, 1966.
       Director: Edward A. Mason, M.D.   Distributor: Docu-
       mentaries for Learning.
              A public-health nurse consults with a psychiatrist
       about a family with a terminally ill father.   Illustrates
       "consultee-centered case discussion" technique.   Training
       film.   C, Prof

436   THE EXCUSE
      16 min. , color, 1975.
      Producer: Sidney Wolinsky. Distributor: University of
      California, Extension Media Center.
           A portrait of American poet Ruth Stone; shot in and
      around her Vermont farmhouse. Includes recollections of
      her creativity in childhood, encouragement from parents,
      and talk about her daughters, her widowhood, her love for
      her husband, and how his suicide affected her. C-A

437   EXECUTIVE DECISION
      28 min. , color, 1975.
      Producer: Woroner Films, Inc. Distributor: MTI Tele-
      programs.
           Security tips for business and government executives
      and their families to protect them from terrorist attack
      while living and working overseas. Training film. See
      also PERSONAL AND FAMILY SECURITY (1102). From
      the Anatomy of Terrorism series. A

438   EXPLORING CHILDHOOD: FAMILY AND SOCIETY SERIES
      see
           AROUND THE WAY WITH KAREEMA   106
           AT THE DOCTOR'S   109
           CRAIG AT HOME   322
           FAMILIES REVISITED: JENNY IS FOUR; RACHEL IS
               SEVEN   452
           HOWIE AT HOME   674
           JEFFREY AT HOME   765
           MICHELLE AT HOME (HI, DADDY!)   923
           OSCAR AT HOME   1068
           RACHEL AT HOME   1170
           RAISING A FAMILY ALONE (DANIEL)   1171
           RAISING MICHAEL ALONE   1172
           SEIKO AT HOME   1249

439   EXPLORING CHILDHOOD: SEEING DEVELOPMENT SERIES
      see
           BILL AND SUZI: NEW PARENTS   153
           GABRIEL IS TWO DAYS OLD   554

440   EXPLORING CHILDHOOD: WORKING WITH CHILDREN
      SERIES see
           SARA HAS DOWN'S SYNDROME   1231

441   EXPRESSIVE MOVEMENTS (AFFECTOMOTOR PATTERNS)
      IN INFANCY
      42 min. , b&w, sil. , 1958.
      Producer: Dr. Bela Mittelmann. Distributor: New York
      University.
           The development of expressive movements during the
      first year of life. C, Prof

From <u>The Fable of He and She</u>.   Courtesy Learning Corp.
of America.

442   THE FABLE OF HE AND SHE
       11 min. , color, 1974.
       Director: Eliot Noyes, Jr.   Distributor: Learning Corp.
       of America.
           A non-sexist fable executed in clay animation.
       Disaster strikes the Island of Baramel, cutting off the
       males--Hardybars--from the females--Mushamels.   Thus,
       the Hardybars must learn to cook and care for the kids,
       and the Mushamels must hunt and slay animals for food.
       Blue Ribbon, American Film Festival.   E-A

443   THE FAILING MARRIAGE
       20 min. , color, 1977.
       Director: Alan L. Summers, M.D. , Ph. D.   Distributor:
       Transactional Dynamics Institute.
           A husband and wife argue over the wife's sister.
       Key sequences are replayed to show the deeply entrenched
       problems in their relationship, which is about to disinte-
       grate due to a breakdown in communication and a power
       struggle.   C, Prof

444   FALL RIVER LEGEND
       10 min. , color, 1972.
       Director: Bob Shanks.   Distributor: Paramount Communi-
       cations.
           Capsule version of the ballet by Agnes de Mille,
       based on the legend of Lizzie Borden, the woman accused
       of murdering her father and stepmother.   CINE Golden
       Eagle.   J-A

445   FAMILIES
       $9\frac{1}{2}$ min. , color, 1970.
       Director: Sy Wexler.   Distributor: Perennial Education.

Stresses the "family of man" theory, as well as the nature of individual families and the fact that they are essential to children.   Animation.   CINE Golden Eagle. Chris Award, Columbus Film Festival.   E

446   FAMILIES: ALIKE AND DIFFERENT
15 min. , color, 1976.
Directors: George McQuilkin, James Kennedy, & Jane Treiman.   Distributor: Churchill Films.
Opening film in a series that compares and contrasts three different family life-styles: an American, a Japanese, and a Mayan Indian family in Mexico.   This film introduces the families and home settings, showing the children at home, playing, and at family gatherings.   Narrated by the children.   From the Families series.   E

447   FAMILIES ARE DIFFERENT AND ALIKE
13 min. , color, 1971.
Producer: Coronet Films.   Distributor: Coronet Films.
Three families of differing sizes are shown to be different and, in many ways, similar in daily activities, life-styles, etc.   E

448   FAMILIES: EARNING AND SPENDING
15 min. , color, 1976.
Directors: George McQuilkin, James Kennedy, & Jane Treiman.   Distributor: Churchill Films.
Cross-cultural comparison of three families: an American, a Japanese, and a Mayan Indian family in Mexico. Narrated by the children, this film depicts how money is earned and spent for family needs.   From the Families series.   E

449   FAMILIES: FOOD AND EATING
15 min. , color, 1976.
Directors: George McQuilkin, James Kennedy, & Jane Treiman.   Distributor: Churchill Films.
Part of a cross-cultural series on three families: an American, a Japanese, and a Mayan Indian family in Mexico.   This film shows the family's source of foods: home gardens, frozen foods, markets, supermarkets. Preparation of food and eating utensils are compared. Narrated by the children.   From the Families series. E

450   FAMILIES GET ANGRY
9 min. , color, 1972.
Director: John Simons.   Distributor: Paramount Communications.
A family quarrel resulting from financial difficulties confuses the young son.   He finally realizes that his family's problems have nothing to do with a lack of love.   I-J, A

451   FAMILIES: HELPING OUT
        15 min. , color, 1976.
        Directors: George McQuilkin, James Kennedy, & Jane
        Treiman. Distributor: Churchill Films.
                Cross-cultural comparison of three families--an
        American, a Japanese, and a Mayan Indian family--narrated
        by the children. Here, the responsibilities of the children
        in each family are noted. From the Families series. E

452   FAMILIES REVISITED: JENNY IS FOUR; RACHEL IS
        SEVEN
        18 min. , b&w, 1977.
        Director: Henry Felt. Distributor: Education Development
        Center.
                Three years after Rachel and her family were first
        filmed--see RACHEL AT HOME (1170)--she was filmed
        again to see how she had changed and also stayed the same.
        The baby in the first film is four here. From the Explor-
        ing Childhood: Family and Society series. J-A

453   FAMILIES SERIES   see
                FAMILIES: ALIKE AND DIFFERENT   446
                FAMILIES: EARNING AND SPENDING   448
                FAMILIES: FOOD AND EATING   449
                FAMILIES: HELPING OUT   451
                FAMILIES: TEACHING AND LEARNING   454

454   FAMILIES: TEACHING AND LEARNING
        15 min. , color, 1976.
        Directors: George McQuilkin, James Kennedy, & Jane
        Treiman. Distributor: Churchill Films.
                Last in a series of cross-cultural films on three
        families: an American, a Japanese, and a Mayan Indian
        family. Narrated by the children, as they learn various
        skills from their parents, grandparents, and each other,
        e. g. , tree pruning, origami, model building. From the
        Families series. E

455   FAMILY
        29 min. , b&w, 1959.
        Producer: KETC-TV. Distributor: Indiana University,
        Audio-Visual Center.
                The changing structure of the American family. In-
        cludes comments from Dr. Margaret Mead and Dr. Bertram
        Beck. From the Search for America: Part 2 series. S-C

456   FAMILY
        30 min. , b&w, 1971.
        Director: Hubert Smith for the National Institute of Mental
        Health. Distributor: National Audiovisual Center.
                Explores the role of the nuclear family as a social-
        izing agency, with focus on the lives of an upper-middle-
        class Anglo Southern California family of five. From the
        Social Seminar series. C-A

From <u>Family</u>.   Courtesy Wombat Productions.

457   FAMILY
        14 min., color, 1972.
        Director: Gene Feldman.   Distributor: Wombat Produc-
        tions.
              Various aspects of the changing role of the family
        in American society today are discussed by members of
        a semi-rural farm family, a female college professor, a
        college student, a black man, a middle-aged woman, and a
        grandmother.   J-C

458   FAMILY
        21 min., color, 1973.
        Director: Bob Conroy for CTV News.   Distributor: Films
        Inc.
              How the family has adapted to changes in contempo-
        rary values and life-styles.   Includes a brief history, com-
        ments from psychiatrists and Dr. Spock, who predicts the
        survival of family life.   From the <u>Human Journey</u> series.
        S-A

459   A FAMILY AFFAIR
        31 min., b&w, 1955.
        Director: Irving Jacoby.   Cast: Frances Sternhagen,
        Augusta French, Allen Nourse.   Distributor: International
        Film Bureau.
              A caseworker helps a family understand their ado-
        lescent son's behavior problems, relating them to problems
        between the husband and wife.   C-A, Prof

460   FAMILY ALBUM
        18 min., color, 1975.
        Producer: Clayton-Davis Inc.   Distributor: Paramount
        Communications.

Stresses the loss suffered by a family if a family member is killed or maimed for life in an auto accident. Recreates several accidents and notes what caused the tragedies.   J-A

461   A FAMILY ALBUM
10 min. , color, p. 1971, r. 1973.
Producer: Sheila Nevins for NET.   Distributor: Indiana University, Audio-Visual Center.
How a divorce after 18 years of marriage affected four members of a family.   Aims to provide insight into reasons for the disintegration of the marriage.   S-A

462   THE FAMILY: AN APPROACH TO PEACE
17 min. , b&w, 1949.
Distributor: Kit Parker Films (rental only).
Families in France, Germany, Japan, Russia, and the U.S. are observed; purpose is to show similarity and generate world understanding.   From the March of Time series.   S-A

463   THE FAMILY CHOOSES A PET
13 min. , color, 1971.
Producer: Latham Foundation.   Distributor: AIMS Instructional Media Services.
A country family moves to the city and tries to find a suitable pet.   How to select, raise, and care for family pets, who are also considered to be family members.   Avail. in Spanish.   E-J

464   FAMILY FOLLIES
21 min. , color, 1974.
Director: Joan Horvath for Guidance Associates/Motion Media.   Distributor: Xerox Films.
A musical revue on the pleasures and problems of family relationships.   I-J

465   A FAMILY FOR NOW
$13\frac{1}{2}$ min. , b&w, 1965.
Director: Leo Trachtenberg.   Distributor: Harvest Films.
The story of David, age nine, a victim of a broken home: his father deserted and his mother had a nervous breakdown.   Placed in a foster home through the Jewish Child Care Association, he and his foster parents must make a lot of adjustments.   C-A

466   THE FAMILY IN THE PURPLE HOUSE
13 min. , color, 1970.
Producer: King Screen Productions.   Distributor: BFA Educational Media.
Seven-year-old Johnny Morris comments on the daily life of his single-parent family.   E-J, A

467   A FAMILY IS BORN
        27 min. , color, 1975.
        Sponsor: Borden Inc.   Distributor: Association Films.
            Study of male and female reproductive organs,
        physiology of reproduction, and embryonic development.
        A family is followed from pregnancy through labor and
        delivery.   S-A

468   FAMILY LIFE OF THE NAVAJO INDIANS
        31 min. , b&w, sil. , 1946.
        Producers: Margaret E. Fries, M.D. , & Paul J. Woolf,
        M.S. Distributor: New York University.
            How Navajo children retain the culture of their
        forebears.   From the Studies on Integrated Development:
        Interaction Between Child and Environment series.   C, Prof

469   THE FAMILY: LIFESTYLES OF THE FUTURE
        21 min. , color, 1976.
        Producer: Philip S. Hobel.   Distributor: Document Asso-
        ciates.
            New family life-styles--group and communal families.
        Comments by Dr. Margaret Mead indicate why the family
        unit is undergoing a transition.   Avail. in French.   S-A

470   FAMILY MATTERS
        $14\frac{1}{2}$ min. , color, 1975.
        Director: Robert Gardner.   Distributor: Agency for In-
        structional TV.
            When a teenage girl invites her divorced parents to
        watch her swim in a race, a series of unpleasant confronta-
        tions result.   From the Self Incorporated series.   J

471   A FAMILY OF FRIENDS
        25 min. , color, 1975.
        Director: Richard D. Field.   Distributor: Richfield Pro-
        ductions.
            The relationship between residents of a group home
        for the mentally retarded, their natural parents, house
        managers, and neighbors.   Focuses on the lives of seven
        home members who are active community members.   C-A

472   FAMILY PLANNING
        10 min. , color, 1968.
        Producer: Walt Disney Productions with the Population
        Council.   Distributor: Walt Disney Educational Media Com-
        pany.
            Explains that the ultimate goal of family planning is
        the enrichment, not the restriction, of life.   Points out
        that the real mark of a man is how well he can provide
        for his children, not how many children he can produce.
        Animated.   For unsophisticated audiences.   S-A

473   FAMILY PLANNING: CHILDREN BY CHOICE
        18 min. , color, 1973.
        Director: Noel Nosseck. Distributor: American Educa-
        tional Films.
              Asks the questions: Do you want to have children?
        How many? Are you mature enough to cope with a family?
        Notes the effects of children on a marriage and what re-
        sponsibilities to expect if one raises children. Reproduction
        and contraception methods are also explained. Avail. in
        Spanish. J-C

474   FAMILY PLANNING--MORE THAN A METHOD
        27 min. , b&w, 1971.
        Producer: Office of Economic Opportunity. Distributor:
        National Audiovisual Center.
              About family planning and some human barriers to
        acceptance. A

475   FAMILY PORTRAIT SITTINGS
        103 min. , b&w with color, 1975.
        Director: Alfred Guzzetti. Distributor: Alfred Guzzetti.
              Monumental study of four living generations of the
        filmmaker's Italian American family and their roots in
        Italy. Incorporates home movies, photographs, and reveal-
        ing dialogues/monologues by his father and mother and his
        maternal great-uncle. S-A

476   A FAMILY TALKS ABOUT SEX
        28 min. , color, 1977.
        Director: Larry Yust for Wexler Film Productions. Dis-
        tributor: Perennial Education.
              Various family situations in which parents either dis-
        cuss sex with their children (toddler through college age),
        or answer questions from the children. First Prize, Na-
        tional Educational Film Festival. Second Place Award,
        National Council on Family Relations. C-A, Prof

477   FAMILY TEAMWORK AND YOU
        13 min. , color, 1966.
        Director: Robert Lusby. Distributor: AIMS Instructional
        Media Services.
              Compares two families--one that makes choices as a
        family; the other lets Mom make them. Avail. in Spanish.
        E-I

478   THE FAMILY THAT DWELT APART
        8 min. , color, 1973.
        Director: Yvon Mallette for the National Film Board of
        Canada. Writer/Narrator: E. B. White. Distributor:
        Learning Corp. of America.
              The seven Pruitts live an independent, happy life
        on an island off the New England coast. They are marooned
        during a winter freeze, but are content and have enough pro-

From Family Portrait Sittings.   Courtesy Alfred Guzzetti.

visions. When well-meaning mainlanders decide the Pruitts need saving, the family is in for it. Animation. J-A

From The Family That Dwelt Apart. Courtesy Learning Corp. of America.

479   THE FAMILY: THE BOY WHO LIVED ALONE
11 min., color, 1968.
Producer: Maclovia Rodriguez. Distributor: Encyclopaedia Britannica Educational Corp.
      A 9-year-old runs away from home because he feels mistreated. Lonely and in discomfort, he thinks about his comfortable home. He and his family are reunited in the morning. E-I

From Fannie Bell Chapman: Gospel Singer. Courtesy Center for Southern Folklore.

480   FANNIE BELL CHAPMAN: GOSPEL SINGER
      42 min. , color, p. 1974, r. 1975.
      Directors: Judy Peiser & Bill Ferris. Distributor: Center for Southern Folklore.
            Three generations of Chapman's Mississippi family discuss her music and healing powers. Black family. S-A

481   A FAR CRY FROM YESTERDAY
      20 min. , color, 1973.
      Director: Steven R. Dreben. Distributor: Perennial Education.
            Teenage couple accepts an unplanned pregnancy; their story is told through flashbacks. J-A

482   FAREWELL TO WELFARE
      20 min. , color, 1976.
      Producer: Employment and Training Administration, Dept. of Labor. Distributor: National Audiovisual Center.
            Notes how the work-incentive program places welfare mothers and other recipients in better-paying jobs. Highlights three welfare mothers in non-traditional jobs and the reactions of their employers. A

483   THE FARM
      24 min. , color, 1976.
      Director: Rift Fournier for NBC-TV. Narrator: Will Geer. Distributor: Films Inc.
            A replica of a 1770s farm in Turkey Run, Va. , where a family of four live as their pre-Revolutionary forebears did. Intercuts snippets on a modern family to contrast the enormous difference between life then and now. E-I

484   THE FARM COMMUNITY
      14 min. , color, 1969.
      Producer: Irving Rusinow. Distributor: Encyclopaedia Britannica Educational Corp.
            The activities of one farm family who work and live as a unit, their contributions to the community and services they receive in return. E

485   FARM FAMILY IN AUTUMN (1967); FARM FAMILY IN SPRING (1968); FARM FAMILY IN SUMMER (1968); FARM FAMILY IN WINTER (1967) (4 films)
      15 min. each, color.
      Producer: Thomas G. Smith. Distributor: Encyclopaedia Britannica Educational Corp.
            Farm and rural community activities conducive to the season and shared by members of a family. E

486   FARM LIFE see
      COUNTRY FAMILIES 320

487   FARMING AND THE LAND
       29 min., color, 1977, r. 1978.
       Director: Michael Hall. Distributor: Image Resources.
           Six different small family farms in New Hampshire
       are threatened by population growth, increased taxes, and
       low earnings.   A

488   FAST-TALKING JOBS
       11 min., color, 1975.
       Producer: WGBH-TV, Boston. Distributor: Films Inc.
           Two short portraits of real-life American kids;
       vignettes include: AUCTIONEERS--Stefan and Steven are
       identical twins whose father is teaching them the business
       of farm machinery auctions.   TAXI DISPATCHER--Karen
       dispatches taxis at a small taxi company owned and operated
       by women. From the Best of Zoom series.   E-I

489   FATHER/DAUGHTER
       10 min., color, 1975.
       Director: Nicholas Frangakis. Distributor: TeleKETICS.
           A documentary that explores the relationship--past
       and present--between a California doctor and his 18-year-
       old daughter, who he found was using drugs.   J-A

490   FATHER MARTIN LECTURE SERIES   see
       ALCOHOLISM AND THE FAMILY   42

491   FATHER/SON
       12 min., color, 1975.
       Director: Fred Kelleher, Jr. Distributor: Diocese of
       Buffalo, Office of Communications.
           A father and his college-age son talk about their
       estrangement. The son pleads with his father to quit
       drinking; the father explains his reasons--disappointment
       in life and a weak nature. Dramatic film. From the I and
       Thou series.   I-A

492   FATHERS--WHAT THEY DO
       11 min., color, p. 1967, r. 1968.
       Producer: Films/West. Distributor: FilmFair Communica-
       tions.
           The workday of three fathers--a gas-station attendant,
       a carpenter, and a hardware-store owner. Also covers how
       each father's wages are used to buy family staples. Open-
       ended.   E

493   FEARS OF CHILDREN
       29 min., b&w, 1952.
       Director: Francis Thompson. Producer: Julien Bryan.
       Distributor: International Film Bureau.
           Common fears experienced by a normal 5-year-old
       and how they become accentuated when his parents are over-
       protective or severe.   C-A

494   FEELING LEFT OUT (A FILM ABOUT DIVORCE)
        15 min. , color, 1975.
        Producer: Charles Cahill & Associates.   Distributor:
        AIMS Instructional Media Services.
                Bobby, age 11, faces his parents' upcoming divorce
        with confusion.   A classmate, who went through the same
        situation and adjusted, tries to help; and his teacher ex-
        plains that marital problems aren't caused by children.   E-J

495   FEELINGS see
        LEARNING TO LIVE SERIES   810

496   FEET ARE FOR WALKING
        60 sec. , color, 1968.
        Directors: Tim Hildebrandt & Greg Hildebrandt.   Distribu-
        tor: TeleKETICS.
                The first tentative steps of a baby toward the hopeful,
        outstretched arms of its father.   Dramatic vignette.   From
        the TeleSPOTS series.   I-A

497   FELIPA--NORTH OF THE BORDER
        17 min. , color, 1971.
        Director: Bert Salzman.   Distributor: Learning Corp. of
        America.
                A young bilingual girl of Mexican heritage lives in
        the Chicano barrio of Tucson.   She has ambitions of be-
        coming a teacher and volunteers to help her uncle learn
        English for a driver's test and new job.   From the Many
        Americans series.   E-I, A

498   THE FEMALE LINE
        58 min. , color, 1978.
        Director: Robin Hardy.   Distributor: PRP Productions.
                Three women from one well-born American family--
        civil-rights activist Mrs. Malcolm Peabody, former U. N.
        Ambassador Marietta Tree, and Pulitzer Prize winner
        Frances Fitzgerald--discuss everything from abortion to
        religion.   Separate interviews; life-styles contrasted.   S-A

499   FERTILIZATION AND BIRTH
        10 min. , color, 1967.
        Producer: Wexler Film Productions.   Distributor: Peren-
        nial Education.
                The reproductive system of a fish and a simple ex-
        planation of the reproductive system of humans.   Includes
        birth and suckling of young in both humans and animals.
        Follow-up to HUMAN AND ANIMAL BEGINNINGS (677).   E

500   FETAL ALCOHOL SYNDROME
        13 min. , color, 1976.
        Director: William B. Hill for NBC-TV.   Distributor:
        Films Inc.
                The damaging and irreversible effects on prenatal

development due to mother's heavy drinking while pregnant. With research and living babies who show the mental and physical defects.   Blue Ribbon, American Film Festival. C-A, Prof

501   FIFTH STREET
27 min. , color, 1970.
Director: Bob McAndrews. Distributor: CRM /McGraw-Hill Films.
Interviews with skid-row inhabitants reveal problematic relationships with mothers, weak fathers, bad marriages, etc.   J-A

502   A FIFTY-FIFTY CHANCE
28 min. , color, 1967.
Producer: National Medical Audiovisual Center.   Distributor: National Audiovisual Center.
Aims to motivate families to immunize against tetanus.   Dramatic film.   A

503   THE 51ST STATE TV SERIES   see
THE AGED   24

504   THE FIGHT FOR LIFE
70 min. , b&w, 1940.
Director: Pare Lorentz for the U.S. Film Service.   Distributors: National Audiovisual Center; Audio Brandon Films (rental only).
The story of a young doctor's disillusionment at the loss of a mother in childbirth.   Follows his work at a maternity clinic in the slums.   A plea for better obstetrical pre- and postnatal care in the slums.   C-A

505   FILM FOR MY SON
28 min. , color, 1975.
Director: Nadja Tesich-Savage.   Distributor: Serious Business Company.
Manhattan filmmaker films her 4-year-old son to show him what she sees.   Includes her thoughts on her childhood in rural Yugoslavia during WWII.   A

506   FILM STUDIES OF THE PSYCHOANALYTIC RESEARCH PROJECT ON PROBLEMS IN INFANCY SERIES   see
ANXIETY: ITS PHENOMENOLOGY IN THE FIRST YEAR OF LIFE   98
BIRTH AND THE FIRST FIFTEEN MINUTES OF LIFE 158
GENESIS OF EMOTIONS   560
GRIEF   595
MOTHER LOVE   959
PSYCHOGENIC DISEASES IN INFANCY: AN ATTEMPT AT THEIR CLASSIFICATION   1152

SHAPING THE PERSONALITY: THE ROLE OF MOTHER-
CHILD RELATIONS IN INFANCY 1265
SMILE OF THE BABY 1291
SOMATIC CONSEQUENCES OF EMOTIONAL STARVATION
IN INFANTS 1300

507   FIRE--NOT IN MY HOUSE!
11 min. , color, 1972.
Producer: Alfred Higgins Productions. Distributor: Alfred Higgins Productions.
The most common causes of home fires and the
simple actions required to remove the hazards. A

508   FIRE PREVENTION AND THE HOME
25 min. , color, 1968.
Producer: Dept. of the Air Force. Distributor: National
Audiovisual Center.
Illustrates home hazards that cause fires, and how
carelessness and panic can lead to tragedy for a family. A

509   FIRE SAFETY--HALL OF FLAME
15 min. , color, 1973.
Producer: Sagen Arts. Distributor: AIMS Instructional
Media Services.
Touches on safety measures for home fires. E-I

510   FIRE--TWO WAYS OUT
11 min. , color, 1973.
Producer: Alfred Higgins Productions. Distributor:
Alfred Higgins Productions.
Illustrates home escape planning for fires in one-
and two-family homes and apartments. Notes what happens
to families if they fail to practice escape planning. E-A

511   FIRST CHILD--SECOND THOUGHTS
28 min. , color, p. 1978, r. 1979.
Director: Bill Wadsworth. Distributor: Miller Productions.
Examines the varying life-styles of four couples
during the year following the birth of their first child. A

512   FIRST FOODS
14 min. , color, 1977.
Director: Jamil Simon. Distributor: Society for Nutrition
Education.
Nutritional needs of babies during the first year of
life, with a demonstration of home preparation of baby food
and advice on selection of commercial baby food. A sequel to GREAT EXPECTATIONS (590). A

513   FIRST IT SEEMED KINDA STRANGE
6 min. , color, 1975.
Producer: WGBH-TV, Boston. Distributor: Films Inc.
A portrait of a real-life American child. Lee lives

with his mother; his parents are divorced. He visits his father and stepmother on weekends and vacations. He understands the situation better now and is in touch with his feelings. From the Best of Zoom series. E-I

514 FIRST STEPS
24 min. , color, 1977.
Producer: Colin Low for the National Film Board of Canada. Distributor: CRM/McGraw-Hill Films.
Emphasizes need for early training/stimulation for educably retarded children. Studies their integration into regular school systems and the development of family, teacher, and non-handicapped peer relationships. From the Special Education series. S-A

515 FIRST TWO WEEKS OF LIFE
17 min. , color, 1973.
Director: Robert Goldman. Sponsor: Pampers Division, Procter & Gamble. Distributor: Association Films.
Day-to-day with Jane, Fred, and their first baby, Rebecca. Aims to reduce anxiety of first-time parents. S-A

516 THE FIRST VISIT TO THE DOCTOR
30 min. , b&w, 1956.
Producer: WQED, Pittsburgh. Distributors: Association Films (rental only); Indiana University, Audio-Visual Center (rental only).
Initial visit when pregnancy is suspected. Step-by-step description of pelvic exam. From the Months Before Birth series. A

517 FIRST YEAR, A. D.
14 min. , color, 1975.
Director: Bernard Selling. Distributor: TeleKETICS.
Divorced parents are brought together when their asthmatic child is hospitalized. Their hostility is examined by a sympathetic nurse, and the real cause of their son's attacks is revealed. National Council on Family Relations Award. S-A

518 THE FIRST YEARS TOGETHER--TO BEGIN A CHILD
28 min. , color, 1972.
Producer: Office of Education. Distributor: National Audiovisual Center.
Demonstrates the parents' role as the first and most important educators of their children. A

519 FIVE WOMEN FIVE BIRTHS
29 min. , b&w, 1978.
Director: Suzanne Arms. Distributor: Davidson Films.
Choices available to women, i. e. , birth alternatives. Shows a birth in a labor room with midwives and physician,

a vaginal birth in a delivery room for a breech delivery,
and a cesarean for a breech.   One home birth includes
two generations of a family, with midwives attending.
Another home birth involves the couple and their physician.
C-A

520   FLYING A KITE
       7 min. , color, 1952.
       Producer: John Barnes.   Distributor: Encyclopaedia
       Britannica Educational Corp.
            Some happy family adventures to be shared.   E

521   FOCUS ON ACTIVE LEARNING SERIES   see
          HERBERT'S BABIES   642

522   FOG PUMAS
       25 min. , color, 1967.
       Directors: Gunvor Nelson & Dorothy Wiley.   Distributor:
       Serious Business Company.
            Housewife drudge revolts and seeks relief in fantasy.
       C-A

523   FOLLOW THE NORTH STAR
       47 min. , color, 1975.
       Producer: Gerber & Beckwith.   Distributor: Time-Life
       Multimedia.
            Benjy is a young Northerner whose family helps
       with the Underground Railroad.   He risks his life to re-
       unite a slave woman and her son.   An ABC Afterschool
       Special, from the Teenage Years series.   Christopher
       Award.   I-J

524   FOLLY   see
          MY LIFE IN ART   990

525   FOOD AND MONEY
       20 min. , color, 1973.
       Producer: Cost of Living Council.   Distributor: National
       Audiovisual Center.
            The economics of food, from farmer to consumer.
       Examines what causes price increases, the costs built into
       a loaf of bread, and how the consumer can cope with rising
       prices.   A

526   FOOD FOLLIES
       23 min. , color, 1977.
       Director: David Burke for Consumers Union.   Distributor:
       Films Inc.
            Guidelines for obtaining wholesome, nutritious food
       at full value for the dollar.   From the Consumer Reports
       series.   J-C

527   THE FOOD STORE (2nd Edition)
      13 min. , color, 1957.
      Producer: Hal Kopel. Distributor: Encyclopaedia Britan-
      nica Educational Corp.
           A mother and her two children go to a neighborhood
      food store and make selections. E

528   FOOT-STOMPIN' MUSIC
      12 min. , color, 1975.
      Producer: WGBH-TV, Boston. Distributor: Films Inc.
           Two short portraits of real-life American kids;
      vignettes include: APPALACHIAN FIDDLER--Jimmy Ed-
      monds, age 12, is a third-generation fiddler who performs
      regularly with his family and has won over 70 prizes.
      COUNTRY SINGER--Tammy Richard plays guitar and sings
      Spanish, Cajun, and Country-Western songs.   From the
      Best of Zoom series.   E-I

529   FOR CHILDREN--BECAUSE WE CARE
      13 min. , color, 1965.
      Producer: Creative Arts Studios, for U.S. Public Health
      Service.   Distributor: National Audiovisual Center.
           Dr. Benjamin Spock discusses community water
      fluoridation and its safety and low-cost in reducing dental
      problems.   With statistics from fluoridated and non-fluori-
      dated communities.   A

530   FOR LOVE OR MONEY
      12 min. , color, 1975.
      Producer: WGBH-TV, Boston. Distributor: Films Inc.
           Two short portraits of real-life American kids;
      vignettes include: ANOTHER DAY IN THE GAS STATION--
      Dale works part time in his father's gas station.   Covers
      his workday and relationship with his father.   RAILROAD
      DREAMS--Mary Ann drives a steam engine on a passenger
      train.   From the Best of Zoom series.   E-I

531   FOR THE BENEFIT OF THE COUNTRY HEREAFTER
      29 min. , color with b&w, 1976.
      Director: Robert Radycki.   Distributor: Radom Productions.
           Overview of notable, all-but-forgotten Polish-Ameri-
      cans who made vital contributions to our culture.   Inter-
      weaves their story with the filmmaker's story and that of
      his Polish-American family.   With home movies.   J-A

532   FOR THE LOVE OF ANNIE
      $27\frac{1}{2}$ min. , color, 1976.
      Director: Buzz Kulik.   Cast: John Astin, Patti Duke Astin,
      Hal Gould.   Distributor: Paulist Productions.
           A lonely, self-centered man finally finds a wife.   Yet
      he treats her badly because he can't believe that she really
      loves him.   She has a heart attack, and he reaches out to
      help her.   From the Insight series.   J-A

533   FOREST TOWN FABLES   see
         PARENTS--WHO NEEDS THEM?   1093

534   THE FORGOTTEN AMERICAN
         25 min. , color, 1968.
         Producer: Phil Lewis for CBS-TV News.   Distributors:
         Carousel Films; Kit Parker Films (rental only).
         Filmed in the Southwest and in the urban Indian
         communities of Los Angeles and Chicago.   Documents the
         despair and poverty of the American Indian.   I-A

535   FOSTER FAMILY HOMES FOR ADULTS
         8 min. , color, 1974.
         Producer: Washington State Dept. of Social & Health Ser-
         vices.   Distributor: National Audiovisual Center.
         Foster home program in the State of Washington that
         provides space for adults who are discharged from institu-
         tions: the elderly and the mentally and physically handi-
         capped.   C-A

536   FOUR CHILDREN
         20 min. , b&w, 1968.
         Producer: Quest Productions for Office of Economic Op-
         portunity.   Distributor: National Audiovisual Center.
         A look at four Head Start children and their home
         lives.   C-A, Prof.

537   FOUR CHILDREN
         50 min. , color, 1973.
         Director: Thomas Robertson.   Distributor: Multimedia
         Program Productions.
         Life-styles of four American children: a black child
         from the inner city; a girl from Appalachia; an Apache
         Indian boy from an Arizona reservation; and a Chicano girl
         who travels with her migrant family.   From the Young
         People's Specials series.   E-J

538   FOUR WOMEN ARTISTS
         25 min. , color, 1977.
         Director: Bill Ferris.   Distributor: Center for Southern
         Folklore.
         Quiltmaker Pecolia Warner discusses how she learned
         to quilt from her mother.   Ethel Mohamed's memories of
         home and family shape her embroidered pictures.   Painter
         Theora Hamblett reminisces about life on her father's farm,
         her brother's death, and her psychic abilities.   Eudora
         Welty is also shown.   All four women are senior citizens.
         C-A

539   FOUR YOUNG WOMEN
         20 min. , color, 1973.
         Directors: David Espar & Leonard C. Schwarz.   Distribu-
         tor: Perennial Education.

Four women discuss their abortions: an unmarried
black woman; a young married woman who can only afford
her one child; a teenager; an unmarried student who will
marry the father when they've finished school.   With an
epilogue on basic abortion procedures.   S-A

540   FRANCESCA, BABY
46 min. , color, 1976.
Director: Larry Elikann.   Distributor: Walt Disney Educational Media Company.
Francesca's mother drinks to cover her grief for
her dead son and marital problems.   Teenage Francesca
is responsible for her younger sister and the household.
She finds help (ALA-TEEN) to overcome the family problems.
Dramatic film.   An ABC Afterschool Special.   Blue Ribbon, American Film Festival.   J-A

541   FRANK FILM
9 min. , color, 1973.
Director: Frank Mouris.   Distributor: Direct Cinema.
Autobiographical collage animation that traces the
maturation process of a white, middle-class Catholic boy
through the Fifties and Sixties.   Academy Award.   Blue
Ribbon, American Film Festival.   Grand Prix, World Animation Film Festival in Annecy.   Silver Phoenix, Atlanta
Film Festival.   J-A

542   THE FREAK
29 min. , color or b&w, 1972.
Director: Paul Stanley.   Cast: Ed Asner, Tim Matheson.
Distributor: Paulist Productions.
A 19-year-old boy returns home a Jesus Freak after
a year's estrangement.   When he starts prayer meetings
in his bedroom and installs a telephone line for runaways,
his father kicks him out, only to find that his only daughter
has also run away.   From the Insight series.   J-A

543   FREE GROWTH
36 min. , b&w, 1970.
Director: Alan Gorg.   Distributor: University of California,
Extension Media Center.
A range of personal histories demonstrate ways that
regimentation and discipline can hurt children at school and
at home.   Focuses on a black ghetto dropout; a Hopi grandfather; an ambitious, white middle-class college student;
and a young hippie.   C-A

544   FREE TO BE ... YOU AND ME
42 min. , color, 1974.
Director: Bill Davis.   Producers: Marlo Thomas & Carole
Hart.   Distributor: McGraw-Hill Films.
Animated and musical-comedy vignettes entertain
while instilling non-sexist, kid-lib messages.   Such stars

as Marlo Thomas, Alan Alda, Harry Belafonte, Mel Brooks, Rita Coolidge, Roberta Flack, Rosey Grier, Michael Jackson, and Cicely Tyson participate.   Emmy Award.   National Council on Family Relations Award.   Chris Bronze Plaque, Columbus Film Festival.   E-A

545   FREE TO CHOOSE
16 min. , color, 1974.
Director: Ben Norman.   Distributor: FilmFair Communications.
Breaks down stereotyped conceptions of jobs for men and women, and encourages pursuit of career goals regardless of sex-role stereotypes of the past.   Examples include a young homemaker, who asks for respect of her choice of a traditional life-style, and a working couple, who share child care and household duties and decision making. J-C

546   FROM GENERATION TO GENERATION
11 min. , color, p. 1974, r. 1977.
Directors: Kate Taylor & Jane Weaver for WGBH-TV, Boston.   Distributor: Films Inc.
Two short portraits of real-life American kids; vignettes include: CELEBRATING PASSOVER--Alisa Israel's family prepares to celebrate a seder.   Shows that being Jewish is a way of life.   GOSPEL SINGING--Spencer Seaphus sings gospel music with a family group called "Gospel Stars Number Two."   From the Best of Zoom series.   E-I

547   FROM START TO FINISH: THE NATURE TRAIL
11 min. , color, 1971.
Director: Frank Jacoby.   Distributor: Paramount Communications.
A little girl and her family visit a nature center. Key sentences from the girl's narration of what they see appear on the screen.   Captioned film.   From the Read On! series.   E

548   FROM THE TOWER
10 min. , color, 1974.
Producers: Mary Louise Love & Robert Blaisdell.   Distributor: University of California, Extension Media Center.
Poet Robinson Jeffers' poem for his granddaughter Una, who is seen in this film at 18, climbing to her grandfather's favorite lookout over the Pacific ocean.   C-A

549   FRONTIER BOY OF THE EARLY MIDWEST
15 min. , color, 1962.
Producer: William Deneen.   Distributor: Encyclopaedia Britannica Educational Corp.
Frontier life in the Midwest during the early 1800s, focusing on the everyday life of one family.   I-J

550 THE FRONTIER EXPERIENCE
25 min., color, 1975.
Director/Star: Barbara Loden. Distributor: Learning
Corp. of America.
The dramatic story of Delilah Fowler's first year
on the Kansas frontier, circa 1869. She and her husband
and four children left a comfortable Pennsylvania life-style
to live in a sod hut on the plains. Her husband soon dies,
and she and the children face and survive the winter alone.
J-A

551 FRUIT AND VEGETABLE STAND see
MY FAMILY BUSINESS 983

552 FUN WITH DAD
$28\frac{1}{2}$ min., color, 1976.
Producer: WTTW/Chicago for the Par Leadership Training
Foundation. Distributors: Perennial Education; National
Audiovisual Center (rental only).
Various everyday activities that fathers and their
preschool children can share to help the children grow up
happier with a strong self-image. From the Look at Me!
series. A

553 A FURTHER GLIMPSE OF JOEY
28 min., b&w, 1967.
Director: Don Owen for the National Film Board of Canada.
Distributor: International Film Bureau.
The boy from the NFBC's 1966 film JOEY (772) is
a year older here, having lived as part of an adopted
family. Highlights problems and situations faced by a
child who was cast off by his natural mother and is now
adjusting to a family who want him. C-A, Prof

554 GABRIEL IS TWO DAYS OLD
15 min., b&w, 1974.
Producer: Education Development Center. Distributor:
Education Development Center.
A new mother talks with noted pediatrician Dr. T.
Berry Brazelton (Harvard) about her newborn son. While
the child is examined, she discusses her initial reactions
to motherhood, her fears and joys, and the fact that she
is responsible for another human being. From the Exploring Childhood: Seeing Development series. CINE Golden
Eagle. J-A, Prof

555 GALS, GUYS AND DOLLS
4 min., color, p. 1972, r. 1975.
Director: Jack Sameth for WNET/13. Distributor: Benchmark Films.
A satiric drama using animated Barbie dolls to point
out sex-role stereotypes in married life. With Marshall
Efron. S-A

556   THE GAME
17 min. , b&w, 1967.
Director: Roberta Hodes.   Distributor: Grove Press Film
Division.
      Black and Puerto Rican teens reenact their hopeless
lives in New York City tenements.   From the play by
George Houston Bass.   S-A

557   GAMES   see
LEARNING TO LIVE SERIES   810

558   THE GARDEN PARTY
24 min. , color, 1974.
Director: Jack Sholder.   Story: Katherine Mansfield.
Distributor: Paramount Communications.
      In post-World War II New England, a young girl
is exposed to death for the first time when a neighboring
farmer is killed in an accident on the day of her mother's
party.   Dramatic film.   Red Ribbon, American Film Festival.   Silver Plaque, Chicago International Film Festival.
Chris Bronze Award, Columbus Film Festival.   Special
Jury Award, San Francisco International Film Festival.   J-A

559   GAUCHO
47 min. , color, 1978.
Director: Robert Lieberman.   Distributor: Time-Life
Multimedia.
      A Puerto Rican boy tries to raise money to take
his mother back to Puerto Rico.   Set in New York City.
An ABC Afterschool Special, from the Teenage Years series.   Blue Ribbon, American Film Festival.   I-J

560   GENESIS OF EMOTIONS
30 min. , b&w, sil. , 1948.
Producer: René A. Spitz, M.D.   Distributor: New York
University.
      Shows how a child develops interest in human beings
by the end of his first month.   From the Film Studies of
the Psychoanalytic Research Project on Problems in Infancy.
series.   C, Prof

561   GENETIC DEFECTS: THE BROKEN CODE
87 min. , color, p. 1973, r. 1975.
Producer: Steve Gilford for WNET.   Distributor: Indiana
University, Audio-Visual Center.
      Three ways that genetic diseases are passed from
parent to child--the recessive, dominant, and sex-linked
patterns of inheritance.   S-A

562   GENTLE BIRTH
15 min. , color, 1976.
Director: Alvin Fiering.   Distributor: Polymorph Films.
      Observes the roles of mother, father, baby, and

obstetrician during Lamaze-Leboyer deliveries.   Illustrates
family-centered maternity practice.   Two families shown.
Blue Ribbon, American Film Festival.   S-A

From The Georges of New York City (Six American Families
series).   Courtesy Carousel Films.

563   THE GEORGES OF NEW YORK CITY
        53 min. , color, 1976.
        Producer: Arthur Barron for Westinghouse Broadcasting
        Corp.   Distributor: Carousel Films.
                Documentary portrait of a middle-class, black family.
        With three children and both parents working, the family
        lives in a pleasant neighborhood but are always aware that
        they are second-class citizens.   Strain on the family also
        results from the fact that Mr. George is a cop and his wife
        fears for his safety.   From the Six American Families
        series.   S-A

564   GERONIMO JONES
        21 min. , color, 1970.
        Director: Bert Salzman.   Distributor: Learning Corp. of
        America.
                An American Indian boy is caught in a conflict be-
        tween pride in his heritage and his future as a modern
        American.   Filmed at the Papago Indian Reservation in
        Arizona.   From the Many Americans series.   CINE Golden
        Eagle.   E-I, A

565   GETTING AROUND   see
                THE STROKE PATIENT COMES HOME SERIES   1328

566   GETTING MARRIED
        16 min. , color, 1975.
        Director: Michael Creedman.   Distributor: BFA Educational Media.
                Dramatic scenes, interviews, and silent film clips
        give reasons for success and failure in marriage, as well
        as reasons why people marry in the first place.   Two
        couples are briefly studied.   S-A

From Getting Married.   Courtesy Pyramid Films.

567   GETTING MARRIED
        26 min. & 48 min. , color, 1976.
        Director: Charles Braverman.   Narrator: Cloris Leachman.
        Distributor: Pyramid Films.
                Cinema vérité look at weddings across America,
        from New York to Hawaii; and the rituals before, during,
        and after civil and religious ceremonies.   Shows how
        weddings are exploited as big business, and couples com-
        ment on their reasons for marriage.   J-A

568   GETTING READY FOR THE DENTIST
        11 min. , b&w, 1945.
        Producer: Dr. Alice Keliher.   Distributor: New York
        University.
                A 3-year-old child is prepared for her first visit
        to the dentist through the use of dramatic play.   From
        the Parent-Child Relations in the Early Years series.
        C-A

569   GETTING TOGETHER SERIES   see
            ADOLESCENT RESPONSIBILITIES: CRAIG AND MARK 18
            PARENTAL ROLES: DON AND MAE   1083

570   THE GIFT
11 min. , color, 1976.
Director: William Crain. Distributor: Barr Films.
A young girl learns about the real nature of gift
giving on her mother's birthday.   E

571   THE GIFT
18 min. , color, 1977.
Director: Douglas G. Johnson. Distributor: Brigham
Young University.
During the Depression, a 12-year-old boy has only
39 cents to buy a Christmas gift for his father. He buys
him a modest tie, and also gets up early on Christmas
morning and does all the chores before his father gets
up--the most lasting gift of all.   I-A

572   GIRL IN FREE FALL
$27\frac{1}{2}$ min. , color, 1976.
Director: Dick Bennett. Cast: Leslie Ackerman, Lynn
Carlin, Bob Hogan. Distributor: Paulist Productions.
A 16-year-old is pregnant and is pressured into an
abortion by her family. She suffers greatly from guilt and
turns to Jesus for solace. From the Insight series.   J-A

573   GIRL OF THE NAVAJOS
$14\frac{1}{2}$ min. , color, 1977.
Director: Norman Nelson. Distributor: Coronet Films.
A young Navajo girl recalls her feelings of fear and
loneliness the first time she had to herd her family's sheep into
the canyon. Red Ribbon, American Film Festival. E-I

574   GIRLS AT 12
30 min. , color, 1974.
Director: Joyce Chopra. Distributor: Education Development Center.
Documents the lives of three young friends who live
in a small industrial city near Boston. Shows the forces--
both formal and informal--that shape them into women, as
well as their expectations, role models, ideals, and stereotyped images. Catches how they relate to peers and family.
See also VIGNETTES (GIRLS AT 12) (1450). From the
Role of Women in American Society series. Blue Ribbon,
American Film Festival. J-S, A

575   GIVE IT A TRY
33 min. , color, 1976.
Director: Mary Briggs for the University of Minnesota.
Distributor: Multi Media Resource Center.
Problematic relationship between a quadraplegic male
and his healthy wife several months after his release from
the hospital. They seek counseling because they're emotionally and sexually frustrated. (Distributor claims no sex.)
A, Prof

576 GLOVE STORY
15 min. , b&w, 1977.
Director: Eliot Noyes, Jr. Distributor: Eliot Noyes
Productions.
A dependent young man loses his sanity and takes
it out on his mother. S-A

577 GOD AND YOUR CHILDREN
23 min. , color, 1976.
Director: Bruce Baker. Distributor: TeleKETICS.
Interviews with three Catholic couples bring out how
and when they teach their children about God. Covers the
importance of stable family relationships, forgiveness,
family prayer, and participation in church/community activities. With a discussion facilitator. From the Storyscape series. A

578 GOD MOMENTS
4 min. , color, 1976.
Director: Donald McDonald. Distributor: TeleKETICS.
Five short vignettes show how people find God in
ordinary human relationships. From the Meetings with
God/Storyscape series. I-A

579 GOING HOME SKETCHBOOK
3 min. , color, 1975.
Director: Mary Beams. Distributor: Serious Business
Company.
Autobiographical animation that explores the impor-
tance of family relationships. Based on a family reunion.
S-A

580 THE GOLDEN MOUNTAIN ON MOTT STREET
34 min. , color, 1968.
Producer: Merrill Brockway for CBS-TV, News. Distributor: Carousel Films.
Problems faced by Chinese Americans in Chinatowns
throughout the U.S. The people question whether immigra-
tion was worth the price: the loss of family and ethnic
ties. I-A

581 THE GOOD, GOOD, GOOD, GOOD LIFE
11 min. , color, 1975.
Director: Rolf Forsberg. Distributor: TeleKETICS.
A man is happily retired until his family decides,
to the contrary, that he is unhappy and introduces him to
the materialistic "good life." Musical-comedy touches.
U.S. Conference of Mayors/Focus on Aging Certificate of
Excellence. J-A

582 GOODBYE LYNN
21 min. , color, 1972.
Director: Harold A. Harvey. Distributor: Centron Films.

Director: Harold A. Harvey. Distributor: Centron Films.
 An unwed, pregnant teenager faces family, friends, teachers, doctors, and boyfriend. Her emotional stresses are delineated as they result from the social reactions to her pregnancy. Silver Hugo, Chicago International Film Festival. Honorable Mention, National Council on Family Relations. Gold Camera Award, U.S. Industrial Film Festival. J-A

583 GOSPEL SINGING see
  FROM GENERATION TO GENERATION 546

584 THE GRANDMOTHER
  34 min., color, p. 1970, r. 1973.
  Director: David Lynch. Distributor: Time-Life Multi-media.
   An abused child fantasizes a grandmother-companion to comfort him. Theater-of-the-absurd drama. C-A

585 GRANDMOTHER AND LESLIE
  $28\frac{1}{2}$ min., color, 1976.
  Producer: WTTW/Chicago for the Par Leadership Training Foundation. Distributors: Perennial Education; National Audiovisual Center (rental only).
   Everyday activities that can be shared by grandparents and their preschool grandchildren to strengthen ties and a child's self-image. From the Look at Me! series. A

586 GRANDPA
  29 min., b&w, 1977.
  Directors: Stephen L. Forman & Paul Desaulniers. Distributor: Films Inc.
   Benjamin Forman is a self-made businessman, octogenarian, and the filmmaker's grandfather. Here, he good-naturedly clashes with this grandson, who seems to lack direction (he's not interested in business), and lovingly interacts with his son, the filmmaker's father. CINE Golden Eagle. S-A

587 THE GRAPES OF WRATH (REVISITED)
  26 min., color, 1967.
  Producer: Arthur Barron for CBS-TV. Distributor: Kit Parker Films (rental only).
   Parallels a Tennessee migrant family of today with the plight of those from John Steinbeck's mise-en-scène. From the Great American Novel series.

588 GRAVITY IS MY ENEMY
  26 min., color, 1977.
  Director: John Joseph. Distributor: Churchill Films.
   Mark Hicks fell from a tree as a child and lost virtually all muscle and nerve function below his neck. Despite his handicap, he became a noted artist, but his sur-

vival continues to depend on the love and selfless devotion
to his family.   Academy Award.   Blue Ribbon, American
Film Festival.   J-A

589   GREAT AMERICAN NOVEL SERIES   see
        THE GRAPES OF WRATH (REVISITED)   587

590   GREAT EXPECTATIONS
        22 min. , color, 1975.
        Director: Jamil Simon.   Distributor: Society for Nutrition
        Education.
              Proper nutrition for pregnant and nursing women;
        with women and infants from a variety of social and ethnic
        backgrounds.   See also   FIRST FOODS (512).   Bronze
        Award, Cleveland Film Festival.   S-A

591   GREAT THEMES OF LITERATURE SERIES   see
        CRIME AND THE CRIMINAL   323

592   THE GREENBERGS OF CALIFORNIA
        58 min. , color, 1976.
        Director: Mark Obenhaus for Westinghouse Broadcasting
        Corp.   Distributor: Carousel Films.
              Documents the impact of a broken marriage on an
        affluent Mill Valley family.   The children have a week-
        end father now, and wish the family could be back together
        again.   From the Six American Families series.   Red Rib-
        bon, American Film Festival.   S-A

From Greene Valley Grandparents.   Courtesy Center for
Southern Folklore.

593   GREENE VALLEY GRANDPARENTS
        10 min. , b&w, 1973.

Directors: Judy Peiser & Bill Ferris.   Distributor: Center for Southern Folklore.

Retired men and women work with mentally retarded youngsters as part of the innovative Foster Grandparent Program at Greene Valley Hospital and School, Greeneville, Tenn.   Red Ribbon, American Film Festival.   C-A, Prof

594   GREY GARDENS
94 min. , color, 1974.
Directors: David Maysles, Albert Maysles, Ellen Hovde, Muffie Meyer, Susan Froemke.   Distributor: Maysles Films.

Documentary about two slightly faded society belles-- Edith Bouvier Beale and daughter Edie--aunt and cousin, respectively, of Jackie Onassis.   The middle-aged daughter and elderly mother make startling and sometimes funny revelations to two brothers--the filmmakers.   C-A

595   GRIEF
30 min. , b&w, sil. , 1947.
Producer: René A. Spitz, M. D.   Distributor: New York University.

The effect of the prolonged absence of a mother on an infant.   From the Film Studies of the Psychoanalytic Research Project on Problems in Infancy series.   C, Prof

596   GRIST MILLER
15 min. , color, 1975.
Producers: Philip Courter & Gay Courter.   Distributor: Paramount Communications.

A family mill in Stillwater, N. J. , dating back to 1844.   From the Yesterday and Today series.   CINE Golden Eagle.   I-A

597   GROW OLD ALONG WITH ME
12 min. , color, 1977.
Director: Coni Beeson.   Distributor: Focus International Inc.

A middle-aged couple, after having raised their children and tended to grandchildren, find that they have to get to know one another all over again.   They begin to court and their new life begins.   (One explicit sexual sequence, according to distributor.)   S-A

598   GROWING PAINS
12 min. , color, 1973.
Director: Noel Nosseck.   Distributor: Pyramid Films.

Question-and-answer discussion on sexuality, masturbation, dating, and love.   Actress Denise Nicholas offers advice, and Dr. Danielle Borut of the Los Angeles Child's Hospital discusses the physiological aspects of puberty.   J-S

599   GROWING UP FEMALE: AS SIX BECOME ONE
        50 min. , b&w, 1971.
        Directors: Julia Reichert & James Klein.   Distributor:
        New Day Films.
            The socialization of the American female; six women--
        ages four to 35, representing various racial and socioeco-
        nomic groups--are profiled.   Classic consciousness-raising
        film.   J-A

600   GROWING UP ON THE FARM TODAY
        15½ min. , color, 1972.
        Director: Harold A. Harvey.   Distributor: Centron Films.
            Profile of a contemporary farm family in the Ameri-
        can Midwest who operate a highly sophisticated business.
        From the Real World series.   E-I

601   GROWING UP TOGETHER: FOUR TEEN MOTHERS AND
        THEIR BABIES
        28½ min. & 55 min. , color, 1974.
        Director: Karen Crommie.   Distributor: Children's Home
        Society of California.
            The daily lives of four teenage mothers and their
        parents, friends, and views on their lives with their babies.
        Silver Plaque, Chicago International Film Festival.   S-C

602   GUESS WHO'S PREGNANT?
        60 min. , color, 1977.
        Producer: WTTW/Chicago.   Distributor: Indiana University,
        Audio-Visual Center.
            Two case studies and sex-ed experts and profession-
        als cover the high statistics of pregnant teenagers (ages 15-
        19) in America today.   Alfred I. Du Pont/Columbia Uni-
        versity Citation in Broadcast Journalism.   Ohio State Award,
        Ohio State University, Institute for Education by Radio-
        Television.   C-A

603   GUIDANCE FOR THE 70S: KIDS, PARENTS, PRESSURES
        16 min. , color, 1971.
        Producer: Robert Sande Productions, Inc.   Distributor:
        BFA Educational Media.
            Teens attending a PACE Seminar attest to everyday
        pressures and tensions; they learn to work out positive ways
        of improving their attitudes.   J-A

604   THE GUILTY
        18 min. , color, 1978.
        Director: William N. Burch.   Cast: Tina Cole, Gordon
        Jump.   Distributor: Brigham Young University.
            A young, pregnant girl is alone and away from home.
        She returns home looking for forgiveness and finds that forgive-
        ness entails much more than just returning home.   S-A

605   GUILTY BY REASON OF RACE
        51 min. , color, 1972.

Director: Fred Flamenhaft-NBC-TV. Distributor: Films Inc.
Japanese Americans reflect on their internment in
U.S. detainment camps after the attack on Pearl Harbor.
They and their grown children discuss the past and the
consequences. Blue Ribbon, American Film Festival. J-A

606 H. E. MATHENY: MUSICAL INSTRUMENT MAKING, A
400-YEAR TRADITION
15 min. , color, 1978.
Director: J. Mark Turner. Distributor: Carousel Films.
Mr. Matheny, age 68, gives an oral history of
musical instrument making in his family, which can be
traced back to France about 400 years ago, prior to their
settling in West Virginia in 1750. J-A

607 HAD YOU LIVED THEN: LIFE IN A MIDWESTERN SMALL
TOWN 1910
18 min. , color, 1976.
Director: Maria Moraites. Distributor: Paramount Communications.
A woman recalls her childhood in a small Midwestern
town at the turn of the century. Filmed in Greenfield Village, Mich. I-A

608 HAD YOU LIVED THEN: LIFE IN AMERICA 1800
16 min. , color, 1969.
Dir. : E. Scharf. Distributor: Paramount Communications.
Shows how a farm family lived in central New York state
at the beginning of the 19th century. Filmed in Cooperstown,
N.Y. Captioned film. I-A

609 HAD YOU LIVED THEN: LIFE IN AN EASTERN SEAPORT
TOWN 1870
17 min. , color, 1976.
Director: Richard Wormser. Distributor: Paramount Communications.
Daily life of a family in this town underscores the
importance of the sailing ship to the economy of the area
and the country. CINE Golden Eagle. Chris Bronze
Plaque, Columbus Film Festival. I-A

610 HAD YOU LIVED THEN: LIFE IN THE WOODLANDS BE-
FORE THE WHITE MAN CAME
12 min. , color, 1976.
Directors: Hugo Harper & Nelson Reed. Distributor:
Paramount Communications.
Indian family life as it involved the environment in
the eastern and Great Lakes regions of the country. In-
cludes tasks and roles of family members. Contemporary
American Indians reenact the life-style. Captioned film. I-A

611 HANDLE WITH CARE
28 min. , b&w, 1965.
Producer: John Sutherland Productions with the U.S. Public
Health Service. Narrator: Burt Lancaster. Distributor:

National Audiovisual Center.
Notes the varied services available to selected mentally retarded people in the greater Los Angeles area. Stresses the importance of a facility on which the families of the mentally retarded can depend for early diagnosis and evaluation and continued assistance.   A, Prof

612   HANDS IN INNOCENCE
22 min. , b&w, n. d.
Producer: Dept. of Cinema, USC.   Distributor: University of Southern California.
Dramatization of a schizophrenic girl's first night home from a mental hospital (from her point of view). Patterns of parent-child conflicts that are typical in families with problem children are recognizable.   C-A

From Hansel and Gretel, An Appalachian Version.   Courtesy Tom Davenport Films.

613   HANSEL AND GRETEL, AN APPALACHIAN VERSION
16 min. , color, 1975.
Director: Tom Davenport. Distributor: Tom Davenport Films.
Live-action, dramatic version of the fairy tale.   Set in the Appalachian mountains of Virginia during the Depression.   CINE Golden Eagle.   PS-I

614   HAPPY BIRTHDAY LENNY
8 min. , color, 1965.
Director: Lenny Lipton. Distributor: Canyon Cinema Cooperative.

Lenny's mom vents her pent-up anger and complaints and, in conclusion, wishes her son a happy birthday.   C-A

615   HAPPY BIRTHDAY, MARVIN
28 min. , color or b&w, 1973.
Director: Hal Cooper.   Cast: Bob Newhart, Anne Francis.
Distributor: Paulist Productions.
        A man panics as he nears his 40th birthday.   His wife tries to deal with his irrational fears and help him through this traumatic time.   A comedy, from the Insight series.   J-A

616   HARLAN COUNTY, U.S.A.
103 min. , color with b&w, 1976.
Director: Barbara Kopple.   Distributor: Cinema 5--16mm.
        Some 180 coal-mining families in Harlan County, Ky. , fight to win a United Mine Workers contract at the Brookside Mine (1974).   Wives and children take front-line, militant parts in the strike.   Academy Award.   Blue Ribbon & Emily Award & John Grierson Award, American Film Festival.   J-A

617   HARMONIZE--FOLKLORE IN THE LIVES OF FIVE FAM-
ILIES
22 min. , color, 1976.
Directors: Paul Wagner & Steve Zeitlin.   Distributor:
Smithsonian Institution.
        Five American families discuss and enact traditions created by and unique to each family.   E-A

618   HAROLD--A CHARACTER DISORDER IN THE MAKING
FROM PRE-CONCEPTION TO 32 YEARS
35 min. , b&w, sil. , 1973.
Producers: Margaret E. Fries, M.D. , & Paul J. Woolf, M.S.   Distributor: New York University.
        Predictions based on his active, healthy constitution interacting with a disturbed family.   From the Studies on Integrated Development: Interaction Between Child and En-vironment series.   C, Prof

619   HARVEST OF SHAME
54 min. , b&w, 1961.
Producer: CBS-TV News.   Narrator: Edward R. Murrow.
Distributor: McGraw-Hill Films.
        Classic television documentary that exposes the plight and deplorable life-style of migrant workers through-out the United States.   Men, women, and their children move from state to state, live in unsanitary conditions, and work for pitiful wages.   Representatives of farmers and workers speak.   S-A

620   THE HAUNTING OF SEVEN DRAGON AVENUE
23 min. , color, 1978.

Director: Peter E. Wittman. Distributor: Home Owners Warranty Corp.

The process used by new home owners and home builders to settle conflicts under The Home Owners Warranty System.   A

621   HAVE A HEALTHY BABY: LABOR AND DELIVERY
29 min. , color, 1978.
Director: Jane Treiman. Distributor: Churchill Films.

From onset of false labor, through the stages of true labor and delivery.   Animation used to clarify each step.   Focuses on two couples.   Blue Ribbon, American Film Festival.   S-A

622   HAVE A HEALTHY BABY: PREGNANCY (Revised Edition)
22 min. , color, 1978.
Director: Jane Treiman. Distributor: Churchill Films.

Notes how damage occurs, by tracing the development of the child from conception.   Good health habits and nutrition during pregnancy are promoted.   Animation.   J-A

623   HAVE ANOTHER DRINK, ESE?
15 min. , color, 1977.
Director: Jesus Trevino. Distributor: AIMS Instructional Media Services.

Framed by the story of a young Chicano family man who is a recovered alcoholic, the film covers alcoholism in the Chicano community and examines successful approaches to treatment and recovery.   C-A

624   HAVE I TOLD YOU LATELY THAT I LOVE YOU?
16 min. , b&w, 1957.
Director: Stuart Hanisch. Distributor: University of Southern California.

A family is enslaved by automatic gadgets in their home and business.   C-A

625   HAVING TWINS
22 min. , color, 1978.
Director: Alvin Fiering. Distributor: Polymorph Films.

Common problems faced while caring for newborn twins--feeding, rivalry, getting help, scheduling, etc.   Includes delivery, and parents of twins discussing their lives. A

626   HE LEARNS SELF-RELIANCE   see
THE STROKE PATIENT COMES HOME SERIES   1328

627   HE LIVED WITH US, HE ATE WITH US, WHAT ELSE, DEAR?
26 min. , color, 1968.
Director: Seymour Robbie for Paulist Productions.   Cast: Efrem Zimbalist, Jr. , Robert Random.   Distributor: The Media Guild.

An affluent teenager is continually bought out of trouble by busy, shallow parents.   Finally, the boy gets in serious trouble, and the father decides that his son must be responsible for his own actions.   From the Insight series.   J-A

628   HEAD START AT SCHOOL SERIES   see
        PARENTS ARE TEACHERS, TOO   1091

629   HEALTH CARE WORTH FIGHTING FOR   see
        THE CHICAGO MATERNITY CENTER STORY   241

630   THE HEALTH FOOD MOVEMENT
        $16\frac{1}{2}$ min. , color, 1973.
        Producer: Norman Siegel.   Distributor: FilmFair Communications.
              Three health-food advocates detail the movement. A young mother, who represents the consumer in the food chain, sees health food as a way of life.   E-A

631   HEALTH FOR THE AMERICAS SERIES   see
        INFANT CARE AND FEEDING   724

632   HEALTHCARING FROM OUR END OF THE SPECULUM
        32 min. , color, p. 1974-76, r. 1976.
        Directors: Denise Bostrom & Jane Warrenbrand for Women Make Movies, Inc.   Distributor: Serious Business Company.
              Documents the abuse and exploitation of women by the medical profession.   Pushes women to educate themselves about their bodies and their gynecological exams so as not to be intimidated.   A health-consumer primer.   Blue Ribbon, American Film Festival.   S-A

633   HEALTHY MOTHER, HEALTHY BABY
        16 min. , color, 1975.
        Director: Jon Bloom.   Distributor: Alfred Higgins Productions.
              Nutritional and medical advice for pregnant women.
        J-A

634   HEALTHY TEETH
        11 min. , color, 1967.
        Producer: Charles Cahill & Associates.   Distributor: AIMS Instructional Media Services.
              The Stewart family practices good dental care.   E

635   HEAR US O LORD!
        51 min. , color or b&w, 1968.
        Producer: Elizabeth Farmer for NET.   Distributor: Indiana University, Audio-Visual Center.
              School District 151 in Cook County, Ill. became the first incorporated suburb in the U.S. ordered to desegregate its schools by busing.   In this film, reporters spend time

with the Dan Lang family, their two children, and neighbors
in South Holland, Ill.   Lang discusses his reasons for not
wanting his children to go to school with blacks.   S-A

636   THE HEART OF TEACHING SERIES   see
          THE PARENT CRUNCH   1080

637   HELP ME! THE STORY OF A TEENAGE SUICIDE
          25 min. , color, 1977.
          Director: Gerald Schiller.   Distributor: S-L Film Produc-
          tions.
                A high-school student commits suicide, and her
          friends, family, and teachers learn, in retrospect, how
          they could have eased her through her depression and pos-
          sibly prevented her death.   Dramatic film.   S-A

638   HELPERS WHO COME TO OUR HOUSE   see
          WORKERS WHO COME TO OUR HOUSE (2nd Edition)
          1547

639   HELPING MY PARENTS
          6 min. , color, 1978.
          Producer: WGBH-TV, Boston.   Distributor: Films Inc.
                Alberta's parents are deaf, but she knows they can
          lead normal lives.   She wants to work with deaf people when
          she grows up, to share what she's learned from her par-
          ents.   From the Best of Zoom series.   E-I, A

640   HENRY ... BOY OF THE BARRIO
          30 min. , b&w, 1968.
          Director: Bernard Selling.   Distributor: Atlantis Produc-
          tions.
                A Mexican American boy's search for identity as he
          grows up in conflict with his mother, his Mexican heritage,
          and the Anglo society in which he lives.   Documentary.
          Chris Award, Columbus Film Festival.   S-A

641   HENRY FORD'S AMERICA
          57 min. , color, p. 1976, r. 1977.
          Director: Donald Brittain.   Distributor: National Film
          Board of Canada.
                The dynasty, the current Henry, and the automobile.
          Red Ribbon, American Film Festival.   J-A

642   HERBERT'S BABIES
          7 min. , color, 1970.
          Director: Stan Smith.   Distributors: Macmillan Films;
          Association Films (rental only).
                Herbert has a chickèn, a cat, and a mother who all
          have babies.   Explains that human babies take a long time
          to grow up, unlike baby cats.   Animation and live action.
          From the Focus on Active Learning series.   E

643 HERE I GREW UP
28 min., color, 1968.
Producer: National Park Service, Division of Audiovisual
Arts. Distributor: National Audiovisual Center.
Senator Everett Dirksen narrates this visual essay
on the place where young Abe Lincoln lived. I-A

644 HEREDITY AND ENVIRONMENT
27 min., color, 1978.
Producer: McGraw-Hill Films & Coast Community College.
Distributor: CRM/McGraw-Hill Films.
Covers genetics and environmental forces before
birth--mother-to-be's diet, emotions, physical health, and
psychological well-being--and after birth that affect a child's
mental, social, and emotional development. From the Developmental Psychology series. S-A

645 THE HIDDEN ALCOHOLICS: WHY IS MOMMY SICK?
22 min., color, 1977.
Producer: WLS-TV, Chicago. Distributor: McGraw-Hill
Films.
Docu-drama about alcoholism in women, with two case
histories. Illustrates common reasons for drinking, symptoms, effects on family, and where to go for help. S-A

646 HIDE 'N' SEEK
30 min., color, 1977.
Director: Martha Moran. Distributor: Counterpoint Films.
Toby becomes very introspective due to his parents'
divorce. He is possessive of his mother and threatened by
her new boyfriend. J-A

647 HIGH SCHOOL
75 min., b&w, 1969.
Director: Frederick Wiseman. Distributor: Zipporah
Films.
Cinema vérité study of life inside the walls of an
urban Philadelphia high school. Classroom, hallway, guidance, and front-office encounters between students, teachers,
and/or counselors and parents speak for themselves. Non-
narrated. S-A

648 THE HILLCREST FAMILY: STUDIES IN HUMAN COMMU-
NICATION SERIES
See min. below, color, 1968.
Producer: Eastern Pennsylvania Psychiatric Institute. Distributor: The Pennsylvania State University.
In this series, four therapists interview the Hillcrest
family (husband, wife, four children). Both parents were
married before; three of the four children are from former
marriages. Problems with the children forced them to seek
psychiatric help. In the Assessment Interviews (28-32 min.
each), the family is interviewed, and problems and causes

are brought out. In the Assessment Consultations (11-16
min. each), each therapist discusses the dynamics of his
interview session and the rationale for his interview approach. C, Prof

649   HIS PHYSICAL WELL-BEING see
      THE STROKE PATIENT COMES HOME SERIES
      1328

650   HIS RETURN TO THE COMMUNITY see
      THE STROKE PATIENT COMES HOME SERIES
      1328

651   THE HISTORY OF MISS ANNIE ANDERSON
      28 min. , color, 1975.
      Director: Diane Orr for KUTV. Distributor: Films Inc.
         At 94, she reflects on her arrival in Utah in a
      covered wagon and homesteading on a small farm, where
      she struggled to make a bare existence and raise her
      children. Blue Ribbon, American Film Festival.   J-A

652   HISTORY OF THE NEGRO PEOPLE SERIES see
      OMOWALE--THE CHILD RETURNS HOME 1051

653   HITCH
      90 min. , color, 1972.
      Director: Irving Jacoby for the Mental Health Film Board.
      Distributor: International Film Bureau.
         Hitch moves to Harlem (N. Y.) with his fatherless
      family from a small Southern town. Initially, he's excited
      by the street action; but when he nearly kills a cab driver,
      he realizes that this life for blacks is not in line with his
      past value system. Documentary. Chris Award, Columbus
      Film Festival.   J-A

654   HOLDING ON
      5 min. , color, 1969.
      Producer: Warren Brown. Distributor: Encyclopaedia
      Britannica Educational Corp.
         A small boy is terrified when he becomes separated
      from his father when they visit Fisherman's Wharf and a
      carnival. From the Magic Moments series. PS-I

655   THE HOLLOW
      64 min. , color, 1975.
      Director: George T. Nierenberg. Distributor: Phoenix
      Films.
         The Allen family and the Kathan family settled in
      the Southern Adirondack Mountains of New York State in
      the early 19th century. Through intermarriage, these
      families have become one family. Current residents of
      the "Hollow" discuss their lives as descendants of the orig-
      inal families and their fear of the outside world. S-A

656   HOME FOR LIFE
       58 min. & 86 min. , b&w, 1967.
       Director: Gerald Temaner.   Distributor: Films Inc.
            Two elderly people suffer through a bewildering
       period as they adjust to life inside the Drexel Home for
       the Aged in Chicago.   C-A

657   HOME LIFE   see
       18TH CENTURY LIFE IN WILLIAMSBURG, VIRGINIA   411

658   HOME SAFE HOME
       20 min. , color, 1977.
       Director: Dennis Marlas.   Distributor: Dennis Films.
            Children learn how to make their home a safe place.
       Host: Barbara Eden.   E

659   HOME SWEET HOME
       14½ min. , color, 1972.
       Director: John Allman for KETC-TV.   Distributor: Agency
       for Instructional TV.
            Eddie is abused by his parents, and Steve's parents
       are strict.   Both boys run away from home.   Captioned
       version avail.   From the Inside/Out series.   I

660   HOME SWEET HOME IMPROVEMENTS   see
       THE CONSUMER FRAUD SERIES   312

661   HOME TO STAY
       48 min. , color, 1978.
       Director: Delbert Mann.   Cast: Henry Fonda, Kristen
       Vigard.   Distributor: Time-Life Multimedia.
            A spunky teenager fights her family's decision to
       institutionalize her grandfather.   From the Teenage Years
       series.   I-A

662   HOMEFIRES
       28 min. , b&w, 1967.
       Director: Irving Jacoby for the Mental Health Film Board.
       Distributor: International Film Bureau.
            Three case histories delineate the work of the Home-
       maker-Home Health Aide Service, a form of assistance pro-
       vided by health and welfare agencies when a family or indi-
       vidual cannot maintain living and housekeeping during a time
       of stress or crisis.   C-A, Prof

663   HOMEWRECKER
       28 min. , color, 1973.
       Producer: Social and Rehabilitation Service, Dept. of
       Health, Education and Welfare.   Distributor: National
       Audiovisual Center.
            Three teens tell what it's like to live with an alco-
       holic parent.   Three adults tell of their own involvement
       with alcoholism, either as alcoholics or as a member of an
       alcoholic's family.   From the No Place Like Home series.   J-A

664   HONEYMOON
        10 min. , color, 1974.
        Director: Ron Floethe.   Distributor: Paramount Communi-
        cations.
              A young girl's gradual adjustment to her mother's
        remarriage and her new stepbrother and stepfather.   E-I

665   HONEYMOON HOTEL   see
              AMERICA: EVERYTHING YOU'VE EVER DREAMED OF
              61

666   HORSES--TO CARE IS TO LOVE
        12 min. , color, 1974.
        Producer: Latham Foundation.   Distributor: AIMS Instruc-
        tional Media Services.
              A girl helps raise a horse with her father, a horse-
        breeder.   J-S

667   THE HOSPITAL
        12 min. , color, 1976.
        Producer: Filmation Studios for CBS-TV.   Distributor:
        McGraw-Hill Films.
              Bill and his brother Russell must go to the hospital
        for the first time (for a tonsillectomy).   They're scared,
        but learn that hospitals are not nearly as bad as they feared.
        From the Learning Values with Fat Albert and the Cosby
        Kids series.   Animation.   E-I

668   THE HOUSE OF THE SEVEN GABLES
        41 min. , b&w, 1940.
        Director: Joe May.   Cast: Vincent Price, George Sanders.
        Distributor: Indiana University, Audio-Visual Center.
              The sinister influence of the house on Jaffrey Pyn-
        cheon, and his unscrupulous efforts to take over its control
        from his family.   Excerpt from the feature film of the same
        name (1779).   S

669   THE HOUSE THAT MARK BUILT
        26 min. , color, 1971.
        Director: Philip Mikan for Rophel Associates.   Distributor:
        Fenwick Productions.
              A visit to the Hartford home (1873-1891) of Mark
        Twain--writer, husband, father, family man.   He closed
        the house after the death of his daughter.   S-A

670   HOW ABOUT SATURDAY?
        20 min. , color, p. 1978, r. 1979.
        Producer: Richard Steinbrecker.   Distributor: MTI Tele-
        programs.
              The anger, frustration, peer problems, guilt, and
        feelings of abandonment felt by children of divorced or di-
        vorcing parents.   Stresses the importance of dealing with
        divorce as a family problem.   Dramatic film.   E-J, A

671   HOW BABIES LEARN
        35 min. , color, 1966.
        Producers: Dr. Bettye M. Caldwell & Julius Richmond.
        Distributor: New York University.
               The effect of mother-child relationships on develop-
        mental advances made by babies during the first year of
        life. C, Prof

672   HOW CLOSE CAN YOU GET?
        10 min. , color, 1971.
        Director: Kent Mackenzie. Distributor: Churchill Films.
               Young people discuss their expectations of marriage.
        Open-ended. From The Searching Years: Dating and Mar-
        riage series. J-A

673   HOW TO MAKE A WOMAN see
           TOGETHER SWEETLY 1406

674   HOWIE AT HOME
        13 min. , b&w, p. 1973, r. 1975.
        Directors: John Friedman & Henry Felt. Distributor:
        Education Development Center.
               A 4-year-old black child with his working-class
        family during mealtime. From the Exploring Childhood:
        Family and Society series. J-A

675   HOW'S SCHOOL, ENRIQUE?
        18 min. , color, 1970.
        Director: Stanley R. Frager. Distributor: AIMS Instruc-
        tional Media Services.
               An intelligent Mexican American boy is encouraged
        by his parents and a Chicano teacher to go to college. A
        white teacher frustrates his chances. Blue Ribbon, Ameri-
        can Film Festival. C-A

676   HUBERT HUMPHREY'S SOUTH DAKOTA see
           MY CHILDHOOD, PART I 979

677   HUMAN AND ANIMAL BEGINNINGS
        13 min. , color, 1966.
        Producer: Wexler Film Productions. Distributor: Peren-
        nial Education.
               Basic human reproduction and family-life concepts.
        Includes animal and human babies. With animation. See
        follow-up film FERTILIZATION AND BIRTH (499). E

678   HUMAN BIRTH
        22 min. , color, 1973.
        Director: Dean Fenley, for the School of Nursing and Dept.
        of Obstetrics and Gynecology, School of Medicine, University
        of Missouri. Distributor: J. B. Lippincott Company.
               Seven birth complications are shown: Vertex De-
        livery, Spontaneous; Vertex Delivery, with Forceps; Breech
        Delivery, Assisted; Breech Delivery, with Forceps; Breech

Delivery, Extraction; Cesarean Delivery; Multiple Birth: Twins.   C-A

679   HUMAN GROWTH III
20 min. , color, 1976.
Producer: Wexler Film Productions.   Distributor: Perennial Education.
Interviews with fifth and sixth graders, junior and senior high students, and young married couples concerning sexual development are interspersed between animated sequences on sexual development and reproduction.   With one birth scene.   I-J

680   HUMAN HEREDITY (Revised Edition)
21 min. , color, 1969.
Producer: Wexler Film Productions.   Distributor: Perennial Education.
Sex determination, sex roles, and sex attitudes. Animation and live action.   CINE Golden Eagle.   J, C-A, Prof

681   THE HUMAN JOURNEY SERIES   see
FAMILY   458

682   HUNGER IN AMERICA
54 min. , color or b&w, 1968.
Producer: CBS-TV News.   Reporters: David Culhane & Charles Kuralt.   Distributors: Carousel Films; Twyman Films (rental only).
Documents hunger and malnutrition suffered by a Chicano family (Texas); a poor, white tenant farm family (Washington, D. C.); a Navajo family (Ariz.); and a black sharecropper family (Ala.).   Emmy Award.   Peabody Award. I-A

683   HUNGER KNOWS MY NAME
27 min. , color or b&w, 1975.
Director: James Sheldon for Paulist Productions.   Cast: Lynn Carlin, William Daniels, Tim Matheson.   Distributor: The Media Guild.
A young, affluent American man joins the Peace Corps against his parents' wishes.   He dies from a disease contracted while abroad, and his parents are embittered until they learn of their son's good work and commitment in the Corps.   From the Insight series.   S-A

684   HYPERACTIVE CHILDREN
14 min. , color, 1976.
Producer: Mary Drayne for CBS-TV News.   Distributor: Carousel Films.
Dr. Ben Feingold, a San Francisco allergist, questions drug treatment of hyperactive children.   He recommends a special diet, without foods containing artificial flavoring or

coloring.   Parents provide testimony to this treatment.
S-A

685   I AIN'T PLAYIN' NO MORE
61 min. , b&w, 1970.
Director: Michel Chalufour.   Distributor: Education Development Center.
　　　　The Morgan Community School, a Washington, D. C. ,
public elementary school, operates under a community
school board.   Records the process of education for parents, teachers, and students.   CINE Golden Eagle.   Blue
Ribbon, American Film Festival.   C-A

686   I AM ME
16 min. , color, 1976.
Producer: Paramount Television.   Distributor: Paramount
Communications.
　　　　Jan Brady wants to best her sister's accomplishments.
Jan wins an essay contest, but only because of a mistake in
the scoring.   From the Brady Bunch Values and Guidance
series.   E-I

687   I AND THOU SERIES   see
　　　　AMERICAN GOTHIC 65
　　　　FATHER /SON   491

688   I DON'T WANT TO SELL BABE
$19\frac{1}{2}$ min. , color, 1972.
Producer: John H. Secondari Productions.   Distributor:
Xerox Films.
　　　　A glimpse of Kansas farm and family life.   A farm
girl raises her calf for 4-H competition, and then must sell
the 960-pound pet.   From the Come Over to My House
series.   CINE Golden Eagle.   E-I

689   I HATE ELEVATORS
60 sec. , color, 1968.
Director: Bruce Baker.   Distributor: TeleKETICS.
　　　　A frightened, pregnant young woman arouses fear and
hostility on a crowded elevator.   Only one woman reaches
out to help her.   Dramatic vignette.   From the TeleSPOTS
series.   I-A

690   I JUST DON'T DIG HIM
$11\frac{1}{2}$ min. , color, 1970.
Director: Irving Jacoby for the Mental Health Film Board.
Distributor: International Film Bureau.
　　　　A 14-year-old boy and his father quarrel when the
boy comes home late one night.   Open-ended.   Presents
both points of view--the boy's search for identity and independence and the father's worry and concern.   J-S

691   I JUST WANT TO LIVE WITH MY KIDS LIKE I USED TO
      11 min. , color, 1975.
      Producer: Blackside for the Assistance Payments Adminis-
      tration, Dept. of Health, Education & Welfare. Distributor:
      National Audiovisual Center.
            An interview with an apprehensive applicant for
      assistance. The interviewer must determine if desertion
      has occurred. Training film. From the Essential Ele-
      ments of Interviewing series. C, Prof

692   I OWE YOU NOTHING!
      10 min. , color, 1971.
      Director: Kent Mackenzie. Distributor: Churchill Films.
            A group rap session on the question of what obliga-
      tions exist between adolescents and parents. Includes role
      playing. From The Searching Years: The Family series.
      J-A

693   I WANT TO DIE
      25 min. , color, 1977.
      Director: Ralph Senensky for Paulist Productions. Cast:
      Grant Goodeve, Jean Cooper, Laurie Walters. Distributor:
      The Media Guild.
            A young college man home for Thanksgiving recess
      tells his family that he intends to kill himself. His step-
      father dismisses the threat; his psychiatrist-mother is un-
      sure. He blames both parents and rejects his sister's
      help. From the Insight series. S-A

694   IF YOU LOVED ME
      54 min. , color, p. 1977, r. 1978.
      Director: Gerald T. Rogers. Distributor: Modern Talking
      Picture Service.
            Drama showing the effects of alcoholism on the
      family. Notes that the spouse of an alcoholic can cope,
      with help from AL-ANON. S-A

695   I'LL NEVER GET HER BACK
      24 min. , b&w, p. 1965, r. 1969.
      Director: Dennis Goulden for WKYC-TV. Distributor:
      Twyman Films (rental only).
            A young unwed mother's story--from arrival at a
      maternity home, to birth and the signing of adoption papers.
      Catholic Broadcasters Gabriel Award. National Press
      Photographers Award. Radio & TV Council of Cleveland
      Award. S-A

696   I'LL ONLY CHARGE YOU FOR THE PARTS   see
            THE CONSUMER FRAUD SERIES   312

697   I'M A PARENT NOW
      17 min. , color, 1977.
      Producer: National Institute of Mental Health. Distributor:

National Audiovisual Center.
Responsibilities, traumas, and satisfactions.   A

698   I'M O.K. --YOU'RE O.K.:   CAN TRANSACTIONAL ANALY-
SIS FREE THE CHILD IN US?
20 min., color, 1976.
Producer: Philip S. Hobel.   Distributor: Document Associates.
        Features the author of the best-selling book on
T.A., Dr. Thomas A. Harris, plus conversations with
psychologists Craig Johnson and Arthur Janov, who believe
that neurosis is simply pain long forgotten from childhood.
C-A

699   I'M READY MOM, ARE YOU?
8 min., color, 1974.
Producer: Communications Group West for the Exceptional
Children's Foundation, Los Angeles.   Distributor: AIMS
Instructional Media Services.
        Steps to successful toilet training.   Designed for
use with retarded children, or any child handicapped by an
over-anxious mother.   S-A

700   I'M 17, I'M PREGNANT ... AND I DON'T KNOW WHAT
TO DO
$28\frac{1}{2}$ min., color, 1970.
Director: David Crommie for Lee Mendelson Film Productions.   Distributor: Children's Home Society of California.
        A pregnant 17-year-old must face painful alterna-
tives--forced marriage, abortion, keeping the baby, or
adoption.   Her friends and family give her conflicting advice.
She decides to keep the baby, but after about a year, she
puts him up for adoption.   Dramatic film based on case history.   Silver Reel, San Francisco International Film Festival.   Silver Award, International Film & TV Festival of
New York.   J-C

701   I'M SOMEBODY SPECIAL
15 min., color, 1977.
Producer: Attila Domokos.   Distributor: AIMS Instructional
Media Services.
        Vignettes underscore the specialness of various chil-
dren: Patricia and her family help each other in small
and big ways.   Cesar likes to dance to his relatives' music.
Nicole cares for her younger siblings while her mother's
at work.   K-I

702   I'M SORRY BABY
25 min., color, p. 1973, r. 1974.
Director: Charles Davis.   Distributor: Association Films.
        Shows how smoking by a pregnant woman can effect
her unborn child's development and her grown child's life
if she dies prematurely due to a smoking-related illness. S-A

703   I'M SORRY, I NEED YOUR BROTHER'S ANSWER, SO
        COULD YOU TRANSLATE?
        18 min. , color, 1975.
        Producer: Blackside for the Assistance Payments Adminis-
        tration, Dept. of Health, Education & Welfare. Distributor:
        National Audiovisual Center.
              How to assess a family's eligibility for aid if they
        have dependent children and a language barrier. Training
        film. From the Essential Elements of Interviewing series.
        C, Prof

704   THE IMMIGRANT EXPERIENCE: THE LONG, LONG
        JOURNEY
        28 min. , color, 1973.
        Director: Joan M. Silver. Distributor: Learning Corp.
        of America.
              Dramatized story of one Polish family who arrived
        in America at the early part of this century. Focuses
        on the boy, Janek, who at first has difficulty adapting to
        American language and customs, and who, in the end, is
        an old man reflecting on his past and the future of his
        grandchildren. I-A

705   THE IMPACT OF THE KENNEDYS: THE PAST
        26 min. , color, 1973.
        Directors: Mert Koplin & Charles Grinker. Distributor:
        Pictura Films.
              The effect of the Kennedy family on America. Notes
        that their strength comes from faith and family love, not
        political power or money. S-A

706   IMPLOSION
        20 min. , b&w, 1973.
        Director: Dick Bay. Distributor: Time-Life Multimedia.
              Disintegration of a marriage. Comic relief. C-A

707   IN BUSINESS FOR MYSELF
        10 min. , color, p. 1974, r. 1977.
        Directors: Michel Chalufour & Nancy Porter for WGBH-TV.
        Distributor: Films Inc.
              Two short portraits of real-life American kids;
        vignettes include: TOYMAKER--Todd manufactures wooden
        toys. POPCORN VENDORS--Tony and his brother sell
        popcorn at Fenway Park in Boston. From the Best of Zoom
        series. E-I

708   IN DARK PLACES: REMEMBERING THE HOLOCAUST
        58 min. , color, 1978.
        Director: Gina Blumenfeld. Distributor: Phoenix Films.
              Includes young American Jews who are attempting
        to face up to the horrors suffered by parents and other
        family members in the concentration camps and ghettos.
        S-A

709   IN MY MEMORY
       15 min. , color, 1973.
       Producer: KETC-TV. Distributor: Agency for Instruc-
       tional TV.
            Linda tries to understand what effect her grand-
       mother's death will have on her life. Captioned version
       avail. From the Inside/Out series. I

710   IN SEARCH OF HELP--WELFARE OR SURVIVORS' BENE-
       FITS
       12 min. , color, 1975.
       Producer: Blackside for the Assistance Payments Adminis-
       tration, Dept. of Health, Education & Welfare. Distribu-
       tor: National Audiovisual Center.
            A recently widowed woman applies for aid. Shows
       how to determine alternative financial resources available
       to such an applicant. Training film. From the Essential
       Elements of Interviewing series. C, Prof

711   IN THE BEGINNING
       29 min. , color, 1976.
       Producer: No. Virginia Educational Telecommunications
       Assoc. , for the National Institute on Alcohol Abuse & Alco-
       holism. Distributor: National Audiovisual Center.
            An engaged couple become estranged over their
       respective parents' contrary views about alcohol at their
       wedding reception. In a second vignette, a mother tries
       to introduce her daughter to social drinking. From the
       Dial A-L-C-O-H-O-L series. S-A

712   IN THE BEGINNING: THE PROCESS OF INFANT DEVEL-
       OPMENT
       15 min. , color, 1978.
       Director: Roy Cox. Distributor: Davidson Films.
            Traces the stages of development (minds, bodies,
       senses) during the first two years of life, and stresses
       the important role of care-givers in this development. C-A

713   IN THE BEST INTERESTS OF THE CHILDREN
       53 min. , color, p. 1976, r. 1977.
       Directors: Frances Reid, Elizabeth Stevens, Cathy Zheutlin.
       Distributor: Iris Films.
            Eight lesbian mothers, their children and two pro-
       fessionals (social workers, attorneys) discuss realities of
       being a lesbian or having one for a mother. Blue Ribbon,
       American Film Festival. S-A

714   IN TOUCH WITH GOD
       3 min. , color, 1976.
       Director: Donald McDonald. Distributor: TeleKETICS.
            A frustrated young mother finds a quiet place to be
       with God without going far from home. From the Meetings
       with God/Storyscape series. I-A

715   INCEST: THE VICTIM NOBODY BELIEVES
       23 min. , color, 1976.
       Director: J. Gary Mitchell. Distributor: MTI Telepro-
       grams.
              Three young women rap about the sexual abuse they
       experienced as children and some effects on them as adults.
       Red Ribbon, American Film Festival. C-A

716   INDIAN BOY IN TODAY'S WORLD
       13 min. , color, 1971.
       Producer: New Document Productions. Distributor: Cor-
       onet Films.
              A 9-year-old Makah Indian boy has lived on the
       reservation all his life, and now is moving to Seattle to
       join his father. I-S

717   INDIAN BOY OF THE SOUTHWEST
       15 min. , color, 1963.
       Director: Wayne Mitchell. Distributor: BFA Educational
       Media.
              Hopi Indian boy Toboya talks about his home, life,
       family, and other families in the pueblo and how they make
       a living. I

718   INDIAN FAMILY OF LONG AGO (BUFFALO HUNTERS OF
       THE PLAINS)
       14 min. , color, 1957.
       Producer: Hal Kopel. Distributor: Encyclopaedia Britan-
       nica Educational Corp.
              Recreates the life of the Plains Indians in the Da-
       kotas and surrounding territories 200 years ago. Focuses
       on a summer day in the life of a Sioux family traveling to
       a large buffalo-hunting camp. I-J

719   INDIVIDUAL AND FAMILY ACTIONS ON WARNING
       18 min. , color, 1965.
       Producer: Office of Civil Defense. Distributor: National
       Audiovisual Center.
              An American family discusses the need for survival
       plans in the event of a nuclear attack. A, Prof

720   INDIVIDUAL PSYCHOLOGY: A DEMONSTRATION WITH A
       PARENT, A TEACHER AND A CHILD, PARTS I AND II
       70 min. , color, 1969.
       Director: Dr. John M. Whiteley. Distributor: American
       Personnel and Guidance Association.
              Rudolph Dreikurs (eminent psychiatrist and pupil /col-
       laborator of Alfred Adler) demonstrates, through interviews
       with a problem child, his mother, and his teacher, how in-
       dividual psychology may be applied to counseling education.
       Training film. C-A, Prof

721   INFANCY
        21 min. , color, 1972.
        Director: Glen Howard for Baystate Film Productions.
        Distributor: Harper & Row Media.
                Behavior and cognitive patterns characteristic of
        the first 18 months of life.   Discusses separation anxiety
        and touches on Harlow mother surrogate experiments.
        From the Development of the Child series.   CINE Golden
        Eagle.   Chris Statuette, Columbus Film Festival.   C-A

722   INFANCY
        19 min. , color, 1973.
        Director: Barbara Jampel.   Distributor: CRM/McGraw-
        Hill Films.
                Babies in home and experimental settings cope with
        their surroundings, maneuver their environment, and com-
        municate.   Attachment to mother is also examined.   From
        the Developmental Psychology series.   Chris Bronze Plaque,
        Columbus Film Festival.   S-A

723   INFANT AND CHILD CARE
        14 min. , color, 1965.
        Producer: Public Health Service.   Distributor: National
        Audiovisual Center.
                Teaches parents how to care for medical and health
        needs for the time when assistance may not be available.
        From the Medical Self-Help series.   A

724   INFANT CARE AND FEEDING
        9 min. , color, 1946.
        Producer: Walt Disney Productions.   Distributor: National
        Audiovisual Center.
                What to do during prenatal period, while baby is
        nursing, and when baby changes from liquid to solid diet.
        Animation.   From the Health for the Americas series.   A

725   INFANT PSYCHOLOGY SERIES   see
            EIGHT INFANTS: TENSION MANIFESTATIONS IN
                RESPONSE TO PERCEPTUAL STIMULATION   410
            SOME OBSERVATIONS CONCERNING THE PHENOMENOL-
                OGY OF ORAL BEHAVIOR IN SMALL INFANTS   1302

726   INFLATION--ONE COMPANY FIGHTS THE BATTLE
        14 min. , color, 1975.
        Producers: Ann Medina & Stan Opotowsky for ABC-TV
        News.   Narrator: Frank Reynolds.   Distributor: Phoenix
        Films.
                The effects of inflation on a $2-billion-a-year busi-
        ness, the Georgia-Pacific Paper Company, and also on the
        modest home of a Georgia-Pacific employee and his family.
        Edited from a 54-min. film entitled CLOSEUP: INFLATION.
        C-A

727   INFLATION: PASSING THE BUCK
        25 min. , b&w, 1969.
        Producer: CBS-TV.   Narrator: Roger Mudd.   Distributor:
        Carousel Films.
            A young Wisconsin couple's combined salaries all
        but disappear with inflation, rising prices, and taxes.
        Includes interviews with the president of their bank, a labor
        union rep. , and various storekeepers with whom the couple
        trade.   I-A

728   INHERITING YOUR PHYSICAL TRAITS
        11½ min. , color, 1970.
        Producer: Don Foster.   Distributor: Coronet Films.
            Traces the inheritance of physical traits through
        chromosomes and genes.   I-J

729   INNER CITY DWELLER: HEALTH CARE
        23 min. , color, 1971.
        Director: Philip Stockton for Indiana University A-V Center
        and Center for Urban Affairs.   Distributor: Indiana Uni-
        versity, Audio-Visual Center.
            Dramatization of an inner-city incident--a young wel-
        fare mother tries to receive routine medical treatment for
        her child and encounters red tape and dehumanizing treat-
        ment.   S-A

730   INNER CITY DWELLER: WORK
        19 min. , color, 1972.
        Director: Philip Stockton for Indiana University A-V Center
        and Center for Urban Affairs.   Distributor: Indiana Uni-
        versity, Audio-Visual Center.
            A young unemployed black man must provide for his
        wife and children, so he gets into a job-training program,
        gets a decent-paying job, and is then laid off--continuing
        the cycle.   S-A

731   THE INNER WOMAN SERIES   see
            CONCEPTION AND PREGNANCY   301
            PHYSIOLOGY OF MISCARRIAGE AND ABORTION   1106

732   INSIDE/OUT SERIES   see
            BREAKUP   190
            BROTHERS AND SISTERS   197
            CAN DO/CAN'T DO   212
            HOME SWEET HOME   659
            IN MY MEMORY   709
            LIVING WITH LOVE   840
            LOVE, SUSAN   861
            A SENSE OF JOY   1254
            TRAVELIN' SHOES   1416

733   INSIGHT SERIES   see
            ALL OUT   50

THE ALLELUIA KID   53
BOSS TOAD   176
BOURBON IN SUBURBIA   177
A BOX FOR MR. LIPTON   178
CELEBRATION IN FRESH POWDER   231
THE COMING OF THE CLONE   292
THE CRIME OF INNOCENCE   327
CUM LAUDE, COME LONELY   333
EDDIE   406
FOR THE LOVE OF ANNIE   532
THE FREAK   542
GIRL IN FREE FALL   572
HAPPY BIRTHDAY, MARVIN   615
HE LIVED WITH US, HE ATE WITH US, WHAT ELSE,
    DEAR?   627
HUNGER KNOWS MY NAME   683
I WANT TO DIE   693
THE LAST OF THE GREAT MALE CHAUVINISTS   798
LEROY   817
THE MAN IN THE CAST IRON SUIT   878
NO TEARS FOR KELSEY   1027
THE PRODIGAL FATHER   1146
REHEARSAL   1188
RIDE A TURQUOISE PONY   1203
SAM   1227
SECOND CHORUS   1244
SEVENTEEN FOREVER   1257
A SLIGHT DRINKING PROBLEM   1290
SOMEWHERE BEFORE   1305
THE THEFT   1364
THE WAR OF THE EGGS   1459
WELCOME HOME   1478
WHEN YOU SEE ARCTURUS   1505
WHERE WERE YOU DURING THE BATTLE OF THE
    BULGE, KID?   1509

734   INTERDEPENDENCE
9 min. , color, 1972.
Producer: Art Evans Productions. Distributor: Paramount
Communications.
        An Oregon family experiences great hardships during
a local flood. They temporarily lose access to staples of
life they ordinarily take for granted. From the Economics
for Elementary series. E-I

735   INTERNATIONAL EDUCATION OF THE HEARING-IMPAIRED
CHILD: AMERICAN SERIES see
    PARENT EDUCATION PROGRAMS   1081

736   INTERNATIONAL POPULATION PROGRAMS SERIES see
    COMMUNICATING FAMILY PLANNING--SPEAK, THEY
    ARE LISTENING   294

737   THE INTERVIEW
      35 min. , color, 1977.
      Producer: National Center on Child Abuse & Neglect, HEW.
      Distributor: National Audiovisual Center.
            The relationship between an abusive mother and her
      child is revealed in an interview with Dr. Eli Newberger,
      pediatrician with Children's Hospital Medical Center, Bos-
      ton. Training film. From the We Can Help series. C,
      Prof

738   INTERVIEW WITH DR. R. D. LAING, PART I: THE
      DILEMMA OF MENTAL ILLNESS
      30 min. , color, 1976.
      Director/Interviewer: Dr. Richard I. Evans. Distributor:
      Macmillan Films.
            Psychiatrist R. D. Laing believes that mentally ill
      persons may be "tragic victims" of mixed signals of love
      and rejection from their families (i. e. , double bind).
      From the Notable Contributors to the Psychology of Per-
      sonality series. C-A, Prof

739   INTERVIEWING THE ABUSED CHILD
      $21\frac{1}{2}$ min. , color, 1978.
      Producer: Cavalcade Productions. Distributor: MTI Tele-
      programs.
            Interviews with abused children illustrate the delicate
      interaction needed between the vulnerable child and the pro-
      fessional interviewer--doctor, nurse, social worker, teacher.
      Shows the balance to be taken between respect of a child's
      privacy and ferreting out the information. Training film.
      C, Prof

740   THE INVENTION OF THE ADOLESCENT
      28 min. , b&w, 1968.
      Producers: Guy Glover & Cecily Burwash for the National
      Film Board of Canada. Distributor: Perennial Education.
            Traces the characteristic dilemmas of adolescence
      through various periods of Western history. Animation.
      J-A

741   INVESTIGATING CASES OF CHILD ABUSE AND NEGLECT
      28 min. , color, 1977.
      Producer: National Center on Child Abuse & Neglect, HEW.
      Distributor: National Audiovisual Center.
            Two dramatized investigations--one by a Child Pro-
      tective Service worker in cooperation with hospital staff;
      the other by police. Training film. From the We Can
      Help series. C, Prof

742   IRA SLEEPS OVER
      17 min. , color, 1977.
      Director: Andrew Sugerman. Distributor: Phoenix Films.
            Ira is excited about his first invitation to sleep over

at a friend's house. His older sister tells him that he'll
be laughed at if he brings his teddy bear. His parents
and sister advise him about the bear, but he makes up his
own mind. E

From The Irish (Storm of Strangers series).   Courtesy
Macmillan Films.

743   THE IRISH
       30 min. , color, p. 1975, r. 1977.
       Director: Chris Jenkyns. Distributor: Macmillan Films.
              Narrator Edmund O'Brien is the voice of Dennis
       Mulligan who fled famine-plagued Ireland in 1855 for America
       with his bride. Pinpoints the rise of Irish Americans in a
       new land, from poverty to the Presidency. From the
       Storm of Strangers series. CINE Golden Eagle. S-A

744   ISSUES IN JUVENILE DELINQUENCY SERIES see
           DELINQUENCY: THE PROCESS BEGINS 356

745   IT HAPPENS
       23 min. , color, 1972.
       Director: Noel Nosseck. Distributor: Pyramid Films.
              A white, pregnant 15-year-old must weigh her al-
       ternatives. The stress of such responsibility is highlighted.
       Open-ended. S-A

746   IT HAPPENS TO US
       30 min. , color, 1972.
       Director: Amalie R. Rothschild. Distributor: New Day
       Films.
              Candid interviews with various women who have had
       illegal abortions, and some horrifying experiences. In-
       cludes a description of four legal procedures and pertinent

medical statistics.   Variety of ethnic and socioeconomic
levels represented.   S-A

747   IT TAKES A LOT OF GROWING
$9\frac{1}{2}$ min. , color, 1969.
Director: Joe Clair.   Distributor: Carousel Films.
     The place of children in the family unit; physiological
differences between fathers, mothers, boys, and girls.
See also ALL KINDS OF BABIES (49).   PS-E

748   ITALIANAMERICAN
26 min. , color, p. 1974, r. 1976.
Director: Martin Scorsese.   Distributor: Macmillan
Films.
     The film director's profile of his parents, a New
York Italian American couple who reminisce about the old
days, Little Italy, and their respective families.   From
the Storm of Strangers series.   J-A

749   IT'S ALL US
28 min. , color, p. 1975, r. 1976.
Directors: Lauren Stell & Susanne Rostock.   Distributor:
Mass Media Ministries.
     Filmed at the Emerson Primary School in Berkeley,
Calif. , where third-grade children, with their teachers and
parents, enact various aspects of the African culture of
Yoruba.   The families continue the life-style in their homes
as well.   E-A

750   IT'S HARDER FOR PATRICK
7 min. , color, p. 1974, r. 1977.
Director: Mary Benjamin Blau for WGBH-TV.   Distributor:
Films Inc.
     How the Reardon family copes with Patrick, their
retarded child.   His older brother and sister assume a lot
of responsibility for Patrick; they talk about their feelings.
From the Best of Zoom series.   E-A

751   IT'S MY TURN
19 min. , color, 1972.
Producer: Linda Martin Enterprises.   Distributor: Film-
Fair Communications.
     The most effective means of contraception (pill,
IUD, diaphragm, foam, condom, rhythm, vasectomy, tubal
ligation), safety, side effects, and pros and cons are in-
formally discussed by a group of married and single women.
S-A

752   IT'S NOT ME
26 min. , color, 1975.
Director: Deborah Wian.   Distributor: Phoenix Films.
     After a severe emotional crisis, a woman leaves
her children, home, and job to go out into the mountains

near Anchorage, Aka., to be alone and paint and come to
terms with her life. Documentary. J-A

753   IT'S OKAY TO BE DEAF, DENISE
      28 min., color, 1975.
      Director: Karen Whitfield for the David T. Siegel Ear
      Research Institute, Los Angeles. Distributor: Viewfinders.
          Denise's parents talk about raising a deaf child,
      and how the family finally learned to communicate with her.
      At seven, Denise attends school with other deaf children,
      but plays with hearing youngsters in her neighborhood. S-A

754   IT'S ONLY BOOZE
      28 min., color, p. 1975, r. 1976.
      Director: Larry L. Badger for KNBC-TV. Distributor:
      Films Inc.
          Includes interviews with several alcoholic teens, as
      well as with professionals and family members trying to
      deal with the problem. J-A

755   IT'S THEIR WORLD, TOO
      22 min., color, 1976.
      Producer: President's Committee on Mental Retardation.
      Distributor: National Audiovisual Center.
          Profiles the parents of a 3-year-old retarded girl;
      a mildly retarded young woman, who works and plans to
      move from a group home to her own apartment; and a
      moderately retarded, middle-aged man who now lives in a
      group home and works. C-A, Prof

756   IT'S WHAT YOU CAN'T SEE ... THAT HURTS
      16 min., color, 1978.
      Producer: Rainbow Productions for the Illinois Children's
      Home and Aid Society. Distributor: MTI Teleprograms.
          Documents the work of the Perceptual and Ego De-
      velopment Project (PEP), an Illinois program specifically
      designed to help reverse developmental deficiencies and to
      heal psychological wounds suffered by foster children. C-A,
      Prof

757   IVAN AND HIS FATHER
      $13\frac{1}{2}$ min., color, 1971.
      Producer: Dimension Films. Distributor: Churchill Films.
          Ivan and his father can't communicate. Ivan role
      plays to be able to say what he'd like to say to his father.
      Open-ended. From The Searching Years: The Family se-
      ries. J-A

758   J. T.
      51 min., color or b&w, 1970.
      Director: Robert M. Young. Cast: Jeanette Dubois, Kevin
      Hooks, Theresa Merritt. Distributors: Carousel Films;
      Twyman Films (rental only).

A lonely, Harlem boy devotes himself to a mangy alley cat, and in the process learns about trust and love from family and neighbors.   From the CBS Children's Hour TV series.   E-J

759   JACKSON JUNIOR HIGH SERIES   see
   LIKE FATHER, LIKE SON   828

760   JADE SNOW WONG
   27 min. , color, 1976.
   Director: Ron Finley for WNET-TV.   Distributor: Films Inc.
    A Chinese American woman worked her way through college, so she could lead a modern American life.   Her immigrant father hoped she would be a dutiful daughter, follow his old-line dictates and grow up in traditional Chinese ways.   Dramatic film; from the Ourstory series.   Red Ribbon, American Film Festival.   J-S

761   JAMES BALDWIN'S HARLEM   see
   MY CHILDHOOD, PART II   979

762   JAMES THURBER'S THE NIGHT THE GHOST GOT IN
   $15\frac{1}{2}$ min. , color, 1976.
   Producer: Robert Stitzel for TBF Productions.   Distributor: BFA Educational Media.
    Young Thurber heard a mysterious noise in his house one night.   He told his brother, who told their mother, who misunderstood.   Shots were fired; the police arrived; chaos resulted.   J-A

763   JAMIE
   15 min. , color, 1976.
   Director: Phillip Blake.   Distributor: The Media Guild.
    A behavior-modification program implemented with a 5-year-old.   His behavior is controlled, and the relationship between the child and his parents is renewed and strengthened.   Subtitled "A Behavioral Approach to Family Intervention. "   From the Behavior Modification Special Education series.   C-A, Prof

764   JANIE'S JANIE
   25 min. , b&w, 1972.
   Directors: Geri Ashur & Peter Barton.   Distributor: Odeon Films.
    Documentary portrait of a Newark, N.J. , welfare mother of five who is forced to raise her children alone.   She married at 15 to escape her family, and talks of her father and former husband who were depressed with their low lot in life and took it out on their families.   S-A

765   JEFFREY AT HOME
   11 min. , b&w, p. 1974, r. 1975.

Director: John Friedman.   Distributor: Education Development Center.

A 4-year-old, white Midwestern child at home during mealtime.   He lives with his working mother and baby brother.   From the Exploring Childhood: Family and Society series.   J-A

766   JENNY
19 min. , color, 1977.
Director: Ginny Hashii.   Distributor: Carousel Films.

How a New York Japanese American family blend their cultural heritage with that of modern American living, and pass it all on to the two young daughters.   Three generations are observed here.   E-A

767   JESSE FROM MISSISSIPPI
14 min. , color, 1971.
Producer: Maclovia Rodriguez.   Distributor: Encyclopaedia Britannica Educational Corp.

Adjustment problems faced by a black family who move to a northern city from rural Mississippi.   The father must work two jobs and the mother must work also, which leaves their young son without adequate supervision.   From the Newcomers to the City series.   I-J

768   JEWISH AMERICAN
26 min. , b&w, 1970.
Director: Ben Maddow.   Distributor: Macmillan Films.

An old Jewish man reflects on life in the early 1900s, when he and many other immigrants settled and built up businesses on the Lower East Side of New York. Originally released under the title A STORM OF STRANGERS. Now, a part of the series A Storm of Strangers.   Blue Ribbon, American Film Festival.   CINE Golden Eagle. Chris Award, Columbus Film Festival.   Gold Medal, Atlanta International Film Festival.   S-A

769   JIMMY'S KITE
$11\frac{1}{2}$ min. , color, 1976.
Producer: Gilbert Altschul Productions.   Distributor: Journal Films.

A father and son build a kite from scratch.   The boy cherishes the experience and stops envying the kids with slick, store-bought kites.   E-I

770   JOE AND MAXI
81 min. , color, p. 1973-78, r. 1978.
Directors: Maxi Cohen & Joel Gold.   Distributors: Maxi Cohen & Joel Gold.

When Maxi was 24, her mother died of cancer.   In order to get closer to her father at this time, Maxi made this exploratory film about him.   Her father is also struck down with cancer, and she and her two younger brothers

must readjust their lives and goals to accommodate their
father's last days.   Documentary.   Blue Ribbon, American
Film Festival.   S-A

771   JOEY
      54 min. , color, p. 1975, r. 1976.
      Director: Luis San Andres.   Cast: Carla Pinza, Jean
      Paul Delgado, Niger Akoni, Jane Fontanez, Joseph Fon-
      tanez.   Distributor: Institutional Cinema.
            Young son of a New York Puerto Rican family is
      humiliated in the streets and beaten by toughs after the
      family moves to a new neighborhood.   Through the support
      of his family and training in martial arts, the boy is able
      to overcome his fear and take care of himself.   I-J

772   JOEY
      28 min. , b&w, 1966.
      Director: Graham Parker for the National Film Board of
      Canada.   Distributor: International Film Bureau.
            Joey is abandoned by his mother and placed in a
      shelter.   A placement worker finally finds the 7-year-old
      a suitable home.   See also A FURTHER GLIMPSE OF
      JOEY (553).   C-A, Prof

773   JOEY AND ME
      10 min. , color, 1976.
      Producer: Charles Cahill & Associates.   Distributor:
      AIMS Instructional Media Services.
            A seventh-grade boy remembers his good friend
      Joey, who dated his older sister, dealt admirably with
      personal and family problems (his mother's alcoholism),
      and was subsequently killed in a car driven by a drunken
      friend.   I-S

774   JOHNNY FROM FORT APACHE
      15 min. , color, 1971.
      Producer: Maclovia Rodriguez.   Distributor: Encyclopaedia
      Britannica Educational Corp.
            An Indian family must make many adjustments to
      their move from a reservation to San Francisco.   Crowded
      apartment living, new schools and friends, and a longing
      for the old way of life must be dealt with.   From the New-
      comers to the City series.   I-J

775   JOSHUA'S CONFUSION
      24 min. , color, 1977.
      Director: Tom Robertson.   Distributor: Multimedia Pro-
      gram Productions.
            A young Amish boy lives surrounded by his chums'
      TV sets, cars, and other modern conveniences.   He wants
      to take part, too.   When he disobeys his father's orders
      and goes to a party, he is punished and runs away.   From
      the Young People's Specials series.   Blue Ribbon, American
      Film Festival.   E-J

776   JOYCE AT 34
        28 min. , color, 1972.
        Directors: Joyce Chopra & Claudia Weill. Distributor:
        New Day Films.
                The filmmaker had a baby in her mid-thirties, and
        had to deal with the changes this new individual wrought
        in her marriage and her filmmaking career. Her mother
        and husband comment. Blue Ribbon, American Film Festi-
        val. S-A

777   JUMP!
        25 min. , color, 1971.
        Producer: Visual Concepts. Distributor: BFA Educational
        Media.
                How parental and group pressure can influence a
        young person's decision to take or not to take drugs. I-S

778   JUNG SAI: CHINESE AMERICAN
        29 min. , color, p. 1975, r. 1976.
        Directors: Frieda Lee Mock & Terry Sanders. Distribu-
        tor: Macmillan Films.
                A young Chinese American journalist travels through
        the West interviewing relatives and other Chinese about the
        history of the Chinese in America and the formation of
        Chinatowns. From the Storm of Strangers series. Red
        Ribbon, American Film Festival. CINE Golden Eagle.
        Cindy Award, Information Film Producers of America. J-A

779   JUVENILE COURT
        144 min. , b&w, 1973.
        Director: Frederick Wiseman. Distributor: Zipporah
        Films.
                Cinema vérité documents the daily routine of a
        Memphis & Shelby County (Tenn.) Juvenile Court--e.g. ,
        arrests, charges, confrontations of offenders with their
        families, social workers, probation officers, and psychia-
        trists. DuPont Award, Columbia University School of
        Journalism. C-A, Prof

780   KATY
        17 min. , color, 1974.
        Producer: Monica Dunlap. Distributor: BFA Educational
        Media.
                Katy takes over her brother's newspaper route when
        he goes to camp. When she is harassed by other newsboys
        and her boss, she and her mother discuss women's lib. I

781   THE KENNEDYS DON'T CRY
        100 min. , color, 1975.
        Director: R. Abramovitz. Distributor: Document Asso-
        ciates.
                The rise of the Kennedys: from the escape from the
        Irish potato famine; from saloon keeper's son to Ambassador

to father of a U.S. President. Also covers Jack, Bobby, and last surviving son, Ted. S-A

782   THE KENNEDYS OF ALBUQUERQUE
59 min. , color, 1976.
Director: Bill Jersey for Westinghouse Broadcasting Corp.
Distributor: Carousel Films.
        Documentary profile of an upper-middle-class professional family with three children, one of whom is retarded. The father designs nuclear weapons and crusades for the rights of retarded. The daughter has a hard time living up to her father's high expectations. The wife, age 40, wants to expand her life outside the home. From the Six American Families series. S-A

783   KENTUCKY: KITH AND KIN
52 min. , color, 1972.
Director: Christian Blackwood. Distributor: Blackwood Productions.
        The activities of the Combs family of Kentucky. Begins with a family reunion and then focuses on various members of the clan: a wealthy horsebreeder; a poor, disabled miner; an ex-Governor; a preacher; and a TV sports announcer. S-A

784   KENTUCKY PIONEERS (2nd Edition)
29 min. , color, 1969.
Producer: Thomas G. Smith. Distributor: Encyclopaedia Britannica Educational Corp.
        A family of five travels down the Ohio river to Kentucky in 1790. Lured by the rich land, they clear the forest, build a log cabin, and lose their eldest son in an Indian attack. I-J

785   A KEY OF HIS OWN
9 min. , color, 1969.
Producer: William Shippey. Distributor: BFA Educational Media.
        Jeff tries to understand the loneliness he feels when his parents work late hours and he's left in the house alone. I-J

786   KID BROTHER
27 min. , b&w, 1958.
Director: Irving Jacoby for the Mental Health Film Board.
Distributor: International Film Bureau.
        An adolescent is forced to attend his older brother's engagement party. He expresses his anger by over-drinking. J-A

787   KIM'S LOOKING GLASS (NEW BABY AT HOME)
$11\frac{1}{2}$ min. , color, 1976.
Producer: Ferguson Films. Distributor: Coronet Films.

A 7-year-old feels slighted by the attention her new baby sister is getting. I-S

788   KINDERBOX
20 min. , color, 1975.
Producer: David Irving. Distributor: Films Inc.
Symbolic study of mother/daughter conflict. S-A

789   KINSHIPS
12 min. , color, 1973.
Producer: Mike Rhodes for Paulist Productions. Distributor: The Media Guild.
Dramatic vignettes point out differing approaches to parent/teenager relationships and communication. From the Vignette series. J-A

790   KIRSA NICHOLINA
16 min. , color, 1970.
Director: Gunvor Nelson. Distributor: Serious Business Company.
Records the home birth of a child named Kirsa Nicholina. The father assists, with the physician's help. C-A

791   THE KISS
60 sec. , color, 1969.
Director: Bruce Baker. Distributor: TeleKETICS.
A day in the life of a married couple ends with a slow-motion kiss. From the TeleSPOTS series. S-A

792   KURT: A RETARDED CHILD IN THE FAMILY
12 min. , b&w, 1973.
Director: Ray Priest for WITF-TV. Distributor: Polymorph Films.
A mother talks about the effects on the family of raising a mentally retarded child. S-A

793   LABOR
$2\frac{1}{2}$ min. , color, sil. , 1976.
Director: Josie Ramstad. Distributor: Serious Business Company.
Childbirth from the mother's (the filmmaker's) point of view: insensitivity of doctors, cesarean experience, nursing, supportive father. Animation. C-A

794   LABOR OF LOVE: CHILDBIRTH WITHOUT VIOLENCE
27 min. , color, 1977.
Producers: Menta & Dr. Art Ulene. Distributor: Perennial Education.
Documents Dr. Frederick Leboyer's method of delivery without violence: from pre-delivery activities to postnatal review. With pros and cons and comparison to traditional delivery. Also covers birth trauma and its effects on later life. Emmy Award. S-A

795   LAMENT OF THE RESERVATION
        24 min. , color, 1971.
        Director: Ross Devenish.   Narrator: Marlon Brando.
        Distributor: McGraw-Hill Films.
            Records the misery of life on an American Indian
        reservation, where poverty, unemployment, hunger, and
        high infant mortality exist.   From the series The North
        American Indian--Part III.   S-A

796   THE LAND, THE SEA, THE CHILDREN THERE
        24 min. , color, 1975.
        Director: Tom Robertson.   Distributor: Multimedia Pro-
        gram Productions.
            Family life-styles of two American children: a farm
        girl from Nebraska and a boy whose family makes a living
        from lobstering off Maine.   From the Young People's
        Specials series.   E-J

797   THE LAST MONTHS OF PREGNANCY
        30 min. , b&w, 1956.
        Producer: WQED, Pittsburgh.   Distributors: Association
        Films (rental only); Indiana University, Audio-Visual Center
        (rental only).
            Fetal development during the later months.   Care
        and well-being of expectant mother.   From the Months Be-
        fore Birth series.   S-A

798   THE LAST OF THE GREAT MALE CHAUVINISTS
        27 min. , color, 1975.
        Director: Dick Bennett for Paulist Productions.   Cast: Kim
        Hunter, Don Porter, Jerry Houser.   Distributor: The Me-
        dia Guild.
            A middle-aged wife suffers the empty-nest syndrome.
        Her husband is too rigid to understand what she's going
        through.   Tragedy results.   From the Insight series.   S-A

799   LAST RITES
        30 min. , color, p. 1978, r. 1979.
        Director: Joan Vail Thorne.   Distributor: Filmakers Li-
        brary.
            A young boy can't understand his mother's death, so
        he tries to bring her back with magic rites.   Dramatic
        film.   S-A

800   LAST STAND FARMER
        25 min. , color, 1975.
        Director: Richard Brick.   Distributor: Silo Cinema.
            Profile of an elderly Vermont subsistence farmer
        and his wife, who shun modern equipment and just barely
        survive.   Blue Ribbon & John Grierson Award, American
        Film Festival.   S-A

801   LAST SUMMER
        17 min. , color, 1978.
        Director: Miriam Weinstein. Distributor: Perennial Edu-
        cation.
                Three young, very pregnant women are shown try-
        ing to maneuver their bodies through a round of summer
        sports, being bombarded with others' pregnancy horror
        stories, and finally holding their newborns and talking about
        the responsibilities of motherhood. Fictional film. S-A

802   THE LAST TABOO
        28 min. , color, 1977.
        Producer: Cavalcade Productions. Distributor: MTI Tele-
        programs.
                Six victims work through early sexual abuse during
        a weekend therapy session. A public-awareness film based
        on the same cases in the training film CHILDHOOD SEXUAL
        ABUSE: FOUR CASE STUDIES (259). CINE Golden Eagle.
        Best of Category Award, National Council on Family Rela-
        tions. S-A

803   LATE FOR DINNER: WAS DAWN RIGHT?
        8 min. , color, 1970.
        Producer: Gary Bergland. Distributor: Encyclopaedia
        Britannica Educational Corp.
                Dawn is late for dinner and is scolded before she
        has a chance to explain why. E

804   THE LATER YEARS OF THE WOODLEYS
        30 min. , b&w, 1969.
        Producer: The Social and Rehabilitation Service, U.S. Dept.
        of Health, Education & Welfare. Distributor: National
        Audiovisual Center.
                The effects of a mild stroke on an elderly woman
        and her husband, and how a social worker can deal effec-
        tively with proud, aged people who can no longer care for
        themselves. Dramatic film, for training purposes. C,
        Prof

805   LATON GOES TO SCHOOL
        15 min. , color, 1978.
        Producer: Calvin Communications. Distributor: Calvin
        Communications.
                Laton is handicapped, but with the help of his par-
        ents and teachers, he moves from a Head Start program
        into the first grade. Stresses parental involvement in edu-
        cating special children. C-A, Prof

806   LAY MY BURDEN DOWN
        60 min. , b&w, 1966.
        Producer: Jack Willis for NET. Distributor: Indiana
        University, Audio-Visual Center.
                The economic and educational plight of black tenant

farmers in the South.   Families lead meager existences
and are always in debt to white landowners.   Schools are
inadequate, and thus the children have little hope of breaking out.   S-A

807   THE LAZY EYE
      13½ min. , color, 1977.
      Director: Amram Nowak.   Distributor: National Society
      for the Prevention of Blindness.
            Mothers discuss the importance of early eye exams
      for their children.   A

808   LEAGUE SCHOOL FOR SERIOUSLY DISTURBED CHILDREN
      SERIES   see
            ONE HOUR A WEEK   1059

809   LEARNING TO BE HUMAN SERIES   see
            ANGEL AND BIG JOE   88
            BIG HENRY AND THE POLKA DOT KID   150
            DEATH OF A GANDY DANCER   351
            LUKE WAS THERE   866
            THE SHOPPING BAG LADY   1270
            THE SKATING RINK   1286
            THE TAP DANCE KID   1350
            VERY GOOD FRIENDS   1446

810   LEARNING TO LIVE SERIES (8 Films)
      30 min. each, color, 1974.
      Producer: Jeffrey Weber.   Distributor: Mass Media
      Ministries.
            A practicing Transactional Analysis therapist joins
      a rap group in discussion and role-play of negative and
      positive positions.   Titles in the series include: EGO
      STATES, TRANSACTIONS, STROKES, TIME STRUCTURES,
      FEELINGS, GAMES, ACQUIRING LIFE SCRIPTS, and
      CHANGING LIFE SCRIPTS.   S-A

811   THE LEARNING TO LOOK SERIES   see
            WHAT IS A FAMILY?   1496

812   LEARNING VALUES WITH FAT ALBERT AND THE COSBY
      KIDS SERIES   see
            THE HOSPITAL   667
            UNCLE MONTY'S GONE   1431

813   LEE SUZUKI--HOME IN HAWAII
      19 min. , color, 1973.
      Director: Bert Salzman.   Distributor: Learning Corp. of
      America.
            Lee is of Hawaiian-Japanese-Filipino-Irish-Swedish de-
      scent.   He enables his grandfather to keep his prized boat when
      it is almost lost because the ill old man can't afford to keep up
      payments.   From the Many Americans series.   E-J, A

814   LEGACY SERIES   see
        COMMIT OR DESTRUCT   293

815   THE LEGEND OF PAULIE GREEN
        29 min. , color, 1976.
        Producer: No. Virginia Educational Telecommunications
        Assoc. , for the National Institute on Alcohol Abuse & Al-
        coholism.   Distributor: National Audiovisual Center.
               Flashbacks show how Paulie came to have a drinking
        problem; Karen is introduced to ALA-TEEN, a group which
        helps young people deal with alcoholic parents.   From the
        Dial A-L-C-O-H-O-L series.   S-A

816   THE LEGEND OF THE SNOW BABY
        $8\frac{1}{2}$ min. , color, 1978.
        Directors: Lyle Bebensee & Philip Hudsmith.   Distributor:
        Kinetic Film Enterprises.
               On September 12, 1893, Marie Peary, daughter of
        Lieut. Commander Robert E. Peary, U. S. N. , and his wife
        Josephine, was born in Greenland.   She was the first white
        child to be born among the Polar Eskimos and the first
        American girl to be born so close to the North Pole.   She
        was given an Eskimo name.   E-J

817   LEROY
        25 min. , color, 1977.
        Producer: Mike Rhodes.   Cast: Albert Salmi, Miriam
        Byrd-Nethery, Steve Franken.   Distributor: Paulist Pro-
        ductions.
               A poor, illiterate white couple have only one real
        possession--their shabby house, which is sold out from
        under them due to an unpaid medical bill.   The husband
        is embittered and feels no one cares, but he learns dif-
        ferently.   From the Insight series.   S-A

818   LET ME SEE
        20 min. , color, 1951.
        Directors: William Mehring & Herbert Skoble.   Distributor:
        University of Southern California.
               Visits a nursery school for visually handicapped
        children in Los Angeles.   Questions what parents can do
        to help their blind children.   A

819   LET YOUR CHILD HELP YOU
        11 min. , b&w, 1946.
        Producer: Josef Bohmer for NYU.   Distributor: New
        York University.
               Shows that even young children can feel a sense of
        achievement and increase their capabilities if allowed to
        help out at home.   From the Parent-Child Relations in the
        Early Years series.   C-A, Prof

820   LETTER FROM A MOTHER
        10 min. , b&w, 1955.
        Producer: U.S. Dept. of the Army.   Distributor: National
        Audiovisual Center.
                An American mother understands the role her son
        must play in defense of America.   C-A

821   LIFE AROUND US SERIES see
        ROCK-A-BYE-BABY 1210

822   LIFE CYCLE
        8 min. , color, 1971.
        Director: Joe Zinn.   Distributor: Paramount Communica-
        tions.
                Animated dots enact the human life cycle, from birth
        through marriage and old age.   I-A

823   THE LIFE YOU SAVE (FIRST AID)
        17 min. , color, 1973.
        Director: Alan Burks.   Distributor: FilmFair Communica-
        tions.
                First-aid vignettes, some of which are: A girl
        can save the life of her father because she knows the four
        main pressure points to stop arterial bleeding.   A boy saves
        his small sister, who has swallowed poison.   J-A

824   A LIGHT FOR JOHN
        22 min. , b&w, 1956.
        Director: Warren Brown.   Distributor: University of
        Southern California.
                Two days in the life of a retarded man and his
        mother.   Depression, hopelessness, and worry are the key
        emotions here.   C-A, Prof

825   THE LIGHT HERE KINDLED
        26 min. , color, 1966.
        Producer: WGN-TV, Chicago, with Plymouth Plantation.
        Distributor: International Film Bureau.
                Recreation of the Pilgrim's trek to the New World
        and their struggle to survive once they arrived.   Gold
        Medal, Freedoms Foundation.   Grand Prize, New York In-
        ternational Film Festival.   I-S

826   THE LIGHTHOUSE
        12 min. , color, 1952.
        Producers: Cynthia Chapman, Hal Albert, Wilbur T. Blume
        for New Horizon Films.   Distributor: Encyclopaedia Britan-
        nica Educational Corp.
                The life of a California lighthouse keeper's son.
        Notes the equipment used in the lighthouse, the work per-
        formed there, and the daily activities of the keeper and his
        family.   E-I

827   LIKE FATHER, LIKE SON
      60 sec. , color, 1967.
      Director: Bruce Baker.   Distributor: TeleKETICS.
            When a man lies about his son's age to get a cheaper
      theater ticket, the son realizes a double standard.   Dra-
      matic vignette.   From the TeleSPOTS series.   I-A

828   LIKE FATHER, LIKE SON
      15 min. , color, 1976.
      Producer: No. Virginia Educational Telecommunications
      Assoc. , for the National Institute on Alcohol Abuse and Al-
      coholism.   Distributor: National Audiovisual Center.
            A boy tries to approach his father, a problem
      drinker, about his alcoholism.   The father at first refuses
      to listen, but finally promises to change.   From the Jack-
      son Junior High series.   J-A

829   LILY: A STORY ABOUT A GIRL LIKE ME
      14 min. , color, p. 1976, r. 1977.
      Director: Elizabeth Grace.   Distributor: Davidson Films.
            Documentary portrait of Lily Grace, a Down's syn-
      drome child and the filmmaker's daughter, who has been
      raised in a normal home environment and mainstreamed
      for six years in a public school.   CINE Golden Eagle.   C-A

830   LINCOLN--THE KENTUCKY YEARS
      18 min. , color, 1972.
      Producer: Image Associates, for the National Park Ser-
      vice.   Narrator: Burgess Meredith.   Distributor: National
      Audiovisual Center.
            Aims to provide insights into his humble beginnings
      and the relationship that shaped his character.   I-A

831   LINDA AND BILLY RAY FROM APPALACHIA
      15 min. , color, 1970.
      Producer: Maclovia Rodriguez.   Distributor: Encyclopaedia
      Britannica Educational Corp.
            A family moves from the Appalachian hills of Ken-
      tucky to city living in Cincinatti, Ohio.   Compares job op-
      portunities, environment, living quarters, prices, schools,
      fears, and struggles of the children, mother, and father.
      From the Newcomers to the City series.   I-J

832   LINDA AND JIMMY
      $16\frac{1}{2}$ min. , color, 1977.
      Producer: Deirdre Walsh.   Distributor: Coronet Films.
            Explores one woman's feelings about herself and her
      role in society.   Linda, her mother, and sister discuss
      how Linda and her husband are examining marital roles
      also.   From the Changing Scene series.   J-A

833   LISA'S WORLD
      30 min. , color, 1969.

Producers: Barbara Roos & Bill La Crosse. Distributor: University of Michigan, Media Resources Center.
  The mother of a retarded 7-year-old discusses the child's daily life and her effect on other family members. Second Prize, International Rehabilitation Film Festival. J-A

834   LISTEN, LADY
60 sec., color, 1967.
Director: Bruce Baker. Distributor: TeleKETICS.
  A husband and his wife are virtual strangers. She falls asleep while her husband rattles on about his successful work day. Dramatic vignette, from the TeleSPOTS series. A

835   LISTEN, MAN
60 sec., color, 1967.
Director: Bruce Baker. Distributor: TeleKETICS.
  A husband's pressure and worry over work causes him to ignore his wife's problems. Dramatic vignette, from the TeleSPOTS series. A

836   LITTLE RED HEN
27 min., color, p. 1967, r. 1974.
Director: Wetzel O. Whitaker. Distributor: Brigham Young University.
  The story of a school teacher (Ettie Lee) who saved her money and used it to provide family-type homes for over 3,000 unwanted, incorrigible boys. I-A

837   LIVES & LIFESTYLES
12 min., color, 1973.
Director: Alvin Fiering. Distributor: Polymorph Films.
  Representatives of four unrelated generations of people living off the land and sea in Maine--a lobsterman, a great-grandmother, young members of a commune, and a dairy farming family--discuss urban vs. rural life-styles, generational differences, and economic self-reliance. J-A

838   LIVING OFF THE LAND
32 min., color, 1972.
Director: Bruce Davidson. Distributor: Time-Life Multimedia.
  A father and son make a living by scavenging scrap metal from New York garbage dumps. Documentary. S-A

839   LIVING THE GOOD LIFE WITH HELEN AND SCOTT NEARING
30 min., color, p. 1976, r. 1977.
Director: John Hoskyns-Abrahall. Distributor: Bullfrog Films.
  An elderly couple pride themselves on their independent life-style in the wilderness. Free from dependence

on the market economy, they grow their own food and build
their own houses (New England).   She is 74; he is 93.   J-A

840   LIVING WITH LOVE
15 min. , color, 1973.
Producer: WVIZ-TV.   Distributor: Agency for Instructional TV.
Dorothy Smith and the children who live in her foster
home show true family feeling.   From the Inside /Out series.
I

841   LIVING WITH PETER
22 min. , color, 1973.
Director: Miriam Weinstein.   Distributors: Miriam Weinstein; Serious Business Company.
Anxieties and self-doubts suffered by the filmmaker
and her boyfriend while living together without marriage.
Companion film to WE GET MARRIED TWICE (1468).   S-A

842   A LOBSTERMAN LIKE HIS FATHER   see
      WORKING WITH MY DAD   1550

843   LOCKED UP, LOCKED OUT
30 min. , color, 1974.
Producer: Isaac Kleinerman for CBS-TV News.   Distributor: Carousel Films.
How the justice system treats youthful offenders
from poor families.   Records a 10-year-old white boy's
experience at a children's treatment center in Atlanta.   C-A

844   LONELINESS ... AND LOVING
16 min. , color, 1972.
Director: Bob Rafelson.   Cast: Jack Nicholson.   Distributor: Learning Corp. of America.
A young drifter returns home to visit his estranged
family, to come to terms with conflicts and repressed emotions.   But his father is paralyzed with a stroke, and the
drifter can't communicate with his sister and brother either.
Specially edited from the feature film 5 EASY PIECES.
From the Searching for Values series.   J-A

845   THE LONG CHRISTMAS DINNER
37 min. , color, 1976.
Producer: Larry Yust.   Play: Thornton Wilder.   Distributor: Encyclopaedia Britannica Educational Corp.
Traces 90 years in the life of the Bayard family,
through a series of Christmas dinners.   Emphasizes re-
curring themes in their shared experiences.   From the
Short Play Showcase series.   J-A

846   THE LONGS: A LOUISIANA DYNASTY
50 min. & 22 min. , b&w, 1965.
Director: Alan Landsburg for Metromedia Producers Corp.

Distributor: Films Inc.
A look at a political family. Huey Long became Governor of Louisiana in 1928 and began a flamboyant political dynasty. His son Russell grew to be a power in the U.S. Senate. Short version is entitled THE LONGS OF LOUISIANA. S-A

847   LONNIE'S DAY
14 min. , color, 1969.
Producer: New Document Productions. Distributor: Coronet Films.
Documentary about a typical day in the life of an 8-year-old black boy--in his high-rise housing complex, at school, in the neighborhood, and with his family. E-C

848   LOOK AT ME! SERIES see
CHILD/PARENT RELATIONSHIPS   252
EVERYDAY PARENTING   434
FUN WITH DAD   552
GRANDMOTHER AND LESLIE   585
THE SINGLE PARENT   1280
THE WORKING MOTHER   1548

849   LOSING JUST THE SAME
60 min. , b&w, 1966.
Producer: KQED-TV, San Francisco. Distributor: Indiana University, Audio-Visual Center.
Highlights the plight of poor blacks in America by focusing on the life of one urban family. The mother supports her ten kids on welfare, but dreams of their successful future. Her 17-year-old son is accused of arson and jailed. S-A

850   LOST & FOUND: A SEARCH FOR OUR ETHNIC HERITAGE
30 min. , color, p. 1976, r. 1977.
Director: Dick Roberts. Distributor: The Dick Roberts Film Co.
Interviews with first-, second-, and third-generation immigrants highlight their feelings about being, or being related to, immigrants. Pride, poverty, shame, roots, and cultural advantages are revealed. S-A

851   LOST LOST LOST (6 Reels)
30 min. each, b&w and color, 1949-63.
Filmmaker: Jonas Mekas. Distributor: Film-Makers' Cooperative.
The filmmaker filmed this personal diary footage, with voice-over narration, beginning in 1949. Reel 1 documents his struggle as a displaced person (Lithuanian immigrant) in a new land (Brooklyn/America) and is of especial interest. Part of a larger work entitled DIARIES, NOTES & SKETCHES. C-A

852   THE LOST PHOEBE
        30 min. , color, 1974.
        Director: Mel Damski. Story: Theodore Dreiser. Dis-
        tributor: Perspective Films.
             A senile old man searches the town for his wife,
        who is dead. S-A

853   LOST PUPPY
        14 min. , color, 1970.
        Director: George McQuilken. Distributor: Churchill
        Films.
             A child disobeys her mother and leaves the house
        to search for her runaway puppy. From the Values for
        Grades K-3 series.

854   THE LOTTERY
        18 min. , color, 1969.
        Director: Larry Yust. Story: Shirley Jackson. Distri-
        butor: Encyclopaedia Britannica Educational Corp.
             Fictional townspeople, who seemingly live normal
        family lives, are caught up in the frenzy of a terrifying
        town ritual. J-A

855   LOUISIANA STORY
        77 min. , b&w, 1948.
        Director: Robert J. Flaherty. Cast: Joseph Boudreaux,
        Lionel Le Blanc, Frank Hardy. Distributor: Films Inc.
             Family and daily life of a young Cajun boy, who ex-
        plores the Louisiana Bayou and watches as men set up an
        oil rig in the bayou and drill for oil. S-A

856   LOVE AND DUTY: WHICH COMES FIRST?
        18 min. , color, 1975.
        Director: Robert Stevenson. Cast: Tommy Kirk, Dorothy
        McGuire. Distributor: Walt Disney Educational Media Company.
             A teenager has no trouble caring for the family
        farm in his father's absence until the beloved family dog
        is stricken with rabies and must be destroyed. Excerpt
        from the 1957 film OLD YELLER (1905). From the Ques-
        tions! ! ! Answers?? Set 1 series. I-J

857   LOVE IS A PLANNED FAMILY
        19 min. , color, 1972.
        Director: Richard Tyson. Distributor: Paramount Com-
        munications.
             Family planning is characterized as an expression of
        love and concern for the quality of life. The reasons for
        family planning and a discussion of the effectiveness of
        various birth control methods are given. Avail. in Spanish.
        S-A

858   LOVE IS A SURPRISE
        60 sec. , color, 1978.

Director: Tony Frangakis.   Distributor: TeleKETICS.
A hassled businessman almost forgets his wedding
anniversary.   His sense of humor pulls him through.   Dramatic vignette, from the TeleSPOTS series.   A

859   LOVE IS FOR THE BYRDS
28 min. , color, 1965.
Director: W. O. Whitaker.   Distributor: Brigham Young
University.
A young couple drift apart because they can't communicate.   When they frankly express their feelings, their
marriage is renewed.   Dramatic film.   Chris Award, Columbus Film Festival.   S-A

860   LOVE IT LIKE A FOOL: A FILM ABOUT MALVINA REY-
NOLDS
28 min. , color, 1977.
Director: Susan Wengraf.   Distributor: New Day Films.
Profile of 76-year-old musician, composer, and
folksinger Malvina Reynolds.   She performs, records, re-
hearses, and discusses how she evolved from a housewife
and mother into a successful musician.   Blue Ribbon &
John Grierson Award, American Film Festival.   Jury Award,
San Francisco International Film Festival.   J-A

861   LOVE, SUSAN
14½ min. , color, 1973.
Producer: WNVT-TV.   Distributor: Agency for Instructional TV.
Susan wants her father to look at the portrait she
just painted.   He's preoccupied.   Captioned version avail.
From the Inside/Out series.   I

862   LOVE'S BEGINNING
10 min. , color, 1972.
Producer: Charles Cahill & Associates.   Distributor:
AIMS Instructional Media Services.
How love makes life richer, especially family love.
E, A

863   LOVING PARENTS
24 min. , color, 1978.
Director: Herman J. Engel.   Distributor: Texture Films.
Raises questions parents most often ask about sex-
educating their kids, i. e. , projecting the proper sexuality
to their kids, guidance for sexual development, how to talk
with them about sex, what kind of sex info is needed, etc.
I-A

864   LOW VIEW FROM A DARK SHADOW
30 min. , b&w, 1968.
Director: Larry Long for WMVS-TV.   Distributor: Indiana
University, Audio-Visual Center.
Case study of a child following the breakup of his

home.   The child reacts predictably to his temporary placement in a home with other foster children and then his placement with a foster family.   Studies his perceptions and reactions to these changes and a new set of parents.   S-A

865   LUCY
         13 min. , color, 1971.
         Director: Alfred Wallace.   Distributor: Pictura Films.
                An unwed, pregnant Puerto Rican teenager decides to have her baby and not have an abortion.   The choices available to her are delineated as are the tensions raised within her family.   S-A

866   LUKE WAS THERE
         32 min. , color, 1976.
         Director: Richard Marquand.   Distributor: Learning Corp. of America.
                A young black boy who is continually abandoned by adults (father, stepfather, hospitalized mother) finally learns to trust another--a counselor at a children's shelter. From the Learning to Be Human series and the Special Treat TV series.   ACT Achievement in Children's Television Award.   E-A

867   LULLABY: ANOTHER DAY
         30 sec. , color, 1970.
         Director: Tony Frangakis.   Distributor: TeleKETICS.
                An old Southern lullaby counterpoints portraits of poor mothers and their children.   From the TeleSPOTS series.   S-A

868   MADE FOR EACH OTHER   see
         ANIMATED WOMEN SERIES   92

869   MADSONG
         5 min. , color, 1976.
         Director: Kathleen Laughlin.   Distributor: Serious Business Company.
                Live-action, animation, optical printing, and multiple soundtrack are used to explore such areas in a woman's life as childbirth, male/female bonding, and the mother / child relationship.   C-A

870   THE MAGIC HOUSE
         $16\frac{1}{2}$ min. , color, 1970.
         Producer: King Screen Productions.   Distributor: BFA Educational Media.
                Two children cast a magic spell to stop their parents from caring about chores, meals, and neatness.   E-I

871   MAGIC MOMENTS SERIES   see
         HOLDING ON   654

872   THE MAGIC MOTH
        22 min. , color, 1976.
        Director: James Pearce. Distributor: Centron Films.
              A father has to explain to his younger children why
        their older sister will not get well. She has a terminal
        illness. CINE Golden Eagle. E-A

873   THE MAILBOX
        24 min. , color, p. 1976, r. 1977.
        Director: Dr. David Jacobs. Distributor: Brigham Young
        University.
              An elderly woman waits patiently for letters from
        her self-absorbed children and grandchildren. Their letters
        never come; she never gives up hope. Dramatic film. I-A

874   MAKE A WISH
        4 min. , color, 1973.
        Producer: Gerontology Center, Pennsylvania State Univer-
        sity. Distributor: The Pennsylvania State University.
              Vignette of a family birthday party for a grandmother,
        age 75, and her granddaughter, age 5. Simulates the re-
        stricted sensory feedback experienced by the elderly woman
        due to sight and hearing loss. C-A

From <u>Make-Believe Marriage.</u>   Courtesy Highgate Pictures /
Learning Corp. of America.

875   MAKE-BELIEVE MARRIAGE
        33 min. & 50 min. , color, p. 1978, r. 1979.
        Director: Robert Fuest. Distributor: Learning Corp. of
        America.
              A high-school jock and the class feminist are paired
        off in their "trial marriage" class. As they face the reali-
        ties and tests of "married life," they grow as individuals
        and fall in love. Dramatic film. An <u>ABC Afterschool Spe-
        cial.</u> Blue Ribbon, American Film Festival. S-A

876   MAKE TODAY COUNT
        29 min. , color, p. 1975, r. 1976.
        Director: Rhoden Streeter.   Distributor: Brigham Young
        University.
             Orville Kelly, journalist and family man is dying
        of cancer, although the disease is in remission at the time
        of the filming.   The diagnosis caused him to rearrange his
        priorities.   A workaholic, he began spending more time
        with his family, and also organized a "Make Today Count"
        lifeline for other cancer patients.   S-A

877   A MAN
        21 min. , b&w, 1976.
        Directors: Len Grossman & Michael Chait.   Distributor:
        Polymorph Films.
             A young man in a men's consciousness-raising group
        works through the death of his father.   Shows the "group
        support process" in action.   From video.   S-A

878   THE MAN IN THE CAST IRON SUIT
        27 min. , color, 1976.
        Director: Paul Stanley for Paulist Productions.   Cast:
        John McLiam, Joshua Bryant.   Distributor: The Media
        Guild.
             Three generations of one family seek fulfillment.
        The grandfather has found the secret of life and is happy.
        But he makes his son and grandson uncomfortable because
        they seek their happiness through material wealth and physi-
        cal prowess.   From the Insight series.   S-A

879   THE MANAGEMENT DEVELOPMENT SERIES   see
             CONSTRUCTIVE USE OF THE EMOTIONS   307

880   MANDY'S GRANDMOTHER
        30 min. , color, 1978.
        Director: Andrew Sugerman.   Cast: Maureen O'Sullivan,
        Amy Levitan, Kathryn Walker.   Distributor: Phoenix Films.
             A young girl and her grandmother meet for the first
        time and must work through their stereotyped preconcep-
        tions of what granddaughters and grandmothers should and
        should not be.   E-J

881   THE MANY AMERICANS SERIES   see
             FELIPA--NORTH OF THE BORDER   497
             GERONIMO JONES   564
             LEE SUZUKI--HOME IN HAWAII   813
             MATTHEW ALIUK--ESKIMO IN TWO WORLDS   905
             MIGUEL--UP FROM PUERTO RICO   928
             SIU MEI WONG--WHO SHALL I BE?   1281
             TODD--GROWING UP IN APPALACHIA   1404

882   MAPLE SUGAR FARMER
        30 min. , color, p. 1972, r. 1973.

Producers: W. Craig Hinde & Robert Davis.   Distributor:
Paramount Communications.
 Sherman Graff, an elderly Illinois farmer, keeps
alive a six-generation family tradition of making maple
syrup and sugar.   From the Yesterday and Today series.
Blue Ribbon, American Film Festival.   Bronze Medal,
Atlanta Film Festival.   Gold Plaque, Chicago International
Film Festival.   CINE Golden Eagle.   Chris Statuette, Co-
lumbus Film Festival.   First Prize, San Francisco Inter-
national Film Festival.   I-A

883 THE MARCH OF TIME SERIES see
  THE FAMILY: AN APPROACH TO PEACE 462
  MARRIAGE & DIVORCE 888

884 MARCO
 83 min. , b&w, 1970.
 Directors: Gerald Temaner & Gordon Quinn.   Distributor:
 Film Images.
  Documents the birth of a young couple's first child
 by the Lamaze method.   Covers pre-labor exercises, visits
 with the doctor, and talks with friends about their experiences.   Also, labor, delivery, and family bonding.   Blue
 Ribbon, American Film Festival.   S-A

885 MARIA OF THE PUEBLOS
 15 min. , color, 1971.
 Director: Maurice Prather.   Distributor: Centron Films.
  Maria Martinez, a Pueblo Indian of New Mexico, and
 her family form, decorate, glaze, and fire their iridescent,
 black pottery by a process that has made Maria an important potter.   From the North American Indians Today series.   Chris Statuette, Columbus Film Festival.   I-A

886 MARRIAGE see
  BIG TOWN 151

887 MARRIAGE
 17 min. , color, 1971.
 Director: Sy Wexler.   Distributor: Perennial Education.
  Covers wedding through golden anniversary.   Animation.   I-A

888 MARRIAGE & DIVORCE
 15 min. , b&w, 1948.
 Distributor: Kit Parker Films (rental only).
  Increased divorce rate since 1900, as well as other
 statistics relating to effects of modern age on marriage.
 From The March of Time series. S-A

889 MARRIAGE IS A PARTNERSHIP see
  ANATOMY OF A TEEN-AGE MARRIAGE 78

890   MARRIAGE PROBLEMS
30 min. , b&w, 1964.
Producer: NET. Host: Dr. Maria Piers. Distributor:
Indiana University, Audio-Visual Center.
Two unhappily married sisters are highlighted.   One
is recently married; the other is pregnant with her second
child.   Dr. Piers points out the unrealistic expectations of
young couples.   Stresses that maturity and independence
are needed to form a good marriage.   From the About
People series.   S-A

891   MARRIAGE, WHAT KIND FOR YOU?
25 min. , color, 1969.
Director: Wetzel O. Whitaker. Distributor: Brigham
Young University.
An engaged couple observe four married couples at
a party.   The couples represent a wide range of marital
relationships; they also offer marital advice.   S-A

892   MARRIED LIVES TODAY
19 min. , color, 1975.
Directors: Joseph Shields & Jaryl Lane. Distributor: BFA
Educational Media.
Three young, middle-class couples discuss what
marriage means to them: a childless couple, a black
couple with two children, and a separated couple with one
small child.   S-A

893   MARSHA
24 min. , color, 1977.
Director: Eugene Wheeler. Distributor: Atlantis Productions.
The mother of a mentally retarded teenage girl discusses her daughter's special problems and singular achievements.   S-A

894   MARTHA
11 min. , color, p. 1973, r. 1974.
Director: Jennifer Mead. Distributor: Perennial Education.
Portrait of a middle-aged suburban woman caught
between traditional roles and values and changing family relationships and sexual roles.   S-A

895   MARY CASSATT: IMPRESSIONIST FROM PHILADELPHIA
28 min. , color, 1977.
Director: Perry Miller Adato. Distributor: Films Inc.
Biography of the 19th-century artist--with much on
the upper-class family expectations and restrictions that
Cassatt had to contend with when she set out to become a
painter.   Also includes an interview with her niece, who
once modeled for Cassatt.   From The Originals: Women
in Art series.   S-A

896   MASCULINE OR FEMININE: YOUR ROLE IN SOCIETY
          $18\frac{1}{2}$ min. , color, 1971.
          Director: J. William Walker. Distributor: Coronet Films.
                Questions contemporary male /female roles, e. g. ,
          what roles the man should play at home and the woman in
          business. Chris Award, Columbus Film Festival. S-A

897   A MASTURBATORY STORY
          15 min. , color, 1978.
          Producers: Chris Morse & Judy Doonan. Distributor:
          Perennial Education.
                Lighthearted approach to male masturbation; aims to
          alleviate parent-induced guilt in growing boys. S-A

898   MATCHES
          9 min. , color, 1971.
          Producer: Dave Bell Associates. Distributor: FilmFair
          Communications.
                A 7-year-old boy fears for his 5-year-old sister's
          life when she runs off with a book of matches. E

899   MATERNITY CARE--LABOR AND DELIVERY
          37 min. , color, 1964.
          Producer: U.S. Dept. of the Navy. Distributor: National
          Audiovisual Center.
                Aims to educate pregnant women about labor and
          delivery, so they'll know what to expect and be able to con-
          tribute to their own comfort and the baby's safety. A

900   MATERNITY CARE--MEDICAL EXAMINATIONS DURING
          PREGNANCY
          28 min. , color, 1963.
          Producer: U.S. Dept. of the Navy. Distributor: National
          Audiovisual Center.
                The nature and purpose of medical examinations for
          pregnant women. A

901   MATERNITY CARE--PERSONAL CARE DURING PREGNANCY
          41 min. , color, 1964.
          Producer: U.S. Dept. of the Navy. Distributor: National
          Audiovisual Center.
                Explains normal physiological changes during preg-
          nancy and provides a regimen to follow. A

902   MATINA HORNER: PORTRAIT OF A PERSON
          16 min. , color, 1974.
          Directors: Joyce Chopra & Claudia Weill. Distributor:
          Phoenix Films.
                The life and work of the president of Radcliffe Col-
          lege, showing how she balances roles of mother, wife,
          academic, and administrator. S-A

903   MATTER OF CHANCE
        28 min. , color, 1977.
        Producer: Veterans Administration.   Distributor: National
        Audiovisual Center.
            A hospital-based sickle cell anemia counseling pro-
        gram.   Points out the chances of hereditary transmission
        among blacks.   C-A

904   A MATTER OF HONOR: SAM HOUSTON
        27 min. , b&w, p. 1953, r. 1967.
        Director: Arthur Hilton.   Distributor: Indiana University,
        Audio-Visual Center.
            A misunderstanding between Sam Houston and his
        wife forces him to resign his office and depart for Texas
        rather than dishonor her.   From the Cavalcade of America
        series.   S

905   MATTHEW ALIUK--ESKIMO IN TWO WORLDS
        18 min. , color, 1973.
        Director: Bert Salzman.   Distributor: Learning Corp. of
        America.
            Although Matthew has adjusted well to city life in
        Anchorage, his uncle cannot adjust and must return north
        From the Many Americans series.   E-J, A

906   MAXINE
        13 min. , b&w, 1975.
        Director: Sarah Snider.   Distributor: Iris Films.
            A wife and mother of two sons is dying in her rural
        home with her family all around her.   C-A

907   ME AND DAD'S NEW WIFE
        33 min. , color, 1976.
        Director: Larry Elikann.   Cast: Kristy McNichol.   Dis-
        tributor: Time-Life Multimedia.
            When 12-year-old Nina finds that her new math
        teacher is also her dad's new wife, she is angry and re-
        sentful and takes it out on those around her.   An ABC
        Afterschool Special; from the Teenage Years series.   CINE
        Golden Eagle.   I-A

908   ME, MYSELF & MAYBE
        $14\frac{1}{2}$ min. , color, 1974.
        Producer: KETC-TV.   Distributor: Agency for Instruc-
        tional TV.
            A girl lacks self-confidence at school until her aunt
        helps her learn some new skills.   From the Bread & But-
        terflies series.   I-J

909   THE MEANING OF ENGAGEMENT   see
            ANATOMY OF A TEEN-AGE ENGAGEMENT   77

910   MEDICAL-LEGAL COMPONENT SERIES   see
            CHILDBIRTH AND PROBLEMS OF CHILD PATIENTS   257

911   MEDICAL SELF-HELP SERIES   see
       EMERGENCY CHILDBIRTH   417
       INFANT AND CHILD CARE   723

912   THE MEDICAL WITNESS
       35 min., color, 1977.
       Producer: National Center on Child Abuse & Neglect, HEW.
       Distributor: National Audiovisual Center.
           Dramatization of a physician's experience in prepar-
       ing for and testifying in court on a child-abuse case.   In-
       cludes do's and don'ts while testifying.   Training film;
       from the We Can Help series.   C, Prof

913   MEET LISA
       5 min., color, 1971.
       Producer: The Learning Garden.   Distributor: AIMS In-
       structional Media Services.
           The world through the eyes of a brain-injured child
       and her parents.   Shows potential for happiness and pro-
       ductivity.   I, A, Prof

914   MEET YOUR PARENT, ADULT, CHILD (A FILM ABOUT
       TRANSACTIONAL ANALYSIS)
       9 min., color, 1975.
       Producer: CBS-TV.   Distributor: BFA Educational Media.
           Analyzes the "parent," "child," and "adult" ego
       states developed in early childhood and carried through to
       adulthood.   How to manage them effectively in interpersonal
       relationships.   Animation.   From the Transactional Analysis
       series.   J-A

915   MEETINGS WITH GOD/STORYSCAPE SERIES   see
       GOD MOMENTS   578
       IN TOUCH WITH GOD   714
       TAPESTRY OF FAITH   1351

916   MEMORIES AND CONVERSATIONS
       90 min., b&w, 1974.
       Director: Hans Schaal.   Distributor: Serious Business
       Company.
           Cinema vérité study of a Greek American, middle-
       aged blue-collar couple.   C-A

917   MEMORIES OF FAMILY
       24 min., color, 1977.
       Director: Alvin Fiering.   Distributor: Polymorph Films.
           Six vignettes recreate typical family situations in
       which we learn about love and trust, disappointment, rejec-
       tion, being old and young, being a mother and a father.
       Explores a range of family relationships.   S-A

918   MEN'S LIVES
       43 min., color, 1974.

Directors: Josh Hanig & Will Roberts. Distributor: New Day Films. The socialization of the American boy into the American man. Questions the traditional stereotypic male role models, as taught by family, school, and society. Blue Ribbon, American Film Festival. Family Life Award, National Council on Family Relations. S-A

919 METER PARK SERIES see
TAKING MEASURE 1345

920 METHODS OF FAMILY PLANNING
18 min., color, 1972.
Director: Jan Stean. Distributor: Paramount Communications.
Methods of contraception explained: rhythm, the pill, diaphragm, intrauterine devices, vaginal spermicides, and condoms; also covers the vasectomy and tubal ligation. Couples and doctors discuss the medical pros and cons of each method. Avail. in Spanish. Silver Award, New York International Film Festival. S-A

921 A MEXICAN-AMERICAN FAMILY
17 min., color, 1970.
Producer: Bernard Selling. Distributor: Atlantis Productions.
A Mexican American family, its traditions and interrelationships, adjustments to a new language and society, and efforts to maintain family unity. Chris Award, Columbus Film Festival. J-A

922 MEXICAN OR AMERICAN
17 min., color, 1970.
Producer: Bernard Selling. Distributor: Atlantis Productions.
Focuses on the question of cultural conflict: is it possible to enjoy the opportunities of America without completely giving up the heritage of one's parents? Chris Award, Columbus Film Festival. J-A

923 MICHELLE AT HOME (HI, DADDY!)
10 min., color, p. 1974, r. 1975.
Director: John Friedman. Distributor: Education Development Center.
An afternoon with a family: the father, who is a lobster fisherman; the mother; 4-year-old Michelle; and her 5-year-old brother. From the Exploring Childhood: Family and Society series. J-A

924 MICROCULTURAL INCIDENTS IN TEN ZOOS
34 min., color, 1971.
Producers: R. L. Birdwhistell & J. D. Van Vlack.
Distributor: Pennsylvania State University.

A pioneer in non-verbal communication analyzes footage of families shot in ten different zoos in seven countries. He makes a cross-cultural comparative study of family structure, teaching styles, body motion, and attitudes. English, American, and Italian families are among those studied. C-A

925   THE MIDDLE MONTHS OF PREGNANCY
       30 min., b&w, 1956.
       Producer: WQED, Pittsburgh. Distributors: Association Films (rental only); Indiana University, Audio-Visual Center (rental only).
              Birthmarks, deformities, morning sickness, clothing changes, relieving constipation, dizziness, etc. From the Months Before Birth series. A

926   MIGHTY MOOSE AND THE QUARTERBACK KID
       31 min., color, 1977.
       Director: Tony Frangakis. Distributor: Time-Life Multimedia.
              A father tries to push his son into Little League football, although his son obviously lacks the talent and interest to make a go of it. Dramatic film. An ABC Afterschool Special, from the Teenage Years series. I-A

927   MIGRANT
       52 min., color, 1970.
       Director: Martin Carr for NBC-TV. Narrator: Chet Huntley. Distributor: Films Inc.
              Plight of migrant farm families in America. Red Ribbon, American Film Festival. Christopher Award. Peabody Award. Robert F. Kennedy Journalism Award. J-C

928   MIGUEL--UP FROM PUERTO RICO
       15 min., color, 1970.
       Director: Bert Salzman. Distributor: Learning Corp. of America.
              Young Miguel was born in Puerto Rico, but now lives in New York City with his family. He has adjustments to make. From the Many Americans series. E-J, A

929   MILD RETARDATION: A FAMILY PROFILE
       14 min., color, 1977.
       Director: Patricia Rambasek. Distributor: Case Western Reserve University, Health Sciences Communications Center.
              How a 21-year-old retarded man functions at home, work, and in social situations; with thoughts from his mother, father, brother, and the young man himself. J-A

930   MINNIE REMEMBERS
       5 min., color, 1976.
       Directors: Kay Henderson, Phil Arnold, & Wayne Smith. Distributor: Mass Media Ministries.

A lonely old widow longs for the past: her childhood, youth, and marriage. J-A

931 A MINOR ALTERCATION
30 min., color, p. 1976, r. 1977.
Director: Jackie Shearer. Distributor: Tricontinental
Film Center.
Dramatizes a real-life incident that occurred during
the throes of the Boston school desegregation controversy.
A black mother and a white mother meet after their daugh-
ters have a dispute at school. J-A

932 MINORITY OF ONE
28 min., color, p. 1975, r. 1976.
Director: Mike Gavin for KNBC-TV. Distributor: Films
Inc.
Shows parents who search endlessly for a cure for
their children's autism. Examines behavior modification,
a controversial method of handling the disorder. Blue Ribbon, American Film Festival. S-A

933 MINORITY YOUTH: AKIRA
14½ min., color, 1971.
Director: Stuart Roe. Distributor: BFA Educational Media.
A Japanese American youth is torn between the culture of his parents and that of his friends. Explores his
family activities, his traditional Japanese life-style at home,
and his strictly American life-style at school. I-S

934 MINORITY YOUTH: ANGIE
10½ min., color, 1971.
Director: Stuart Roe. Distributor: BFA Educational Me-
dia.
Angie discusses her life as a Mexican American.
She takes pride in her Mexican American home. I-S

935 MINORITY YOUTH: FELICIA
11½ min., b&w, 1966.
Director: Stuart Roe. Distributor: BFA Educational Media.
A high-school junior lives in a modest home in Watts,
a black suburb of Los Angeles, with her mother, brother,
and sister. She is highly motivated to make something of
her life and finds strength in her family. I-S

936 THE MIRACLE OF BIRTH
30 min., color, 1974.
Director: Roger S. Olson. Distributor: Brigham Young
University.
Shows three couples: one experiencing Primiparous
(first birth) with an Episiotomy; one a Multiparous (second
birth); and another a Forceps delivery. C-A

937   A MISERABLE MERRY CHRISTMAS
       15 min. , color, 1974.
       Producer: WNET/13.   Distributor: Encyclopaedia Britan-
       nica Educational Corp.
           Based on a chapter from the Autobiography of Lin-
       coln Steffens, in which the journalist recalled a childhood
       Christmas when his family tricked him into believing that
       he would receive no gifts and then gave him the best gift
       ever.   I-S

938   MISS, MRS. OR MS. --WHAT'S IT ALL ABOUT?
       25 min. , color, 1977.
       Producer: Vern Diamond for CBS-TV News.   Distributor:
       Carousel Films.
           Covers traditional sex-role stereotypes, and notes
       that they no longer have meaning.   I-S

939   MRS. COP
       15 min. , color, 1973.
       Director: Joe De Cola.   Distributor: MTI Teleprograms.
           A sergeant on the Washington, D. C. , police force
       and her husband, also a police officer, discuss her job in
       a traditionally male field, how their marriage survives with
       two cops in the family, etc.   S-A, Prof

940   THE MITT
       17 min. , color, p. 1976, r. 1977.
       Director: Michael Brownstone.   Distributor: Learning
       Corp. of America.
           A 12-year-old boy earns money to buy a new base-
       ball mitt, but uses the money instead to buy his mom
       something she needs and wants.   E-J

941   MOBILE HOME FIRE SAFETY
       15 min. , color, 1977.
       Director: David Hoffman.   Distributor: Film Communicators.
           Potential problem areas are reviewed and ways to
       correct them are given.   S-A

942   MODERN WOMEN: THE UNEASY LIFE
       60 min. , b&w, 1966.
       Producer: NET.   Distributor: Indiana University, Audio-
       Visual Center.
           Frustrations and satisfactions of women who combine
       motherhood with careers; women who are solely housewives
       and mothers; and women who are solely career-oriented.
       Also explores attitudes of husbands and unmarried men
       towards educated women.   S-A

943   MOHAWK NATION
       45 min. , color, p. 1976, r. 1977.
       Director: Allan Siegel.   Distributor: Third World News-
       reel.

In 1974, Mohawk Indians seized abandoned land in New York State that was originally part of their ancestral land and supposedly ceded to the state in the 18th century. They contest this treaty and reestablish their roots in this film, which shows families setting up new homes, reclaiming dignity lost in reservation life.   C-A

944   MOM AND DAD CAN'T HEAR ME
47 min. , color, 1978.
Director: Larry Elikann. Cast: Priscilla Pointer, Stephen Elliott, Rosanna Arquette. Distributor: Time-Life Multimedia.
When a family moves to a new town, the teenage daughter fears that her deaf and overly strict parents will cause her to be ostracized. She concocts various lies to hide them from her new friends. An ABC Afterschool Special; from the Teenage Years series.   J-A

945   MOM, WHY WON'T YOU LISTEN?
13 min. , color, 1971.
Director: Kent Mackenzie. Distributor: Churchill Films.
Young people wonder how to get their parents to listen to them. From The Searching Years: The Family series.   J-A

946   THE MONEY TREE
19 min. , color, 1971.
Director: Durrell R. Crays for Hanna-Barbera Productions. Distributor: AIMS Instructional Media Services.
Points out the importance of financial planning and awareness of economic responsibility in family life and marriage in general. Avail. in Spanish.   I-A

947   THE MONTHS BEFORE BIRTH SERIES see
THE BEGINNING OF PREGNANCY 135
THE BIRTH OF THE BABY 162
THE FIRST VISIT TO THE DOCTOR 516
THE LAST MONTHS OF PREGNANCY 797
THE MIDDLE MONTHS OF PREGNANCY 925
NUTRITION AND DENTAL CARE IN PREGNANCY 1043
THE PHYSIOLOGY OF REPRODUCTION 1107
THE WEEKS AFTER BIRTH 1477

948   MOONBIRD
10 min. , color, 1959.
Directors: John Hubley & Faith Hubley. Distributor: Films Inc.
Two young brothers share a fantasy adventure. Animation with the voices of the filmmakers' two young sons. I, S-A

949   MORAL DECISION MAKING SERIES see
AGGRESSION-ASSERTION 25
RESPONSE TO MISBEHAVIOR 1195

950   MORAL JUDGMENT AND REASONING
      17 min. , color, 1978.
      Producer: McGraw-Hill Films & Coast Community College.
      Distributor: CRM/McGraw-Hill Films.
             Covers the origins of moral development in a child
      from three perspectives: the psychoanalytic theory, the
      social learning theory, and the cognitive developmental
      theory.   Vignettes highlight the stages of moral development
      and reasoning.   From the Developmental Psychology series.
      S-A

951   MORE THAN A DREAM
      28 min. , color, 1975.
      Director: Stanley Losak for NBC-TV. Distributor: Films
      Inc.
             Two working-class families--one black, one white--
      who live in Nashville are observed.   Both men hold two
      jobs, both wives work, both families are Baptist, both have
      similar goals and fears.   S-A

952   MORE THAN A SCHOOL
      56 min. , color, 1973.
      Director: Martha Coolidge. Distributor: Films Inc.
             Parents, students, and teachers talk freely about
      their participation in the alternative community high school
      that exists within the traditional Herrick's Long Island
      Senior High (N. Y.).   From the Alternative Education series.
      Blue Ribbon, American Film Festival.   S-A

953   MOTHER-INFANT INTERACTION 1: FORMS OF INTER-
      ACTION AT SIX WEEKS
      49 min. , b&w, 1967-68.
      Directors: Sylvia Brody, Ph. D. , & Sidney Axelrad, D. S. Sc.
      Distributor: New York University.
             Mother-child interaction during feeding.   Series
      (Mother-Infant Interaction) notes long-term effects of mother-
      ing on the emotional and cognitive development of infants
      during the first year of life.   C, Prof

954   MOTHER-INFANT INTERACTION 2: FORMS OF INTER-
      ACTION AT SIX MONTHS
      42 min. , b&w, 1967-68.
      Directors: Sylvia Brody, Ph. D. , & Sidney Axelrad, D. S. Sc.
      Distributor: New York University.
             Mother-child interaction during feeding: the develop-
      ment of tension tolerance.   Series (Mother-Infant Interaction)
      notes long-term effects of mothering on the emotional and
      cognitive development of infants during the first year of
      life.   C, Prof

955   MOTHER-INFANT INTERACTION 3: FEEDING AND OBJECT
      RELATIONS AT ONE YEAR
      40 min. , b&w, 1967-68.

Directors: Sylvia Brody, Ph. D. , & Sidney Axelrad, D. S. Sc.
Distributor: New York University.
　　　　Suggests connections between modes of mother-infant
experience and the infant's relationships to persons and
things at age one. Series (Mother-Infant Interaction) notes
long-term effects of mothering on the emotional and cognitive development of infants during the first year of life.
C, Prof

956　　MOTHER-INFANT INTERACTION 4: FEEDING AND FUNC-
　　　　TION--PLEASURE IN THE FIRST YEAR OF LIFE
　　　　42 min. , b&w, 1967-68.
　　　　Directors: Sylvia Brody, Ph. D. , & Sidney Axelrad, D. S. Sc.
　　　　Distributor: New York University.
　　　　　　　Relationships between types of maternal behavior and
　　　　the degree of excitement with which the infant responds to
　　　　stimuli. Series (Mother-Infant Interaction) notes long-term
　　　　effects of mothering on the emotional and cognitive develop-
　　　　ment of infants during the first year of life. C, Prof

957　　MOTHER-INFANT INTERACTION 5: MATERNAL BEHAVIOR
　　　　AND THE INFANT'S OBJECT CATHEXIS IN THE FIRST
　　　　YEAR OF LIFE
　　　　41 min. , b&w, 1967-68.
　　　　Directors: Sylvia Brody, Ph. D. , & Sidney Axelrad, D. S. Sc.
　　　　Distributor: New York University.
　　　　　　　The way an infant is mothered during feeding is re-
　　　　lated to the quality, quantity, and stability of his investment
　　　　in the outer world of objects. Series (Mother-Infant Inter-
　　　　action) notes long-term effects of mothering on the emotional
　　　　and cognitive development of infants during the first year
　　　　of life. C, Prof

958　　MOTHER-INFANT INTERACTION 6: RESEMBLANCES IN
　　　　EXPRESSIVE BEHAVIOR
　　　　41 min. , b&w, 1971.
　　　　Directors: Sylvia Brody, Ph. D. , & Sidney Axelrad, D. S. Sc.
　　　　Distributor: New York University.
　　　　　　　Suggests that an infant's expressive behavior is de-
　　　　rived, to an important extent, from the maternal behavior
　　　　he experiences during feeding. Series (Mother-Infant Inter-
　　　　action) notes long-term effects of mothering on the emo-
　　　　tional and cognitive development of infants during the first
　　　　year of life. C, Prof

959　　MOTHER LOVE
　　　　20 min. , b&w, sil. , 1952.
　　　　Producer: René A. Spitz, M. D. Distributor: New York
　　　　University.
　　　　　　　Social relations between mother and child, plus ef-
　　　　fects of separation/deprivation. From the Film Studies
　　　　of the Psychoanalytic Research Project on Problems in In-
　　　　fancy series. C, Prof

960   MOTHER LOVE
        20 min. , b&w, 1959.
        Director: Harold Mayer for CBS-TV. Distributor: Ca-
        rousel Films.
                Dr. Harry F. Harlow tests the reactions of newborn
        rhesus monkeys to unusual and inanimate mother substitutes.
        Shows the long-term psychological effects of denial of
        mother love. From the Conquest TV series. J-A

961   MOTHER OF THE KENNEDYS: A PORTRAIT OF ROSE
        FITZGERALD KENNEDY
        47 min. , color, 1974.
        Producer: Radharc, Inc. Distributor: Mass Media Min-
        istries.
                The 83-year-old Rose Kennedy shares her attitudes,
        ideals, and enriching experiences. Her daughter Eunice
        and son Ted also talk about their mother. J-A

962   MOTHER TIGER, MOTHER TIGER
        11 min. , color, 1974.
        Director: Rolf Forsberg. Distributor: TeleKETICS.
                Flashbacks reveal a mother reliving her joy at the
        expected birth of her child and the anger and frustration
        she experiences when she gives birth to a severely handi-
        capped child. CINE Golden Eagle. S-A

963   MOTHER TO DINNER
        18 min. , color, 1976.
        Director: Elisabeth Nonas. Distributor: Crystal-Nonas
        Films.
                Dilemma of a young bride who is pulled between
        conflicting demands of her possessive mother and her young
        husband. Dramatic film. S-A

964   MOTHERS AFTER DIVORCE
        20 min. , color, 1976.
        Directors: Henry Felt & Marilyn Felt. Distributor: Poly-
        morph Films.
                Four middle-aged women (with teenaged children)
        once led sheltered lives; now they are divorced. They dis-
        cuss their fearful new lives and relationships with their kids
        as single parents. S-A

965   MOTHERS AND TODDLERS: HUMANIZING THE GROWTH
        EXPERIENCE
        17 min. , b&w, 1970.
        Director: David Altschul. Distributor: Journal
        Films.
                Documents the preschool program "Toddlers Lab,"
        which was initiated by the Martin Luther King Family Cen-
        ter, a black social agency. Based on the notion that par-
        ents must experience a sense of competence before they
        can effectively encourage their children. C-A

966 MOTHER'S DAY
     23 min. , b&w, 1948.
     Director: James Broughton. Distributors: Serious Busi-
     ness Company; Grove Press Film Division.
          Recollection of childhood, family, and friends of
     filmmaker. C-A

967 MOTHER'S DIET AND HER BABY'S FUTURE
     23 min. , color, 1969.
     Producer: U.S. Dept. of the Navy. Distributor: National
     Audiovisual Center.
          What effect the lack of protein in the diet of preg-
     nant rats has on their offspring. Relates findings to hu-
     mans. C-A

968 MOTHERS--WHAT THEY DO
     11 min. , color, 1968.
     Producer: Films/West. Distributor: FilmFair Communi-
     cations.
          The work of three mothers is shown--a full-time
     housewife, a mother who works full-time, and a mother who
     works part-time. E

969 A MOTHER'S WORRY
     33 min. , color, 1978.
     Director: Gary Schlosser. Distributor: Gary Schlosser.
          Documents a mother's stress and its affects as a
     result of her 2-year-old's hospitalization. Red Ribbon,
     American Film Festival. C-A, Prof

970 MOTILITY IN PARENT-CHILD RELATIONSHIPS
     40 min. , b&w, sil. , 1959.
     Producer: Dr. Bela Mittelmann. Distributor: New York
     University.
          Important role of motor ability in the development
     of interpersonal relationships during the first year-and-a-
     half of life. C, Prof

971 MOUNTAIN COUSINS see
     COUNTRY FAMILIES 320

972 MOUNTAIN PEOPLE
     52 min. , color, 1978.
     Director: Cinda Firestone. Distributor: Cinema 5--16mm.
          Focuses on some elderly people and their families
     in rural West Virginia. Notes that things are changing and
     younger family members are moving away, leaving the old
     to carry on the traditions. Red Ribbon, American Film
     Festival. S-A

973 THE MOUNTAIN PEOPLE
     24 min. , color, 1974.
     Director: Dennis Mitchell for Granada International TV,
     London. Distributor: Wombat Productions.

Pride and strength of exploited southern Appalachian poor. One impoverished family is highlighted. Blue Ribbon, American Film Festival. Gold Medal, Virgin Islands Film Festival. Chris Award, Columbus Film Festival. J-A

974   MOUNTAINS OF GREEN, STREETS OF GOLD
27 min. , color, 1978.
Director: Dennis Goulden for WKYC-TV. Distributor: Films Inc.
Some Appalachians who left good jobs in the city (Cleveland) to return to the mountains of West Virginia for peace of mind. J-A

975   MUGGERS!
15 min. , color, p. 1973, r. 1974.
Director: Philip Abbott. Narrator: Rosey Grier. Distributor: Walt Disney Educational Media Company.
A youth with no arrest record reluctantly helps his drug-addicted older brother get money to support his habit. From Under the Law, Series 1. J-S

976   MURIEL NEZHNIE HELFMAN
17 min. , b&w, 1977.
Director: Carol Greenfield. Distributor: Carol Greenfield.
Helfman is a St. Louis tapestry weaver and designer. Since she is also a wife and mother and works at home, various problems must be solved to balance career and home life. S-A

977   MY BIG BROTHER see
ALONE IN THE FAMILY 58

978   MY BROTHER'S KEEPER
12 min. , color, 1976.
Producer: Paramount Television. Distributor: Paramount Communications.
Marcia hires her brother for a job at the ice cream shop and then has to fire him because he's irresponsible. From The Brady Bunch Values and Guidance series; specially edited from The Brady Bunch TV series. E-I

979   MY CHILDHOOD, PARTS I & II: HUBERT HUMPHREY'S SOUTH DAKOTA and JAMES BALDWIN'S HARLEM
51 min. , b&w, 1964.
Producer: Arthur Barron. Distributor: Benchmark Films.
In Part I, HUBERT HUMPHREY'S SOUTH DAKOTA (26 min.), Humphrey talks about growing up in a small Midwestern town and his love for his family. In Part II, JAMES BALDWIN'S HARLEM (25 min.), Baldwin bitterly recalls his tortured father, his Harlem poverty, and his strong will to leave the ghetto. Best of Festival, Martin Luther King Film Festival. CINE Golden Eagle. Blue Ribbon, American Film Festival. J-A

980   MY COUNTRY, RIGHT OR WRONG?
        15 min. , color, 1972.
        Director: Anthony Newley.   Cast: Jack Warden, Michael
        Douglas.   Distributor: Learning Corp. of America.
                A young man disagrees with his parents over a de-
        cision to avoid the draft and flee to Canada.   His father
        sees to it that his son ends up in the Army.   Although the
        son is killed in action, the father feels he did the right
        thing.   Questions parents' right to force a possible life-and-
        death decision.   Edited from the 1971 film SUMMERTREE
        (2029).   From the Searching for Values series.   J-A

981   MY DAD'S A COP
        18 min. , color, 1976.
        Directors: William Brose & David Moses.   Distributors:
        MTI Teleprograms; William Brose Productions.
                Problems, joys, and pride shared by black family of
        a cop.   Documentary.   E-J

982   MY DEAR UNCLE SHERLOCK
        24 min. , color, 1978.
        Director: Arthur H. Nadel.   Distributor: ABC Wide
        World of Learning.
                A young boy's talent for detective work--acquired
        from his amateur-sleuth uncle--almost costs him his life.
        Dramatic film.   An ABC Weekend Special.   E-J

983   MY FAMILY BUSINESS
        12 min. , color, 1975.
        Producer: WGBH-TV, Boston.   Distributor: Films Inc.
                Two short portraits of real-life American kids;
        vignettes include: FRUIT AND VEGETABLE STAND--Ralph
        Lavita works at the family fruit stand in Boston's Italian
        North End.   CHINESE RESTAURANT--Mei Ling Lee is a
        waitress in her parents' New Jersey restaurant.   From the
        Best of Zoom series.   E-I

984   MY FATHER, MY BROTHER AND ME
        24 min. , color, 1978.
        Director: Tom Robertson.   Distributor: Multimedia Pro-
        gram Productions.
                A father's devotion to his mentally retarded son and
        how this love makes life bearable for his migrant family.
        His daughter tells the story.   From the Young People's
        Specials series.   E-J

985   MY FATHER THE DOCTOR
        18 min. , color, 1972.
        Director: Miriam Weinstein.   Distributor: Miriam Wein-
        stein.
                Studies past and present relationship between the
        filmmaker and her father.   Includes old photos and home
        movies.   C-A

986   MY GIRLFRIEND'S WEDDING
         60 min. , color, 1970.
         Director: James McBride. Distributor: New Yorker Films.
              The British girlfriend of the filmmaker discusses
         her love for her father, her son, and for the filmmaker:
         she wants to marry an American so she can stay in this
         country. C-A

987   MY GRANDSON LEW
         13 min. , color, 1976.
         Director: Donald MacDonald. Distributor: Barr Films.
              A mother encourages her young son to cherish
         memories of his deceased grandfather. E-J, A

988   MY HUSBAND LEFT OUT ON US
         23 min. , color, 1975.
         Producer: Blackside for Assistance Payments Administra-
         tion, Dept. of Health, Education & Welfare. Distributor:
         National Audiovisual Center.
              An interview situation with a woman in her thirties
         who has six kids and has been deserted by her husband.
         The interviewer must determine whether actual desertion
         has occurred. Training film. From the Essential Ele-
         ments of Interviewing series. C, Prof

989   MY HUSBAND STOPPED SUPPORT PAYMENTS
         22 min. , color, 1976.
         Producer: Blackside for Assistance Payments Administra-
         tion, Dept. of Health, Education & Welfare. Distributor:
         National Audiovisual Center.
              An interview focusing on the welfare regulations that
         cover child support, as well as the responsibility of the
         client and the agency. Training film. From the Essential
         Elements of Interviewing series. C, Prof

990   MY LIFE IN ART (Series of 8 Films)
         30 min. total, color, 1969-73.
         Directors: Freude; with Gunvor Nelson & Scott Bartlett.
         Distributor: Serious Business Company.
              A diary on film documenting the filmmaker's friends,
         husband, child, feminism, and life in California. Titles
         are: PROMISE HER ANYTHING BUT GIVE HER THE
         KITCHEN SINK (3 min.); SHOOTING STAR (5 min.); STAND-
         UP & BE COUNTED (3 min.); ADAM'S BIRTH (2 min.);
         SWEET DREAMS (3 min.); FOLLY (3 min.); WOMEN &
         CHILDREN AT LARGE (7 min.); ONE AND THE SAME (4
         min.). C-A

991   MY MAIN MAN
         14 min. , color, 1975.
         Producer: Mike Rhodes for Paulist Productions. Distri-
         butor: The Media Guild.
              A black boy sulks and ultimately endangers his father's

life because he'd rather play basketball than help his father
save the family business. The boy runs away, but father and
son are reconciled in the morning. From the Bloomin' Human
series. CINE Golden Eagle. E-J

992   MY MOM'S HAVING A BABY
       47 min. , color, 1977.
       Director: Larry Elikann. Distributor: Time-Life Multimedia.
              Nine-year-old Petey's mom is pregnant. Dr. Len-
       don Smith (a real-life pediatrician) calls Petey and his
       friends into his office to see a film about childbirth, so
       the boy can understand the process and adjust to the new
       arrival. An ABC Afterschool Special; from the Teenage
       Years series. I-J, A

993   MY NAME IS DAVID ... AND I'M AN ALCOHOLIC
       23½ min. , color, 1977.
       Producer: Gordon-Kerckhoff Productions. Distributor:
       AIMS Instructional Media Services.
              A middle-aged alcoholic goes through a 28-day stay
       at an AA rehabilitation center rather than be dismissed
       from his job. Highlights help available to wives (AL-ANON)
       and children of alcoholics (ALA-TEEN). S-A

994   MY NAME IS OONA
       10 min. , b&w, 1969-70.
       Director: Gunvor Nelson. Distributor: Serious Business Co.
              Portrait of the filmmaker's 9-year-old daughter and
       her dawning of self-knowledge. S-A

995   MY TURTLE DIED TODAY
       8 min. , color, 1968.
       Producer: Stephen Bosustow Productions. Distributor:
       BFA Educational Media.
              When a pet turtle dies and kittens are born, a boy's
       father, teacher, and a pet-store owner try to help the child
       understand the cycle of life. E

996   MYSTO THE GREAT
       25 min. , color, 1976.
       Director: Eric Edson. Distributor: Perspective Films.
              A widower refuses to be a grief-stricken, docile old
       man. Against his son's wishes, he drives off in the search
       of a new life, perhaps with a new wife. Dramatic film. S-A

997   NAMES OF SIN
       11 min. & 18 min. , color, 1975.
       Director: Rolf Forsberg. Distributor: TeleKETICS.
              A little girl breaks the window of a sick neighbor on
       a dare from her friends. She "wins" a charm bracelet as
       a reward, but feels responsible when she learns the woman
       is dying. Her mother reassures her. Longer version in-
       cludes a discussion leader to initiate questions after viewing.
       From the Storyscape series. I-A

From Nana, Mom and Me.   Courtesy Amalie R. Roth-
schild/New Day Films.

998   NANA, MOM AND ME
       47 min. , color, 1974.
       Director: Amalie R. Rothschild. Distributor: New Day
       Films.
             Three generations of Jewish women are profiled here
       (the filmmaker, her mother, the elderly grandmother).
       Life-style choices are compared and contrasted. The film-
       maker's somewhat younger sister and their father also
       make an appearance. S-A

999   NANA: UN PORTRAIT
       25 min. , color, 1973.
       Director: Jamil Simon. Distributor: Third Eye Films.
             The filmmaker's grandmother reminisces at age 80
       about her early family life in Baghdad, her husband, tri-
       umphs and tragedies. In French, with English subtitles.
       C-A

1000   NANOOK OF THE NORTH
       64 min. , b&w, sil. with music, 1922.
       Director: Robert J. Flaherty. Distributor: Films Inc.
             Classic saga of an Eskimo family, as they go about
       their daily life in continual battle with the elements. The
       1976 restored version has a new musical score. S-A

1001   NAN'S CLASS
       40 min. , color, 1977.
       Director: Ginny Durrin. Distributor: American Society
       for Psychoprophylaxis in Obstetrics.
             The experiences of five couples and one single parent

who attend childbirth preparation classes. Includes births with Lamaze, Leboyer, and Cesarean deliveries. Blue Ribbon, American Film Festival. S-A

1002 NATIONAL DISTRICT ATTORNEY'S ASSOCIATION EVIDENCE TRAINING SERIES see
CORPUS DELICTI-HOMICIDE 318

1003 NATIONAL KIDS' QUIZ
30 min., color, 1978.
Producer: Bantling Productions, Inc., for NBC-TV. Distributor: Xerox Films.
An audience views dramatized scenes of family and school dilemmas involving such areas as honesty, privacy, and loyalty, and then votes on the most satisfying solutions to the problems. I-J

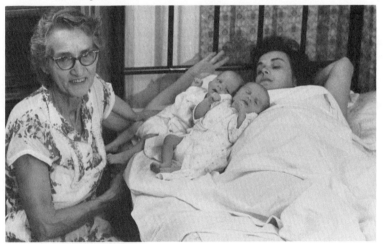

From Nature's Way. Courtesy Appalshop Films.

1004 NATURE'S WAY
20 min., color, 1973.
Director: John Long for the Appalachian Educational Media Project. Distributor: Appalshop Films.
At home with some Appalachian senior citizens and their natural cures and remedies. One woman prepares her family's special ointment. A man discusses his cancer-cure medicine that saved his wife's life. An accomplished midwife delivers a set of twins. S-A

1005 NAVAJO GIRL
20½ min., color, 1973.
Producer: Bobwin Associates. Distributor: Xerox Films.
A Navajo family lives at the poverty level on a reservation and has few, if any, amenities; but 10-year-old

Kathy is happy with her loving family, and knowledgeable about Indian traditions. From the Come Over to My House series. Blue Ribbon, American Film Festival. E-I

1006   THE NAVAJO WAY
52 min. , color, 1974.
Director: Robert Northshield for NBC-TV News. Distributor: Films Inc.
Intercut with the story of Mary Grey Mountain, her son, Robert Lee, and an 85-year-old medicine man, Long Salt, is the story of the plight of the Navajo today and their continual involvement with Navajo tradition. I-A

1007   A NAVAJO WEAVER
22 min. , b&w, sil. , 1966.
Director: Susie Benally. Producers: Sol Worth & John Adair. Distributor: Museum of Modern Art.
In a project conducted by Sol Worth and John Adair in Pine Springs, Ariz. , the Navajo Indians learned to film themselves. Here, Susie Benally films her mother weaving on a loom, as well as focusing on steps prior to weaving. See also SECOND WEAVER (1245). From the Navajos Film Themselves series. C-A

1008   NAVAJOS FILM THEMSELVES SERIES   see
A NAVAJO WEAVER   1007
SECOND WEAVER   1245

1009   THE NEGLECTED
30 min. , b&w, 1965.
Director: Irving Jacoby for the Mental Health Film Board. Distributor: International Film Bureau.
What can be done to salvage families and rehabilitate parents whose children have come under protection of community authorities due to abuse or neglect. C-A, Prof

1010   NEVER A BRIDE
22 min. , color, 1969.
Director: Scott Whitaker. Distributor: Brigham Young University.
An immature girl realizes that it's more important to be the right person than to find the right person for marriage. Dramatic film. S-A

1011   THE NEW ALCHEMISTS
29 min. , color, 1975.
Director: D. T. Henaut for the National Film Board of Canada. Distributor: Benchmark Films.
Some young scientists and their families living near Falmouth, Mass. , successfully work an experimental plant and fish farm where they use only organic fertilizers in an efficient, self-contained ecosystem with solar heat and a windmill for energy. Red Ribbon, American Film Festival. J-A

1012   NEW ENGLAND SEA COMMUNITY
       16 min., color or b&w, 1962.
       Director: Bruce R. Buckley.   Distributor: Indiana University, Audio-Visual Center.
            The daily life of a New England seacoast town, circa 1845, seen through the eyes of a 13-year-old boy. Includes some views of family life.   From the Pioneer Life series.   I-J

1013   THE NEW KID
       11 min., color 1972.
       Producer: King Screen Productions.   Distributor: BFA Educational Media.
            Aims to help children adapt to changes that come when families move.   E-J

1014   A NEW LIFE
       11 min., color, 1976.
       Director: Rocky L. Pearson.   Distributor: Pear Films Company.
            A Vietnamese family adjusts to a new life in America. Points out difficulties encountered.   C-A

1015   THE NEW POLICE--FAMILY CRISIS INTERVENTION
       14 min., color, 1973.
       Producer: Harry Moses Productions.   Distributor: MTI Teleprograms.
            Documents the work of the specially trained family-crisis intervention unit of the Oakland, Calif., police department.   Training film.   C, Prof

1016   NEWBORN
       28 min., color, 1972.
       Director: Bill Jersey.   Sponsor: Johnson & Johnson Baby Products Company.   Distributor: Association Films.
            The first three months of life--the experiences of a first-time mother, father, and their child.   S-A

1017   NEWBORN
       28 min., color, p. 1977, r. 1978.
       Director: Heather Cook for Canadian Broadcasting Corp. Distributor: Filmakers Library.
            Stresses the abilities and senses of the newborn, as well as the importance of mother and baby being together in the first hours after birth to begin the "bonding" process. Includes neonatal research of distinguished researchers, e.g., Dr. Berry Brazelton of Harvard.   Blue Ribbon, American Film Festival.   S-A

1018   NEWCOMERS TO THE CITY SERIES   see
            CHICANO FROM THE SOUTHWEST   242
            JESSE FROM MISSISSIPPI   767
            JOHNNY FROM FORT APACHE   774
            LINDA AND BILLY RAY FROM APPALACHIA   831

1019   A NICE KID LIKE YOU
       38 min. , b&w, 1969.
       Producer: Gene Lichtenstein.   Distributor: University
       of California, Extension Media Center.
       East Coast college students rap about drugs, sex,
       political action, and their relationships with friends and
       parents.   C-A

1020   NIGHTSHIFT
       25 min. , color, p. 1976, r. 1977.
       Director: Jerry Feldman.   Distributor: US Films.
       Explores crisis of a middle-class family man who
       must face the pressures of growing old and retiring from
       a job and life-style he's been comfortable in for many
       years.   C-A

1021   NIMROD WORKMAN: TO FIT MY OWN CATEGORY
       35 min. , b&w, 1975.
       Directors: Scott Faulkner & Anthony Slone.   Distributor:
       Appalshop Films.
       Nimrod Workman worked 42 years in the coal mines
       of West Virginia to support a family of 11.   He talks about
       life in the mines, union organizing, and his family, with
       whom he is seen at home.   Merit Award, Athens Interna-
       tional Film Festival.   S-A

1022   NINE MONTHS IN MOTION
       19 min. , color, 1977.
       Producer: Patti Moore.   Distributor: Perennial Education.
       Key exercises for pregnant women of all ages,
       shapes, and conditions.   A

1023   1900:   PASSING OF AN AGE
       25 min. , b&w, 1975.
       Director: Orson Welles.   Cast: Joseph Cotten, Agnes
       Moorehead, Tim Holt.   Distributor: Films Inc.
       Small-town America and the coming of the automo-
       bile, which rendered old money, and the families who
       possessed it, obsolete.   Extract from the 1942 film THE
       MAGNIFICENT AMBERSONS (1853).   J-S

1024   NIXON'S CHECKERS SPEECH
       30 min. , b&w, televised 1952, r. 1971.
       Distributor: New Yorker Films.
       In 1952, when Richard M. Nixon was Eisenhower's
       running mate, Nixon was accused of "unethically using
       special campaign funds for personal ends." This nation-
       wide telecast cleared his name, as Nixon appealed to Mom
       and Pop America with details of his finances, and dragged
       his wife and two daughters into the act, as well as their
       dog Checkers--the only campaign gift he claimed to have
       retained.   S-A

From Nimrod Workman: To Fit My Own Category. Courtesy Appalshop Films.

From Nixon's Checkers Speech.   Courtesy New Yorker
Films.

1025   NO HIDING PLACE
        51 min. , b&w, 1964.
        Producer: Talent Associates-Paramount, with United Art-
        ists Television & the CBS Television Network.   Cast:
        George C. Scott, Lois Nettleton, Ruby Dee, Joseph Cam-
        panella, Constance Ford.   Distributor: Carousel Films.
            A black family moves into an all-white Northern
        suburb.   A white, Southern-born woman urges her husband
        not to sell their home in the wake of a neighborhood panic
        to sell out.   From the East Side/West Side TV series.
        Blue Ribbon, American Film Festival.   S-A

1026   NO PLACE LIKE HOME SERIES   see
            HOMEWRECKER   663

1027   NO TEARS FOR KELSEY
        27 min. , color, 1969.
        Director: Hal Cooper for Paulist Productions.   Cast: Lloyd
        Bochner, Deborah Winters, Geraldine Brooks, Don Mitchell.
        Distributor: The Media Guild.

An incorrigible 14-year-old runaway is continually apprehended and must face her parents in Juvenile Court. She's a truant, may be pregnant, has used drugs. She blames her parents for her predicament. From the Insight series. S-A

1028 NO TRESPASSING
15 min., color, 1975.
Producer: Robert Crowther for No. Virginia Educational Telecommunications Assoc. Distributor: Agency for Instructional TV.
Alex lives with his family in a city apartment, but he's so fed up with the lack of privacy, that he takes refuge in an abandoned building. From the Self Incorporated series. J

1029 NOBODY IMPORTANT
11 min., color, 1975.
Director: Tony Frangakis. Distributor: TeleKETICS.
The effect of marital discord on a couple's 5-year-old child. The lonely boy runs away looking for a fantasy place where he can be somebody important. J-A

1030 THE NORTH AMERICAN INDIAN--PART III SERIES see
LAMENT OF THE RESERVATION 795

1031 NORTH AMERICAN INDIANS TODAY SERIES see
MARIA OF THE PUEBLOS 885
WHERE HAS THE WARRIOR GONE? 1506

1032 NORTHEAST FARM COMMUNITY
15 min., color or b&w, 1960.
Directors: Louis C. Jones & Frank O. Spinney. Distributor: Indiana University, Audio-Visual Center.
Dramatization of typical farm-family life in northeastern U.S. during the early 1880s. From the Pioneer Life series. I-J

1033 NOT BY CHANCE
22 min., color, 1977.
Director: John Barasa. Distributor: Cinema Medica.
Documents a natural childbirth at home with physician in attendance. Ends with nursing. C-A, Prof

1034 NOT ME ALONE
31 min., color, 1970.
Director: Alvin Fiering. Distributor: Polymorph Films.
Record of one couple's participation in parent prep classes, subsequent labor, and Lamaze delivery. See also CHILDBIRTH (256). C-A

1035 NOT TOGETHER NOW: END OF A MARRIAGE
25 min., color, p. 1974, r. 1975.

Director: Miriam Weinstein. Distributor: Polymorph
Films.
  A young married couple, now separated, discuss
their lives before and during their marriage and the changes
separation has wrought. She's blossomed; he's lonely and
confused. They share responsibility for their three young
children. S-A

1036   NOTABLE CONTRIBUTORS TO THE PSYCHOLOGY OF
  PERSONALITY SERIES see
    INTERVIEW WITH DR. R. D. LAING, PART I: THE
    DILEMMA OF MENTAL ILLNESS 738

1037   NOTES ON AN APPALACHIA COUNTY: VISITING WITH
  DARLENE
  45 min. , b&w, 1974.
  Producers: P. J. O'Connell & Lisa J. Marshall. Distributor: Pennsylvania State University.
    Darlene is a 28-year-old mother of four preschool
  children, with an absent, non-supportive husband. This
  documentary observes her hopeless existence, as she tries
  to survive and retain custody of her children in a home of
  extreme poverty. S-A

1038   NOW WE LIVE ON CLIFTON
  25 min. , color, 1974.
  Producer: Kartemquin Films. Distributor: Haymarket
  Films.
    In the white, working-class Taylor family of Chicago,
  the 10-year-old daughter takes karate lessons, the father
  (a night cab driver) cooks the supper, the 12-year-old son
  praises his multiracial neighborhood, and the mother works
  full-time as a secretary. I-A

1039   NUEVA: AN ALTERNATIVE
  18 min. , color, p. 1971, r. 1974.
  Director: Karen Crommie. Distributor: University of
  California, Extension Media Center.
    Illustrates the educational philosophy and methodology
  of the Nueva Day School and Learning Center in Hills-
  borough, Calif. The school was founded by teachers and
  parents to establish a different approach to educating children with high potential. A

1040   NURSERY SCHOOL CHILD-MOTHER INTERACTION: THREE
  HEAD START CHILDREN AND THEIR MOTHERS
  41 min. , b&w, 1969.
  Producer: Dr. Marianne Marschak. Distributor: New York
  University.
    Head Start activities, interaction patterns, and ma-
  ternal attitudes are observed with three black mothers and
  their 4-year-old boys, two of whom are considered difficult
  and the third well-adjusted. C, Prof

1041   NURSING SERIES   see
       CARE OF THE NEWBORN BABY--THE NURSE'S ROLE
       IN INSTRUCTING THE PARENTS   216

1042   NURTURING
       17 min., color, 1978.
       Director: Roy Anthony Cox.   Distributor: Davidson Films.
       The need for a stimulating environment and emo-
       tional and verbal support for infants.   Pediatrics Award,
       John Muir Medical Film Festival.   C-A

1043   NUTRITION AND DENTAL CARE IN PREGNANCY
       30 min., b&w, 1956.
       Producer: WQED, Pittsburgh.   Distributors: Association
       Films (rental only); Indiana University, Audio-Visual Cen-
       ter (rental only).
       Dietary needs for maintaining mother's and establish-
       ing baby's dental health.   From the Months Before Birth
       series.   A

1044   NUTRITION EDUCATION SERIES   see
       THE BIG DINNER TABLE   149

1045   NUTRITION: THE CONSUMER AND THE SUPERMARKET
       15 min., color, 1976.
       Director: William Crain.   Distributor: Barr Films.
       How to buy the best and most nutritional food avail-
       able.   Discusses the role of advertising, store layout,
       packaging, and labeling to influence purchasing decisions.
       S-A

1046   OF SUGAR CANE AND SYRUP
       15 min., color, 1977.
       Producers: Steve Knudsen & Luella Snyder.   Distributor:
       Perspective Films.
       Highlights the growing of sugar cane and the making
       of syrup, activities that the Stribling family of northeastern
       Louisiana are still involved with.   They use traditional
       methods, equipment, and recipes handed down from past
       generations.   CINE Golden Eagle.   Blue Ribbon, American
       Film Festival.   S-A

1047   THE OKIES--UPROOTED FARMERS
       24 min., b&w, 1975.
       Director: John Ford.   Cast: Henry Fonda, John Carra-
       dine, Jane Darwell.   Distributor: Films Inc.
       The Joad family must leave their home and go off
       to California looking for work in Depression America.
       Extract from the 1940 film THE GRAPES OF WRATH
       (1751).   J-S

1048   OLD ENOUGH TO KNOW
       20 min., color, 1972.

Director: Dick Gilbert. Distributor: Perennial Education. Aims to help parents educate their preschool and early-elementary-age children about sex. Parents' voice-overs recall their own childhood experiences. C-A

1049   OLD-FASHIONED WOMAN
49 min., color, 1974.
Director: Martha Coolidge. Distributor: Films Inc.
Profile of the filmmaker's upper-class Yankee grand-mother Mabel Tilton Coolidge. She reflects on her child-hood, husband, and son (the filmmaker's deceased father). Ends with the family gathered for a Thanksgiving dinner. Blue Ribbon, American Film Festival. CINE Golden Eagle. J-A

1050   OLIVIA: MEXICAN OR AMERICAN--DIFFERENCES IN THE FAMILY
13 min., color, 1973.
Director: Kent Mackenzie for Dimension Films. Distri-butors: Churchill Films; TeleKETICS.
A Mexican American girl protests the restrictive aspects of her Mexican heritage, which she feels are un-just; yet she also needs and wants her parents' love and support. From The Searching Years: Differences series. J-A

1051   OMOWALE--THE CHILD RETURNS HOME
30 min., b&w, 1965.
Producer: NET. Distributor: Indiana University, Audio-Visual Center.
John Williams, a Mississippi-born black novelist, travels to Africa to explore his roots. From the History of the Negro People series. S-A

1052   ON BEING AN EFFECTIVE PARENT (THOMAS GORDON)
45 min., color, 1972.
Director: Dr. John M. Whiteley. Distributor: American Personnel and Guidance Association.
Dr. Thomas Gordon discusses the dynamics and use of PET (Parent Effectiveness Training), a theory he de-veloped to promote mutual understanding and communication between parents and children. Training film for par-ents. A

1053   ON BEING SEXUAL
22 min., color, 1975.
Director: Elaine Millare. Distributor: The Stanfield House.
Notes the necessity of giving accurate, complete sex education to retarded young people, to help them develop responsible and appropriate sexual behavior. With parents, professionals, and retarded young adults. A

1054 ON DEATH AND DYING
58 min., color, 1974.
Director: Martin Hoade for NBC-TV. Distributor: Films
Inc.
Dr. Elisabeth Kubler-Ross, doctor and psychiatrist,
counsels the dying and their families. Here, she discusses these experiences and relates how parents can in-
terpret what their dying children can't verbalize. She
also reads poems by anguished mothers. Christopher
Award. C-A

1055 ON THE RUN
27 min., color, p. 1975, r. 1976.
Director: Robert Richter. Distributor: MTI Teleprograms.
Examines why kids run away from home, by asking
those who have. S-A

1056 ON THE SEVENTH DAY
20 min., b&w, 1961.
Director: Irwin Goldress. Distributor: New York Uni-
versity.
A Jewish family prepares for and celebrates the
Sabbath. S-A

1057 ONE AND THE SAME see
MY LIFE IN ART 990

1058 ONE GENERATION IS NOT ENOUGH
24 min., color, 1979.
Director: Tony De Nonno. Distributor: De Nonno Pix.
A Hungarian and his American-born son work together as violin makers in a small New York City shop.
The son (a fourth-generation violin maker) learns from his
father. S-A

1059 ONE HOUR A WEEK
18 min., color, 1973.
Producer: Bureau of Education for the Handicapped, Dept.
of Health, Education & Welfare. Distributor: National
Audiovisual Center.
Depicts the home-training program of the League
School for Seriously Disturbed Children. Describes the
behavior-modification techniques that parents can practice
at home. From the League School for Seriously Disturbed
Children series. A

1060 ONE MORE TIME
13 min., color, 1977.
Producers: Reba Ann Benschoter & Tom Singarella.
Distributor: Meyer Children's Rehabilitation Institute.
Shows parents of cerebral-palsy children and professionals working together at the Meyer Children's Rehabilitation Institute in Omaha, Neb. C-A, Prof

1061   ONE MORE YEAR ON THE FAMILY FARM?
        21½ min. , color, 1977.
        Director: Henry Blinder.   Distributor: Coronet Films.
        Interviews with two families exemplify the changes
        occurring in farming today.   One family decides to keep
        their small farm.   The other explains the success of their
        large, modernized farm.   From the Changing Scene series.
        J-A

1062   ONE OF A KIND
        58 min. , color, 1978.
        Director: Harry Winer.   Cast: Diane Baker.   Distributor:
        Phoenix Films.
        A troubled mother feels burdened by a daughter,
        whose only problem is the need to feel wanted and loved by
        her mother.   An ABC Afterschool Special.   E-A

1063   ONE SPECIAL DOG
        17 min. , color, 1969.
        Producer: Stephen Bosustow Productions.   Distributor:
        BFA Educational Media.
        Story of a Southwest Indian family and the son's
        special half-wild dog that saves his sister's pet lamb when
        some wild dogs chase it.   E-I

1064   ONE TO GROW ON SERIES   see
        ACT TWO--LINDSEY   13

1065   ORDINARY PEOPLE
        25 min. , color, 1977.
        Producer: Parental Stress Center, University of Pittsburgh.
        Distributor: MTI Teleprograms.
        Delineates symptoms and dynamics of child abuse.
        Focuses on a normal couple who have moved to a small
        town from an urban home.   The wife feels isolated and
        finds herself less able to cope with her young children.
        Her distress signals are pointed out.   Training and public-
        awareness film.   C-A, Prof

1066   THE OREGON TRAIL
        25 min. , b&w, 1956.
        Producer: John Barnes.   Distributor: Encyclopaedia
        Britannica Educational Corp.
        A pioneer family migrates to Oregon from Missouri
        in the 1840s in a wagon train.   Hardships and Indian terror
        are emphasized.   I-S

1067   THE ORIGINALS: WOMEN IN ART SERIES   see
        ANONYMOUS WAS A WOMAN   96
        MARY CASSATT: IMPRESSIONIST FROM PHILADEL-
        PHIA   895

1068   OSCAR AT HOME
        10 min. , b&w, p. 1974, r. 1975.
        Director: John Friedman. Distributor: Education Develop-
        ment Center.
            A 4-year-old at home in Texas during mealtime,
        with his working-class Mexican American family (six chil-
        dren). From the Exploring Childhood: Family and Society
        series.   J-A

1069   OUR FAMILY ALBUM/NUESTRO ALBUM DE LA FAMILIA!
        7 min. , color, 1973.
        Producer: Brentano Foundation. Distributor: Carousel
        Films.
            Children's family photos are presented in a class-
        room setting.   Part of the Bilingual Film Series, Module I:
        Let's Get Ready!, which is designed to teach English to
        Spanish-speaking children. E-I

1070   OUR FAMILY WORKS TOGETHER (2nd Edition)
        11 min. , color, 1978.
        Producer: Keir Cline. Distributor: Coronet Films.
            When their mother returns to school, her son and
        daughter realize that they will all have to work together to
        get the household chores done. E

1071   OUR LITTLE MUNCHKIN HERE
        12 min. , color, 1975.
        Director: Lois Tupper. Distributor: Iris Films.
            An adolescent girl is at odds with her family. J-A

1072   OUR OWN TWO HANDS
        14½ min. , color, 1974.
        Producer: WHRO-TV. Distributor: Agency for Instruc-
        tional TV.
            The Holland family lives and works on a small pig
        farm.   They enjoy the idea of sustaining a farm with their
        own hand labor. From the Bread & Butterflies series.
        I-J

1073   OUR TOTEM IS THE RAVEN
        21 min. , color, 1971.
        Director: Paul Preuss. Cast: Chief Dan George. Dis-
        tributor: BFA Educational Media.
            An American Indian grandfather tries to initiate his
        teenage grandson into manhood on old holy tribal grounds.
        The urban youth has a hard time accepting the seriousness
        of the ritual at first. E-J

1074   OURSTORY SERIES see
        THE DEVIL'S WORK 367
        ELIZA 414
        JADE SNOW WONG 760

1075   P. J. AND THE PRESIDENT'S SON
47 min. , color, 1977.
Director: Larry Elikann.   Cast: Lance Kerwin, Milton
Selzer.   Distributor: Time-Life Multimedia.
Two 15-year-old boys who look alike--P.J. , the son
of a middle-class family, and Preston, the son of the Presi-
dent of the United States--change places for a few days be-
cause they envy each other's life-style.   Adaptation of Mark
Twain's The Prince and the Pauper.   An ABC Afterschool
Special; from the Teenage Years series.   I-A

1076   PKU--PREVENTABLE MENTAL RETARDATION (2nd Edition)
16 min. , color, 1966.
Producer: Carl J. Ross.   Distributor: International Film
Bureau.
Shows how mental retardation caused by phenylketo-
nuria (PKU) can be easily prevented when diagnosed soon
after birth.   Case histories emphasize need to check all
infants for PKU.   C-A, Prof

1077   PAMELA WONG'S BIRTHDAY FOR GRANDMA
8 min. , color, p. 1976, r. 1977.
Producer: Lifestyle Productions, with St. Theresa's
School, Chicago.   Distributor: Encyclopaedia Britannica
Educational Corp.
In an urban Chinese American neighborhood, a young
girl participates in a family party.   E-I

1078   PARENT-CHILD RELATIONS IN THE EARLY YEARS SE-
RIES   see
GETTING READY FOR THE DENTIST   568
LET YOUR CHILD HELP YOU   819

1079   PARENT/CHILD RELATIONSHIPS: IT'S MY DECISION AS
LONG AS IT'S WHAT YOU WANT
14 min. , color, 1974.
Producer: Peter Jordan.   Host: Beau Bridges.   Distributor: CRM/McGraw-Hill Films.
Jane, age 16, wants to spend Saturday evening with
a friend in a nearby state.   She feels she's mature enough
to go, but her mother disagrees and says they should discuss it, while conceding to Jane's right to her own decision.
The contradiction angers Jane.   From Conflict and Awareness: A Film Series on Human Values.   Gold Award, International Film & TV Festival of New York.   S-A

1080   THE PARENT CRUNCH
14½ min. , color, 1976.
Producer: Educational Film Center.   Distributor: Agency
for Instructional TV.
A fourth grader gets A's on his homework and C's
when he does the same work in class.   The child's angry
parent confronts the teacher with this contradiction.   From
the Heart of Teaching series.   Training film.   C, Prof

1081 PARENT EDUCATION PROGRAMS
30 min. , color, 197?.
Producer: Bureau of Education for the Handicapped, Dept.
of Health, Education & Welfare. Distributor: National
Audiovisual Center.
Formal and informal programs for parents of young
hearing-impaired children. Covers family dynamics, parent-child communication, and language development. From
the International Education of the Hearing-Impaired Child:
American series. C-A, Prof

1082 PARENT PROBLEMS: WHEN LOYALTIES CONFLICT
$7\frac{1}{2}$ min. , color, 1969.
Producer: King Screen Productions. Distributor: BFA
Educational Media.
Teenage Mary is forced to choose between her
friendship with Jenny and her mother's disappproval of the
girl who was caught shoplifting. I-S

1083 PARENTAL ROLES: DON AND MAE
29 min. , color, 1973.
Producer: Gregory Heimer. Distributor: Encyclopaedia
Britannica Educational Corp.
Cinema vérité portrait of a middle-class Southern
California family, emphasizing conflicts faced by the par-
ents when dealing with each other and their five children.
See also ADOLESCENT RESPONSIBILITIES: CRAIG AND
MARK. (18) From the Getting Together series. J-S, A

1084 PARENTING CONCERNS: PREPARING YOUR CHILD FOR
KINDERGARTEN
21 min. , color, 1978.
Producer: Cine-Image Films, Ltd. Distributor: Perennial
Education.
Aims to teach parents how to prepare their children
(from age 2) for the social role they will be forced to as-
sume in kindergarten. A

1085 PARENTING CONCERNS: THE FIRST TWO YEARS
21 min. , color, 1977.
Producer: Cine-Image Films, Ltd. Distributor: Perennial
Education.
Child-care and child-rearing suggestions for new and
veteran parents. A

1086 THE PARENTING EXPERIENCE
19 min. , color, 1977.
Producer: The Pampers Professional Services Division of
Procter & Gamble. Distributor: Association Films.
Two couples demonstrate how both mother and father
can carry out basic infant care. Also stresses the profound
effect of physical and emotional closeness between parent
and child. S-A

1087   PARENTING: GROWING WITH CHILDREN
       22 min. , color, 1976.
       Director: Peter Schnitzler.   Distributor: FilmFair Com-
       munications.
           The realities, rewards, and responsibilities of par-
       enting, with focus on four different family units--single
       parent, working parents, young couple with new baby, large
       family with traditional parenting roles.   Shows there is no
       single "right way" to be a successful parent.   Chris Bronze
       Plaque, Columbus Film Festival.   J-A

1088   PARENTS
       59 min. , b&w, 1964.
       Producer: George Page for NET.   Distributor: Indiana
       University, Audio-Visual Center.
           Documents the changing problems of America's par-
       ents.   Includes interviews with parents, children, Dr.
       Spock, Betty Friedan, and Paul Popenoe.   S-A

1089   PARENTS
       22 min. , b&w, 1968.
       Directors: Gerald Temaner & Gordon Quinn.   Distributor:
       Film Images.
           A white, middle-class urban (Chicago) youth group
       discusses the generation gap.   A cinema vérité rap session.
       S-A

1090   PARENTS? A BSCS BEHAVIOR FILM
       13½ min. , color, 1974.
       Producer: Biological Sciences Curriculum Studies.   Dis-
       tributor: BFA Educational Media.
           Explores parent/child relationships and parental roles
       in both animal and human worlds.   J-S

1091   PARENTS ARE TEACHERS, TOO
       18 min. , b&w, 1967.
       Producer: Office of Economic Opportunity.   Distributor:
       National Audiovisual Center.
           The role of parents as a child's first and ongoing
       teachers.   From the Head Start at School series.   A

1092   PARENTS' VOICES
       12 min. , color, p. 1972, r. 1976.
       Director: Kent Mackenzie for Dimension Films.   Distributor:
       The Little Red Filmhouse.
           A young guy and girl role-play their feelings "after
       sex, " while other young people in a rap group role-play
       "parents' voices" and values.   Shows how parental influence
       affects sexual behavior.   Open-ended.   From the Sex, Feel-
       ings & Values series.   S-A

1093   PARENTS--WHO NEEDS THEM?
       10 min. , color, 1973.

Producer: Marshall Izen.   Distributor: Coronet Films.
A magic puppet makes a boy invisible so he can
really see the many things his parents do for him and for
the whole family.   Second edition of APPRECIATING OUR
PARENTS, from the Forest Town Fables series.   E-I

From The Pasciaks of Chicago (Six American Families series).   Courtesy Carousel Films.

1094   THE PASCIAKS OF CHICAGO
59 min. , color, p. 1976, r. 1977.
Director: Mark Obenhaus for Westinghouse Broadcasting
Corp.   Distributor: Carousel Films.
A blue-collar Polish American family (six chil-
dren), whose traditions and ethnic background are shaken by
the new life-style of the children.   From the Six American
Families series.   S-A

1095   PAT EXPLORES HIS CITY
14 min. , color, 1971.
Producer: Irving Rusinow.   Distributor: Encyclopaedia
Britannica Educational Corp.
Pat Novak's parents decide to move because their

apartment is too small.   They settle on a new place that,
while not ideal, is within their budget and near the father's
work, etc.   Delineates how the family's needs and budget
determine their choice.   E

1096   PATHWAYS THROUGH NURSERY SCHOOL
25 min., color, 1964.
Director: John R. Bousek.   Distributor: International
Film Bureau.
Notes that the mutual effort of qualified teachers and
interested parents makes for a good nursery school.   C-A,
Prof

1097   PEEGE
28 min., color, p. 1973, r. 1974.
Director: Randal Kleiser.   Cast: Bruce Davison, Barbara
Rush.   Distributor: Phoenix Films.
When a family visits their stroke-enfeebled grandmother in a nursing home on Christmas, the woman is no
match for the vibrant grandmother who floods their memories of times past.   Her favorite grandson is most disturbed by the change.   See also PORTRAIT OF GRANDPA
DOC (1131).   Chris Plaque, Columbus Film Festival.   Best
Film in Family Counseling, T.E.A.M. Film Award Competition.   Top Honor Award, National Council on Family Relations.   J-A

1098   PEER CONDUCTED BEHAVIOR MODIFICATION
24 min., color, 1977.
Director: Phillip Blake.   Distributor: The Media Guild.
Illustrates how a child's schoolmates and their parents are mobilized in a neighborhood effort to modify some
behavioral problems in the child.   Premise is that peers
rather than parents may be responsible for deviant behavior.
From the Behavior Modification Special Education series.
C-A

1099   PEOPLE SOUP
12 min., color, 1970.
Director: Alan Arkin.   Distributor: Learning Corp. of
America.
Two brothers combine some everyday household foods
and substances to formulate a scientific experiment on the
kitchen table.   E-I

1100   PERCEPTION
20 min., color, 1975.
Director: Roger S. Olson.   Distributor: Brigham Young
University.
Guidelines to enable parents to help their children
perceive the environment.   C-A

1101   PERSON TO PERSON IN INFANCY
       22 min., b&w, 1970.
       Producer: Dept. of Health, Education & Welfare. Distri-
       butor: National Audiovisual Center.
          The importance of closeness between infant and
       adult, which is shown to be as viable in group care as at
       home.   C-A

1102   PERSONAL AND FAMILY SECURITY
       25 min., color, 1975.
       Producer: Woroner Films, Inc.   Distributor: MTI Tele-
       programs.
          Security details (at home, while driving, at the office,
       etc.) for protecting business and government executives from
       urban terrorists.   Training film.   See also EXECUTIVE
       DECISION (437).   From the Anatomy of Terrorism series.
       S-A

1103   PERSONALITY: EARLY CHILDHOOD
       20 min., color, 1978.
       Producer: McGraw-Hill Films & Coast Community College.
       Distributor: CRM/McGraw-Hill Films.
          Four aspects of preschool personality: dependency,
       identification, aggression, anxiety.   Shows that TV violence
       and family aggression are examples of aggressive models,
       and that emotional and instrumental dependency, especially
       in young girls, occurs because of adult encouragement.
       From the Developmental Psychology series.   S-A

1104   PERSONALITY: MIDDLE CHILDHOOD
       19 min., color, 1978.
       Producer: McGraw-Hill Films & Coast Community College.
       Distributor: CRM/McGraw-Hill Films.
          The transition period (ages 6-12), from home to so-
       ciety.   Stresses family environment as the one in which
       encouragement, appreciation, and training of the child can
       motivate him or her to achieve.   From the Developmental
       Psychology series.   S-A

1105   THE PHENOMENA OF ROOTS
       52 min., color, 1978.
       Producer: David L. Wolper Productions.   Host: Louis
       Gossett, Jr.   Distributor: Films Inc.
          The impact of the TV film on the American public.
       Tells how the first 12-hour miniseries was made from Alex
       Haley's book.   S-A

1106   PHYSIOLOGY OF MISCARRIAGE AND ABORTION
       28 min., color, 1977.
       Producer: WXYZ-TV.   Distributor: McGraw-Hill Films.
          Covers the termination of pregnancy--spontaneous and
       induced--as well as danger signals in pregnancy and after-
       effects of each procedure.   Aims to dispel common miscon-

ceptions about miscarriage.   From the Inner Woman series.
S-A

1107   THE PHYSIOLOGY OF REPRODUCTION
30 min. , b&w, 1956.
Producer: NET.   Distributors: Indiana University, Audio-
Visual Center (rental only); Association Films (rental only).
Explains the function of hormones in sexual matura-
tion and in the processes of ovulation and fetal development.
From the Months Before Birth series.   S-A

1108   PICNIC
8 min. , color, 1971.
Director: Jim Burroughs.   Distributor: Paramount Communications.
A family picnics by a lake in the woods and cooks a
meal over an open fire.   A captioned film that teaches the
words picnic, grass, green, find, frog, turtle, fire, hot,
eat, drink.   From the Starting to Read series.   E

1109   PILGRIM JOURNEY
24 min. , color, 1973.
Director: Tom Robertson.   Distributor: Multimedia Program Productions.
The voyage of the Mayflower, as seen through the
eyes of a young female passenger.   From the Young People's
Specials series.   E-J

1110   THE PINBALLS
31 min. , color, p. 1976, r. 1977.
Producer: Martin Tahse.   Cast: Kristy McNichol.   Distributor: Walt Disney Educational Media Company.
Three alienated, depressed kids (ages 15, 13, and 8)
share the same foster home.   Their nurturing foster parents provide an environment where they can learn to care
about others and especially about themselves.   An ABC
Afterschool Special.   I-J

1111   A PIONEER HOME
10½ min. , color, 1948.
Producer: Coronet Films.   Distributor: Coronet Films.
The physical surroundings, home furnishings, hard
work, and simple pleasures of pioneer home life.   E-I

1112   PIONEER JOURNEY ACROSS THE APPALACHIANS
13 min. , color, 1957.
Producer: Coronet Films.   Distributor: Coronet Films.
A North Carolina family makes the trek before the
Revolutionary War.   Dramatizes the reasons why and how the
early settlers moved West.   Chris Award, Columbus Film
Festival.   I-J

1113 PIONEER LIFE SERIES see
NEW ENGLAND SEA COMMUNITY 1012
NORTHEAST FARM COMMUNITY 1032

1114 PIONEER LIVING: HOME CRAFTS
10 min., color, 1971.
Producer: Moreland-Latchford Productions. Distributor:
Coronet Films.
Explores the many craft skills needed by a pioneer
family in the early 1800s. I-S

1115 PIONEER LIVING: PREPARING FOODS
9½ min., color, 1971.
Producer: Moreland-Latchford Productions. Distributor:
Coronet Films.
In autumn in the early 1800s, preparations for win-
ter began, i. e., preserving apples, churning butter, making
maple sugar, and baking bread. Chris Award, Columbus
Film Festival. I-S

1116 PIONEER LIVING: THE HOME
10½ min., color, 1971.
Producer: Moreland-Latchford Productions. Distributor:
Coronet Films.
The tasks of a pioneer family of the early 1800s as
they select a site and build a home, cook their food, and
make candles and soap. E-J

1117 A PLACE FOR AUNT LOIS
17 min., color, 1973.
Director: Gene Feldman. Distributor: Wombat Productions.
A family pressures a divorced, unattractive aunt to
shape up and look for a new husband. She'd rather go to
school and stay the way she is. Her niece thinks her aunt
is great the way she is, too. Chris Award, Columbus
Film Festival. E-J

1118 A PLACE TO COME BACK
35 min., color, p. 1976, r. 1977.
Director: Ellen Lorbetske. Distributor: Ellen Lorbetske.
Documentary shot on a family-owned (75 years) dairy
farm in northern Wisconsin. Focuses on the wife/mother
of six who has lived her whole life on this land and who
struggles to prepare for changes in her life: none of the
six children wants to continue the operation of the farm
when their parents retire. J-A

1119 PLANNING CREATIVE PLAY EQUIPMENT FOR YOUNG
CHILDREN: OUTDOOR
16 min., color, 1959.
Director: O. E. Patterson. Distributor: University of
California, Extension Media Center.

More than 120 families worked together to build a creative community nursery school for their children.   The play yard is cooperatively supervised by mothers and teachers.   C-A

From A Place for Aunt Lois.   Courtesy Wombat Productions.

1120 PLAY THE SHOPPING GAME
20 min. , color, 1977.
Producer: Donald Klugman.   Distributor: Encyclopaedia Britannica Educational Corp.
Six young game-show contestants leave the TV studio to shop for food, housing, clothing, transportation, recreation, and personal care.   To win the game, they must deal effectively with ads, labels, salespeople, etc.   From the Consumers in a Changing World series.   J-S

1121 PLAYING WITH FIRE
16 min. , color, 1975.
Director: Frank Cantor.   Distributor: National Fire Protection Association.
The consequences of playing with fire as seen through the eyes of a child.   E-I, A

1122   THE PLUTOCRATS
        51 min., color, 1971.
        Producer: BBC-TV. Distributor: Time-Life Multimedia.
            Documentary on several Texas millionaires and
        their families. S-A

1123   POISON PREVENTION FOR PRIMARY
        10 min., color, 1977.
        Director: Michael Halperin. Distributor: Paramount
        Communications.
            Poison hazards in the home, and how children can
        make their homes "poison proof" to protect themselves
        and their younger brothers and sisters. E-I

1124   THE POISON PROBLEM
        10 min., color, 1977.
        Producer: Associated Film Services. Distributor: AIMS
        Instructional Media Services.
            Alerts children to the misuse of medicines, spray
        paints, gardening supplies, car preps, bleaches and sham-
        poos, furniture polish, varnish, play dough, moth flakes,
        matches, and roach powder. K-I

1125   POISONS ALL AROUND US
        11 min., color, 1977.
        Director: Alfred Higgins. Distributor: Alfred Higgins
        Productions.
            What to do in case of poisoning with common house-
        hold substances. I-S

1126   POLICE MARRIAGE--FILM I: HUSBAND/WIFE PERSONAL
        ISSUES
        20 min., color, 1976.
        Director: Robert Karpas. Distributor: Harper & Row
        Media.
            Shows how the stress of being a cop affects the
        husband/wife relationship and puts a strain on the best of
        marriages. Training film. C-A, Prof

1127   POLICE MARRIAGE FILM II: THE POLICEMAN'S FAMILY
        20 min., color, 1976.
        Director: Robert Karpas. Distributor: Harper & Row
        Media.
            Tackles the special problems of the police officer
        as father and husband, and the stresses that may crop up.
        Training film. C-A, Prof

1128   POLICE MARRIAGE FILM III: SOCIAL ISSUES; THE
        FAMILY IN THE COMMUNITY
        20 min., color, 1976.
        Director: Robert Karpas. Distributor: Harper & Row
        Media.
            Personal stresses faced by police officers in their

interaction with other officers, friends, relatives, neighbors, and society.   Training film.   C-A, Prof

1129   POPCORN VENDORS   see
        IN BUSINESS FOR MYSELF   707

From The Popovich Brothers of South Chicago.   Courtesy Jill Godmilow.

1130   THE POPOVICH BROTHERS OF SOUTH CHICAGO
        60 min. , color, 1978.
        Director: Jill Godmilow.   Distributor: Balkan Arts Center.
            While the primary focus is the Popovich family, and especially the Popovich Brothers' remarkable 50-year career with their tamburitza orchestra, the entire South Chicago Serbian American community provides the backdrop. Red Ribbon, American Film Festival.   S-A

1131   PORTRAIT OF GRANDPA DOC
        28 min. , color, 1977.
        Director: Randal Kleiser.   Cast: Melvyn Douglas, Bruce Davison, Barbara Rush, Anne Seymour.   Distributor: Phoenix Films.
            A young artist prepares an exhibit as a tribute to his deceased grandfather, the man who encouraged the artist's talents as a child.   Memory flashbacks highlight their special relationship.   See also PEEGE (1097).   Red Ribbon, American Film Festival.   I-A

1132   POWER AND THE LAND
        39 min. , b&w, 1940.
        Director: Joris Ivens.   Commentary: Stephen Vincent Benét.   Distributors: National Audiovisual Center (sale only); Museum of Modern Art (rental only).

Classic documentary that explores the daily life and
work on a typical family farm (the Parkinson family farm
in St. Clairsville, Ohio) before and after electrification.   S-A

From <u>Portrait of Grandpa Doc.</u>   Courtesy Phoenix Films.

1133   PREGNANCY AFTER 35
       22 min. , color, 1978.
       Director: Gwen Brown.   Distributor: Polymorph Films.
           The physical and emotional realities of late preg-
       nancy.   Deals with the commonly expressed fears of Down's
       syndrome, amniocentesis, etc.   C-A, Prof

1134   PREGNANCY IN MOTION
       15 min. , color, 1977.
       Director: Mai Cramer.   Distributor: Mai Cramer.
           The yogic approach to natural childbirth.   A

1135   PREJUDICE: HATRED OR IGNORANCE?
       $23\frac{1}{2}$ min. , color, 1976.
       Director: Herschel Daugherty.   Cast: Carol Lynley, James
       MacArthur.   Distributor: Walt Disney Educational Media.

A white youth, who was captured and raised by Indians, must now go and live with white settlers. He is torn by mixed loyalties and the prejudice against him. Vignette from the Disney feature THE LIGHT IN THE FOREST. From the Questions!!! Answers?? Set II series. I-J

1136   PRENATAL CARE
24 min., color, 1977.
Director: Ted Robbins. Distributor: Pyramid Films.
Good prenatal care increases the chances of a happy, satisfying birth experience and lessens anxieties of parents-to-be. Animation, live-action, and graphics show how to achieve this. S-A

1137   PRENATAL DEVELOPMENT
23 min., color, 1974.
Director: Barbara Jampel. Distributor: CRM/McGraw-Hill Films.
Stages of fetal development, research statistics, importance of nutrition, effects of drugs, and influence of mother's environment on the psychological development of the fetus. From the Developmental Psychology series. Silver Award, International Film & TV Festival of New York. CINE Golden Eagle. S-A

1138   PRENATAL DEVELOPMENT
26 min., color, 1975.
Director: Roger S. Olson. Distributor: Brigham Young University.
Prenatal development from conception through fetal stage. Stresses importance of seeing an obstetrician early and regularly. A

1139   PREPARATION FOR MARRIAGE SERIES see
ARE YOU THE ONE? 105

1140   PREPARING FOR CHILDBIRTH
24 min., color, 1976.
Distributor: Association Films.
An expectant couple goes to classes to prepare for the Lamaze delivery of their child. Active role of husband underscored. S-A

1141   PRESENTING THE CASE
32 min., color, 1977.
Producer: National Center on Child Abuse & Neglect, HEW.
Distributor: National Audiovisual Center.
A social worker/witness presents evidence at a child-abuse hearing before the juvenile court. Dramatized training film. From the We Can Help series. C, Prof

1142   PRESSURE MAKES PERFECT
        15 min. , color, 1975.
        Director: John Allman for KETC-TV. Distributor: Agency
        for Instructional TV.
            At her piano recital, Nan rebels against parental
        pressure to excel by playing a short simple piece, banging
        her fists on the keyboard, and shouting at the audience.
        From the Self Incorporated series.   J

1143   PRIMUM NON NOCERE
        18 min. , color, 1976.
        Director: John Barasa. Distributor: Cinema Medica.
            A natural childbirth at home, with attending physi-
        cian, and with no medication, medical apparatus, prep of
        mother or stitches.   From parents' point of view.   Chicago
        International Film Festival Award.   C-A

1144   PRISONERS OF CHANCE
        20 min. , color, 1978.
        Producers: Marc Stirdivant & Thom Eberhart.   Distribu-
        tor: FilmFair Communications.
            Focuses on two teenagers who become pregnant.
        One girl raises her son at home with her mother; her boy-
        friend denies responsibility.   The other girl marries her
        boyfriend.   Dramatic film, based on real incidents.   J-A

1145   PROBLEM? TO THINK OF DYING
        59 min. , color, 1977.
        Director: Denny Spence for KTCA-TV.   Distributor: In-
        diana University, Audio-Visual Center.
            The personal experiences, feelings, and coping
        mechanisms of two people who have faced death--widow
        Lynn Caine and terminal cancer patient Orville Kelly.   S-A

1146   THE PRODIGAL FATHER
        27 min. , color, 1975.
        Director: Marc Daniels for Paulist Productions.   Cast:
        Jim McMullan, Biff McGuire, Eileen Brennan.   Distributor:
        The Media Guild.
            A young man must reconsider his lifelong hatred of
        the alcoholic father who deserted him and has reappeared.
        From the Insight series.   S-A

1147   PROFESSIONAL DRUG FILMS SERIES   see
            COUNSELING--A CRITICAL INCIDENT   319

1148   PROGRAMMED INSTRUCTION IN MEDICAL INTERVIEWING
        SERIES   see
            PROGRAMMED INTERVIEW INSTRUCTION, NO. 3,
            MRS. CARSON   1149

1149   PROGRAMMED INTERVIEW INSTRUCTION, NO. 3, MRS.
        CARSON
        18 min. , b&w, 1970.

Producer: University of Southern California, School of Medicine. Distributor: National Audiovisual Center.

The effective use of silence (by an interviewer) to permit a harassed housewife with continuous headaches to speak on her own initiative and to come to an understanding of her complaints. Training film. From the Programmed Instruction in Medical Interviewing series. C, Prof

1150   THE PROMISE
15 min., color, p. 1976, r. 1977.
Producer: Charles Paulich for Paulist Productions. Distributor: The Media Guild.

A young girl's trust in her father is shaken when he is forced to break a promise repeatedly. But she seeks the reason why. From the Bloomin' Human series.   E-A

1151   PROMISE HER ANYTHING BUT GIVE HER THE KITCHEN SINK   see
MY LIFE IN ART   990

1152   PSYCHOGENIC DISEASES IN INFANCY: AN ATTEMPT AT THEIR CLASSIFICATION
20 min., b&w, sil., 1952.
Producer: René A. Spitz, M.D. Distributor: New York University.

Relates a series of psychogenic diseases to infants' relationships with their mothers. From the Film Studies of the Psychoanalytic Research Project on Problems in Infancy series.   C, Prof

1153   PSYCHOLOGICAL HAZARDS IN INFANCY
22 min., b&w, 1970.
Producer: Office of Child Development, Dept. of Health, Education & Welfare. Distributor: National Audiovisual Center.

The vital experiences in infancy may be hampered by inadequate stimulation, insufficient warm attention, or inappropriate handling not geared to changing developmental needs. Shows resultant mild and severe psychological damage and means of prevention.   C-A, Prof

1154   PSYCHOLOGICAL IMPLICATIONS OF BEHAVIOR DURING THE CLINICAL VISIT
20 min., b&w, sil., 1944.
Producers: Margaret E. Fries, M.D., & Paul J. Woolf, M.S. Distributor: New York University.

Notes that one can spot clues to a child's emotional state by observing overt behavior while awaiting and during physical and dental exams, I.Q. tests, play group, and interaction with mother. From the Studies on Integrated Development: Interaction Between Child and Environment series.   C-A, Prof

1155   PSYCHOLOGY TODAY SERIES   see
        DEVELOPMENT   362
        SOCIAL PSYCHOLOGY   1296

1156   A PSYCHONEUROSIS WITH COMPULSIVE TRENDS IN THE
        MAKING   see
        A CHARACTER NEUROSIS WITH DEPRESSIVE AND COM-
        PULSIVE TRENDS IN THE MAKING: LIFE HISTORY
        OF MARY FROM BIRTH TO FIFTEEN YEARS   239

1157   PSYCHOSOCIAL ASPECTS OF DEATH
        39 min. , b&w, 1971.
        Director: Dr. Kenneth Gene Faris.   Distributor: Indiana
        University, Audio-Visual Center.
            Dramatized story of a leukemia patient, his preg-
        nant wife, and a nursing student who is facing patient death
        for the first time.   C-A, Prof

1158   THE PUBLIC HEALTH NURSE AND THE MENTALLY RE-
        TARDED CHILD
        24 min. , color, 1960.
        Producer: University of Oklahoma, for the Oklahoma State
        Dept. of Health.   Distributor: International Film Bureau.
            How public-health nurses can help parents with re-
        tarded children.   Training film.   C, Prof

1159   PUEBLO VILLAGE   see
        ROOTED IN THE PAST   1214

1160   THE PURITAN EXPERIENCE: FORSAKING ENGLAND
        28 min. , color, 1975.
        Director: Richard Marquand.   Cast: David Warner, Sian
        Phillips.   Distributor: Learning Corp. of America.
            Puritanism through the eyes of one family--the Hig-
        gins--who leave their English home for life in the New
        World.   John, Anne, and daughter Charity are looking for
        freedom of religious expression.   See also THE PURITAN
        EXPERIENCE: MAKING A NEW WORLD (1161).   J-A

1161   THE PURITAN EXPERIENCE: MAKING A NEW WORLD
        31 min. , color, 1975.
        Director: Richard Marquand.   Distributor: Learning Corp.
        of America.
            Continues the saga of the Higgins family--see THE
        PURITAN EXPERIENCE: FORSAKING ENGLAND (1160)--
        in 17th-century Massachusetts.   Daughter Charity is now a
        teenager and rebels against Puritan doctrine.   She is cap-
        tured by the Indians and forcibly returned to her community,
        where she admits to outrage against the Puritans' treatment
        of the Indians.   J-A

1162   PURITAN FAMILY OF EARLY NEW ENGLAND
        10½ min. , color, 1955.

Producer: Coronet Films. Distributor: Coronet Films.
Daily activities of a Puritan family living in a small,
New England coastal village. Freedoms Foundation Award.
E-J

1163   PURPOSES OF FAMILY PLANNING
15 min. , color, 1972.
Director: Hector J. Lemieux. Distributor: Paramount
Communications.
Covers health, emotional maturity, economic stability, and the need to provide each child with love. Avail.
in Spanish. S-A

1164   THE PUZZLE CHILDREN
59 min. , color, 1976.
Director: Bill Davis for WQED-TV, Pittsburgh. Distributor: Indiana University, Audio-Visual Center.
Designed to alert parents and teachers to signs of
learning disabilities. Four children are profiled; their
parents, teachers, and special educators comment. With
Julie Andrews and Bill Bixby. S-A

1165   THE QUESTION OF TELEVISION VIOLENCE
55 min. , color, 1973.
Director: Graeme Ferguson for the National Film Board of
Canada. Distributor: Phoenix Films.
The important role of parents in controlling their
children's TV fare is stressed by such notables as Peggy
Charren (Action for Children's Television), Dean Burch
(FCC Chairman), Julian Goodman (president of NBC), and
Elton Rule (president of ABC). Edited version of the four-
day 1972 U.S. Senate Hearings on Television Violence. S-A

1166   QUESTIONS !!! ANSWERS?? SET I SERIES see
ALCOHOLISM: WHO GETS HURT? 45
LOVE AND DUTY: WHICH COMES FIRST? 856
RESPONSIBILITY: WHAT ARE ITS LIMITS? 1196
STEPPARENTS: WHERE IS THE LOVE? 1318

1167   QUESTIONS !!! ANSWERS?? SET II SERIES see
DEATH: HOW CAN YOU LIVE WITH IT? 349
PREJUDICE: HATRED OR IGNORANCE? 1135
YOUR CAREER: YOUR DECISION? 1570

1168   THE QUIET ONE
68 min. , b&w, 1948.
Director: Sidney Meyers. Producer: Janice Loeb. Commentary & Dialog: James Agee. Cast: Donald Thompson,
Sadie Stockton, Estelle Evans, Clarence Cooper. Distributors: Texture Films; Audio Brandon Films (rental only);
Images (rental only).
Docu-drama about a young withdrawn black boy who
is sent to the Wiltwyck School for Boys for treatment be-

cause he is emotionally battered by his indifferent parents and grandmother. First Prize, Venice International Film Festival. Best Picture of the Year, Protestant Motion Picture Council. S-A

1169 THE QUIET REVOLUTION OF MRS. HARRIS
21 min., color, 1976.
Producer: Cinemalore Co., Calif. Distributor: The Media Guild.
After 11 years of marriage and four kids, Gloria Harris attempts to change her life by freeing herself from societal constrictions, completing her M.A. and working as a counselor. From the Women Today series. S-A

1170 RACHEL AT HOME
11 min., b&w, 1974.
Director: John Friedman. Distributor: Education Development Center.
A white, urban professional family at home during mealtime. Four-year-old Rachel has a baby sister. See also FAMILIES REVISITED: JENNY IS FOUR, RACHEL IS SEVEN (452). From the Exploring Childhood: Family and Society series. J-A

1171 RAISING A FAMILY ALONE (DANIEL)
9 min., color, 1977.
Director: Henry Felt. Distributor: Education Development Center.
Daniel is Puerto Rican, and raises his five sons alone in a northeastern city, with the help of community services. From the Exploring Childhood: Family and Society series. J-A

1172 RAISING MICHAEL ALONE
17 min., color, p. 1976, r. 1977.
Director: Henry Felt. Distributor: Education Development Center.
Eleven-year-old Michael and his mother live in a large city. She talks about her life alone with Michael, her job, etc. From the Exploring Childhood: Family and Society series. J-A

1173 RAPPORT
12 min., color, 1973.
Producer: Mike Rhodes for Paulist Productions. Distributor: The Media Guild.
Dramatic vignettes probe crises in modern marriage, responsibilities, alternatives to problems, and changing attitudes toward marriage and family during this century. From the Vignette series. J-C

1174 RAPUNZEL, RAPUNZEL
18 min., color, p. 1977, r. 1978.

Director: Tom Davenport.   Distributor: Tom Davenport
Films.
Adapted from the Brothers Grimm fairy tale; set
in America.   Live-action.   K-J

1175   A RAY OF HOPE
10 min. , color, 1977.
Director: David A. Tapper.   Distributor: American Cancer Society.
Describes positive results achieved with Radiation
Therapy in treatment of Hodgkin's Disease.   Two young
mothers relate their experiences as patients.   After their
recovery, their family life, medical exams and treatments
are followed.   S-A

1176   READ BEFORE YOU WRITE
6 min. , color, 1972.
Producer: Ben Norman.   Distributor: FilmFair Communications.
A young married couple, in the process of shopping
for a new TV, learn about installment buying and properly
drawn contracts.   J-A

1177   READ ON! SERIES see
AND THEN WHAT HAPPENED?   STARRING DONNA,
ALICE AND YOU 85
FROM START TO FINISH: THE NATURE TRAIL   547

1178   READ THE LABEL--AND LIVE! (2nd Edition)
13 min. , color, 1977.
Director: Lee Rhoads. Distributor: Alfred Higgins Productions.
Dramatic sequences emphasize common problems
that result when people don't read labels of household
products, e.g. , hair sprays, insecticides, paint thinners,
medicines, etc.   Safe handling practices are underscored.
I-S

1179   READIN' AND WRITIN' AIN'T EVERYTHING
26 min. , color, 1975.
Director: Terry Kelley.   Distributor: The Stanfield House.
Documents the lives of three families with retarded
children, as well as that of a retarded adult.   CINE Golden
Eagle.   Bronze Medal, International Film & TV Festival of
New York.   C-A

1180   READING READINESS SERIES   see
BABY RABBIT   114

1181   THE REAL WORLD SERIES   see
GROWING UP ON THE FARM TODAY   600

1182   THE REALLY BIG FAMILY
       50 min. , b&w, 1965.
       Director: Alex Grasshoff for David L. Wolper.   Narrator:
       Henry Fonda.   Distributor: Films Inc.
            Joys, trials, and triumphs of feeding and clothing a
       family of 18 children.   A week in the life of this 20-mem-
       ber family is shown.   C-A

1183   THE REAPER
       28 min. , color, 1970.
       Producer: USC, Dept. of Cinema.   Distributor: Univer-
       sity of Southern California.
            Dramatic film set in Wyoming in the 1870s, with
       focus on a dirt-farming family and its struggle to survive
       in the midst of a hostile environment and a plague.   C-A

1184   REFERRED FOR UNDERACHIEVEMENT
       35 min. , b&w, 1966.
       Director: Edward A. Mason, M.D.   Distributor: Docu-
       mentaries for Learning.
            An interview with a family of seven, who have been
       referred to a psychiatric clinic because their 12-year-old
       son has been underachieving in school.   Training film.   C,
       Prof

1185   REFLECTIONS
       15 min. , color, 1968.
       Director: Noel Black.   Distributor: Pyramid Films.
            A 12-year-old Chinese boy living on the Lower East
       Side of New York is rejected by peers due to lack of athletic
       ability.   A Puerto Rican girl befriends him, but the preju-
       dices of her mother and his father cause the boy to retreat
       from the friendship.   CINE Golden Eagle.   First Prize,
       Locarno Film Festival.   I-J

1186   REFLECTIONS SERIES   see
       THIS ONE FOR DAD   1377

1187   REGIONAL INTERVENTION PROGRAM SERIES   see
       TODDLER MANAGEMENT   1405

1188   REHEARSAL
       27 min. , color, p. 1976, r. 1977.
       Producer: John Meredyth Lucas for Paulist Productions.
       Cast: Jamie Smith-Jackson, Cliff De Young, Janet McLach-
       lan.   Distributor: The Media Guild.
            A group of teenagers participate in a psychodrama
       guided by a psychologist.   Several teens are able to work
       out their hostilities toward their parents and appreciate
       their parents' point of view.   From the Insight series.   S-A

1189   RELEASE
       28 min. , color, 1974.

Director: Susanne Szabo Rostock. Distributor: Odeon
Films.
The story of a woman, who, after spending four
years in prison on a drug charge, is released to a difficult
reunion with her three sons, who had been placed in foster
homes. CINE Golden Eagle. A

1190   THE RELUCTANT DELINQUENT
24 min., color, 1977.
Director: Ira Eisenberg. Distributor: Lawren Productions.
A 17-year-old locked in maximum security in Juvenile Hall is paroled to his mother so that he can attend a
special school for students with learning disabilities. S-A

1191   REMINISCENCES OF A JOURNEY TO LITHUANIA
82 min., color, 1971-72.
Director: Jonas Mekas. Distributors: Film-Makers' Cooperative; Canyon Cinema Cooperative.
A film diary reflecting the immigrant Mekas brothers'
(Jonas and Adolfas) first days in America in the early Fifties, immigrant life in Brooklyn, and return to Lithuania
in 1971 for the first time in 25 years for a family reunion.
C-A

1192   RENE SPITZ: ABOUT HIS OWN WORK
22 min., color, 1977.
Director: Thomas Sand. Distributor: Parents' Magazine
Films.
Spitz (d. 1974) was known for his studies of the
effects of emotional deprivation on child development. He
underscored the mother's role in setting the child's development. Here, he lectures, interacts with a child, and is
discussed by colleagues. C-A, Prof

1193   THE REPORT CARD: HOW DOES RICCARDO FEEL?
5 min., color, 1970.
Producer: Gary Bergland. Distributor: Encyclopaedia
Britannica Educational Corp.
Riccardo has worked hard and achieved a good re-
port card. His mother's misdirected anger confuses him.
He has to learn to read emotions more carefully to realize
when and if he is really the source of his mother's anger.
E-I

1194   REPORT ON DOWN'S SYNDROME
21 min., color, 1962.
Producer: Carl J. Ross. Distributor: International Film
Bureau.
General characteristics, treatment, and genetic find-
ings. Sequences of two mongoloid children over a six-year
period examine advantages and rewards of family life. C-A,
Prof

1195   RESPONSE TO MISBEHAVIOR
8 min., color, 1972.
Producer: John Churchill for Moreland-Latchford Productions. Distributor: Paramount Communications.
A brother and sister fight and break a vase while left alone in the house. They have four ways to handle their predicament. Open-ended. From the Moral Decision Making series. I-J

1196   RESPONSIBILITY: WHAT ARE ITS LIMITS?
19 min., color, 1975.
Director: Norman Tokar. Cast: Brian Keith, Vera Miles. Distributor: Walt Disney Educational Media Company.
A man's dream of establishing a wild-bird sanctuary interferes with the development of a hunting resort. He is accidently shot while taking the law into his own hands. This tragedy is a burden on his family. Questions how one person's value system can affect others. Excerpt from the 1964 film THOSE CALLOWAYS (2047). From the Questions!!! Answers?? Set 1 series. I-J

1197   RESTRICTED NEIGHBORHOOD
60 sec., color, 1969.
Director: Bruce Baker. Distributor: TeleKETICS.
A white couple turn down the offer of a dream house because the neighborhood is restricted. Dramatic vignette from the TeleSPOTS series. S-A

1198   RETIREMENT
50 min., color, 1978.
Director: Cinda Firestone. Distributor: Cinema 5--16mm.
Examines three retirement communities (in Arizona and Florida), and notes how the residents have or have not adapted to life there. C-A

1199   REVELATION: ULLA
4 min., color, 1971.
Director: Amelia Anderson. Distributor: Creative Film Society.
Vignettes reveal relationship of model Ulla Anderson Jones to her mother, father, grandmother, girlfriend, lover, and child. A

1200   REWARD AND PUNISHMENT
14 min., color, 1974.
Producer: Peter Jordan. Distributor: CRM/McGraw-Hill Films.
Designed to show parents and teachers how to reward and punish their children effectively and use these principles to modify existing behavior. Abuses of punishment are also covered. From the Behavior Modification series. S-A

1201   RICHIE
        31 min. , color, 1978.
        Director: Paul Wendkos. Cast: Ben Gazzara, Robby Ben-
        son. Distributor: Learning Corp. of America.
            A man is forced to kill his own son when the boy
        becomes uncontrollable due to heavy involvement with drugs.
        Based on a true story, and edited from the 1977 TV film
        THE DEATH OF RICHIE (1686). S-A

1202   RICKY AND ROCKY
        15 min. , color, 1973.
        Directors: Tom Palazzolo & Jeff Kreines. Distributor:
        Canyon Cinema Cooperative.
            Ricky is Italian; Roxann is Polish; they are engaged,
        and surprised by a backyard wedding shower given by
        Ricky's working-class family. Cinema vérité in suburbia.
        S-A

1203   RIDE A TURQUOISE PONY
        28 min. , color or b&w, 1971.
        Director: Hal Cooper. Cast: Belinda Montgomery, Jan
        Clayton, John Larch. Distributor: Paulist Productions.
            A young woman, who has spent two years working
        with the Navajos as a VISTA volunteer, comes home to
        find a bitter, dying grandmother and a warmonger fiancé.
        But she learns through the loving and forgiving actions of
        her father that God still exists in others. From the In-
        sight series. S-A

1204   THE RIGHT TO CHOOSE
        $27\frac{1}{2}$ min. , color, 1975.
        Sponsor: Association for the Study of Abortion. Distribu-
        tor: Association Films.
            Abortion experts discuss the emotional, social, legal,
        medical, and religious issues involved; and a college stu-
        dent, a housewife, a mother, and a grandmother personalize
        the issues. C-A

1205   RILEY FAMILY
        59 min. , b&w, 1967.
        Producer: The School of Social Welfare, University of
        California, Berkeley. Distributor: University of California,
        Extension Media Center.
            An application interview with a real family--father,
        mother and 15-year-old son. The family crisis surround-
        ing the developmental stages of the child, his physical dis-
        ability (mild epilepsy), and its consequences are noted. A
        kinescope. C, Prof

1206   RIPPLES SERIES see
        DAD AND I 335

1207 THE RIVER
29 min., color, p. 1976, r. 1978.
Director: Barbara Noble. Story: Flannery O'Connor.
Distributor: Phoenix Films.
A lonely little boy, neglected by his hedonistic parents, is taken under the wing of a babysitter who is also
into fundamentalist religion. His baptism in the river gives
him such a feeling of belonging that he returns to the river
alone tragically to relive the experience. C-A

1208 THE ROAD NEVER ENDS
15 min., color, 1976.
Director: Arthur Drooker. Distributor: Texture Films.
What life is like for the wife and sons of a truck
driver who spends most of his time on the road. J-A

1209 ROBIN ... A RUNAWAY
32 min., color, 1976.
Director: Thom Eberhardt. Distributor: FilmFair Communications.
A 14-year-old runaway is arrested while hitchhiking.
Flashbacks show why she felt she had to run away from
home. Best in Category, National Council on Family Relations. J-A

1210 ROCK-A-BYE-BABY
30 min., color, 1971.
Director: Richard Ellison. Producer: Lothar Wolff. Dis-
tributor: Time-Life Multimedia.
Examines the psychological effects of mothering and
lack of mothering on infant development. Avail. in Spanish.
From the Life Around Us series. Blue Ribbon & Emily
Award, American Film Festival. CINE Golden Eagle. S-A

1211 THE ROLE OF WOMEN IN AMERICAN SOCIETY SERIES
see
CLORAE AND ALBIE 283
GIRLS AT 12 574
SALLY GARCIA AND FAMILY 1226
VIGNETTES (GIRLS AT 12) 1449

1212 RONNIE'S TUNE
18 min., color, 1977.
Director: Gene Feldman. Distributor: Wombat Productions.
Julie's beloved cousin Ronnie has committed suicide;
and Julie, at 11, tries to hold onto her good memories of
the boy, and understand her aunt's strange reaction to her
son's death. Blue Ribbon, American Film Festival. I-A

1213 ROOKIE OF THE YEAR
47 min., color, 1975.
Producer: Daniel Wilson. Cast: Jodie Foster. Distributor: Time-Life Multimedia.

An 11-year-old girl's parents are supportive of her desire to fill a vacancy on an all-male Little League baseball team. Her brother, however, is embarrassed and angry; and the other parents and kids resent her. She plays in spite of all the rejection. An ABC Afterschool Special, from the Teenage Years series. Blue Ribbon, American Film Festival. Emmy Award. Christopher Award. I-A

1214   ROOTED IN THE PAST
13 min., color, 1975.
Producer: WGBH-TV, Boston. Distributor: Films Inc.
Two short portraits of real-life American kids; vignettes include: PUEBLO VILLAGE--Laverne Concha lives in an Indian village where a stream supplies the family's water, and bread is baked in outdoor ovens. She translates one of her grandparent's stories. WESTERN RANCH--Ray Spears visits his grandfather's cattle ranch. His grandfather encourages him to practice rodeo bull riding. From the Best of Zoom series. E-I

1215   ROSE KENNEDY REMEMBERS--THE BEST OF TIMES ...
THE WORST OF TIMES
52 min., color, 1975.
Producer: BBC-TV. Distributor: Time-Life Multimedia.
What it's like to be the matriarch of the Kennedy clan. Chris Award, Columbus Film Festival. S-A

1216   ROSEDALE: THE WAY IT IS
57 min., color, 1976.
Producer: WNET-TV. Distributor: Indiana University, Audio-Visual Center.
Documents racial tensions in this predominantly white, middle-class neighborhood in Queens, N.Y. S-A

1217   ROSELAND
$12\frac{1}{2}$ min., color, 1973.
Director: Royanne Rosenberg. Distributor: Serious Business Company.
Documentary portrait of Rose Oliver--an overweight, unmarried welfare mother of three, who lives in the projects of Chicago. Includes the birth of one of her children. C-A

1218   RUFUS M., TRY AGAIN
13 min., color, 1977.
Producer: Martha Moran. Distributor: BFA Educational Media.
Dramatizes Chapter 1 in Rufus M, the third book about the Moffat family by Eleanor Estes. When Rufus's older brother and sister taunt him because he can't read, Rufus learns to use the library. E

1219 THE RUNAWAY PROBLEM
27 min., color, p. 1976, r. 1977.
Producer: Miller Productions. Distributor: Miller Productions.
Interweaves young runaways' stories of life in the streets, with stories from parents, who discuss their helplessness. Promotes the use of national runaway hotline--"Peace of Mind"--which is a message center for communication to parents. J-A

1220 RUNAWAYS
10 min., color, 1969.
Producer: Sid Davis Productions. Distributor: Sid Davis Productions.
Dramatized stories of two teenagers who run away from home, for different reasons. J

1221 RUNAWAYS
25 min., color, 1975.
Director: Donald McDonald. Distributors: The Little Red Filmhouse; MTI Teleprograms.
Focuses on Kathy, who runs away from home after a family argument; and on Debbie, an experienced runaway who meets Kathy. J-A

1222 SSI CAN MAKE THE DIFFERENCE
20 min., color, 1977.
Producer: Social Security Administration. Distributor: National Audiovisual Center.
Four case histories highlight facts about eligibility for Supplemental Security Income. Cases include: a young blind boy; a widow; an elderly couple living in a rural area; and a Spanish-surnamed man drawing both Social Security and SSI. A

1223 SAFE BICYCLING
13 min., color, 1959.
Producer: Crawley Films, with cooperation of Mass. Safety Council & Safe Bicycle Committee. Distributor: International Film Bureau.
Rules for safe bicycling, stressing parental responsibility for the safety of the bikes themselves. E-I, A

1224 SAFETY ... HOME-SAFE-HOME
14 min., color, 1972.
Producer: Charles Cahill & Associates. Distributor: AIMS Instructional Media Services.
Covers fire, electricity, poisons, slips and falls, and cuts and bruises. Avail. in Spanish. E-I

1225 SALESMAN
90 min., b&w, 1969.
Directors: David Maysles, Albert Maysles, Charlotte Zwerin.

Distributor: Maysles Films.
Four door-to-door Bible salesmen invade some American middle-class homes to try to convince families to buy The Book. Cinema vérité documentary. C-A

1226 SALLY GARCIA AND FAMILY
35 min., color, 1977.
Director: Joyce Chopra. Distributor: Education Development Center.
A 40-year-old housewife and mother of five decided to change her life. She attends evening school to get her B.A., and works as a career counselor. Highlights conflicts that she and her family face as a result of this lifestyle change. She is Puerto Rican; her husband is Mexican American. From the Role of Women in American Society series. J-A

1227 SAM
28½ min., color, 1969.
Director: Jack Shea for Paulist Productions. Cast: Jack Albertson, Michael-James Wixted. Distributor: The Media Guild.
In the next millennium, the only human being left alive is given a computer for a wife. When "she" announces that an experimental computer baby has been ordered, the man smashes her and escapes. From the Insight series. J-A

1228 SAM
20 min., b&w, 1973.
Director: Margaret Bach. Distributor: University of California, Extension Media Center.
Sam, a Japanese American gardener, and his wife discuss their past--horrifying World War II experiences both here and in Japan, and resulting smashed goals--and family life. C-A

1229 SANDBOX
10 min., b&w, 1965.
Producer: USC, Dept. of Cinema. Distributor: University of Southern California.
An adaptation of Edward Albee's play, which comments on "contemporary American family relationships" and especially "their attitude towards the elderly." C-A

1230 SANDY AND MADELEINE'S FAMILY
30 min., color, 1973.
Directors: Sherrie Farrell, John Gordon Hill, & Peter M. Bruce. Distributor: Multi Media Resource Center.
A lesbian couple, who were sued for divorce and child custody by their husbands, try to sustain life as a family after they win custody, but are ordered by the court to maintain separate residences. Includes domestic life and interviews with the children. C-A

1231   SARA HAS DOWN'S SYNDROME
16 min., color, 1974.
Directors: John Friedman & Henry Felt. Distributor:
Education Development Center.
    Six-year-old Sara has Down's syndrome, but she
lives at home with her parents, three sisters, and brother.
Family support has enabled Sara to do things despite her
severe handicaps. From the Exploring Childhood: Working
with Children series. J-A, Prof

1232   SARAH AT $2\frac{1}{2}$
20 min., color, 1978.
Director: John Temple. Distributor: Urbanimage Corp.
    The everyday life of a $2\frac{1}{2}$-year-old. With voice-over
commentary by family members, including her 92-year-old
great-grandmother, concerning their expectations for the
child and aspects of parenting. Notes how values are trans-
ferred from generation to generation. S-A

1233   SARA'S SUMMER OF THE SWANS
33 min., color, 1976.
Director: James B. Clark. Distributor: Time-Life Multimedia.
    A 14-year-old is suffering through a lonely summer,
with braces on her teeth and a little brother to annoy her.
She rejects family and friends and withdraws, until a boy
helps her find her lost brother and herself. An ABC Afterschool Special; from the Teenage Years series. CINE
Golden Eagle. I-A

1234   SATURDAY AFTERNOON
11 min., color, 1975.
Director: John Stewart. Distributor: TeleKETICS.
    A comic mime of a married couple mechanically per-
forming their usual Saturday-afternoon rituals. S-A

1235   SATURDAY MORNING
88 min., color, 1971.
Director: Kent Mackenzie for Dimension Films. Distributors: Churchill Films; Mass Media Ministries (rental
only); Twyman Films (rental only).
    Record of discussions at a six-day encounter group
of young people who focus on feelings about parents, dating,
sex and morality, and their search for personal identity and
love. Best Film of the Year Award, National Council on
Family Relations. J-S, A

1236   SAY YES TO LOVE
30 sec., color, 1969.
Director: Bruce Baker. Distributor: TeleKETICS.
    Dramatic vignette in which a little girl removes all
distractions from her father so they can share a quiet moment of love. From the TeleSPOTS series. E-A

1237   SCHMEERGUNTZ
15 min. , b&w, 1966.
Directors: Gunvor Nelson & Dorothy Wiley.   Distributor:
Serious Business Company.
Contrasts media images of womanhood with real-life
roles and duties of motherhood and married life.   S-A

1238   SCOTT GOES TO THE HOSPITAL
11 min. , color, 1973.
Producer: Alfred Higgins Productions.   Distributor: Alfred Higgins Productions.
Designed to allay children's fears about going to the
hospital for treatment.   E

1239   SEARCH FOR AMERICA: PART 2 SERIES   see
FAMILY   455

1240   SEARCHING FOR VALUES   see
LONELINESS ... AND LOVING   844
MY COUNTRY, RIGHT OR WRONG?   980
WHEN PARENTS GROW OLD   1504
WHETHER TO TELL THE TRUTH   1511

1241   THE SEARCHING YEARS: DATING AND MARRIAGE SE-
RIES   see
HOW CLOSE CAN YOU GET?   672

1242   THE SEARCHING YEARS: DIFFERENCES SERIES   see
OLIVIA: MEXICAN OR AMERICAN--DIFFERENCES IN
THE FAMILY   1050

1243   THE SEARCHING YEARS: THE FAMILY SERIES   see
CAN A PARENT BE HUMAN?   211
I OWE YOU NOTHING!   692
IVAN AND HIS FATHER   757
MOM, WHY WON'T YOU LISTEN?   945
WAIT UNTIL YOUR FATHER GETS HOME!   1452

1244   SECOND CHORUS
25 min. , color, 1978.
Director: Russ Petranto.   Cast: John Astin, Patty Duke
Astin, Marcia Wallace.   Distributor: Paulist Productions.
After 16 years of marriage, a couple get divorced.
They meet on their way to their son's marriage, but their
son cancels his wedding plans because he fears he can't
have an honest, open relationship the way his parents did.
They're shocked to realize their marriage was so strong
and decide to try again.   From the Insight series.   S-A

1245   SECOND WEAVER
9 min. , b&w, sil. , 1966.
Director: Mrs. Benally.   Producers: Sol Worth & John
Adair.   Distributor: Museum of Modern Art.

A companion film to A NAVAJO WEAVER (1007). In this film, Mrs. Benally turns her camera on her daughter, Susie, who is weaving a belt. Part of a project conducted by Sol Worth and John Adair with Navajo Indians in Pine Springs, Ariz. From the Navajos Film Themselves series. C-A

1246   THE SECRET LIFE OF T. K. DEARING
47 min., color, 1978.
Producer: Daniel Wilson. Cast: Jodie Foster, Eduard Franz. Distributor: Time-Life Multimedia.
At first, Theresa Dearing resents her grandfather when he comes to live with her family. Then, she learns that both he and she have a lot in common. They become confidants. An ABC Afterschool Special; from the Teenage Years series. J-A

1247   THE SECRET LOVE OF SANDRA BLAIN
28 min., color, 1971.
Producer: Don Hoster. Distributors: AIMS Instructional Media Services; Image Associates; FMS Productions.
A wife/mother becomes an alcoholic and begins deceiving her friends, family, doctor, and herself. Avail. in Spanish. S-A

1248   SEEDS OF TRUST
29 min., color, p. 1978, r. 1979.
Director: Vicky Wingert. Distributor: Victoria Films.
Four families and their childbirth experiences. All are supported by nurse-midwives. S-A

1249   SEIKO AT HOME
12 min., color, 1974.
Directors: Henry Felt & John Friedman. Distributor: Education Development Center.
A 4-year-old Japanese American girl with her family. She has two younger sisters; her father is an architect. From the Exploring Childhood: Family and Society series. J-A

1250   SELF IDENTITY/SEX ROLES: I ONLY WANT YOU TO BE HAPPY
16 min., color, 1975.
Producer: Steve Katten. Host: Beau Bridges. Distributor: CRM/McGraw-Hill Films.
Drama involving a mother and her two grown daughters. They conflict on their definitions of "the female role." From Conflict and Awareness: A Film Series on Human Values. Silver Award, International Film & TV Festival of New York. S-A

1251   SELF INCORPORATED SERIES see
CHANGES 235

DIFFERENT FOLKS   373
DOUBLE TROUBLE   392
FAMILY MATTERS   470
NO TRESPASSING   1028
PRESSURE MAKES PERFECT   1142
TWO SONS   1428
WHAT'S WRONG WITH JONATHAN?   1502

1252   THE SELLIN' OF JAMIE THOMAS (PART I)
24 min. , color, 1975.
Director: Tom Robertson.   Distributor: Multimedia Program Productions.
A slave auction breaks up a family; but the family
members endure great hardship to reunite.   Continued in
Part II.   From the Young People's Specials series.   E-J

1253   THE SELLIN' OF JAMIE THOMAS (PART II)
24 min. , color, 1977.
Director: Tom Robertson.   Distributor: Multimedia Program Productions.
Continuation of Part I.   Now, the slave family tries
to escape North through the Underground Railroad.   They
settle in a Quaker town.   From the Young People's Specials
series.   E-J

1254   A SENSE OF JOY
14½ min. , color, 1973.
Producer: WVIZ-TV.   Distributor: Agency for Instructional
TV.
A boy wanders leisurely to the beach while his sister
rushes to the beach by a different route.   From the Inside/
Out series.   E-I

1255   SEPARATION/DIVORCE: IT HAS NOTHING TO DO WITH
YOU
14 min. , color, 1974.
Producer: Steve Katten.   Host: Beau Bridges.   Distribu-
tor: CRM/McGraw-Hill Films.
Larry's parents have decided to separate, and he
is faced with choosing between them.   Dramatic film.
From Conflict and Awareness: A Film Series on Human
Values.   Gold Award, International Film & TV Festival
of New York.   S-A

1256   THE SEVEN WISHES OF JOANNA PEABODY
29 min. , color, 1978.
Director: Stephen Foreman.   Cast: Butterfly McQueen,
Star-Shemah, Garrett Morris.   Distributor: Learning Corp.
of America.
A "fairy godmother" grants some wishes to a 12-year-
old Harlem girl.   She wishes for a quiet baby brother, clean
dishes, etc. , until she realizes that she's too self-absorbed
and should think of others.   An ABC Weekend Special.   I

1257   SEVENTEEN FOREVER
       27 min., color, 1975.
       Director: Hal Cooper for Paulist Productions.   Cast: Rue
       McClanahan, Lee Purcell, John Rudolph.   Distributor: The
       Media Guild.
            A family--daughter, mother, and grandfather--are ob-
       sessed with youth.   They dress outlandishly young for their
       ages.   They quarrel and realize the truth about inner beauty.
       From the Insight series.   S-A

1258   1776:   AMERICAN REVOLUTION ON THE FRONTIER
       22 min., color, 1976.
       Director: John Ford.   Cast: Henry Fonda, Claudette Col-
       bert, Edna May Oliver.   Distributor: Films Inc.
            The story of homesteader Gilbert Martin and his
       bride at the time of the American Revolution in upstate New
       York.   Extract from the 1939 film DRUMS ALONG THE
       MOHAWK (1698).   J-S

1259   SEX, FEELINGS & VALUES SERIES   see
       PARENTS' VOICES   1092

1260   SEX ROLE DEVELOPMENT
       23 min., color, 1974.
       Producer: Barbara Jampel.   Distributor: CRM/McGraw-
       Hill Films.
            How sex-role stereotypes are taught to children.   Ob-
       serves the daily routine of a family with a 3-year-old son.
       They are attempting non-sexist, non-traditional sex-role
       socialization.   From the Developmental Psychology series.
       S-A

1261   THE SEXES: WHAT'S THE DIFFERENCE
       28 min., color, p. 1972, r. 1978.
       Producer: Canadian Broadcasting Corp.   Distributor:
       Filmakers Library.
            Surveys the research of leading child developmental-
       ists: Dr. Jerome Kagan (Harvard), Dr. Eleanor Maccoby
       (Stanford), and Drs. Jeanne and Jack Block (National Insti-
       tute of Mental Health) on the subject of inborn vs. learned
       male/female traits.   Explores influence of parents.   S-A

1262   SEXUAL ABUSE: THE FAMILY
       30 min., color, 1977.
       Producer: National Center on Child Abuse & Neglect, HEW.
       Distributor: National Audiovisual Center.
            A physician, social worker, and a psychologist dis-
       cuss sexual abuse of children.   Includes a training inter-
       view with a sexually abused child and her family.   From
       the We Can Help series.   Training film.   C, Prof

1263   SEXUALITY: THE HUMAN HERITAGE
       59 min., color, p. 1975, r. 1976.

Director: Al Mifelow for NET. Distributor: Indiana University, Audio-Visual Center.

Development of sexual identity, from uterine prenatal sex hormones to family and societal influences. Also notes male/female roles in marriage. From The Thin Edge series. S-A

1264 THE SEXUALLY ABUSED CHILD: IDENTIFICATION/INTERVIEW
8 min., color, 1978.
Producer: Cavalcade Productions. Distributor: MTI Teleprograms.

Illustrates methods of developing a bond with an abused child so as to establish the facts behind possible sexual abuse. Training film. C, Prof

1265 SHAPING THE PERSONALITY: THE ROLE OF MOTHER-CHILD RELATIONS IN INFANCY
20 min., b&w, sil., 1953.
Producer: René A. Spitz, M.D. Distributor: New York University.

Forms of mother/child interaction and how they affect the child. Demonstrates how the feeding and play methods of five breastfeeding mothers express their wishes of what their children should be like. From the Film Studies of the Psychoanalytic Research Project on Problems in Infancy series. C, Prof

1266 SHELLEY WHITEBIRD'S FIRST POWWOW
8 min., color, p. 1976, r. 1977.
Producer: Lifestyle Productions. Distributor: Encyclopaedia Britannica Educational Corp.

An American Indian girl prepares for her first Powwow. Her family lives in a big city, but they continue the old traditions. E-I

1267 SHOOTING STAR see
MY LIFE IN ART 990

1268 SHOPLIFTING: SHARON'S STORY
25 min., color, 1978.
Director: Yvonne Chotzen. Distributor: Learning Corp. of America.

A teenager is picked up for shoplifting in a department store. Shows what she must endure after arrest-- booking, confrontation with parents, etc. J-A

1269 SHOPPERS
27 min., color, 1977.
Director: Robert Newman. Distributor: Robert Newman, United Church Board for Homeland Ministries.

Young, white Americans discuss life-style options open to them--marriage, non-marital relationships, male/

female roles, communal life, work and urban life vs. country and rural living, personal and interpersonal values. S-A

1270 THE SHOPPING BAG LADY
21 min., color, p. 1974, r. 1975.
Director: Bert Salzman. Distributor: Learning Corp. of America.
A teenager and her friends harass a New York City shopping-bag lady. The teen finally reaches out to the old lady and reexamines her relationship with her own grandmother. From the Learning to Be Human series. Chris Statuette & President's Award, Columbus Film Festival. Red Ribbon, American Film Festival. E-A

1271 SHORT PLAY SHOWCASE SERIES see
THE LONG CHRISTMAS DINNER 845

1272 SHRIMPIN'S NOT A REAL GOOD LIFE see
WORKING WITH MY DAD 1550

1273 SIBLINGS AS BEHAVIOR MODIFIERS
25 min., color, 1976.
Director: Phillip Blake. Distributor: The Media Guild.
The story of a mentally retarded child whose family keep him home rather than institutionalize him. Studies sibling involvement. From the Behavior Modification Special Education series. C-A

1274 SICKLE CELL ANEMIA AND SICKLE CELL TRAIT
28 min., color, 1973.
Producer: Hinton Productions for the U.S. Job Corps.
Distributor: National Audiovisual Center.
Aims to answer common questions about sickle-cell anemia and sickle-cell trait. S-A

1275 SIGN OF PROFIT
20 min., color, 1964.
Producer: U.S. Dept. of Agriculture. Distributor: National Audiovisual Center.
A farmer and his wife dream of bettering their farm. A

1276 SIGNS OF LIFE
60 sec., color, 1970.
Director: Bruce Baker. Distributor: TeleKETICS.
An only child is delighted to learn that she'll soon have a new baby brother or sister. Dramatic vignette. From the TeleSPOTS series. E-A

1277 SINCERITY
Reel One: 25 min., color, sil., 1973.
Reel Two: 40 min., color, sil., 1975.

Director: Stan Brakhage. Distributors: Brakhage Films; Film-Makers' Cooperative; Canyon Cinema Cooperative. Reel One covers "childhood and youth." Reel Two covers "the first years of marriage." Filmmaker's auto-biography. C-A

1278   SINGLE FATHERING
8 min., color, 1977.
Director: Ron Taylor. Distributor: Canyon Cinema Co-operative.
        A single man adopts a baby girl. As he cares for her, he discusses his reasons for adopting and his philoso-phy of life. Includes nudity. Special Merit Award, Athens Film Festival. S-A

1279   SINGLE PARENT
40 min., color, 1976.
Director: Hubert Smith. Distributor: The Media Guild.
        Cinema vérité exploration of a single-parent family (three children) as they go about their daily lives. The mother tries to care for her home and children and begin dating once again. From the Women Today series. S-A

1280   THE SINGLE PARENT
28½ min., color, 1976.
Producer: WTTW/Chicago for the Par Leadership Training Foundation. Distributors: Perennial Education; National Audiovisual Center (rental only).
        Family activities for single-parent families with pre-school children. From the Look at Me! series. A

1281   SIU MEI WONG--WHO SHALL I BE?
17 min., color, 1970.
Producer: Michael Ahnemann. Distributor: Learning Corp. of America.
        A young Chinese American girl wants to be a ballerina, but when her ballet lessons conflict with her Chinese les-sons, she's forced to confront her father about his old-world attitudes. Set in Los Angeles. In Chinese, with English subtitles. From The Many Americans series. I-J, A

1282   SIX AMERICAN FAMILIES SERIES   see
        THE BURKS OF GEORGIA   199
        THE GEORGES OF NEW YORK CITY   563
        THE GREENBERGS OF CALIFORNIA   592
        THE KENNEDYS OF ALBUQUERQUE   782
        THE PASCIAKS OF CHICAGO   1094
        THE STEPHENSES OF IOWA   1316

1283   SIX FILMMAKERS IN SEARCH OF A WEDDING
13 min., color, 1971.
Producer: Envision Corp. Distributors: Pyramid Films; Polymorph Films (rental only).

A traditional family wedding is filmed by six different filmmakers, each using a different style, i.e., collage/animation, pixilation, home movie, cinema vérité, wedding-photo montage. J-A

1284 SIXTEEN IN WEBSTER GROVES
47 min., b&w, 1966.
Producer: Arthur Barron for CBS-TV News. Distributor: Carousel Films.
In 1966, Webster Groves, Mo., was an affluent, suburban community on the outskirts of St. Louis. CBS-TV and Charles Kuralt examined the lives, attitudes, and values of 16-year-olds living in this community. They found materialistic, conforming, insulated young people who parroted their parents' rigid attitudes. See follow-up film WEBSTER GROVES REVISITED (1472). Blue Ribbon, American Film Festival. S-A

1285 60 MINUTES TV SERIES see
COPS 317
THREE'S A CROWD 1386

1286 THE SKATING RINK
27 min., color, p. 1974, r. 1975.
Director: Larry Elikann. Distributor: Learning Corp. of America.
A moody, stammering teenager exasperates his father, brothers, and sister with his behavior. When he is taken under the wing of the new skating-rink owner, he gains skill as a skater and confidence as a person, enabling him to express love for his family for the first time. Dramatic film. An ABC Afterschool Special; from the Learning to Be Human series. E-A

1287 A SLAVE'S STORY: RUNNING A THOUSAND MILES TO FREEDOM
29 min., color, 1972.
Director: John Irvin. Distributor: Learning Corp. of America.
Based on an "authentic narrative" by William and Ellen Craft and introduced by their great-granddaughter. Dramatizes the Crafts' courageous escape from slavery in 1848, and follows them from the South to freedom in Philadelphia. J-A

1288 SLED DOGS see
ANIMAL PARTNERS 91

1289 SLEEPY WORLD
60 sec., color, 1967.
Director: Bruce Baker. Distributor: TeleKETICS.
A boy attempts to awaken his parents with a kiss. Dramatic vignette; from the TeleSPOTS series. E-A

1290   A SLIGHT DRINKING PROBLEM
       25 min. , color, 1977.
       Director: Hal Cooper for Paulist Productions.   Cast: Patty
       Duke Astin, James Hampton, Rue McClanahan.   Distribu-
       tor: Southerby Productions.
           A man and his wife deny the existence of his alco-
       holism, but she is hurt by his drunken escapades.   She at-
       tends an AL-ANON meeting, where she learns to let her
       husband face the consequences of his own actions.   From
       the Insight series.   S-A

1291   SMILE OF THE BABY
       30 min. , b&w, sil. , 1948.
       Producer: René A. Spitz, M. D.   Distributor: New York
       University.
           Indicates that parents' love creates a special atmos-
       phere that the baby associates with pleasure, play, food,
       and relief from discomfort.   From the Film Studies of the
       Psychoanalytic Research Project on Problems in Infancy
       series.   C, Prof

1292   SO FAR APART
       21 min. , color, 1974.
       Producer: KBTV-9 Combined Communications Corp.   Dis-
       tributor: Screen Education Enterprises.
           Conflicting values between parents and teenagers can
       cause trouble.   Some kids run away.   Focuses on a real
       family facing such problems.   Open-ended.   J-S, A

1293   SO I TOOK IT
       10 min. , color, 1975.
       Producer: Sid Davis.   Distributor: MTI Teleprograms.
           Preteen Sally's first shoplifting offense is initiated
       by peer pressure, and finally results in her involving both
       herself and her younger brother.   E-S

1294   THE SOAP BOX DERBY SCANDAL
       24 min. , color, p. 1974, r. 1975.
       Director: Bob Cihi.   Distributor: Weston Woods.
           A boy's derby car is rigged by his uncle, who is also
       the boy's guardian.   The boy goes on to win the 1973 All-
       American Soap Box Derby National Championship in Akron,
       Ohio, but he is disqualified.   The annual championship was
       discontinued as a result of this scandal.   I, A

1295   A SOCIAL LEARNING APPROACH TO FAMILY THERAPY
       see
           CHILDHOOD AGGRESSION: A SOCIAL LEARNING AP-
               PROACH TO FAMILY THERAPY   258

1296   SOCIAL PSYCHOLOGY
       33 min. , color, 1971.
       Producer: Carole Hart.   Distributor: CRM/McGraw-Hill
       Films.

How parents reacted to the first busing of black children to previously all-white schools in middle-class Westport, Conn. From the Psychology Today series. Bronze Award, International Film & TV Festival of New York. S-A

1297 SOCIAL SEMINAR SERIES see
      BRIAN AT SEVENTEEN 193
      FAMILY 456

1298 SOFT IS THE HEART OF A CHILD
      28 min., color, p. 1978, r. 1979.
      Director: Gerald T. Rogers. Distributor: Modern Talking Picture Service.
      Effects of parents' alcoholism on preteen children. Dramatic film. Blue Ribbon, American Film Festival. E-J, A

1299 SOLDIER'S HOME
      $41\frac{1}{2}$ min., color, p. 1976, r. 1977.
      Director: Robert Young. Story: Ernest Hemingway. Distributor: Perspective Films.
      A young soldier returns from World War I and struggles with a sense of alienation from his mother, community, and neighbors. From the American Short Story series. Silver Hugo, Chicago International Film Festival. J-A

1300 SOMATIC CONSEQUENCES OF EMOTIONAL STARVATION IN INFANTS
      30 min., b&w, sil., 1949.
      Producer: René A. Spitz, M.D. Distributor: New York University.
      A clinical study of two infants during the first four months: one a desired, loved child in a middle-class home; the other raised in a foundling home. Also compares the children between the ages of 13 and 14 months, to show the ravages of emotional deprivation on the institutionalized child. From the Film Studies of the Psychoanalytic Research Project on Problems in Infancy series. C, Prof

1301 SOME BASIC DIFFERENCES IN NEWBORN INFANTS DURING THE LYING-IN PERIOD
      20 min., b&w, sil., 1944.
      Producers: Margaret E. Fries, M.D., & Paul J. Woolf, M.S. Distributor: New York University.
      Observes three normal newborns who are responding differently during nursing. Notes importance of mothers' attitudes. From the Studies on Integrated Development: Interaction Between Child and Environment series. C, Prof

1302 SOME OBSERVATIONS CONCERNING THE PHENOMENOLOGY
OF ORAL BEHAVIOR IN SMALL INFANTS
20 min. , b&w, sil. , 1951.
Producers: Sibylle Escalona, Ph.D. , & Mary Leitch, M.D.
Distributor: New York University.
Documents variations in oral behavior in a number of
infants under 24 weeks of age. From the Infant Psychology
series. C, Prof

1303 SOMEDAY A FUTURE
27 min. , color, 1977.
Director: Rhoden Streeter. Distributor: WAVE-TV.
The experiences of three widows at different points
in their recovery from grief. Examines a community widows' self-help program that enables widows to reach out
to one another as counselors and friends. C-A

1304 SOMETIMES I WONDER WHO I AM
5 min. , b&w, 1970.
Director: Liane Brandon. Distributor: New Day Films.
A young housewife/mother dreams of the career
she could have had. C-A

1305 SOMEWHERE BEFORE
27 min. , color or b&w, 1975.
Director: Paul Stanley. Cast: Ron Howard, Cindy Williams. Distributor: Paulist Productions.
A young woman in labor is rushed to the hospital.
She despairs over the desertion of her boyfriend, and this
despair is slowly killing the child. From the Insight series. S-A

1306 SONG FOR MY SISTER
45 min. , b&w, 1968.
Director: John Klein. Distributor: New York University.
A teenager and her brother wander through the streets
of New York City.

1307 SOON THERE WILL BE NO MORE ME
10 min. , color, 1972.
Director: Larry Schiller. Distributor: Churchill Films.
The story of a 19-year-old mother who is dying of
cancer and writing a diary as a legacy for her daughter.
S-A

1308 SOUTHERN ACCENTS, NORTHERN GHETTOS
50 min. , b&w, 1969.
Producer: ABC-TV. Distributor: Benchmark Films.
A black woman and her 11 children are profiled in
this case study. The family migrated north to Chicago
hoping to leave subsistence life behind. They must go on
welfare in Chicago. Chris Award, Columbus Film Festival. J-A

1309   SPEAKING OF MEN
        20 min., color, 1977.
        Directors: Christine M. Herbes & Ann-Carol Grossman.
        Distributor: Polymorph Films.
            Three women discuss their relationships with and at-
        titudes toward men. The women are young, single pro-
        fessionals, but reveal different points of view.   S-A

1310   SPECIAL EDUCATION SERIES see
        FIRST STEPS 514

1311   SPECIAL TREAT SERIES see
        BIG HENRY AND THE POLKA DOT KID 150
        LUKE WAS THERE 866
        THE TAP DANCE KID 1350

1312   THE SPRING AND FALL OF NINA POLANSKI
        10 min., color, p. 1975, r. 1976.
        Director: Kathleen Shannon for the National Film Board
        of Canada. Distributor: The Media Guild.
            Animation noting what a woman thinks of her hus-
        band and children, and how they perceive her. Also touches
        on what to do with one's life once the kids are grown.
        Open-ended. From the Women Today series. S-A

1313   STANDUP & BE COUNTED see
        MY LIFE IN ART 990

1314   STARTING NURSERY SCHOOL: PATTERNS OF BEGINNING
        23 min., b&w, 1959.
        Producer: L. Joseph Stone, for the Child Study Dept.,
        Vassar College. Distributor: New York University.
            A child's gradual introduction to a college laboratory
        nursery school without the sudden stress of abrupt separation
        from mother. From the Vassar Studies of Normal Per-
        sonality Development series. C, Prof

1315   STARTING TO READ SERIES see
        PICNIC 1108

1316   THE STEPHENSES OF IOWA
        58 min., color, p. 1976, r. 1977.
        Producers: Arthur Barron & Mark Obenhaus for Westing-
        house Broadcasting Corp. Distributor: Carousel Films.
            A documentary profile of a third-generation farm
        family with six children, whose good life is threatened by
        the great costs of running a farm. From the Six American
        Families series. S-A

1317   STEPPARENTING: NEW FAMILIES, OLD TIES
        25 min., color, 1976.
        Directors: Henry Felt & Marilyn Felt. Distributor: Poly-
        morph Films.

Stepparents and professionals discuss the tensions and challenges in raising other people's children. C-A, Prof

1318   STEPPARENTS: WHERE IS THE LOVE?
16 min., color, 1975.
Producer: Walt Disney Productions. Cast: Ron Howard, Earl Holliman. Distributor: Walt Disney Educational Media Company.
A teenager has a tough time accepting his stepfather, so he runs away. Vignette from the feature film SMOKE (1970). From the Questions!!! Answers?? Set 1 series. I-J

1319   THE STEPS OF AGE
25 min., b&w, 1950.
Director: Ben Maddow for the Mental Health Film Board.
Distributor: International Film Bureau.
Jimmy Potter retires and as a result goes into a depression and soon dies. His widow, on the other hand, was always able to cope with old age and retirement until her husband died and left her alone and a burden on the children. C-A

1320   A STORM OF STRANGERS SERIES see
THE IRISH   743
ITALIANAMERICAN   748
JEWISH AMERICAN   768
JUNG SAI: CHINESE AMERICAN   778

1321   STORY
7 min., color, p. 1964, r. 1969.
Director: Homer Groening. Distributor: Paramount Communications.
A boy relates a story to his younger sister. The filmmaker--the father of these kids--taped his son's spontaneous story and his daughter's responses and then shot visuals to illustrate the story. Avail. in Spanish. E

1322   STORY OF OUR NEW BABY
$10\frac{1}{2}$ min., color, 1971.
Producer: Coronet Films. Distributor: Coronet Films.
The story of birth as told to a little girl who expects a new baby brother or sister. Traces development in womb, changes in mother's body, and how the family prepares for birth. E-I

1323   STORY OF PEGGY AT THE FARM
16 min., color, 1957.
Producer: Calvin Productions. Distributor: International Film Bureau.
An 8-year-old city child visits her cousin's farm. She learns that almost all the food eaten by the family and animals comes directly from the farm itself. E

1324 STORYSCAPE SERIES see
GOD AND YOUR CHILDREN 577
NAMES OF SIN 997
TO BE A FAMILY 1395
THE WAY HOME 1464

1325 STRANGERS IN THEIR OWN LAND: THE PUERTO RICANS
14 min., color, 1971.
Director: John E. Johnson, Jr., for ABC-TV News. Distributor: Xerox Films.
Documents the difficulties faced by Puerto Rican families in New York City and the attempts of social agencies to solve the problems. S-A

1326 THE STREET
10 min., color, 1976.
Director: Caroline Leaf. Story: Mordecai Richler. Distributor: National Film Board of Canada.
Reactions of various family members in a Jewish Canadian household to the dying and death of the grandmother. All from the point of view of her young grandson, who is experiencing death for the first time. Animation. Blue Ribbon, American Film Festival. J-A

1327 STREET CORNER REFLECTIONS
11 min., color, 1976.
Director: Rodney Thompson. Cast: Sandra Richards, Benny Harris, Ronald Wilkerson, Edward Ferdinand, Joe Fegan. Distributor: Kit Parker Films (rental only).
A black boy stays out of school to care for his sick grandmother. She warns him to stay out of trouble, yet she continues to keep him out of school to quell her loneliness.

1328 THE STROKE PATIENT COMES HOME SERIES (6 Films)
29 min. each, b&w, 1966.
Producer: Rehabilitation Committee of the Chicago Heart Association. Distributor: International Film Bureau.
Intended for stroke patients, their families, and professionals involved with their care. Titles include: UNDERSTANDING HIS ILLNESS; UNDERSTANDING HIS PROBLEMS; HIS PHYSICAL WELL-BEING; GETTING AROUND; HE LEARNS SELF-RELIANCE; and HIS RETURN TO THE COMMUNITY. C-A

1329 STROKES see
LEARNING TO LIVE SERIES 810

1330 THE STRUGGLE FOR CONTROL see
THE CHICAGO MATERNITY CENTER STORY 241

1331   STUDIES ON INTEGRATED DEVELOPMENT: INTERACTION
       BETWEEN CHILD AND ENVIRONMENT SERIES see
          ANNA N: LIFE HISTORY FROM BIRTH TO FIFTEEN
          YEARS; THE DEVELOPMENT OF EMOTIONAL PROB-
          LEMS IN A CHILD REARED IN A NEUROTIC EN-
          VIRONMENT 94
          A CHARACTER NEUROSIS WITH DEPRESSIVE AND
          COMPULSIVE TRENDS IN THE MAKING: LIFE HIS-
          TORY OF MARY FROM BIRTH TO FIFTEEN YEARS
          239
          FAMILY LIFE OF THE NAVAJO INDIANS 468
          HAROLD--A CHARACTER DISORDER IN THE MAKING
          FROM PRE-CONCEPTION TO 32 YEARS 618
          PSYCHOLOGICAL IMPLICATIONS OF BEHAVIOR DURING
          THE CLINICAL VISIT 1154
          SOME BASIC DIFFERENCES IN NEWBORN INFANTS
          DURING THE LYING-IN PERIOD 1301
          TWO CHILDREN: CONTRASTING ASPECTS OF PER-
          SONALITY DEVELOPMENT 1425

1332   SUBVERSION?
       30 min. , color, 1971.
       Director: Barry Brown for KQED, San Francisco. Distri-
       butor: FilmWright.
            Three generations of Japanese Americans review the
       long-term effects of the U.S. detainment camps for Japanese
       Americans after Japan's attack on Pearl Harbor. S-A

1333   SUDDEN INFANT DEATH SYNDROME
       4 min. , color, 1976.
       Producer: Amram Nowak Associates for Bureau of Com-
       munity Health Services, Public Health Service. Distributor:
       National Audiovisual Center.
            Documents the cases of SIDS each year in America,
       how it can be predicted or prevented, as well as the guilt
       and grief suffered by SIDS parents. From the Sudden In-
       fant Death Syndrome series. C-A

1334   SUDDEN INFANT DEATH SYNDROME SERIES see
          AFTER OUR BABY DIED 21
          A CALL FOR HELP 208
          SUDDEN INFANT DEATH SYNDROME 1333
          YOU ARE NOT ALONE 1561

1335   SUGAR AND SPICE
       32 min. , color, 1974.
       Producers: Eric Breitbart, Vicki Breitbart, & Alan Jacobs.
       Distributor: Odeon Films.
            Explores three (in New York and Massachusetts) day-
       care centers where parents and teachers work together to
       create a non-sexist environment for learning. S-A

1336 THE SUGAR CEREAL IMITATION ORANGE BREAKFAST
8 min., color, p. 1972, r. 1975.
Director: Jack Sameth for WNET/13. Distributor: Benchmark Films.
Host Marshall Efron looks at the ways children
manipulate their mothers into buying brand-name, frosted,
sugar-coated cereals even though they're bad for teeth and
low in nutrition. Chris Plaque, Columbus Film Festival.
I-A

1337 SUICIDE AT 17
18 min., color, 1977.
Director: Ira Eisenberg. Sponsor: Suicide Prevention &
Crisis Center of San Mateo (Calif.) County. Distributor:
Lawren Productions.
Questions why 17-year-old Bobby Benton took his life
and how it might have been prevented. Interviews with his
parents, teammates, neighbors, and the director of the
Suicide Prevention & Crisis Center aim to add insight into
the problem of adolescent suicide. S-A

1338 SUNDAY FATHER
11 min., color, 1973.
Director: Paul Leaf. Cast: Dustin Hoffman. Distributor:
Films Inc.
A divorced man takes his daughter on a once-a-week
Sunday outing in New York's Central Park. S-A

1339 SUPERJOCK
15½ min., color, 1978.
Director: Scott Brown. Distributor: Journal Films.
An overweight, middle-aged ex-athlete and his equally
flabby son learn that improper diet, smoking, and lack of
exercise lower one's sense of well-being and endanger life.
They are motivated to begin a new pattern of good diet and
exercise. S-A

1340 SUSAN
5 min., b&w, 1971.
Producer: Conal Films for Human Resources Research
Organization. Distributor: National Audiovisual Center.
A quiet, withdrawn child of nine is brought to school
against her will by her insistent mother. The child becomes erratic, destructive, and classified as mentally retarded. The head of the school interviews the child. C-A,
Prof

1341 SWEDES IN AMERICA
16 min., b&w, 1943.
Producer: Office of War Information. Narrator: Ingrid
Bergman. Distributor: National Audiovisual Center.
The lives and contributions of Swedes in America,
particularly the Swedish American families in Minnesota.
Features Carl Sandburg. S-A

1342   SWEET DREAMS see
       MY LIFE IN ART 990

1343   SYLVIA, FRAN AND JOY
       25 min. , b&w, 1973.
       Director: Joan Churchill. Distributor: Churchill Films.
          Compares the life-style choices of three young
       women: one discontented mother who chooses to work while
       her unemployed husband assumes child-care duties; one
       contented mother/housewife who is fulfilled in a traditional
       role; and a young woman who is separated from her hus-
       band and seeking her identity in pleasing hobbies and work.
       Red Ribbon, American Film Festival. S-J

1344   TAKING CARE OF BUSINESS
       14½ min. , color, 1974.
       Producer: KETC-TV, St. Louis. Distributor: Agency for
       Instructional TV.
          David starts mowing lawns to earn extra money and
       as a result neglects his home responsibilities. From the
       Bread & Butterflies series. I-J

1345   TAKING MEASURE
       15 min. , color, 1976.
       Producer: Orsatti Productions. Distributor: Educational
       Film Systems.
          A young girl and her family learn how to use metrics
       in everyday life. Animation. From the Meter Park series.
       E

1346   A TALE OF TODAY
       10 min. , color, 1972.
       Directors: Fred Gebauer & Phyllis Gebauer. Distributor:
       Mass Media Ministries.
          A husband/wife team made this film to promote
       their life-style on a rural commune. S-A

1347   TALENT FOR TONY
       13 min. , color, 1971.
       Director: Bruce Baker. Distributor: TeleKETICS.
          An artist tries to get his children preoccupied with
       paper and crayons, as he prepares his work for an exhibit.
       E

1348   TALKING ABOUT BREASTFEEDING
       17 min. , color, 1972.
       Director: Alvin Fiering. Distributor: Polymorph Films.
          Some nursing mothers who have overcome medical
       problems and social pressures to breastfeed talk about their
       experiences. A

1349   TALKING TOGETHER
       20 min. , b&w, 1967.

Producer: Bank Street College of Education, Dept. of
Communications for the Office of Economic Opportunity.
Distributor: National Audiovisual Center.
Discussion between parents and teachers highlights
why their exchange of ideas is essential to their children's
development.   C-A, Prof

1350   THE TAP DANCE KID
30 min. & 50 min., color, 1978.
Director: Barra Grant. Cast: Claudia McNeil, Charles
Honi Coles, Danielle Spencer, James Pelham. Distributor:
Learning Corp. of America.
A young black boy dreams of becoming a tap dancer
like his uncle, but his parents have other plans for him.
His sister, who wants to be a lawyer, defends her broth-
er's right to choose. A TV Special Treat; from the Learn-
ing to Be Human series.   J-A

1351   TAPESTRY OF FAITH
2 min., color, 1976.
Director: Donald McDonald. Distributor: TeleKETICS.
A handicapped child watches his grandmother make
a tapestry for him. When he runs his fingers over the
stitches, he learns what true beauty really is. From the
Meetings with God/Storyscape series.   I-A

1352   TEACHERS, PARENTS AND CHILDREN
17 min., color, 1974.
Producer: Davidson Films. Distributor: Davidson Films.
Explains how alliances between families and teachers ease a child's entrance into school and support and
encourage his growth. Importance of link between home
and school stressed. From the Early Childhood Development series.   C-A

1353   THE TEACHING TRIAD
19 min., color, 1973.
Producer: Dubnoff Center for Child Development and Educational Therapy. Distributor: AIMS Instructional Media
Services.
A positive teaching triad (teacher-child-parent) is
depicted. The teacher provides individual attention to
meet the needs of the family, i.e., home visits, parent
meetings, etc.   C-A, Prof

1354   TEENAGE FATHER
30 min., color, 1978.
Director: Taylor Hackford. Distributor: Children's Home
Society of California.
A 17-year-old boy and his 15-year-old girlfriend expect a baby. After hearing contrary opinions from their
families and being advised by a social worker, they have the
baby. But the girl refuses to see her boyfriend; she wants

to raise the baby alone. Dramatic film based on case histories. Red Ribbon, American Film Festival. S-A

From Teenage Mother: A Broken Dream. Courtesy.
Carousel Films.

1355 TEENAGE MOTHER: A BROKEN DREAM
15 min., color, 1977.
Producer: Mary Drayne for CBS-TV News. Distributor:
Carousel Films.
A 15-year-old Grand Rapids, Mich., girl is an unwed teenage mother. Her boyfriend wouldn't marry her, so the baby was put in a foster home and she's in a detention home trying to finish her education so she can get a job. J-A

1356 THE TEENAGE YEARS SERIES see
THE BRIDGE OF ADAM RUSH 195
THE ESCAPE OF A ONE-TON PET 427
FOLLOW THE NORTH STAR 523
GAUCHO 559
HOME TO STAY 661
ME AND DAD'S NEW WIFE 907
MIGHTY MOOSE AND THE QUARTERBACK KID 926
MOM AND DAD CAN'T HEAR ME 944
MY MOM'S HAVING A BABY 992
P.J. AND THE PRESIDENT'S SON 1075
ROOKIE OF THE YEAR 1213
SARA'S SUMMER OF THE SWANS 1233
THE SECRET LIFE OF T. K. DEARING 1246
TELL ME MY NAME 1358

1357 TELESPOTS SERIES see
A BOY'S MAN 187

CAN I TALK TO YOU, DAD?   213
FEET ARE FOR WALKING   496
I HATE ELEVATORS   689
THE KISS   791
LIKE FATHER, LIKE SON   828
LISTEN, LADY   834
LISTEN, MAN   835
LOVE IS A SURPRISE   858
LULLABY: ANOTHER DAY   867
RESTRICTED NEIGHBORHOOD   1197
SAY YES TO LOVE   1236
SIGNS OF LIFE   1276
SLEEPY WORLD   1289
WAR GAMES   1457
THE WEDDING   1473

1358   TELL ME MY NAME
52 min. , color, 1978.
Director: Delbert Mann.   Cast: Barbara Barrie, Barnard Hughes, Arthur Hill.   Distributor: Time-Life Multimedia.
A 19-year-old adoptee tracks down her natural mother and is not ready for the rejection she receives from the horrified woman.   The girl upsets both her adopted family and her natural mother's family in the process of coming to terms with her identity.   From the Teenage Years series.   S-A

1359   THE TENEMENT
40 min. , b&w, 1967.
Producer: Jay I. McMullen for CBS-TV News.   Distributors: Carousel Films; Twyman Films (rental only).
Several black families from the tenements of South Chicago are profiled.   There are mothers raising eight to ten children alone with no husbands; the children bear the responsibilities of adults, and hopelessness is the norm. S-A

1360   TENNIS MOTHERS
14 min. , color, 1975.
Producer: Phyllis Bosworth for CBS-TV News.   Distributor: Carousel Films.
The mother of a 12-year-old Staten Island, N. Y. , tennis player is determined to mold her daughter into the next Chris Evert.   The mother devotes her life to the daughter's tennis lessons, tournaments, and practice sessions, but the girl shows the wear and tear of this pressure to succeed.   J-A

1361   TESTAMENT
20 min. , color, 1974.
Director: James Broughton.   Distributors: Serious Business Company; Canyon Cinema Cooperative; Film-Makers' Cooperative.

Sensual, poetic memories of a Victorian childhood spent in San Francisco that may or may not resemble the filmmaker's childhood.   C-A

1362   THAT GREAT FEELING
19 min., color, p. 1976, r. 1977.
Director: Mario Pellegrini. Distributor: United Way of America.
A family faces contemporary problems; shows how United Way agencies can help them deal with those problems.   A

1363   THAT'S OUR BABY
23 min., color, 1975.
Directors: Carrie Aginsky & Yasha Aginsky. Distributors: Serious Business Company; Lawren Productions.
Emphasizes that childbirth can be a natural and rewarding, fear-free event if parents are properly prepared and educated. Carrie Aginsky is the expectant mother and focus of the film. A Lamaze birth is witnessed.   A

1364   THE THEFT
27 min., color, 1974.
Director: Arthur Hiller for Paulist Productions. Cast: Larry Pressman, Sharon Farrell, Lou Antonio. Distributor: The Media Guild.
A suburban couple struggle for a more open and trusting relationship. They fight constantly and are finally reconciled by a thief who gives them advice as he makes off with their valuables. From the Insight series. S-A

1365   THEIR SPECIAL NEEDS
18 min., color, 1976.
Producer: ACTION, Washington, D.C. Distributor: Association Films.
Documents ACTION's foster-grandparent program, which puts older Americans to work with neglected young people who need them--the physically disabled, mentally retarded, emotionally disturbed, etc. A

1366   THEY'RE ATTACKING MY TREE FORT
18 min., color, 1972.
Producer: John H. Secondari Productions. Distributor: Xerox Films.
Brad and Dale Lambert discover that their father's lumber company has doomed their fantastic tree fort.
From the Come Over to My House series. E-I

1367   THIGH LINE LYRE TRIANGULAR
7 min., color, sil., 1961.
Director: Stan Brakhage. Distributors: Brakhage Films; Audio Brandon Films (rental only); Canyon Cinema Cooperative; Film-Makers' Cooperative.
The birth of the filmmaker's second child. C-A

From That's Our Baby. Courtesy Serious Business Company.

1368   THE THIN EDGE SERIES   see
       SEXUALITY: THE HUMAN HERITAGE   1263

1369   THINGS ARE DIFFERENT NOW
       15 min., color, 1978.
       Director: Mike Rhodes for Paulist Productions.   Cast:
       Troy Goudlock, Joel Fluellen.   Distributor: The Media
       Guild.
           A black teenager is full of anger over his parents'
       divorce.   He blames his mother, refuses to talk with his
       father, and gives his friends a hard time.   From the
       Bloomin' Human series.   J-S

1370   THINGS, IDEAS, PEOPLE
       14½ min., color, 1974.
       Producer: WNVT-TV.   Distributor: Agency for Instruc-
       tional TV.
           Three children think their father has lost his job, so
       they make lists of job possibilities.   From the Bread &
       Butterflies series.   I-J

1371   THIRD GENERATION
       6½ min., b&w, 1973.
       Director: Ian Connor.   Distributor: Perspective Films.
           Impressionistic study of events preceding a baby's
       birth in a country house.   S-C

1372   THIRDSTRING
       15 min., color, 1972.
       Producer: USC, Dept. of Cinema.   Distributor: University
       of Southern California.
           A boy suffers under a domineering mother and sister.
       He tries to escape into a fantasy life, but his sister is de-
       termined to stop that, too.

1373   THE 30-SECOND DREAM
       15 min., color, 1977.
       Directors: Terry Brandon & M. Lawrence.   Distributor:
       Mass Media Ministries.
           Montage of TV commercials that shows how TV ad-
       vertisers manipulate viewers into buying their products.
       Four selling techniques are highlighted: success, vitality,
       intimacy, and problem-free families.   J-A

1374   THIS CHILD IS RATED X
       53 min., color, 1971.
       Producer: Martin Carr for NBC-TV News.   Narrator: Ed-
       win Newman.   Distributor: Films Inc.
           Studies abuse of children's rights and inequities of
       juvenile justice.   Focuses on two types of children--the
       child who commits a child's crime (truancy); and the child
       who commits a serious crime (robbery or mugging).   Both
       are usually incarcerated in the same facilities, thereby ex-

posing runaways and truants to hardened criminals.   Emmy·
Award.   Peabody Award.   J-A

1375   THIS IS IT
10 min. , color, 1971.
Director: James Broughton.   Distributors: Serious Business Company; Canyon Cinema Cooperative; Film-Makers'
Cooperative.
Features the filmmaker's 4-year-old son Orion, who
plays while a Zen poem is read by the filmmaker in voice
over.   S-A

1376   THIS IS THE HOME OF MRS. LEVANT GRAHAM
15 min. , b&w, 1971.
Producers: Topper Carew, Eliot Noyes, Jr. , & Claudia
Weill.   Distributor: Pyramid Films.
An urban black mother with her family in cramped
Washington, D.C. , housing.   There are too many people
and children under one roof, unemployment, and drinking
problems.   C-A

1377   THIS ONE FOR DAD
18 min. , color, 1978.
Director: Mike Rhodes for Paulist Productions.   Cast:
Dick Van Patten, Johnny Whitaker.   Distributor: Southerby
Productions.
A boy cuts himself off from all emotion when his
father dies.   When he finishes the cross-country race his
father wanted him to win, he is able to cry and reach out
to others.   From the Reflections series.   J-S

1378   THE THORNE FAMILY FILM
80 min. , color, 1977.
Producer: David Milholland.   Distributor: Center for Urban Education.
Documentary portrait of an Oregon family--the
Thornes--who homesteaded near Pendleton, Ore. , in the
1800s.   Today, approximately 100 of the 300-member clan
still live near this same town.   Covers the history of Pendleton and family traditions, loss of rural ties, and struggle to maintain family ties.   S-A

1379   THORNTON WILDER
30 min. , b&w, 1967.
Director: Harold Mantell.   Distributors: Films for the
Humanities; Indiana University, Audio-Visual Center.
Biography of the man who wrote Our Town.   Includes
interviews with his brother and sisters, family photos, and
family background.   S-A

1380   THOSE MAIL ORDER MILLIONS see
THE CONSUMER FRAUD SERIES 312

1381   THOSE WHO MOURN
        5 min., color, 1971.
        Director: Tony Frangakis. Distributor: TeleKETICS.
        A young widow struggles with grief and memories,
        as she tries to deal with the killing of her husband in a
        campus disturbance. S-A

1382   THOSE WHO STAY BEHIND
        16 min., color, 1969.
        Producer: Social and Rehabilitation Service, Dept. of
        Health, Education & Welfare. Distributor: National Audio-
        visual Center.
        The hardships of isolated, disadvantaged rural fami-
        lies. Focuses on the special problems of one family with
        an afflicted child. C-A

1383   THOUGH I WALK THROUGH THE VALLEY
        30 min., color, 1972.
        Director: Mel White. Distributors: Pyramid Films; Mass
        Media Ministries (rental only).
        The last six months of terminal cancer patient Tony
        Brouwer's life. A relatively young father, he shows how
        he and his family face the stages of death and dying realis-
        tically, yet with hope. Silver Medal, Atlanta Film Festival.
        Film Award, National Council on Family Relations. CINE
        Golden Eagle. Best Documentary of the Year, National
        Evangelical Film Foundation. S-A

1384   THREE FILMS
        7 min., color, sil., 1965.
        Director: Stan Brakhage. Distributors: Brakhage Films;
        Film-Makers' Cooperative; Canyon Cinema Cooperative.
        Birth, nursing, infant masturbation. Experimental
        cinema. C-A

1385   THREE STYLES OF MARITAL CONFLICT
        14 min., color, 1976.
        Directors: Phil Stockton & Dr. John Gottman. Distribu-
        tors: Research Press; Behavioral Images.
        Dramatized vignettes portray couples who display
        three common styles of dysfunctional marital conflict: the
        "passive partner," "overadequate/underadequate," and the
        "hidden agenda." Notes how to clinically observe and
        analyze both verbal and non-verbal marital behavior. Train-
        ing film. C, Prof

1386   THREE'S A CROWD
        13 min., color, 1976.
        Producer: Marion Goldin for CBS-TV News. Distributor:
        Time-Life Multimedia.
        Interviews with several couples who explain why they
        don't want children. From the TV series 60 Minutes. S-A

1387 TILLIE'S PHILODENDRON
7 min., color, 1977.
Director: Mitchell Rose. Distributor: Encyclopaedia
Britannica Educational Corp.
A neglected wife plays a flute to ease her pain.
Her philodendron even enjoys the music. After her husband
leaves her, the woman and the plant thrive. When she
grows old and dies, the plant dies too, but sprouts again
in the spring. Animation. I-A

1388 A TIME FOR DECISION
30 min., color, 1967.
Producer: Don Hoster. Distributors: AIMS Instructional
Media Services; Image Associates; FMS Productions.
Dramatizes the effect on a family if a family mem-
ber is a compulsive drinker. Outside help is recommended.
Avail. in Spanish. S-A

1389 THE TIME HAS COME
22 min., color, 1977.
Director: Jamil Simon. Distributor: Third Eye Films.
Explores a non-sexist approach to child rearing,
with a look at sex-role stereotyping and ways for parents
to expand options for their children. C-A

1390 TIME STRUCTURES see
LEARNING TO LIVE SERIES 810

1391 A TIME TO BE BORN
30 min., color, 1977.
Director: William E. Cohen for BioMed Arts. Distributor: Read Natural Childbirth Foundation.
The labor and birth of a couple's first child. It's
a hospital delivery in which the woman is supported by
her husband, a physician, labor coach, and nurse. S-A

1392 TIME'S LOST CHILDREN
29 min., color, 1973.
Director: Ronald Martin for KPBS-TV, San Diego. Distributor: Indiana University, Audio-Visual Center.
Parents of autistic children discuss their kids: how
they seemed normal until age two or three and then seemed
unable to relate to reality. Shows work with autistic children at San Diego's Los Niños Remedial Center. C-A,
Prof.

1393 TO A BABYSITTER (2nd Edition)
16½ min., color, 1974.
Producer: Alfred Higgins Productions, with the Los Angeles County Medical Assoc. & the American National Red
Cross. Distributor: Alfred Higgins Productions.
A responsible young babysitter is followed through
an evening on the job. Safety precautions are noted. J-A

1394   TO ALL THE WORLD'S CHILDREN
        12 min. , color, 1970.
        Producer: ABC-TV. Distributor: Xerox Films.
        Set on a northern Arizona Navajo reservation,
        where the children and their families preserve their tradi-
        tional culture while also adapting to contemporary American
        life. Christopher Award. E-S

1395   TO BE A FAMILY
        20 min. , color, 1977.
        Directors: John Leveque & Alan Oddie. Distributor: Tele-
        KETICS.
        A discussion leader guides parents and children
        through preparations for First Communion. Vignettes high-
        light what it means to experience community within the im-
        mediate family and its circle of friends. From the Story-
        scape series. E-A

1396   TO BE A MAN
        58 min. , color, p. 1977, r. 1978.
        Director: Christian Blackwood. Distributors: Blackwood
        Productions; Perspective Films (43 min. version).
        Charts roles and attitudes of American men from
        frontier days through contemporary society. Dr. Spock
        talks about his strict upbringing. A New Jersey couple,
        who are recently divorced, try to cope with the factors that
        caused their split. Dr. Lee Salk covers single fatherhood.
        S-A

1397   TO BE A PARENT
        16 min. , color, 1972.
        Director: Frank Moynihan. Distributor: Billy Budd Films.
        Young people consider aspects of parenting. From
        the Circle of Life series. J-S, A

1398   TO BE GROWING OLDER
        15½ min. , color, 1973.
        Director: Frank Moynihan. Distributor: Billy Budd Films.
        Aims to sensitize young people to the problems of
        the elderly. From the Circle of Life series. CINE Golden
        Eagle. S

1399   TO BE MARRIED
        14½ min. , color, 1971.
        Director: Frank Moynihan. Distributor: Billy Budd Films.
        Marriage and communication, signs of affection, di-
        vorce, building together, the wedding day, living together,
        friendship. From the Circle of Life series. S

1400   TO LIFE, WITH LOVE
        13½ min. , color, 1972.
        Sponsor: American Council of Life Insurance. Distributor:
        Association Films.

A young couple learn about the important role that personal financial security, reinforced by life insurance, can play in strengthening their life together. J-C

1401 TO LIVE AGAIN SERIES see
WHERE THERE'S A WILL 1508

1402 TO LIVE AS EQUALS
28 min., color, 1978.
Producer: Lois Goodkind. Distributor: Lodon Films.
Programs and community-support services for mentally retarded citizens of New Jersey. Briefly touches on two retarded parents attempting to raise their healthy baby, and on the parents of retarded individuals. First Prize, International Rehabilitation Film Festival. A

1403 TO NOURISH A CHILD: NUTRITION FROM NEWBORN THROUGH TEENS
20 min., color, 1977.
Director: Ed Schultz. Distributor: Tupperware Home Parties.
The nutritional needs of a child, from prenatal through adolescence, with emphasis on emotional aspects of foods. A

1404 TODD--GROWING UP IN APPALACHIA
12 min., color, 1970.
Director: Herman Engel. Distributor: Learning Corp. of America.
Todd's family barely gets by because his father is an illiterate and unemployed ex-miner who was forced out of work by illness. But when Todd finds food stamps, he returns them because their owner may need them more than his family. From The Many Americans series. E-J, A

1405 TODDLER MANAGEMENT
19 min., color, 1973.
Producer: Airlie Foundation for Bureau of Education for the Handicapped, Dept. of Health, Education & Welfare.
Distributor: National Audiovisual Center.
Shows how mothers are taught to modify unacceptable behavior in their preschool children through a program run entirely by non-professional mothers. From the Regional Intervention Program series. C-A

1406 TOGETHER SWEETLY
15 min., color, 1973.
Directors: Bobbi Ausubel & Alvin Fiering. Distributor: Polymorph Films.
Short version of a filmed play (HOW TO MAKE A WOMAN, 58 min., color, 1972), which depicts a wife giving up her identity to please and serve her husband. Feminist point of view. S-A

1407   TOMMY'S FIRST CAR
11 min. , color, 1972.
Producer: Dan Bessie for Learning Garden.   Distributor:
FilmFair Communications.
Father and son search for a car for the boy.
Father shows son what to look for before buying a used car.
Red Ribbon, American Film Festival.   J-A

1408   TOMORROW WE'LL SEE WHAT HAPPENS
30 min. , b&w, 1973.
Director: William C. Jersey for the Ford Foundation.
Distributor: Films Inc.
Los Angeles teachers, students, administrators, and
parents are involved in a broad collaborative effort to im-
prove their schools.   C-A, Prof

1409   TOMORROW'S CHILDREN
54 min. , b&w, 1934.
Producer: Bryan Foy, Jr.   Distributor: Kit Parker Films
(rental only).
A young woman wants to be married, but some "do-
gooders" want her sterilized because her family are dere-
licts.   An early exploitation drama.   C-A

1410   TOO MANY PEOPLE
8 min. , color, 1973.
Producer: Gordon-Kerckhoff Productions.   Distributor:
Paramount Communications.
Overpopulation problems, in terms a child can understand.   From the Community Life: Caring About Our Community series.   E-I

1411   TRANSACTIONAL ANALYSIS: A DEMONSTRATION WITH
ELAINE
33 min. , color, 1973.
Producer: Dr. John Whiteley.   Distributor: American
Personnel and Guidance Association.
Emily Ruppert demonstrates TA with a young woman
who is engaging in self-defeating behavior: there is a
struggle between Elaine's "critical parent" and "natural
child. "   Training film.   C, Prof

1412   TRANSACTIONAL ANALYSIS: A DEMONSTRATION WITH
PAT
36 min. , color, 1973.
Producer: Dr. John Whiteley.   Distributor: American
Personnel and Guidance Association.
Emily Ruppert demonstrates the TA concept of the
"victim-persecutor-rescuer triangle" with a client who has
a marital problem.   They analyze the game Pat plays with
his wife.   Training film.   C, Prof

1413   TRANSACTIONAL ANALYSIS SERIES   see
MEET YOUR PARENT, ADULT, CHILD   914
WE'RE OK (A FILM ABOUT TRANSACTIONAL ANALY-
SIS)   1485

1414   TRANSACTIONS   see
LEARNING TO LIVE SERIES   810

1415   THE TRAP OF SOLID GOLD
51 min. , b&w, 1969.
Director: Paul Bogart.   Cast: Cliff Robertson, Dina
Merrill, Dustin Hoffman, Conrad Nagel, Ruth White, James
Broderick.   Distributor: International Film Bureau.
A young executive and his family live beyond their
means in a fashionable suburb.   S-A

1416   TRAVELIN' SHOES
15 min. , color, 1973.
Producer: ENVT-TV.   Distributor: Agency for Instructional TV.
A boy's family has mixed feelings about a move
from the country to Washington, D. C.   From the Inside/
Out series.   I

1417   THE TREASURE: INDIAN HERITAGE
13 min. , color, 1970.
Producer: King Screen Productions.   Distributor: BFA Educational Media.
Against their father's wishes, two teenage Indian
brothers trade Indian artifacts for a machine-made canoe.
When their father is arrested for defending tribal fishing
rights, the boys begin to see the value of their heritage.
I-A

1418   TRILOGY SERIES   see
YOU   1558

1419   TROLLSTENEN
125 min. , color, 1976.
Director: Gunvor Nelson.   Distributor: Serious Business
Company.
The filmmaker's family (six brothers and sisters)
reexamine their Swedish upbringing.   With old photos, home
movies, Swedish landscape, and live-action.   C-A

1420   TROUBLE IN THE FAMILY
90 min. , b&w, 1965.
Directors: Harold Mayer & Edmund Levy.   Distributor:
Indiana University, Audio-Visual Center.
A middle-class New England family enter into family
therapy because their bright 15-year-old son is doing poorly
in school.   Includes scenes from nine of 13 therapy sessions
with therapist Dr. Norman L. Paul.   C-A, Prof

From Trollstenen (Photo by Mats Holmstrand).   Courtesy
Serious Business Company.

1421   TROUBLE ON MY PAPER ROUTE
       17 min. , color, 1973.
       Producer: John H. Secondari Productions.   Distributor:
       Xerox Films.
             A 12-year-old Polish American boy in Detroit takes
       over his older brother's paper route, and is harassed by a
       street gang who ridicule his ethnic heritage and threaten
       to steal his money.   From the Come Over to My House
       series.   E-I

1422   THE TROUBLE WITH HUSBANDS
       10 min. , b&w, 1940.
       Director: Leslie Rauch.   Cast: Ruth Lee, Robert Bench-
       ley.   Distributor: Audio Brandon Films (rental only).
             Comic short involving cliché husband/wife quarrels.
       C-A

1423   THE TRYING TIME
       20 min. , color, 1973.
       Director: Dick Gilbert for Planned Parenthood Center,
       Seattle.   Distributor: Perennial Education.
             Young teens at play and work, while parents' voice-
       over recalls their own anxieties while growing up.   A

1424   TWINS
       7 min. , color, p. 1974, r. 1975.
       Director: Barrie Nelson.   Distributor: Learning Corp. of
       America.

A pair of twins--same mother, same home environment--are as different as night and day in personality and career choices. Although both become successful, they both end up searching for new values. Animation. S-A

1425 TWO CHILDREN: CONTRASTING ASPECTS OF PERSON-
ALITY DEVELOPMENT
20 min., b&w, sil., 1943.
Producers: Margaret E. Fries, M.D. & Paul J. Woolf,
M.S. Distributor: New York University.
Differences in constitution of two newborns result
in different responses to stimuli, influencing child-parent
relationships, ego development, defense mechanisms, etc.
From the Studies on Integrated Development: Interaction
Between Child and Environment series. C, Prof

1426 TWO FAMILIES: AFRICAN AND AMERICAN
22 min., color, 1974.
Producers: John H. Secondari & Helen Jean Rogers. Distributor: Learning Corp. of America.
Cross-cultural comparison of an interdependent African tribal family and an independent contemporary New York
City family. From the Comparative Cultures and Geography series. E-S

1427 TWO FARMS: HUNGARY AND WISCONSIN
22 min., color, 1973.
Producers: John H. Secondari & Helen Jean Rogers. Distributor: Learning Corp. of America.
Cross-cultural comparison of an independent Wisconsin farm family and a collective farm family in southeastern
Hungary. From the Comparative Cultures and Geography
series. E-S

1428 TWO SONS
14½ min., color, 1975.
Director: John Allman for KETC-TV. Distributor: Agency
for Instructional TV.
Greg's parents have unconsciously molded him into a
"bad boy" and his brother into a "good boy." Open-ended.
From the Self Incorporated series. J

1429 TWO WORLDS TO REMEMBER
38 min., color, 1970.
Director: Phyllis Chinlund. Distributor: Phoenix Films.
Two elderly ladies adjust to a new life in the Jewish
Home and Hospital for the Aged in New York. One is a
longtime widow; the other is an elderly divorcée. The
transformation is painful for them and their families. S-A

1430 UNCLE BEN
27 min., color, 1978.
Director: David K. Jacobs. Distributor: Brigham Young
University.

An alcoholic takes on the responsibility of his sister's orphaned children. Through great perseverance, he succeeds in overcoming his alcoholism and becomes a father to the children.   J-A

1431   UNCLE MONTY'S GONE
14 min., color, p. 1976, r. 1977.
Directors: D. Towsley, R. Larriva, L. Zucker, & M. Lamore. Distributor: McGraw-Hill Films.
A young girl must learn to deal with the death of a loved one. Animation. From the Learning Values with Fat Albert and the Cosby Kids series.   E

1432   UNCOMMON IMAGES: THE HARLEM OF JAMES VAN DERZEE
22 min., color & b&w, 1977.
Producer: Evelyn Barron for WNBC-TV. Distributor: Filmakers Library.
Black photographer James Van DerZee recorded thousands of family rituals (weddings and funerals) in Harlem over the years. His photographs are now valuable historic documents. Here, at 90, he fondly recalls his career, family, and especially his life with his beloved wife. CINE Golden Eagle. Silver Plaque, Chicago International Film Festival.   S-A

1433   UNDER THE LAW, SERIES 1   see
MUGGERS! 975

1434   UNDERSTANDING HIS ILLNESS   see
THE STROKE PATIENT COMES HOME SERIES   1328

1435   UNDERSTANDING HIS PROBLEMS   see
THE STROKE PATIENT COMES HOME SERIES   1328

1436   UNDERSTANDING LABOR AND DELIVERY
18 min., color, 1978.
Director: Dan Lundmark. Distributor: Film & Video Service.
What to expect during labor, hospital admittance, and delivery.   A

1437   AN UNFINISHED STORY
$13\frac{1}{2}$ min., b&w, 1975.
Sponsor: Association for the Study of Abortion, Inc. Distributor: Association Films.
A young mother considers an illegal abortion when she becomes pregnant with her fourth child. She feels another child would threaten her family's future. Dramatic film.   C-A

1438   A UNICORN IN THE GARDEN
7 min., color, 1969.

Director: William T. Hurtz. Story: James Thurber.
Distributor: Learning Corp. of America. A husband sees a unicorn. His bossy wife does not, and thinks her husband is crazy. She tries to have him committed, with surprising results. Animation. E-A

1439 UNWED MOTHERS IN TODAY'S WORLD
29 min. , color, 1970.
Producer: Lawrence A. Williams. Distributor: Lawren Productions.
Four young women informally discuss with a counselor their experiences as unwed mothers. One girl is keeping her baby, one is giving hers up for adoption, the other two are undecided. Emphasizes need for sensitive counseling and sound prenatal care. Kinescope. S-A

1440 USING MONEY WISELY
18 min. , color, 1971.
Producer: Gilbert Altschul Productions. Distributor: Journal Films.
Ron Webster, a professional money-management counselor, introduces three typical families with money problems to solutions to their money management difficulties. S-A

1441 THE VALENTINE LANE FAMILY PRACTICE: A TEAM APPROACH TO HEALTH CARE
29 min. , color, 1977.
Producer: Philip S. Hobel. Distributor: Document Associates.
The Valentine Lane Family Practice--an affiliate of Montefiore Hospital and Medical Center in White Plains, N. Y. --provides primary health care that emphasizes treatment for the whole family, as well as comprehensive individual care. The team of professionals are shown in action. A

1442 VALUES FOR GRADES K-3 SERIES see
LOST PUPPY 853

1443 THE VANISHING MOMMY
25 min. , color, 1977.
Director: Dennis Goulden for WKYC-TV. Distributor: Films Inc.
Working mothers discuss their relationships with their children and husbands and their ability to fulfill the roles of mother in the home and worker outside the home. S-A

1444 VASECTOMY
17 min. , color, 1972.
Director: Robert Churchill. Distributor: Churchill Films.
Interviews with men and their wives tell of reasons

for having a vasectomy.   With animated explanation of the surgery.   C-A

1445   VASSAR STUDIES OF NORMAL PERSONALITY DEVELOP-
MENT SERIES   see
   ABBY'S FIRST TWO YEARS: A BACKWARD LOOK   6
   ... AND THEN ICE CREAM   84
   STARTING NURSERY SCHOOL: PATTERNS OF BEGIN-
   NING   1314

1446   VERY GOOD FRIENDS
29 min. , color, 1977.
Director: Richard Bennett.   Distributor: Learning Corp.
of America.
   13-year-old Kate must learn to cope with the acci-
dental death of her vibrant 11-year-old sister Joss.   An
ABC Afterschool Special; from the Learning to Be Human
series.   Gold Hugo, Chicago International Film Festival.
J-A

1447   VICTOR
25 min. , color, 1975.
Producers: Marion Krueger & Chris Krueger.   Distributor: Shadowstone Films.
   Victor, age 12, overcomes his special learning
problems enough to begin to experience some success.   His
teachers and parents worry about what will happen when
he enters Junior High, where there are no special-educa-
tion programs.   Narrated by his parents.   C-A, Prof

1448   VIGNETTE SERIES   see
   BEING REAL   143
   DIFFERENT WITH DIGNITY   375
   KINSHIPS   789
   RAPPORT   1173
   WALLS AND WINDOWS   1457

1449   VIGNETTES (GIRLS AT 12)
15 min. , color, 1975.
Director: Joyce Chopra.   Distributor: Education Development Center.
   Interviews with the five adult women who appeared
in the film GIRLS AT 12 (574).   Each are into different
roles and stages of life.   From the Role of Women in
American Society series.   S

1450   A VISIT TO INDIANA
10 min. , color, 1970.
Director: Curt McDowell.   Distributor: Canyon Cinema
Cooperative.
   Parody of a Midwestern family reunion.   Originally
shot in 8mm.   S-A

1451   VOICES FROM WITHIN
        20 min., color, p. 1977, r. 1978.
        Directors: Steven Fischler & Joel Sucher. Producer:
        Long-Termers Committee. Distributor: Pacific Street
        Film Collective.
            A group of women at the Bedford Hills Correctional
        Facility--the Long-Termers Committee, composed of
        women serving sentences of four years to life--speak out
        for benefits for long-termers. They want more contact
        with their parents and children. C-A, Prof

1452   WAIT UNTIL YOUR FATHER GETS HOME!
        11 min., color, 1971.
        Director: Kent Mackenzie for Dimension Films. Distri-
        butors: Churchill Films; TeleKETICS.
            Part of a six-day encounter session in which a
        group of young people discuss feelings, problems, male vs.
        female roles, and questions concerning family. From The
        Searching Years: The Family series. J-A

1453   WAITING FOR BABY
        10 min., b&w, 1941.
        Director: Leslie Rauch. Cast: Robert Benchley, Ruth
        Lee. Distributor: Audio Brandon Films (rental only).
            A nervous husband awaits the delivery of Junior with
        much trepidation. Comic short. C-A

1454   WALK A COUNTRY MILE
        28 min., color, 1975.
        Producer: N.J. Public Broadcasting Authority. Distribu-
        tor: Indiana University, Audio-Visual Center.
            The life-styles and difficulties of poor rural residents
        of New Jersey. S-A

1455   WALK IN THEIR SHOES
        24 min., color, 1968.
        Directors: Richard Neil Evans & Scott Whitaker. Distri-
        butor: Brigham Young University.
            A boy and his younger sister resent their parents'
        interference in their social lives, until the boy is forced to
        assume responsibility for his sister. He then understands
        why his parents act as they do. Avail. in Spanish. J-S

1456   WALKIN'S TOO SLOW: A FILM ABOUT RUNAWAYS
        26 min., color, p. 1976, r. 1977.
        Producer: Bill Pace. Distributor: Bandanna Media.
            Documentary about six American runaway teenagers,
        their reasons for running away, and their experiences in
        crisis centers, juvenile courts, youth homes, and on the
        streets. J-A

1457   WALLS AND WINDOWS
        12 min., color, 1973.

Producer: Mike Rhodes for Paulist Productions. Distributor: The Media Guild.
Dramatic vignettes highlight communication problems between teenagers and their parents. From the Vignette series. J-A

1458   WAR GAMES
60 sec., color, 1967.
Director: Bruce Baker. Distributor: TeleKETICS.
Children overhear their parents fighting. Dramatic vignette, from the TeleSPOTS series. E-A

1459   THE WAR OF THE EGGS
27 min., color, 1971.
Director: Lamont Johnson for Paulist Productions. Cast: Elizabeth Ashley, Bill Bixby, James Olson. Distributor: The Media Guild.
During a marital squabble, the wife pushes her tiny son down the stairs and hurts him badly. The couple claim it was an accident, but a psychiatrist breaks through their defenses to the truth. From the Insight series. National Council on Family Relations Award. S-A

1460   WASHINGTON SQUARE
20 min., b&w, 1953.
Director: William Wyler. Cast: Olivia de Havilland, Montgomery Clift. Distributor: Indiana University, Audio-Visual Center.
A shy, awkward girl is swept off her feet by a fortune hunter, to the dismay of her obnoxious father. Excerpt from the 1949 film THE HEIRESS (1767). S-C

1461   WATCH
12 min., color, 1974.
Producer: Northwestern, Incorporated. Distributor: Encyclopaedia Britannica Educational Corp.
A bored young boy who is home alone invites a friend over. The visitor accidentally breaks a family heirloom, but when the mother returns home, her son is caught holding the broken heirloom. Open-ended. I

1462   WATERGROUND
16 min., color, 1977.
Director: Frances Morton. Distributor: Appalshop Films.
Five generations of one North Carolina family have operated a water-powered gristmill, over a span of 100 years. Today, Walter Winebarger operates the mill. He reflects on the once-great demand for Winebarger Mill's services, his contentment with his life-style, and the clientele he serves today. J-A

1463   WATERMEN
53 min., color, 1972.

Directors: Romas V. Slezas & Holly Fisher. Distributor: Odeon Films. Three generations of fishermen on Chesapeake Bay. C-A

1464 THE WAY HOME
15 min. & 23 min. , color, 1976.
Director: Nicholas Frangakis. Distributor: TeleKETICS.
A rebellious, estranged son returns home and is forgiven by all but his elder brother, who feels cheated because he stayed home like a good boy and worked hard for the family business. The longer version of the film includes a discussion facilitator. From the Storyscape series. J-A

1465 THE WAY WE LIVE
$14\frac{1}{2}$ min. , color, 1974.
Directors: Louise Henry & Michael Switzer for WNVT-TV.
Distributor: Agency for Instructional TV.
Documents the values that shape the lives of a West Virginia family: attitudes toward work, home life, and leisure time. From the Bread & Butterflies series. I-J

1466 WE CAN HELP SERIES see
ABUSIVE PARENTS 10
THE INTERVIEW 737
INVESTIGATING CASES OF CHILD ABUSE AND NEGLECT 741
THE MEDICAL WITNESS 912
PRESENTING THE CASE 1141
SEXUAL ABUSE: THE FAMILY 1262
WORKING TOGETHER 1549

1467 WE DO, WE DO
11 min. , color, 1970.
Director: Bruce Baker. Distributor: TeleKETICS.
A teenage couple about to be married are barraged with aspects of life that threaten a successful marriage, e.g. , money problems, children, in-laws, careers. S-A

1468 WE GET MARRIED TWICE
22 min. , color, 1973.
Director: Miriam Weinstein. Distributors: Serious Business Company; Miriam Weinstein.
The filmmaker marries her live-in boyfriend: once at home with a few friends standing by, and again in a religious ceremony followed by a big family reception. Companion film to LIVING WITH PETER (841). S-A

1469 WE HAVE AN ADDICT IN THE HOUSE
30 min. , color, 1973.
Producer: The Communications Foundation, Inc. Distributors: MTI Teleprograms; Pyramid Films.

Parents and adolescents talk about their conflicts and alienation. Filmed during narcotics-addiction therapy sessions at the Samaritan Society, a drug-counseling center. J-A

1470   WE TIPTOED AROUND WHISPERING
23 min., color, 1973.
Producer: Bureau of Education for the Handicapped, Dept. of Health, Education & Welfare. Distributor: National Audiovisual Center.
Documents what parents of deaf children experience until their deafness is finally diagnosed. From the Western Maryland College series. C-A

1471   WE WON'T LEAVE YOU
17 min., color, 1975.
Director: Edward A. Mason, M.D. Distributor: Documentaries for Learning.
When 5-year-old Heather goes into the hospital (Massachusetts General) for a hernia operation, and a less-than-eight-hour stay, her parents are able to stay with her throughout preparation and anesthesia. Silver Hugo, Chicago International Film Festival. C-A

1472   WEBSTER GROVES REVISITED
53 min., b&w, 1966.
Producer: Arthur Barron for CBS-TV News. Distributor: Carousel Films.
A follow-up telecast to SIXTEEN IN WEBSTER GROVES (1284). Records reactions of the community to the original telecast during and after its airing. Some re-examine their values. S-A

1473   THE WEDDING
60 sec., color, 1977.
Director: Tony Frangakis. Distributor: TeleKETICS.
A bride and groom leave family and friends waiting anxiously at the chapel in order to visit the bride-to-be's grandmother in the hospital. From the TeleSPOTS series. A

1474   A WEDDING IN THE FAMILY
22 min., color, p. 1976, r. 1977.
Director: Debra Franco. Distributor: New Day Films.
The week before the filmmaker's 22-year-old sister marries, members of the Franco family reflect on the upcoming event with diverse expectations. Red Ribbon, American Film Festival. S-A

1475   A WEEK FULL OF SATURDAYS
17 min., color, p. 1978, r. 1979.
Director: Nicholas Dancy. Distributor: Filmakers Library.

Documents the importance of pre-retirement planning. Several men and women discuss housing, finances, family relations, and leisure activities. C-A

From A Wedding in the Family. Courtesy Debra Franco/ New Day Films.

1476 WEEKEND
15 min., color, 1970.
Director: Bruce Baker. Distributor: TeleKETICS.
A middle-aged couple on the verge of estrangement go off for a weekend and are stranded in their motel room. National Council on Family Relations Award. S-A

1477 THE WEEKS AFTER BIRTH
29 min., b&w, 1956.
Producer: WQED, Pittsburgh. Distributors: Association Films (rental only); Indiana University, Audio-Visual Center (rental only).
Care of mother after delivery, exercises to aid recovery, and proper rest and diet. From the Months Before Birth series. A

1478 WELCOME HOME
27 min., color, 1975.
Director: Ralph Senensky for Paulist Productions. Cast: Nan Martin, Dick Van Patten, Jerry Houser. Distributor: The Media Guild.
A young man returns home from juvenile detention camp and must face his domineering mother and non-assertive father, whom he detests. When his father saves his life, the son changes his mind about his father's strengths. From the Insight series. S-A

1479   WELFARE
167 min. , b&w, 1975.
Director: Frederick Wiseman. Distributor: Zipporah
Films.
Cinema vérité study of the day-to-day activities
in a large urban welfare center, where the frustrations
of bureaucratic red tape affect both staff and clients. C-A

1480   THE WELFARE
17 min. , b&w, 1966.
Director: Ernest Rose. Distributor: University of California, Extension Media Center.
Story of a black ghetto family on welfare, and a
new case worker who slogs through the mounds of red tape
to try to help them.   The husband is forced to move out of
the home so his family can qualify for Aid to Needy Children. C-A

1481   WELFARE AND THE FATHERLESS FAMILY
15 min. , color, 1973.
Producer: Isaac Kleinerman for CBS-TV News. Distributor: Carousel Films.
Examines the lives of low-income apartment dwell-
ers. Shows that the welfare system encourages the breakup of families by offering more money to families if fathers
are absent. C-A

1482   WE'LL MAKE OUR OWN TEAM
$21\frac{1}{2}$ min. , color, 1973.
Director: Bert Salzman. Distributor: Xerox Films.
Stewart Collins, a 12-year-old black boy, lives in a
Washington, D. C. , ghetto. He tries to convince his father
to let him be an inventor rather than an upholsterer. From
the Come Over to My House series. E-I

1483   WE'RE DOING OK
5 min. , color, p. 1977, r. 1978.
Director: Tom Rook. Distributor: TeleKETICS.
A young career woman worries about her aging
mother, who lives alone in a deteriorating neighborhood.
J-A

1484   WE'RE NOT THE JET SET
90 min. , color, p. 1975, r. 1977.
Director: Robert Duvall. Distributor: Films Inc.
Documentary profile of the B. A. Peterson family of
Nebraska. Peterson and his six sons continue to live in
the macho tradition of the old West, as rodeo performers
and ranchers. His two daughters and wife are totally domi-
nated by the men. C-A

1485   WE'RE OK (A FILM ABOUT TRANSACTIONAL ANALYSIS)
9 min. , color, 1975.

Producer: Sam Weiss Productions. Distributor: BFA
Educational Media.
Explains the three ego states--"parent," "adult,"
and "child"--as defined by Transactional Analysis. Gives
examples of situations when these behavior patterns might
appear. Animation. From the Transactional Analysis series. J-A

1486 WESTERN MARYLAND COLLEGE SERIES see
WE TIPTOED AROUND WHISPERING 1470

1487 WESTERN RANCH see
ROOTED IN THE PAST 1214

1488 WESTWARD WAGONS
24 min., color, 1973.
Director: Thomas Robertson. Distributor: Multimedia
Program Productions.
The story of a 10-year-old boy and his family's
dangerous trek across the plains in 1870. From the Young
People's Specials series. Red Ribbon, American Film
Festival. E-J

1489 WHAT ABOUT THAD?
9 min., color, 1973.
Director: Keith Atkinson. Distributor: Brigham Young
University.
A shy, troubled boy is neglected by parents, teachers, and peers. He breaks a window, runs away, and col-
lapses. Open-ended. E-A

1490 WHAT COLOR IS THE WIND?
27 min., color, 1973.
Director: Allan Grant. Distributor: Allan Grant Productions.
Study of how a 3-year-old blind boy is taught to
"see" by his parents and sighted twin brother. Blue Ribbon, American Film Festival. S-A, Prof

1491 WHAT DO I KNOW ABOUT BENNY?
10 min., color, p. 1965, r. 1968.
Producers: University of Missouri at Kansas City & Calvin
Productions. Distributor: BFA Educational Media.
A teacher tries to explain to Benny's hostile mother
why the child hasn't done well in school. From the Critical
Moments in Teaching series. Training film. C, Prof

1492 WHAT DO WE DO NOW?--THE NEED FOR DIRECTION
29 min., color, 1976.
Producer: Drew Associates for the Bureau of Education
for the Handicapped, Dept. of Health, Education & Welfare.
Distributor: National Audiovisual Center.
The frustrating problems and obstacles faced by

parents as they try to secure the proper services for their handicapped child.   Introduces a California program entitled "Direction," which assesses a child's needs and attempts to match those needs to available services.   C-A

1493   WHAT DOES OUR FLAG MEAN?
10½ min. , color, 1967.
Producer: Coronet Films.   Distributor: Coronet Films.
When Susy Kim and her family become citizens, the neighborhood kids surprise them with a parade of homemade flags.   Freedoms Foundation Award.   E-I

1494   WHAT FIXED ME
20 min. , color, 1973.
Director: Thomas Rickman.   Distributor: Time-Life Multimedia.
Filmed entirely in western rural Kentucky; reflections of the filmmaker's roots are revealed.   Touches on his mother's suicide, his father's religious fanaticism and disillusionment, and his own escape into fantasy.   S-A

1495   WHAT HARVEST FOR THE REAPER?
59 min. , b&w, 1968.
Producer: Morton Silverstein for NET.   Distributor: Indiana University, Audio-Visual Center.
Documents how a group of farm workers are caught up in a system that keeps them continually in debt.   The growers and processors present their side and are refuted by the Migrant Chairman, Suffolk County Human Relations Commission (N. Y.).   S-A

1496   WHAT IS A FAMILY?
7 min. , color, 1973.
Producer: Ted Lowry.   Distributor: McGraw-Hill Films.
Animation and puppets show that loving and caring make a family, both human and animal.   From the Learning to Look series.   E

1497   WHAT IS NORMAL?
30 min. , b&w, 1964.
Producer: Lloyd Ellingwood for WTTW.   Host: Dr. Maria Piers.   Distributor: Indiana University, Audio-Visual Center.
A young man loses his job just before his marriage. Shows his reactions, as well as those of his fiancée and parents.   From the About People series.   S-A

1498   WHAT MAN SHALL LIVE AND NOT SEE DEATH?
57 min. , color, 1971.
Director: Joan Konner for NBC-TV.   Distributor: Films Inc.
Overview of death and dying attitudes, counseling, etc.   Psychiatrist Dr. Elisabeth Kubler-Ross encourages

the terminally ill to express their feelings and share their responses. Programs that counsel families of dying persons and in particular the children are focused upon. Emmy Award. Family of Man Award. S-A

1499 WHAT MIGHT HAVE BEEN: JEFFERSON DAVIS
20 min. , b&w, p. 1954, r. 1966.
Producer: Teaching Film Custodians. Distributor: Indiana University, Audio-Visual Center.
Lieutenant Jefferson Davis married the daughter of his commanding officer Colonel Zachary Taylor. She encouraged her husband to become a planter; his brother encouraged him to enter politics. After his wife's death, he entered politics. From the Cavalcade of America series. E-J

1500 WHAT PRICE HONESTY?
11 min. , color, 1976.
Producer: Paramount Television. Distributor: Paramount Communications.
A newspaper ad reports a missing wallet. The Brady boys find it and, unfortunately, it contains $1,100. They agonize over a decision. Open-ended. Edited from the Brady Bunch TV series, and a segment in the Brady Bunch Values and Guidance series. E-I

1501 WHAT'S SO GREAT ABOUT BOOKS
14 min. , color, 1977.
Director: Richard Avila. Distributor: Orlando Public Library.
Why parents should read with their children, from infancy on up. Stresses reading together as a warm, sharing experience, that also aids language development and creative thinking. S-A

1502 WHAT'S WRONG WITH JONATHAN?
14½ min. , color, 1975.
Producer: UNIT Productions, Utah State Board of Education. Distributor: Agency for Instructional TV.
Everything has gone wrong for a boy during one whole day, so he angrily explodes at his mother for no apparent reason. From the Self Incorporated series. J

1503 WHEN A CHILD ENTERS THE HOSPITAL
16 min. , color, 1975.
Director: Miriam Weinstein. Distributor: Polymorph Films.
Chronicles the hospitalization of a young girl undergoing minor surgery in Boston. Her parents are encouraged to remain with the child during her stay. C-A, Prof

1504 WHEN PARENTS GROW OLD
15 min. , color, 1973.

Director: Gilbert Cates. Cast: Gene Hackman, Melvyn Douglas. Distributor: Learning Corp. of America.

A man wants to marry and move away from home, but he is burdened with his suddenly widowed, irascible father whose health is failing. Excerpt from the 1970 film I NEVER SANG FOR MY FATHER (1792). From the Searching for Values series. J-A

1505   WHEN YOU SEE ARCTURUS
27 min., color, 1974.
Director: Marc Daniels for Paulist Productions. Cast: Efrem Zimbalist, Jr., William Windom, Mark Hamill. Distributor: The Media Guild.

An affluent, bored architect decides to kill himself. But his son's senseless murder convinces the man of the value of life. From the Insight series. S-A

1506   WHERE HAS THE WARRIOR GONE?
$12\frac{1}{2}$ min., color, 1971.
Producer: Coleman Film Enterprises. Distributor: Centron Films.

Explores the life of Ted Cly, a Navajo father living on a reservation in Utah. He works as a tourist guide, tends sheep, and farms the land; but he lives in a matriarchal society where women hold virtually all property rights and control the home, flock, crops, and children. From the North American Indians Today series. I-S

1507   WHERE IS DEAD?
19 min., color, p. 1975, r. 1976.
Director: Jackie Rivétt-River. Distributor: Encyclopaedia Britannica Educational Corp.

Nine-year-old David dies suddenly, and his 6-year-old sister is sad, confused, and fearful. Her parents try to ease her fears. Blue Ribbon, American Film Festival. E-I, A

1508   WHERE THERE'S A WILL
29 min., color, 1969.
Producer: Social and Rehabilitation Service, Dept. of Health, Education & Welfare. Distributor: National Audiovisual Center.

Two disabled housewives demonstrate how a handicapped person can manage a home. From the To Live Again series. C-A

1509   WHERE WERE YOU DURING THE BATTLE OF THE BULGE, KID?
26 min., color or b&w, 1967.
Director: Seymour Robbie. Cast: Tim O'Connor, Robert Doyle. Distributor: Paulist Productions.

A high-school student boycotts classes because his friend is expelled from school for writing an anti-war piece in the school paper. His father tries to convince him to follow the rules right or wrong. The father is then faced with losing his job unless he takes a key ad campaign for a fraudulent product. From the Insight series. J-A

1510 WHERE'S TOMMY?
11 min., color, 1974.
Director: Ronald Sexton. Distributors: National Fire Protection Association; Alfred Higgins Productions.
What can happen if a child is left alone in the house even for the shortest time, i.e., fire deaths and injuries. J-A

1511 WHETHER TO TELL THE TRUTH
18 min., b&w, 1972.
Director: Elia Kazan. Cast: Marlon Brando. Distributor: Learning Corp. of America.
Focuses on a young, ex-prizefighter's dilemma: whether to be protective of his older brother and his crime connections, or talk to the Crime Commission and obey his conscience. Excerpt from the 1954 film ON THE WATER-FRONT (1906). From the Searching for Values series. J-A

1512 WHILE YOU'RE WAITING
29½ min., color, 1969.
Producer: Centron Films. Distributor: Centron Films.
Proper prenatal care. Insight for husbands about moods and needs of pregnant women. S-A

From Who Are the DeBolts? Courtesy Pyramid Films.

1513 WHO ARE THE DEBOLTS?
54 min. & 72 min., color, 1977.
Director: John Korty. Distributor: Pyramid Films.
Profile of an extraordinary couple who have 19 children--five natural children and the rest adopted, handicapped children of mixed nationalities and racial backgrounds. An upbeat, communal atmosphere pervades their California

home.   Academy Award.   Blue Ribbon, American Film
Festival.   I-A

1514   WHO DO YOU KILL?
51 min. , b&w, 1964.
Producer: Talent Associates-Paramount, in association
with United Artists Television & the CBS-TV Network.
Cast: Diana Sands, James Earl Jones, George C. Scott.
Distributor: Carousel Films.
A young black couple live in the rat-infested Harlem
slums.   Their child is bitten by a rat and dies.   They are
enraged over the conditions in which they are forced to live.
From the East Side/West Side TV series.   S-A

1515   WHO DO YOU TELL?
11 min. , color, 1979.
Producer: J. Gary Mitchell.   Distributor: MTI Teleprograms.
Animation and discussion among young people highlight a variety of problems--fire, lost children, family
violence, child abuse, incest--and the family and community support available for help.   E

1516   WHO REMEMBERS MAMA?
59 min. , color, 1977.
Director: Allen Mondell.   Distributor: Media Projects,
Inc.
Explores the economic and emotional problems faced
by middle-aged housewives and mothers when they are divorced, e.g. , the "displaced homemaker" syndrome.   S-A

1517   WHOSE CHILD IS THIS?
29 min. , color, 1978.
Director: Rhoden Streeter for WAVE-TV.   Distributor:
Learning Corp. of America.
A teacher discovers an abused child in her third grade
class. Follows the procedure involved in reporting the case
and following it through to a successful conclusion. Training
film. Gold Electra, Birmingham Film Festival. C, Prof

1518   WHY FATHERS WORK
14 min. , color, 1969.
Producer: William Kay.   Distributor: Encyclopaedia
Britannica Educational Corp.
A father is shown at work.   Explains how his work
(structural ironworker) helps his family and community.   E

1519   WHY ME?
57 min. , color, 1974.
Director: Joe Saltzman for KNXT-TV, Los Angeles.
Distributor: Carousel Films.
Breast cancer and its aftereffects.   Several women
who've had mastectomies tell of their ordeals, the psycho-

logical repercussions, the need for family understanding
and support. S-A

1520 WHY MOTHERS WORK
19 min. , color, 1976.
Producer: William Kay. Distributor: Encyclopaedia
Britannica Educational Corp.
Two mothers discuss why they work, and their daily
lives are observed. E-J

1521 WHY NOT SNACK?
4 min. , color, 1974.
Sponsor: National Dairy Council. Distributor: Association
Films.
A boy spends his afternoon snacking on junk food,
and then can't eat the nutritious meal his mother prepares
for supper. I-J

1522 WIDOWS
41 min. , b&w, 1972.
Director: Edward A. Mason, M.D. Distributor: Documentaries for Learning.
Several recently widowed women describe their experiences and feelings, single parenting, adaptation to grief,
and subsequent maturity. C-A

1523 WIFE BEATING
27 min. , color, 1976.
Director: Gerald Polikoff for NBC-TV. Distributor: Films
Inc.
Shows how this crime is coming out of the shadows
on all economic levels of society. Includes interviews and
group discussions with victims, psychological causes, and
effects. Blue Ribbon, American Film Festival. S-A

1524 WILD RIVER
52 min. , color, 1970.
Producer: National Geographic Society. Distributor: National Geographic Society.
The Craighead family travels down the white-water
Salmon River in Idaho. Parents and children shoot the
rapids in kayaks and rubber boats, fish for meals, cook
over a campfire, and sleep in tents. I-A

1525 WINDOW WATER BABY MOVING
13 min. , color, sil. , 1959.
Director: Stan Brakhage. Distributors: Brakhage Films;
Film-Makers' Cooperative; Canyon Cinema Cooperative;
Grove Press Film Division.
The natural childbirth of the filmmaker's first child--
a daughter. C-A

1526 WINDY DAY
9 min. , color, 1968.

Directors: John Hubley & Faith Hubley. Distributor:
Films Inc.
Two little girls fantasize about romance, marriage,
and growing up. Animation, with the voices of the film-
makers' daughters. Golden Lion, Venice Film Festival.
S-A

1527   WINGATE, I LOVE YOU
9 min., color, 1976.
Producer: Counterpoint Films. Distributor: Paramount
Communications.
A young man runs away from home due to family
hassles. He meets a man in a bus station who is on his
way to visit his nephew in prison. The uncle asks for ad-
vice--the runaway stresses love. J-A

1528   THE WINGED COLT
66 min., color, 1977.
Director: Tom Armistead for ABC-TV. Distributor: ABC
Wide World of Learning.
The story of a boy and his uncle who become the
owners of a miraculous colt born without wings. In the
course of their dealings with this creature, the two patch
up their estrangement. From the ABC Weekend Specials
series. E-J

1529   WINNIE WRIGHT, AGE 11
26 min., color, 1974.
Producers: G. Quinn, T. Webb, B. Martens, S. Davenport, G. Grieco/Kartemquin Films. Distributor: Haymarket Films.
Cinema vérité look at a white Chicago steelworker's
family, with special focus on the youngest daughter's daily
life and attitudes. J-A

1530   WINTER OF THE WITCH
25 min., color, 1970.
Producer: Parents' Magazine Films. Cast: Hermione
Gingold. Narrator: Burgess Meredith. Distributor: Learning Corp. of America.
A boy and his mom move into a house inhabited by a
pathetic witch. She feels obsolete in a world of unhappy
people. The witch, the boy, and his mother launch a plot
to put the witch back into the business of scaring people.
CINE Golden Eagle. E-J

1531   WISE AND RESPONSIBLE CONSUMERSHIP
13½ min., color, 1973.
Producer: Centron Films. Distributor: Centron Films.
Children accompany their parents to the supermarket
and hardware store, where they learn how to shop wisely.
From the Elementary Consumer Education series. E-J

1532 WITH BABIES AND BANNERS: STORY OF THE WOMEN'S
      EMERGENCY BRIGADE
      46 min., color & b&w, 1978.
      Director: Lorraine Gray for the Women's Labor History
      Film Project. Distributor: New Day Films.
           The victory of the General Motors Sit-Down Strike
      in Flint, Mich., in 1937, was won through the great efforts
      of the Women's Emergency Brigade, made up of working
      women and wives, mothers, sisters, and girlfriends of the
      strikers. Now middle-aged women, the key activists are
      profiled in this film. They reminisce about their heroic
      involvement and the family and work conditions that pre-
      cipitated their involvement. Blue Ribbon & Emily Award
      & John Grierson Award, American Film Festival. S-A

1533 WITH JUST A LITTLE TRUST
      15 min., color, 1975.
      Director: Tony Frangakis. Distributor: TeleKETICS.
           An elderly, arthritic black woman tries to bolster
      the sagging spirits of her young widowed daughter, who is
      trying to raise her three children at the poverty level.
      Dramatic film. Virgin Islands Film Festival Medal. J-A

1534 WOMAN IS
      12 min., color, p. 1974, r. 1975.
      Director: Sandy Ostertag. Distributor: Phoenix Films.
           Traces the history of women's roles in society
      from ancient times to the present. S-A

1535 WOMANCENTERING
      8 min., b&w, 1977.
      Director: Nancy Peck. Distributor: Women Make Movies.
           A young mother's growing interest in feminism, with
      support from other women at a neighborhood women's cen-
      ter. A

1536 WOMANHOUSE
      47 min., color, p. 1973, r. 1974.
      Director: Johanna Demetrakas. Distributor: Serious Busi-
      ness Company.
           Documents a project of the Feminist Art Program
      at the California Institute of the Arts, which refurbished a
      mansion to symbolize women's social and sexual roles:
      housewife, mother, etc. C-A

1537 WOMEN
      15 min., color, 1975.
      Director: Coni Beeson. Distributor: Serious Business
      Company.
           The verbal and visual clichés traditionally used to
      describe women. Includes nudity. C-A

1538 WOMEN & CHILDREN AT LARGE see
      MY LIFE IN ART 990

1539   WOMEN IN PRISON
       54 min. , color, 1974.
       Director: Joe De Cola for ABC-TV News.   Distributor:
       Carousel Films.
               Documents process of dehumanization that occurs
       when women are imprisoned.   Shows an alternative to tradi-
       tional prison life in Des Moines, Iowa, which permits women
       convicts to live at home, stay employed, and care for their
       children.   S-A

1540   WOMEN: THE HAND THAT CRADLES THE ROCK
       20 min. , color, 1976.
       Producer: Philip S. Hobel.   Distributor: Document Asso-
       ciates.
               Contrasts women who are content with their traditional
       roles as wives and mothers with those involved in redefining
       their roles and goals.   Avail. in French and Spanish.   S-A

1541   WOMEN TODAY SERIES   see
       THE QUIET REVOLUTION OF MRS. HARRIS   1169
       SINGLE PARENT   1279
       THE SPRING AND FALL OF NINA POLANSKI   1312

1542   WOMEN WHO DIDN'T HAVE AN ABORTION
       $28\frac{1}{2}$ min. , color, p. 1977, r. 1978.
       Director: Ivan Cury.   Distributor: Martha Stuart Commu-
       nications.
               Various women discuss their unwanted pregnancies.
       They all had their babies because they didn't want to have
       abortions.   C-A

1543   WOMEN'S WORK: ENGINEERING
       26 min. , color, 1974.
       Director: A. Christine Dall.   Distributor: Education De-
       velopment Center.
               Documents the personal and professional lives of
       several engineering students and working engineers.   A
       chemical engineer and her husband discuss the problems
       and benefits of combining a full-time career with the re-
       sponsibilities of family life.   S-A

1544   WOMEN'S WORK: MANAGEMENT
       29 min. , color, 1976.
       Directors: A. Christine Dall & Hiti Salloway.   Distributor:
       Education Development Center.
               Six working women discuss their jobs, concerns, and
       methods of juggling a demanding work schedule and family
       life.   S-A

1545   WOO WHO? MAY WILSON
       33 min. , color, 1970.
       Director: Amalie R. Rothschild.   Distributor: New Day
       Films.

How one woman--a onetime dependent wife/mother--
survived when her husband kicked her out of his life. At
age 60, she came to New York City and forged a new
career as an artist. Now, she's a bohemian sculptor with
young friends and grandchildren. C-A

1546 WOODLAND INDIANS OF EARLY AMERICA
$10\frac{1}{2}$ min. , color, 1958.
Producer: Coronet Films. Distributor: Coronet Films.
The daily life of a Chippewa family. Dramatic film.
E-I

1547 WORKERS WHO COME TO OUR HOUSE (2nd Edition)
10 min. , color, 1975.
Producer: Coronet Films. Distributor: Coronet Films.
The different types of workers who service the home;
points out interdependence of family and community. Second edition of HELPERS WHO COME TO OUR HOUSE. E

1548 THE WORKING MOTHER
$28\frac{1}{2}$ min. , color, 1976.
Producer: WTTW/Chicago for the Par Leadership Training
Foundation. Distributors: Perennial Education; National
Audiovisual Center (rental only).
Games and activities working mothers can share
with their preschool kids. From the Look at Me! series.
A

1549 WORKING TOGETHER
30 min. , color, 1977.
Producer: National Center on Child Abuse & Neglect, HEW.
Distributor: National Audiovisual Center.
Multiagency and multidiscipline approaches to child
abuse and neglect. Covers consultation teams, community
coordinating, and the education of professionals and the
public. Training film. From the We Can Help series.
C-A, Prof

1550 WORKING WITH MY DAD
9 min. , color, 1975.
Producer: WGBH-TV, Boston. Distributor: Films Inc.
Two short portraits of real-life American kids;
vignettes include: A LOBSTERMAN LIKE HIS FATHER--
Craig works in Maine with his father and grandfather on
their boat and tends to his own pots as well. He wants to
continue the work when he grows up. SHRIMPIN'S NOT A
REAL GOOD LIFE--Johnny works on his father's shrimp
boat in the Gulf of Mexico, but he doesn't like the work.
From the Best of Zoom series. E-I

1551 WORKOUT
15 min. , color, 1969.
Director: Bruce Baker. Distributor: TeleKETICS.

A father, upset by recent demonstrations on his son's campus, visits his son and confronts him both physically and verbally. S-A

1552   WORRY: I'M IN BIG TROUBLE NOW
12 min. , color, 1973.
Producer: Guidance Associates/Motion Media. Distributor: Xerox Films.
A boy is entrusted with the care of his little brother, who wanders away while they are in the woods and can't be found. I-J

1553   WOULD YOU KISS A NAKED MAN?
20 min. , color, 1974.
Director: Alan Gough. Distributor: Perennial Education.
Teen attitudes toward sexuality are explored: sexual role playing, values, virginity, sexual games, love, commitment, and pressures and influences of peer groups and parents. Short nude scene. S-C

1554   THE WYETH PHENOMENON
26 min. , color, 1968.
Producer: CBS-TV News. Reporter: Harry Reasoner.
Distributor: BFA Educational Media.
The art of Andrew Wyeth; plus interviews with his artist/sister Henriette and son Jamie, also a noted artist.
S-A

1555   THE YEAR OF THE COMMUNES
52 min. , color, 1969-70.
Producers: Kathleen Rawlings & Nick Chickering. Narrator: Rod Steiger. Distributor: Association Films.
An insider's view of nine communes in the American West. S-A

1556   YESTERDAY AND TODAY SERIES   see
THE BIRCH CANOE BUILDER   155
CIDER MAKER   277
GRIST MILLER   596
MAPLE SUGAR FARMER   882

1557   YOGA   see
BIG TOWN   151

1558   YOU
16½ min. , color, 1973.
Director: Leonard Schneider. Distributor: Centron Films.
Two brothers, ages 12 and 8, of differing temperaments engage in a typical family argument. When they cool off, they try to understand each other's feelings and viewpoints. From the Trilogy series. Bronze Plaque, Columbus Film Festival. E-I

1559 YOU AND YOURS
20 min. , color, 1975.
Producer: National Fire Protection Association. Distributor: National Fire Protection Association.
Burns and fire prevention, detection, control, and escape planning for the home. I-A

1560 YOU ARE EATING FOR TWO
19 min. , color, 1977.
Director: Malca Gillson. Distributor: National Film Board of Canada.
Good prenatal nutrition. S-A

1561 YOU ARE NOT ALONE
27 min. , color, 1976.
Producer: Bureau of Community Health Services, Public Health Service. Distributor: National Audiovisual Center.
Designed to assist families who have lost an infant due to the Sudden Infant Death Syndrome. Explores aspects of physical and emotional grief and attempts to assure parents that they are not to blame. From the Sudden Infant Death Syndrome series. A

1562 YOU CAN'T CATCH IT
40 min. , color, 1973.
Director: William W. Hansard, Jr. Distributor: Education Development Center.
Sickle-cell anemia is hereditary. Professionals comment, and two victims of the anemia are profiled--a 14-year-old girl and a 37-year-old man. For black audiences.

1563 YOU CAN'T MEAN "NOT EVER"
26 min. , color, 1977.
Director: Martha Garrett Russell. Distributor: University of Minnesota, Audio Visual Library Service.
Eric and Liz consider remaining permanently childless; however, they must face questions from friends and relatives. Dramatic film. S-A

1564 YOU DON'T HAVE TO BUY THIS WAR, MRS. SMITH
28 min. , b&w, 1971.
Director: Sally Pugh. Distributor: Kit Parker Films (rental only).
Anti-war speech by Bess Myerson, then Commissioner of Consumer Affairs for New York City, delivered before the 1970 World Mother's Day Assembly of Another Mother for Peace in San Francisco. She encouraged a boycott of war-profiting companies. From video. C-A

1565 YOU HAVEN'T CHANGED A BIT
15 min. , color, 1970.
Director: Bruce Baker. Distributor: TeleKETICS.

A recently married couple quarrel and take separate vacations with their parents, who treat them like children. The couple realize they belong together as adults and should try to work out their problems. National Council on Family Relations Award.   S-A

1566   YOUNG ANDY JACKSON
20 min. , b&w, p. 1954, r. 1965.
Producer: Teaching Film Custodians. Distributor: Indiana University, Audio-Visual Center.
In 1780, the Jackson brothers were captured in guerrilla action against the British. Their mother obtained their releases from military prison in a prisoner exchange, but son Robert and the mother died shortly thereafter. Young Andy Jackson went on to become President of the United States. From the Cavalcade of America series.   E-J

1567   YOUNG MARRIAGE: WHEN'S THE BIG DAY?
14 min. , color, 1975.
Producer: Steve Katten. Host: Beau Bridges. Distributor: CRM/McGraw-Hill Films.
An engaged couple are shocked when they visit their newly married friends and witness signs of trouble in the marriage. But they are naive and confident that their marriage can't help but be a success. From Conflict and Awareness: A Film Series on Human Values.   S-A

1568   YOUNG PEOPLE'S SPECIALS SERIES   see
FOUR CHILDREN   537
JOSHUA'S CONFUSION   775
THE LAND, THE SEA, THE CHILDREN THERE   796
MY FATHER, MY BROTHER AND ME   984
PILGRIM JOURNEY   1109
THE SELLIN' OF JAMIE THOMAS (PT. I & PT. II)
   1252, 1253
WESTWARD WAGONS   1488

1569   YOUNG, SINGLE AND PREGNANT
18 min. , color, 1973.
Directors: David Espar & Leonard C. Schwarz. Distributor: Perennial Education.
Documents the decisions of four single young women when they became pregnant--adoption, abortion, marriage, and single parenthood.   S-A

1570   YOUR CAREER: YOUR DECISION?
$17\frac{1}{2}$ min. ,color, 1976.
Producer: Walt Disney Productions. Distributor: Walt Disney Educational Media Company.
A career conflict arises between a young ballerina and her mother. Questions who should make or influence career choices and how to reconcile opposing points of view. Excerpted from the feature film BALLERINA (1955). From the Questions!!! Answers?? Set II series.   I-J

1571   YOUR CREDIT IS GOOD, UNFORTUNATELY   see
       THE CONSUMER FRAUD SERIES   312

1572   YOUTH UNDER THE INFLUENCE SERIES   see
       ALCOHOLISM: I WAS GOIN' TO SCHOOL DRUNK   43

1573   YUDIE
       20 min. , b&w, 1974.
       Director: Mirra Bank.   Distributor: New Day Films.
       The filmmaker's elderly aunt is self-sufficient and
       proud of it.   She reminisces about growing up a Jew on
       the Lower East Side of New York, her failed marriage, and
       her independence.   Blue Ribbon, American Film Festival.
       S-A

SELECTED DRAMATIC FEATURES

1574 THE ACTRESS
90 min., b&w, 1953.
Director: George Cukor. Cast: Spencer Tracy, Jean
Simmons, Teresa Wright, Anthony Perkins. Distributor:
Films Inc.
Ruth Gordon's early life. Dra-Bio

1575 ADAM AT 6 A. M.
90 min., color, 1970.
Director: Robert Sheerer. Cast: Michael Douglas, Louise
Latham, Joe Don Baker, Lee Purcell, Charles Aidman.
Distributor: Swank Motion Pictures.
A disenchanted young university professor takes off
in search of his roots. Dra

1576 THE ADAMS CHRONICLES SERIES (13 Films)
60 min. each, color, 1976.
Directors: Paul Bogart, James Cellan-Jones, Barry Davis,
Anthony Page, Bill Glenn, Fred Coe. Producer: WNET/13.
Distributors: Indiana University, Audio-Visual Center
(16mm); Films Inc. (video).
Based on The Adams' Papers--300,000 pages of let-
ters, diaries, and journals written by the Adamses, one of
America's First Families. Film titles include: JOHN
ADAMS: LAWYER (1758-1770); JOHN ADAMS: REVOLU-
TIONARY (1770-1776); JOHN ADAMS: DIPLOMAT (1776-
1783); JOHN ADAMS: MINISTER TO GREAT BRITAIN
(1784-1787); JOHN ADAMS: VICE PRESIDENT (1788-1796);
JOHN ADAMS: PRESIDENT (1797-1801); JOHN QUINCY
ADAMS: DIPLOMAT (1809-1815); JOHN QUINCY ADAMS:
SECRETARY OF STATE (1817-1825); JOHN QUINCY ADAMS:
PRESIDENT (1825-1829); JOHN QUINCY ADAMS: CON-
GRESSMAN (1830-1848); CHARLES FRANCIS ADAMS: MIN-
ISTER TO GREAT BRITAIN (1861-1864); HENRY ADAMS:
HISTORIAN (1870-1885); CHARLES FRANCIS ADAMS II:
INDUSTRIALIST (1886-1893). Bio

1577   ADAM'S RIB
101 min., b&w, 1949.
Director: George Cukor. Cast: Spencer Tracy, Katharine
Hepburn, David Wayne, Jean Hagen, Tom Ewell, Judy Holliday. Distributor: Films Inc.
The D.A. vs. his wife, an attorney who takes the
case of a woman charged with shooting her philandering
husband. Com

1578   THE ADVENTURES OF BULLWHIP GRIFFIN
111 min., color, 1967.
Director: James Neilson. Cast: Roddy McDowall, Suzanne Pleshette, Karl Malden, Hermione Baddeley. Distributor: Audio Brandon Films.
A dignified Boston butler and his ward strike it rich
during the California Gold Rush. Com

1579   AH, WILDERNESS!
101 min., b&w, 1935.
Director: Clarence Brown. Cast: Lionel Barrymore,
Mickey Rooney, Wallace Beery. Distributor: Films Inc.
An overly romantic youth grows up in small-town
America. From the play by Eugene O'Neill. Com

1580   ALICE ADAMS
99 min., b&w, 1935.
Director: George Stevens. Cast: Katharine Hepburn,
Fred MacMurray, Frank Albertson, Charley Grapewin,
Fred Stone, Hedda Hopper. Distributor: Films Inc.
Gauche Alice yearns for a wealthy beau all her own.
Dra

1581   ALICE DOESN'T LIVE HERE ANYMORE
112 min., color, 1974.
Director: Martin Scorsese. Cast: Ellen Burstyn, Kris
Kristofferson, Alfred Lutter, Diane Ladd, Harvey Keitel.
Distributor: Swank Motion Pictures.
On the road with a young widow and her precocious
12-year-old son. Dra

1582   ALICE'S RESTAURANT
111 min., color, 1969.
Director: Arthur Penn. Cast: Arlo Guthrie, Pat Quinn,
James Broderick, Pete Seeger. Distributor: United Art-
ists/16.
Based on the autobiographical song by Arlo Guthrie,
which takes him from the bed of his dying father, Woody,
to life in a hippie commune. Sat

1583   ALL FALL DOWN
111 min., b&w, 1962.
Director: John Frankenheimer. Cast: Eva Marie Saint,
Warren Beatty, Karl Malden, Angela Lansbury, Brandon
de Wilde, Constance Ford. Distributor: Films Inc.

Destructive relationship between a man, his wife,
and their two adult sons. Dra

1584   ALL MINE TO GIVE
102 min. , color, 1956.
Director: Allen Reisner. Cast: Glynis Johns, Cameron
Mitchell, Patty McCormack, Hope Emerson, Jon Provost.
Distributor: Universal/16.
True story of a young Scottish couple who settled in
the Wisconsin wilderness in the middle of the 19th century,
died, and left behind six small orphans. Parents' Magazine Special Merit Award. Dra

1585   ALL MY SONS
92 min. , b&w, 1949.
Director: Irving Reis. Cast: Edward G. Robinson, Burt
Lancaster, Howard Duff, Louisa Horton, Mady Christians.
Distributor: Universal/16.
A factory owner manufactures defective airplane
parts during WWII, to the disgust of his son. From the
play by Arthur Miller. Dra

1586   ALL THAT HEAVEN ALLOWS
89 min. , color, 1955.
Director: Douglas Sirk. Cast: Jane Wyman, Rock Hudson,
Agnes Moorehead, Virginia Grey, Conrad Nagel. Distributor: Universal/16.
A widow falls for a younger man and is harassed by
her disapproving children and community. Dra

1587   ALL THE WAY HOME
103 min. , b&w, 1963.
Director: Alex Segal. Cast: Jean Simmons, Robert Preston, Pat Hingle, Aline MacMahon, John Cullum. Distributor: Paramount Pictures Corp.
A few days in the life of a young family in Knoxville,
Tenn. , circa 1915. The father is suddenly killed in an accident, but life goes on. From the book by James Agee
and play by Tad Mosel. Dra

1588   AN AMERICAN ROMANCE
122 min. , color, 1944.
Director: King Vidor. Cast: Brian Donlevy, Ann Richards,
Walter Abel, John Qualen, Stephen McNally. Distributor:
Films Inc.
An immigrant is molded into an American executive
via two wars, his family, and steel. Dra

1589   ... AND NOW MIGUEL
95 min. , color, 1966.
Director: James B. Clark. Cast: Pat Cardi, Michael
Ansara, Guy Stockwell, Clu Gulager, Joe De Santis. Distributors: Universal/16; Twyman Films.

A Mexican American boy wants to be a good sheep-herder like his father. Before he can join his father on the annual sheep-grazing trip, he must prove that he can handle the responsibility. Parents' Magazine Family Medal Award. Dra

1590   ANDY HARDY COMES HOME
80 min., b&w, 1958.
Director: Howard W. Koch. Cast: Mickey Rooney. Distributor: Films Inc.
Andy--now an attorney--returns home and gets into trouble. Com

1591   ANDY HARDY GETS SPRING FEVER
85 min., b&w, 1939.
Director: W. S. Van Dyke II. Cast: Mickey Rooney, Ann Rutherford. Distributor: Films Inc.
Andy falls for an older woman. Com

1592   ANDY HARDY MEETS A DEBUTANTE
89 min., b&w, 1940.
Director: George B. Seitz. Cast: Mickey Rooney, Judy Garland. Distributor: Films Inc.
Andy and his women. Com

1593   ANGEL IN MY POCKET
105 min., color, 1969.
Director: Alan Rafkin. Cast: Andy Griffith, Jerry Van Dyke, Kay Medford, Lee Meriwether, Edgar Buchanan, Margaret Hamilton. Distributor: Universal/16.
A new preacher in a small town has a hard time dealing with his congregation. Com

1594   THE ANGEL LEVINE
107 min., color, 1970.
Director: Jan Kadar. Cast: Zero Mostel, Harry Belafonte, Ida Kaminska, Milo O'Shea. Distributor: Audio Brandon Films.
Down-at-the-heels Morris Mishkin comes home one day to find a black man in his kitchen who claims he can work miracles. Com-Dra

1595   ANNA CHRISTIE
90 min., b&w, 1930.
Director: Clarence Brown. Cast: Greta Garbo, Charles Bickford, Marie Dressler, George Marion, James Mack, Lee Phelps. Distributor: Films Inc.
Harlot meets her father after many years of separation. Based on the play by Eugene O'Neill. Dra

1596   ANOTHER MAN, ANOTHER CHANCE
136 min., color, 1977.
Director: Claude Lelouch. Cast: James Caan, Genevieve

Bujold, Jennifer Warren, Susan Tyrrell. Distributor: United Artists/16.
American widower meets French-born widow on the plains of the Old West. Dra

1597 ANOTHER PART OF THE FOREST
107 min., b&w, 1948.
Director: Michael Gordon. Cast: Fredric March, Dan Duryea, Ann Blyth, John Dall, Edmond O'Brien, Florence Eldridge. Distributor: Universal/16.
The greedy Hubbard clan during the Civil War. See THE LITTLE FOXES (1834) for more on this family. Dra

1598 APARTMENT FOR PEGGY
99 min., color, 1948.
Director: George Seaton. Cast: Jeanne Crain, William Holden, Edmund Gwenn. Distributor: Films Inc.
A student-veteran and his pregnant wife live on campus and struggle to survive. Com

1599 APPLAUSE
80 min., b&w, 1929.
Director: Rouben Mamoulian. Cast: Helen Morgan, Joan Peers, Henry Wadsworth. Distributors: Universal/16; Museum of Modern Art.
Relationship between an aging burlesque star and her cultured daughter. Mus-Dra

1600 ARSENIC AND OLD LACE
118 min., b&w, 1944.
Director: Frank Capra. Cast: Cary Grant, Raymond Massey, Josephine Hull, John Alexander, Jean Adair, Jack Carson, Peter Lorre. Distributor: United Artists/16.
A drama critic discovers that his two elderly aunts are misusing their elderberry wine. Com

1601 ASH WEDNESDAY
99 min., color, 1973.
Director: Larry Peerce. Cast: Elizabeth Taylor, Henry Fonda, Helmut Berger, Keith Baxter. Distributor: Paramount Pictures Corp.
Middle-aged woman undergoes plastic surgery to try to save her marriage. Dra

1602 AUDREY ROSE
113 min., color, 1977.
Director: Robert Wise. Cast: Marsha Mason, Anthony Hopkins, John Beck, Susan Swift, John Hillerman. Distributor: United Artists/16.
A happy New York City family is disrupted by a mysterious stranger who claims their daughter is the reincarnation of his dead child, Audrey Rose. Dra

1603   AUNTIE MAME
143 min. , color, 1958.
Director: Morton DaCosta.   Cast: Rosalind Russell, Forrest Tucker, Fred Clark, Roger Smith, Pippa Scott, Peggy
Cass.   Distributors: Twyman Films; Institutional Cinema.
Sybaritic woman raises her orphaned nephew amidst
a horde of zany friends.   See also   MAME (1856).   Com

1604   THE AUTOBIOGRAPHY OF MISS JANE PITTMAN
110 min. , color, 1974.
Director: John Korty.   Cast: Cicely Tyson, Richard A.
Dysart, Odetta.   Distributors: Learning Corp. of America;
Audio Brandon Films; Swank Motion Pictures; Mass Media
Ministries.
The story of a fictional black woman--from her
childhood as a slave through her death at age 110 in the
early 1960s.   Bio

1605   THE AWFUL TRUTH
92 min. , b&w, 1937.
Director: Leo McCarey.   Cast: Irene Dunne, Cary Grant,
Ralph Bellamy.   Distributor: Audio Brandon Films.
A couple attempt to wreck each other's romances
while waiting for their divorce.   Com

1606   THE BABY MAKER
109 min. , color, 1970.
Director: James Bridges.   Cast: Barbara Hershey, Colin
Wilcox-Horne, Sam Groom, Madge Kennedy.   Distributor:
Swank Motion Pictures.
A free-spirited girl agrees to bear a child for a
childless couple, to be fathered by the husband.   Dra

1607   BABY, THE RAIN MUST FALL
99 min. , b&w, 1965.
Director: Robert Mulligan.   Cast: Lee Remick, Steve
McQueen, Don Murray, Paul Fix, Ruth White, Josephine
Hutchinson.   Distributor: Kit Parker Films.
A woman tries unsuccessfully to save her marriage
to a drifting ex-con.   From a play by Horton Foote.   Dra

1608   THE BACHELOR AND THE BOBBYSOXER
95 min. , b&w, 1947.
Director: Irving Reis.   Cast: Cary Grant, Shirley Temple,
Myrna Loy.   Distributor: Films Inc.
A bachelor is plagued by a girl who has a crush on
him; he falls for her sister.   Com

1609   BACHELOR MOTHER
80 min. , b&w, 1939.
Director: Garson Kanin.   Cast: Ginger Rogers, David
Niven, Charles Coburn.   Distributor: Films Inc.
Misunderstandings over a foundling baby.   See also
BUNDLE OF JOY (1639).   Com

1610 THE BAD SEED
129 min. , b&w, 1956.
Director: Mervyn LeRoy. Cast: Patty McCormack, Nancy
Kelly, Henry Jones, Eileen Heckart. Distributor: Swank
Motion Pictures.
Spoiled, charming little girl turns out to be a closet
psychopath. Dra

1611 THE BANK DICK
74 min. , b&w, 1940.
Director: Edward Cline. Cast: W. C. Fields, Grady
Sutton, Franklin Pangborn. Distributors: Twyman Films;
Swank Motion Pictures.
Egbert Sousé supports his nagging wife, daughter,
and mother-in-law with various money-making schemes.
Com

1612 BAREFOOT IN THE PARK
105 min. , color, 1967.
Director: Gene Saks. Cast: Jane Fonda, Robert Redford,
Mildred Natwick, Charles Boyer. Distributor: Paramount
Pictures Corp.
Young newlyweds and a mother-in-law, in the caverns
of New York City. From the play by Neil Simon. Com

1613 BELLES ON THEIR TOES
89 min. , color, 1952.
Director: Henry Levin. Cast: Myrna Loy, Jeanne Crain,
Debra Paget, Martin Milner, Jeffrey Hunter, Barbara Bates.
Distributor: Films Inc.
The further adventures of the Gilbreth family: mother
decides to carry on father's engineering career, with 12
kids. Sequel to CHEAPER BY THE DOZEN (1652). Com

1614 THE BEST YEARS OF OUR LIVES
170 min. , b&w, 1946.
Director: William Wyler. Cast: Fredric March, Myrna
Loy, Dana Andrews, Teresa Wright, Harold Russell. Distributors: Macmillan Films; Twyman Films.
Three World War II veterans return to American life,
loves and families. Dra

1615 BIG BAD MAMA
84 min. , color, 1974.
Director: Steve Carver. Cast: Angie Dickinson, William
Shatner, Tom Skerritt, Susan Sennett. Distributor: Films Inc.
A lusty widow teaches her two daughters about men,
money, and moonshining in the Texas dust bowl. Com-Dra

1616 THE BIG COUNTRY
166 min. , color, 1958.
Director: William Wyler. Cast: Charles Bickford, Burl
Ives, Gregory Peck, Charlton Heston, Jean Simmons, Carroll

Baker. Distributor: United Artists/16.
Bitter family feud over water rights. Wes

1617   THE BIG FIX
108 min. , color, 1978.
Director: Jeremy Paul Kagan. Cast: Richard Dreyfuss,
Susan Anspach, Fritz Weaver, Bonnie Bedelia, John Lith-
gow, Ofelia Medina. Distributor: Universal/16.
A divorced private eye, whose kids accompany him
on capers. Dra

1618   BIG JAKE
110 min. , color, 1971.
Director: George Sherman. Cast: John Wayne, Maureen
O'Hara, Richard Boone, Patrick Wayne. Distributor: Westcoast Films.
The Duke takes charge when his grandson is kid-
napped and held for ransom. Wes

1619   THE BIGAMIST
80 min. , b&w, 1953.
Director: Ida Lupino. Cast: Ida Lupino, Joan Fontaine,
Edmond O'Brien. Distributor: Ivy Film.
Man is tormented by guilty secret that he's married
to two women. Dra

1620   BIGGER THAN LIFE
95 min. , color, 1956.
Director: Nicholas Ray. Cast: James Mason, Barbara
Rush, Walter Matthau, Christopher Olsen, Pamela Mason,
Kipp Hamilton. Distributor: Films Inc.
A man's cortisone treatments cause a severe person-
ality change, which almost destroys his family. Dra

1621   BILLIE
87 min. , color, 1965.
Director: Don Weis. Cast: Patty Duke, Jim Backus, Jane
Greer, Warren Berlinger, Dick Sargent. Distributor: United
Artists/16.
A 16-year-old high-school track star is constantly
in trouble with her less athletic boyfriend and her father.
Com

1622   BIRCH INTERVAL
104 min. , color, 1976.
Director: Delbert Mann. Cast: Eddie Albert, Rip Torn,
Ann Wedgeworth, Susan McClung. Distributor: Swank
Motion Pictures.
An 11-year-old city girl is sent to live with her
mother's family in Amish country. A grandfather helps
her cope. Dra

1623 THE BLACK ORCHID
      95 min., b&w, 1959.
      Director: Martin Ritt. Cast: Sophia Loren, Anthony
      Quinn, Mark Richman, Ina Balin. Distributor: Paramount
      Pictures Corp.
           Widow of a slain gangster wants to remarry so that
      her son will have a decent father. Her choice is a widower
      with a grown daughter who tries to wreck her father's
      plans. Dra

1624 BLONDIE SERIES
      75 min. each, b&w, 1939-50.
      Directors: Frank R. Strayer, Abby Berlin, Edward Bernds.
      Cast: Penny Singleton, Arthur Lake. Distributor: United
      Films.
           Adventures of the Bumstead family. Various titles
      available. Com

1625 BLOODBROTHERS
      116 min., color, 1978.
      Director: Robert Mulligan. Cast: Paul Sorvino, Tony Lo
      Bianco, Richard Gere, Lelia Goldoni, Marilu Henner. Dis-
      tributor: Swank Motion Pictures.
           A macho New York Italian-American family. Dra

1626 BLUE DENIM
      89 min., b&w, 1959.
      Director: Philip Dunne. Cast: Brandon de Wilde, Carol
      Lynley, MacDonald Carey, Marsha Hunt. Distributor:
      Films Inc.
           Two teenagers faced with a pregnancy are unable to
      confide in their parents. Dra

1627 BLUME IN LOVE
      115 min., color, 1973.
      Director: Paul Mazursky. Cast: George Segal, Susan
      Anspach, Kris Kristofferson, Marsha Mason, Shelley Win-
      ters. Distributor: Westcoast Films.
           A man is desperately in love with his ex-wife and
      plots to regain her love. Com-Dra

1628 BOB & CAROL & TED & ALICE
      104 min., color, 1969.
      Director: Paul Mazursky. Cast: Natalie Wood, Robert
      Culp, Elliott Gould, Dyan Cannon. Distributor: Swank Mo-
      tion Pictures.
           A married couple who've attended an Esalen-type
      institute try to liberate their best friends. Sat

1629 BON VOYAGE!
      125 min., color, 1962.
      Director: James Neilson. Cast: Fred MacMurray, Jane
      Wyman, Michael Callan, Deborah Walley, Jessie Royce

Landis, Tommy Kirk. Distributor: Association Films.
An American family vacations on a luxury liner.
Com

1630   BORN INNOCENT
99 min. , color, 1975.
Director: Donald Wrye. Cast: Linda Blair, Richard
Jaeckel, Joanna Miles, Kim Hunter. Distributor: Learning
Corp. of America.
A teenage runaway is unwanted by her alcoholic
mother and insensitive father. She ends up in a juvenile
detention center with tough, criminal girls. Dra

1631   THE BOTTOM OF THE BOTTLE
88 min. , color, 1956.
Director: Henry Hathaway. Cast: Van Johnson, Ruth
Roman, Joseph Cotten, Jack Carson. Distributor: Films
Inc.
A successful attorney's life is turned upside down
by his alcoholic younger brother. Dra

From A Brand New Life. Courtesy Learning Corp. of
America.

1632   A BRAND NEW LIFE
74 min. , color, 1973.
Director: Sam O'Steen. Cast: Cloris Leachman, Martin
Balsam, Mildred Dunnock, Wilfrid Hyde-White. Distributors: Learning Corp. of America; Mass Media Ministries.
A middle-aged couple are shocked to find that they
are expecting a baby. After much soul-searching, the wife,
who loves her career and her husband very much, decides
to have the baby. See also DO I REALLY WANT A CHILD?
(381). Dra

1633 THE BRIDE CAME C. O. D.
92 min. , b&w, 1941.
Director: William Keighley. Cast: Bette Davis, James
Cagney, Jack Carson, Stuart Erwin, Eugene Pallette. Distributor: United Artists/16.
An heiress and her hectic love life give her father
a run for his money. Com

1634 THE BRIDE GOES WILD
97 min. , b&w, 1948.
Director: Norman Taurog. Cast: June Allyson, Van
Johnson, Butch Jenkins, Arlene Dahl, Hume Cronyn, Una
Merkel. Distributor: Films Inc.
A child-hating author borrows an orphan to win over
a prim teacher who is illustrating his book. Com

1635 THE BRIDE WORE BOOTS
86 min. , b&w, 1946.
Director: Irving Pichel. Cast: Barbara Stanwyck, Robert
Cummings, Diana Lynn, Patric Knowles, Robert Benchley,
Peggy Wood, Natalie Wood. Distributor: Universal/16.
Expert horsewoman and her novelist husband, who
hates horses. Com

1636 BRIGHAM YOUNG--FRONTIERSMAN
115 min. , b&w, 1940.
Director: Henry Hathaway. Cast: Tyrone Power, Linda
Darnell, Dean Jagger, Brian Donlevy, Jane Darwell, John
Carradine, Mary Astor, Vincent Price. Distributor: Films
Inc.
19th-century exodus of the Mormon people from
Illinois to Utah, their promised land. Dra-Bio

1637 THE BROTHERHOOD
96 min. , color, 1968.
Director: Martin Ritt. Cast: Kirk Douglas, Alex Cord,
Irene Papas, Luther Adler, Susan Strasberg. Distributor:
Paramount Pictures Corp.
Tragic study of an Italian American family's involve-
ment with the Mafia. Dra

1638 THE BROTHERS RICO
110 min. , b&w, 1957.
Director: Phil Karlson. Cast: Richard Conte, Kathryn
Grant, Dianne Foster, James Darren, Larry Gates. Dis-
tributor: Institutional Cinema.
The story of three hunted brothers. Dra

1639 BUNDLE OF JOY
98 min. , color, 1956.
Director: Norman Taurog. Cast: Debbie Reynolds, Eddie
Fisher, Adolphe Menjou, Una Merkel, Tommy Noonan, Nita
Talbot. Distributor: Westcoast Films.

An unmarried salesgirl has an unwanted baby on her hands. Remake of BACHELOR MOTHER (1609). Mus-Com

1640   BUSH MAMA
96 min. , b&w, 1975.
Director: Haile Gerima. Distributor: Tricontinental Film Center.
Dorothy is a black woman living on welfare in Watts, Los Angeles. She tries to raise her daughter while her man is in prison for a crime he didn't commit. Dra

1641   THE BUSTER KEATON STORY
91 min. , b&w, 1957.
Director: Sidney Sheldon. Cast: Donald O'Connor, Ann Blyth, Peter Lorre, Rhonda Fleming. Distributor: Paramount Pictures Corp.
Life story of Buster. Bio

1642   BUTTERFLIES ARE FREE
109 min. , color, 1972.
Director: Milton Katselas. Cast: Edward Albert, Goldie Hawn, Eileen Heckart. Distributors: Twyman Films; Swank Motion Pictures.
A young, blind, would-be singer/composer wants a life of his own away from his over-protective mother.
From the play by Leonard Gershe. Com-Dra

1643   BYE BYE BIRDIE
112 min. , color, 1963.
Director: George Sidney. Cast: Dick Van Dyke, Ann-Margret, Janet Leigh, Maureen Stapleton, Paul Lynde, Bobby Rydell. Distributors: Twyman Films; Institutional Cinema.
Teen rock 'n' roll idol is drafted and America goes crazy. One devoted fan wins "one last kiss" from the heartthrob, and her whole family shares her anxiety. Mus-Com

1644   CABIN IN THE SKY
100 min. , b&w, 1943.
Director: Vincente Minnelli. Cast: Ethel Waters, Eddie Anderson, Lena Horne, Louis Armstrong, Rex Ingram. Distributor: Films Inc.
The Lord (assisted by the target's church-going wife) and The Devil (assisted by gamblers, booze, and a floozy) fight for the soul of a man. Mus

1645   CAPE FEAR
106 min. , b&w, 1961.
Director: J. Lee Thompson. Cast: Gregory Peck, Robert Mitchum, Polly Bergen, Martin Balsam, Lori Martin, Jack Kruschen, Telly Savalas. Distributor: Universal/16.
Convicted rapist comes back to terrorize the wife and daughter of the man who testified against him. Dra

1646   CAROUSEL
128 min., color, 1956.
Director: Henry King. Cast: Shirley Jones, Gordon
MacRae, Cameron Mitchell. Distributor: Films Inc.
A carnival barker mistreats the shy girl he marries,
but he loves her and dies trying to provide for their expected baby. Mus

1647   CARRIE
98 min., color, 1976.
Director: Brian DePalma. Cast: Sissy Spacek, Piper
Laurie, Betty Buckley, Amy Irving. Distributor: United
Artists/16.
A religious fanatic abuses her teenage daughter in
the name of Jesus. Hor

1648   CASANOVA BROWN
99 min., b&w, 1944.
Director: Sam Wood. Cast: Gary Cooper, Teresa Wright,
Frank Morgan, Anita Louise, Patricia Collinge. Distributor: United Artists/16.
College professor, whose marriage has been annulled
and who's about to be remarried, finds that he's also about
to become a father by his ex-wife. Com

1649   CAT ON A HOT TIN ROOF
108 min., color, 1958.
Director: Richard Brooks. Cast: Elizabeth Taylor, Paul
Newman, Burl Ives, Judith Anderson, Jack Carson, Madeleine Sherwood. Distributor: Films Inc.
Hothouse family drama on Big Daddy's Southern
plantation, involving strained relations between Big Daddy,
Big Mama, Maggie the Cat, her impotent husband Brick,
and the little no-neck monsters. From the play by Tennessee Williams. Dra

1650   THE CATERED AFFAIR
92 min., b&w, 1956.
Director: Richard Brooks. Cast: Bette Davis, Ernest
Borgnine, Debbie Reynolds, Barry Fitzgerald. Distributor:
Films Inc.
A Bronx mother plans an extravagant wedding the
family can't afford, all to impress the future groom's
mother. Dra

1651   THE CHAMP
86 min., b&w, 1931.
Director: King Vidor. Cast: Wallace Beery, Jackie
Cooper, Irene Rich, Roscoe Ates, Edward Brophy, Hale
Hamilton. Distributor: Films Inc.
Down-and-out boxer and the son who adores him.
Dra

1652   CHEAPER BY THE DOZEN
85 min. , color, 1950.
Director: Walter Lang.   Cast: Clifton Webb, Jeanne
Crain, Myrna Loy.   Distributor: Films Inc.
An industrial engineer tries to introduce efficiency
into his own household of 12 children.   See also   BELLES
ON THEIR TOES (1613).   Com

1653   CHICKEN EVERY SUNDAY
94 min. , b&w, 1949.
Director: George Seaton.   Cast: Dan Dailey, Celeste
Holm, William Frawley, Alan Young.   Distributor: Films
Inc.
A woman filing for divorce thinks back over her
wedding and subsequent 20 years of marriage.   Com

1654   A CHILD IS WAITING
102 min. , b&w, 1963.
Director: John Cassavetes.   Cast: Judy Garland, Burt
Lancaster, Bruce Ritchey, Gena Rowlands, Steven Hill.
Distributor: Audio Brandon Films.
Plight of a mentally retarded boy abandoned by his
parents and placed in a state institution.   Dra

1655   CHRIST IN CONCRETE (SALT TO THE DEVIL)
116 min. , b&w, 1949.
Director: Edward Dmytryk.   Cast: Sam Wanamaker, Lea
Padovani, Kathleen Ryan.   Distributor: Audio Brandon
Films.
Italian American tenement life during the Twenties
and Depression.   Originally titled GIVE US THIS DAY.   Dra

1656   CHRISTMAS HOLIDAY
93 min. , b&w, 1944.
Director: Robert Siodmak.   Cast: Deanna Durbin, Gene
Kelly, Gladys George, Gale Sondergaard, Richard Whorf.
Distributor: Universal/16.
A young singer is tormented by her marriage to a
murderer.   Dra

1657   CINDERELLA LIBERTY
120 min. , color, 1973.
Director: Mark Rydell.   Cast: James Caan, Marsha Mason,
Kirk Calloway.   Distributor: Films Inc.
A seaman on liberty in Seattle falls for a hooker and
becomes surrogate father to her precocious mulatto son.
Com-Dra

1658   CINDERFELLA
88 min. , color, 1960.
Director: Frank Tashlin.   Cast: Jerry Lewis, Judith Anderson, Ed Wynn, Anna Maria Alberghetti.   Distributor:
Twyman Films.

Take-off on the Cinderella myth. Here, Lewis is
Fella, a simple boy about to inherit riches, but not before
his stepmother and stepbrothers make a play for it.
Parents' Magazine Family Medal Award. Com

1659   CITIZEN KANE
       119 min. , b&w, 1941.
       Director: Orson Welles. Cast: Orson Welles, Joseph
       Cotten, Dorothy Comingore, Agnes Moorehead, Ruth War-
       rick. Distributor: Films Inc.
           Flashbacks trace the fictional life of Charles Foster
       Kane, from childhood through two marriages, from wealth
       and power to lonely death. Bio

1660   CITY FOR CONQUEST
       106 min. , b&w, 1940.
       Director: Anatole Litvak. Cast: James Cagney, Ann Sheri-
       dan, Anthony Quinn, Arthur Kennedy, Donald Crisp, Elia
       Kazan. Distributor: United Artists/16.
           A boxer sacrifices all for his younger brother, even
       his eyesight in one last fight. Dra

1661   CLAUDIA
       91 min. , b&w, 1943.
       Director: Edmund Goulding. Cast: Dorothy McGuire,
       Robert Young, Ina Claire, Reginald Gardiner. Distributor:
       Films Inc.
           A child-bride matures when she hears that her
       mother is dying. See also CLAUDIA AND DAVID (1662).
       From the play by Rose Franken. Com-Dra

1662   CLAUDIA AND DAVID
       78 min. , b&w, 1946.
       Director: Walter Lang. Cast: Dorothy McGuire, Robert
       Young, Mary Astor, Rose Hobart. Distributor: Films Inc.
           Claudia and David with their baby in Connecticut.
       Sequel to CLAUDIA (1661). Com

1663   CLAUDINE
       92 min. , color, 1974.
       Director: John Berry. Cast: Diahann Carroll, James
       Earl Jones, Tamu, David Kruger, Yvette Curtis, Eric
       Jones, Adam Wade. Distributor: Films Inc.
           A 36-year-old black, single mother of six, illegally
       supplements her welfare checks by working as a domestic.
       She falls for a garbage collector, but both are afraid of
       permanent relationships. Com-Dra

1664   THE COCKEYED MIRACLE
       81 min. , b&w, 1946.
       Director: S. Sylvan Simon. Cast: Frank Morgan, Keenan
       Wynn, Cecil Kellaway, Audrey Totter, Gladys Cooper. Dis-
       tributor: Films Inc.
           Two spirits return to look after their family. Fan

1665   THE COHENS AND KELLYS IN HOLLYWOOD
78 min., b&w, 1932.
Director: John Francis Dillon. Cast: George Sidney,
Charles Murray, June Clyde, Norman Foster. Distributor:
Universal/16.
The families move to Hollywood, where daughter
Kitty Kelly becomes a movie star. Com

1666   THE COHENS AND KELLYS IN TROUBLE
71 min., b&w, 1933.
Director: George Stevens. Cast: George Sidney, Charlie
Murray, Maureen O'Sullivan, Andy Devine. Distributor:
Universal/16.
The families decide to take a vacation by the sea,
and run into Kelly's gold-digging ex-wife. Com

1667   COME BACK, LITTLE SHEBA
99 min., b&w, 1952.
Director: Daniel Mann. Cast: Shirley Booth, Burt Lancaster, Richard Jaeckel, Terry Moore. Distributor: Paramount Pictures Corp.
An alcoholic and his wife live an empty existence,
always dwelling on what might have been. From the play
by William Inge. Dra

1668   COME BLOW YOUR HORN
115 min., color, 1963.
Director: Bud Yorkin. Cast: Frank Sinatra, Lee J. Cobb,
Molly Picon, Barbara Rush, Jill St. John, Tony Bill.
Distributor: Paramount Pictures Corp.
A swinging bachelor has it made until his younger
brother shows up at his pad and wants a taste of the good
life, too. From the play by Neil Simon. Com

1669   COMING HOME
127 min., color, 1978.
Director: Hal Ashby. Cast: Jane Fonda, Jon Voight,
Bruce Dern, Penelope Milford. Distributor: United Art-
ists/16.
The effects of the Vietnam War on a marriage. Dra

1670   CORNBREAD, EARL AND ME
95 min., color, 1975.
Director: Joe Manduke. Cast: Moses Gunn, Rosalind
Cash, Keith Wilkes, Bernie Casey, Madge Sinclair. Distributor: Swank Motion Pictures.
A black high-school athlete is mistaken for a rapist-
killer and gunned down by the police. His parents set out
to clear their son's name. Dra

1671   THE COUNTRY GIRL
104 min., b&w, 1954.
Director: George Seaton. Cast: Bing Crosby, Grace Kelly,

William Holden, Gene Reynolds. Distributor: Paramount Pictures Corp.
A has-been, alcoholic actor blames his failures on his wife, yet he is totally dependent upon her. From the play by Clifford Odets. Dra

1672 THE COURTSHIP OF EDDIE'S FATHER
117 min., color, 1963.
Director: Vincente Minnelli. Cast: Glenn Ford, Shirley Jones, Stella Stevens, Dina Merrill, Ron Howard, Roberta Sherwood. Distributor: Films Inc.
A widowed father won't remarry until his 6-year-old son approves the choice. Com-Dra

1673 CRAZY MAMA
82 min., color, 1975.
Director: Jonathan Demme. Cast: Cloris Leachman, Stuart Whitman, Ann Sothern, Linda Purl, Jim Backus. Distributor: Films Inc.
When a bill collector takes away her beauty salon, a woman steals his car and takes off with her mother and pregnant daughter. Along the way, they rob banks. Com-Dra

1674 THE CRAZY QUILT
80 min., b&w, 1966.
Director: John Korty. Cast: Tom Rosqui, Ina Mela. Narrator: Burgess Meredith. Distributor: Kit Parker Films.
Two unusual people finally end up a couple--not because of any great passion, but because that's all there is. Com-Dra

1675 THE CROWD ROARS
85 min., b&w, 1932.
Director: Howard Hawks. Cast: James Cagney, Joan Blondell, Ann Dvorak, Eric Linden, Guy Kibbee. Distributor: United Artists/16.
A champion race-car driver teaches the trade to his kid brother, who proceeds to steal away his girlfriend and his success. Dra

1676 DAISY MILLER
91 min., color, 1974.
Director: Peter Bogdanovich. Cast: Cybill Shepherd, Barry Brown, Mildred Natwick, Cloris Leachman, Eileen Brennan. Distributor: Paramount Pictures Corp.
Young American woman, her mother, and bratty brother take Europe by storm, offending all the right rich people and losing in the end. Dra

1677 THE DARK AT THE TOP OF THE STAIRS
124 min., color, 1960.

Director: Delbert Mann. Cast: Robert Preston, Dorothy McGuire, Eve Arden, Angela Lansbury, Shirley Knight. Distributor: Audio Brandon Films.
A salesman and his family in a small Oklahoma town in the Twenties. Seventeen years of marriage-gone-sour, a small son, and an adolescent daughter with growing pains. From the play by William Inge. Dra

1678   THE DARK MIRROR
85 min. , b&w, 1946.
Director: Robert Siodmak. Cast: Olivia de Havilland, Lew Ayres, Thomas Mitchell. Distributor: Ivy Film.
One twin is normal; one is demented. Mys

1679   DAUGHTERS COURAGEOUS
107 min. , b&w, 1939.
Director: Michael Curtiz. Cast: Claude Rains, John Garfield, Rosemary Lane, Lola Lane, Priscilla Lane, Fay Bainter, Jeffrey Lynn. Distributor: United Artists/16.
Daughters try working out the problems of their parents: their father returns after a 20-year absence. See also FOUR DAUGHTERS (1728), FOUR WIVES (1730), and FOUR MOTHERS (1729). Dra

1680   DAYS OF WINE AND ROSES
117 min. , b&w, 1962.
Director: Blake Edwards. Cast: Jack Lemmon, Lee Remick, Charles Bickford, Jack Klugman. Distributor: Twyman Films.
The devastating effects of alcoholism on a marriage. Parents' Magazine Special Merit Award. Dra

1681   DEAR BRAT
82 min. , b&w, 1951.
Director: William A. Seiter. Cast: Mona Freeman, Billy DeWolfe, Edward Arnold, Lyle Bettger. Distributor: Paramount Pictures Corp.
Judge Wilkins is running for reelection to the state Senate. His teenage daughter wants to right the wrongs of the world, so she sets out to rehabilitate ex-cons and hires one as the family gardener. Sequel to DEAR WIFE (1684) and DEAR RUTH (1683). Com

1682   DEAR BRIGITTE
100 min. , color, 1965.
Director: Henry Koster. Cast: James Stewart, Fabian, Glynis Johns, Billy Mumy, Brigitte Bardot. Distributor: Films Inc.
Jimmy Stewart's son has a crush on Bardot. Com

1683   DEAR RUTH
95 min. , b&w, 1947.
Director: William D. Russell. Cast: William Holden,

Joan Caulfield, Mona Freeman, Edward Arnold, Billy De-
Wolfe. Distributor: Universal/16.
A teenager writes love letters to a serviceman using
her sister's name and photo. See also DEAR WIFE (1684)
and DEAR BRAT (1681). Com

1684 DEAR WIFE
98 min., b&w, 1949.
Director: Richard Haydn. Cast: William Holden, Joan
Caulfield, Billy DeWolfe, Mona Freeman, Edward Arnold.
Distributor: Paramount Pictures Corp.
Sequel to DEAR RUTH (1683). Ruth Wilkins is now
married to Bill, but they can't afford to move out of her
parents' house. See also DEAR BRAT (1681). Com

1685 DEATH BE NOT PROUD
99 min., color, 1975.
Director: Donald Wrye. Cast: Arthur Hill, Robby Benson.
Distributors: Learning Corp. of America; Mass Media
Ministries.
True story of the life, dying, and death of John
Gunther's remarkable 16-year-old son. Bio

1686 THE DEATH OF RICHIE
98 min., color, 1977.
Director: Paul Wendkos. Cast: Ben Gazzara, Robby
Benson, Lance Kerwin, Eileen Brennan, Clint Howard.
Distributor: Learning Corp. of America.
Distraught father kills his drug-crazed son. See
also RICHIE (1201). Dra-Bio

1687 A DELICATE BALANCE
134 min., color, 1973.
Director: Tony Richardson. Cast: Katharine Hepburn,
Paul Scofield, Lee Remick, Kate Reid, Joseph Cotten,
Betsy Blair. Distributor: Paramount Pictures Corp.
A wealthy middle-aged couple, her alcoholic sister,
their neurotic daughter, and a frightened pair of neighbors
banter, bicker, and booze in the couple's posh Connecticut
home. From the play by Edward Albee. Dra

1688 DESIGNING WOMAN
118 min., color, 1957.
Director: Vincente Minnelli. Cast: Gregory Peck, Lauren
Bacall, Dolores Gray, Sam Levene. Distributor: Films
Inc.
Marital complications result when a New York sports-
writer marries a fashion designer. Com

1689 DESIRE UNDER THE ELMS
111 min., b&w, 1958.
Director: Delbert Mann. Cast: Sophia Loren, Anthony
Perkins, Burl Ives. Distributor: Paramount Pictures Corp.

A 70-year-old New England patriarch is hated by
his sons, while his young, immigrant wife lusts after his
stepson and his farm.   From the play by Eugene O'Neill.
Dra

1690   DESPERATE CHARACTERS
88 min. , color, 1971.
Director: Frank D. Gilroy.   Cast: Shirley MacLaine,
Kenneth Mars, Gerald S. O'Loughlin, Sada Thompson.   Dis-
tributor: Paramount Pictures Corp.
A childless couple are trapped in a joyless marriage.
Dra

1691   THE DESPERATE HOURS
112 min. , b&w, 1955.
Director: William Wyler.   Cast: Fredric March, Arthur
Kennedy, Humphrey Bogart, Martha Scott, Gig Young.   Distributor: Paramount Pictures Corp.
Three escaped cons terrorize a family's home; the
father does his best to save his family.   From the play/
novel by Joseph Hayes.   Dra

1692   DIAMOND HEAD
107 min. , color, 1962.
Director: Guy Green.   Cast: Charlton Heston, Yvette
Mimieux, George Chakiris, France Nuyen, Aline MacMahon.
Distributor: Audio Brandon Films.
A ruthless, white empire-builder in Hawaii challenges
his defiant sister's romance with a Hawaiian boy.   Dra

1693   DIARY OF A MAD HOUSEWIFE
100 min. , color, 1970.
Director: Frank Perry.   Cast: Richard Benjamin, Carrie
Snodgress, Frank Langella.   Distributors: Universal/16;
Swank Motion Pictures.
A dissatisfied wife is trapped with a monster of a
husband, obnoxious kids, and a narcissistic lover.   Dra

1694   DIVORCE AMERICAN STYLE
109 min. , color, 1967.
Director: Bud Yorkin.   Cast: Dick Van Dyke, Debbie
Reynolds, Jean Simmons, Jason Robards, Van Johnson.
Distributor: Audio Brandon Films.
After 17 years of marriage, a couple end up in a
divorce court.   Com

1695   DODSWORTH
101 min. , b&w, 1936.
Director: William Wyler.   Cast: Walter Huston, Ruth
Chatterton, Mary Astor, David Niven.   Distributor: Audio
Brandon Films.
A middle-aged businessman tries to preserve his
marriage to a selfish woman.   Dra

1696   DOUBLE INDEMNITY
        107 min. , b&w, 1944.
        Director: Billy Wilder. Cast: Fred MacMurray, Barbara
        Stanwyck, Edward G. Robinson. Distributor: Universal/16.
        An insurance agent falls for a conniving blonde, who
        talks him into helping her bump off her husband for the in-
        surance money. Mys

1697   A DREAM OF KINGS
        107 min. , color, 1969.
        Director: Daniel Mann. Cast: Anthony Quinn, Irene
        Papas, Inger Stevens, Sam Levene. Distributor: Swank
        Motion Pictures.
        A Greek American tries to get enough money to-
        gether to bring his dying son back to Greece. Dra

1698   DRUMS ALONG THE MOHAWK
        103 min. , color, 1939.
        Director: John Ford. Cast: Claudette Colbert, Henry
        Fonda, Edna May Oliver, John Carradine, Ward Bond.
        Distributor: Films Inc.
        A young man, his new bride, and subsequent baby
        settle in the backwoods of New York State along the Mohawk
        Trail. They face hostile Indians, the Revolutionary War,
        and a "pretty" flag in the end. See also 1776: AMERI-
        CAN REVOLUTION ON THE FRONTIER (1258). His-Dra

1699   DUEL IN THE SUN
        135 min. , color, 1947.
        Director: King Vidor. Cast: Gregory Peck, Jennifer
        Jones, Joseph Cotten, Lionel Barrymore, Lillian Gish,
        Walter Huston, Herbert Marshall, Butterfly McQueen.
        Distributor: Twyman Films.
        One good brother, one bad brother, and a romance
        with a half-breed Indian girl. Wes

1700   DYNASTY
        99 min. , color, 1976.
        Director: Lee Philips. Cast: Stacy Keach, Sarah Miles,
        Harris Yulin. Distributor: Lucerne Films.
        Two feuding brothers share a woman and a business
        in the Old West. Wes

1701   EAST OF EDEN
        115 min. , color, 1955.
        Director: Elia Kazan. Cast: James Dean, Raymond
        Massey, Jo Van Fleet, Julie Harris, Burl Ives. Distribu-
        tors: Audio Brandon Films; Swank Motion Pictures; Twy-
        man Films.
        Strife between a religious fanatic father and his
        tormented son. Also includes a favored son and a long-
        missing mother. Set in California on the eve of World War
        I. Parents' Magazine Special Merit Award. Dra

1702   THE EFFECT OF GAMMA RAYS ON MAN-IN-THE-MOON
MARIGOLDS
101 min., color, 1972.
Director: Paul Newman.   Cast: Joanne Woodward, Nell
Potts, Roberta Wallach.   Distributor: Films Inc.
Seedy mother torments her two daughters and re-
grets her wasted life.   From the play by Paul Zindel.   Dra

1703   THE EGG AND I
108 min., b&w, 1947.
Director: Chester Erskine.   Cast: Claudette Colbert,
Fred MacMurray, Marjorie Main, Percy Kilbride, Louise
Allbritton.   Distributor: Universal/16.
Stylish city slickers move to a dilapidated chicken
farm, try to raise chickens, and adjust to rural life.   First
appearance of Ma and Pa Kettle.   Com

1704   ELEANOR AND FRANKLIN: THE EARLY YEARS
2 hours, color, 1976.
1705   ELEANOR AND FRANKLIN: RISE TO LEADERSHIP
2 hours, color, 1976.
1706   ELEANOR AND FRANKLIN: THE WHITE HOUSE YEARS
3 hours, color, 1977.
Director: Daniel Petrie.   Cast: Jane Alexander, Edward
Herrmann, Ed Flanders, Rosemary Murphy, Priscilla
Pointer, Walter McGinn.   Distributor: Time-Life Multimedia.
Life stories of Eleanor before Franklin, and Eleanor
and Franklin and family as they rise to the White House.
Bio

1707   THE EMIGRANTS
151 min., color, 1972.
Director: Jan Troell.   Cast: Max von Sydow, Liv Ullmann.   Distributor: Swank Motion Pictures.
Dramatic account of Swedes' emigration to America
in the mid-19th century.   Focuses on Karl Oskar and his
wife Kristina.   See also THE NEW LAND (1893).   His-
Dra

1708   ENTER LAUGHING
112 min., color, 1967.
Director: Carl Reiner.   Cast: Reni Santoni, Jose Ferrer,
Shelley Winters, Elaine May, Jack Gilford.   Distributor:
Audio Brandon Films.
From Carl Reiner's autobiographical novel about a
star-struck Bronx boy who dreams of an acting career,
while his parents push him to keep his job.   Com

1709   EVERYTHING BUT THE TRUTH
86 min., color, 1956.
Director: Jerry Hopper.   Cast: Maureen O'Hara, John
Forsythe, Tim Hovey, Frank Faylen.   Distributor: Uni-
versal/16.

A little boy takes his parents' advice to tell the truth. He throws his whole town into an uproar by exposing political corruption and becoming a national celebrity. Com

1710   THE EXORCIST
121 min. , color, 1973.
Director: William Friedkin. Cast: Ellen Burstyn, Linda Blair, Jason Miller, Lee J. Cobb, Max von Sydow. Distributor: Swank Motion Pictures.
A mother is distraught over her daughter's bizarre fits. Hor

1711   FACES
129 min. , b&w, 1968.
Director: John Cassavetes. Cast: John Marley, Gena Rowlands, Lynn Carlin, Seymour Cassel. Distributor: Budget Films.
The breakdown of a middle-class marriage. Dra

1712   FAMILY HONEYMOON
85 min. , b&w, 1948.
Director: Claude Binyon. Cast: Claudette Colbert, Fred MacMurray, Rita Johnson, William Daniels. Distributor: Universal/16.
A young widow takes her rowdy tots on her honeymoon when she remarries. Com

1713   THE FARMER'S DAUGHTER
97 min. , b&w, 1947.
Director: H. C. Potter. Cast: Loretta Young, Joseph Cotten, Ethel Barrymore. Distributor: Audio Brandon Films.
A Swedish farm girl rises from humble beginnings to become a candidate for Congress. Her boyfriend's mother runs the opposing political machine. Com

1714   FATHER OF THE BRIDE
92 min. , b&w, 1950.
Director: Vincente Minnelli. Cast: Spencer Tracy, Joan Bennett, Elizabeth Taylor, Billie Burke, Leo G. Carroll. Distributor: Films Inc.
A lawyer is a contented man until his daughter announces wedding plans. See also FATHER'S LITTLE DIVIDEND (1715). Com

1715   FATHER'S LITTLE DIVIDEND
82 min. , b&w, 1951.
Director: Vincente Minnelli. Cast: Spencer Tracy, Joan Bennett, Elizabeth Taylor, Don Taylor, Billie Burke, Russ Tamblyn. Distributor: Films Inc.
Months after her wedding, with her father still recuperating, a bride announces that she is pregnant. Sequel to FATHER OF THE BRIDE (1714). Com

1716   FEAR STRIKES OUT
       100 min. , b&w, 1957.
       Director: Robert Mulligan.   Cast: Anthony Perkins, Karl
       Malden, Norma Moore, Adam Williams.   Distributor: Para-
       mount Pictures Corp.
           A hard-driving father pushes his son to practice
       ball everyday so that he'll someday play for the Boston Red
       Sox.   His son cracks up under the strain, just as he's
       about to reach his goal.   Based on Jimmy Piersall's life.
       Bio

1717   FIRE SALE
       88 min. , color, 1977.
       Director: Alan Arkin.   Cast: Alan Arkin, Rob Reiner,
       Vincent Gardenia, Sid Caesar, Kay Medford.   Distributor:
       Films Inc.
           The exploits of the nutty Fikus family.   Com

1718   THE FIRST TIME
       89 min. , b&w, 1952.
       Director: Frank Tashlin.   Cast: Robert Cummings, Bar-
       bara Hale, Jeff Donnell.   Distributor: Institutional Cinema.
           A young couple's life is turned upside down by a new
       baby.   Com

1719   FIVE FINGER EXERCISE
       109 min. , b&w, 1962.
       Director: Daniel Mann.   Cast: Rosalind Russell, Jack
       Hawkins, Maximilian Schell, Richard Beymer.   Distributor:
       Audio Brandon Films.
           A middle-aged wife and mother becomes infatuated
       with her children's refined tutor and disgusted with her
       brash husband.   Dra

1720   FIVE ON THE BLACK HAND SIDE
       96 min. , color, 1973.
       Director: Oscar Williams.   Cast: Leonard Jackson,
       Clarice Taylor, Virginia Capers, Glynn Turman.   Distribu-
       tor: United Artists/16.
           A middle-class black family enlightens their father/
       husband about women's lib and black self-awareness.   Com

1721   FLAMING STAR
       92 min. , color, 1960.
       Director: Don Siegel.   Cast: Elvis Presley, Barbara Eden,
       Steve Forrest, Dolores Del Rio.   Distributor: Films Inc.
           Texas, 1870--a white settler, his Indian wife, their
       half-breed son, and a white son by a previous marriage are
       caught up in an Indian uprising.   Wes

1722   FLOWER DRUM SONG
       131 min. , color, 1961.
       Director: Henry Koster.   Cast: Nancy Kwan, James

Shigeta, Jack Soo, Miyoshi Umeki, Juanita Hall, Benson Fong. Distributor: Universal/16.
A Chinese girl comes to San Francisco to marry a husband selected in a photo; but she falls for someone else. Mus

1723 FOR LOVE OF IVY
102 min., color, 1968.
Director: Daniel Mann. Cast: Sidney Poitier, Abbey Lincoln, Beau Bridges, Nan Martin, Carroll O'Connor. Distributor: Films Inc.
A suburban family is unhappy when their black housekeeper decides to leave them for a secretarial job. Com

1724 FOR LOVE OR MONEY
108 min., color, 1963.
Director: Michael Gordon. Cast: Kirk Douglas, Mitzi Gaynor, Thelma Ritter, Gig Young, William Bendix, Julie Newmar. Distributor: Universal/16.
A wealthy widow tries to marry off her three beautiful daughters. Com

1725 FOR PETE'S SAKE
109 min., color, 1974.
Director: Peter Yates. Cast: Barbra Streisand, Michael Sarrazin, Estelle Parsons, William Redfield, Molly Picon. Distributors: Twyman Films; Swank Motion Pictures.
To save her husband from debt, a woman tries one unsuccessful scheme after another to make money. Com

1726 THE FORTUNE COOKIE
125 min., b&w, 1966.
Director: Billy Wilder. Cast: Jack Lemmon, Walter Matthau, Ron Rich, Judi West. Distributor: United Artists/16.
A TV cameraman is knocked down at a pro ball game, and his shady brother-in-law talks him into pretending real injury and trying to collect. Sat

1727 40 CARATS
110 min., color, 1973.
Director: Milton Katselas. Cast: Liv Ullmann, Edward Albert, Gene Kelly, Binnie Barnes. Distributor: Swank Motion Pictures.
A fortyish divorcée wonders whether to marry a 22-year-old man. She asks her teenage daughter, mother, and ex-husband if they approve. Com

1728 FOUR DAUGHTERS
90 min., b&w, 1938.
Director: Michael Curtiz. Cast: The Lane Sisters, Claude Rains, Gale Page, John Garfield. Distributor: United Artists/16.

Four sisters from a musical family and their love
lives. See also FOUR WIVES (1730), DAUGHTERS COUR-
AGEOUS (1679), and FOUR MOTHERS (1729). Dra

1729   FOUR MOTHERS
86 min. , b&w, 1940.
Director: William Keighley. Cast: The Lane Sisters,
Claude Rains, Eddie Albert, Gale Page, May Robson. Distributor: United Artists/16.
A family reunion is wrecked when a son-in-law's
land-development scheme falls through, and they must struggle to repay investors. See also DAUGHTERS COURA-
GEOUS (1679), FOUR WIVES (1730), and FOUR DAUGHTERS
(1728). Dra

1730   FOUR WIVES
99 min. , b&w, 1939.
Director: Michael Curtiz. Cast: The Lane Sisters, Claude
Rains, Eddie Albert, John Garfield. Distributor: United
Artists/16.
The four daughters are now wives, and suffer love
and other difficulties. See also DAUGHTERS COURA-
GEOUS (1679), FOUR DAUGHTERS (1728), and FOUR
MOTHERS (1729). Dra

1731   FREAKY FRIDAY
95 min. , color, 1977.
Director: Gary Nelson. Cast: Jodie Foster, Barbara Harris, John Astin. Distributor: Swank Motion Pictures.
Mother and daughter reverse roles, and when they
do, they have to cope with the results. Com

1732   FRIENDLY PERSUASION
137 min. , color, 1956.
Director: William Wyler. Cast: Gary Cooper, Dorothy
McGuire, Anthony Perkins. Distributor: Hurlock Cine
World.
The Civil War disrupts the lives of a peace-loving
Indiana Quaker family. Dra

1733   FROM THE TERRACE
144 min. , color, 1960.
Director: Mark Robson. Cast: Paul Newman, Joanne
Woodward, Myrna Loy, Ina Balin, Leon Ames. Distributor:
Films Inc.
Dissolution of a marriage through misunderstanding
and neglect. Moral: Wealth can't buy happiness. Dra

1734   FULL OF LIFE
91 min. , b&w, 1957.
Director: Richard Quine. Cast: Judy Holliday, Richard
Conte, Salvatore Baccaloni. Distributor: Institutional Cinema.
The husband is not a successful writer; his wife is
pregnant; and the house is full of termites. Newlyweds. Com

1735   FUN WITH DICK AND JANE
        95 min., color, 1977.
        Director: Ted Kotcheff. Cast: Jane Fonda, George Segal,
        Ed McMahon. Distributor: Swank Motion Pictures.
            When an upper-middle-class family man loses his
        job, he and his wife maintain their posh life-style with
        part-time jobs as armed robbers. Com

1736   THE GAY SISTERS
        110 min., b&w, 1942.
        Director: Irving Rapper. Cast: Barbara Stanwyck,
        Geraldine Fitzgerald, George Brent, Nancy Coleman, Gig
        Young. Distributor: United Artists/16.
            Three sisters are heiresses, but they need money.
        One marries just to obtain the inheritance. Dra

1737   GENERATION (A TIME FOR GIVING)
        104 min., color, 1969.
        Director: George Schaefer. Cast: David Janssen, Kim
        Darby, Carl Reiner, Pete Duel, Andrew Prine, James
        Coco, Sam Waterston. Distributor: Association Films.
            A pair of newlyweds decide to have their child with-
        out medical assistance, much to the consternation of the
        girl's father. Com

1738   GIANT
        201 min., color, 1956.
        Director: George Stevens. Cast: Elizabeth Taylor, Rock
        Hudson, James Dean, Carroll Baker, Jane Withers, Chill
        Wills, Mercedes McCambridge, Sal Mineo. Distributor:
        Twyman Films.
            Rock owns a huge cattle ranch in Texas. He meets
        and marries Liz, and brings her back to the ranch. She
        has trouble adjusting, but they have a family. Rock's sis-
        ter is the tyrant. Wes-Dra

1739   THE GIFT OF LOVE
        105 min., color, 1958.
        Director: Jean Negulesco. Cast: Lauren Bacall, Robert
        Stack, Evelyn Rudie, Lorne Greene. Distributor: Films
        Inc.
            After the death of his wife, a man adopts a preco-
        cious child who desperately tries to fill the void in his life.
        Dra

1740   GIVE US THIS DAY see
            CHRIST IN CONCRETE (SALT TO THE DEVIL) 1655

1741   THE GLASS MENAGERIE
        104 min., color, 1973.
        Director: Anthony Harvey. Cast: Katharine Hepburn, Sam
        Waterston, Michael Moriarty, Joanna Miles. Distributor:
        Cinema 5--16mm.

Amanda Wingfield was deserted by her husband, but desperately clings to romantic notions and her two grown children--a crippled, shy daughter and a poetic son with wanderlust. From the play by Tennessee Williams. Dra

1742   GO ASK ALICE
74 min., color, 1973.
Director: John Korty. Cast: Jamie Smith-Jackson, Andy Griffith, Ruth Roman, Julie Adams, William Shatner. Distributors: Twyman Films; Swank Motion Pictures.
The descent of a straight teenager into a life of drugs and sex, due to her feelings of inadequacy and loneliness when her family moves to a new neighborhood. Dra

1743   THE GODFATHER
171 min., color, 1972.
1744   THE GODFATHER, PART II
200 min., color, 1974.
Director: Francis Ford Coppola. Cast: Al Pacino, Marlon Brando, James Caan, Robert Duvall, Diane Keaton, Robert De Niro, Richard Castellano. Distributor: Paramount Pictures Corp.
The rise of the Corleone family--first- and second-generation Italian Americans--to positions of power in the Mafia. Dra

1745   GOING HOME
97 min., color, 1971.
Director: Herbert Leonard. Cast: Robert Mitchum, Jan-Michael Vincent, Brenda Vaccaro. Distributor: Films Inc.
After serving a prison term for the murder of his wife, a man tries to go straight, but is deterred by his revenge-seeking son, who witnessed the murder. Dra

1746   THE GOLDBERGS   see
MOLLY   1879

1747   GONE WITH THE WIND
222 min., color, 1939.
Director: Victor Fleming. Cast: Clark Gable, Vivien Leigh, Leslie Howard, Olivia de Havilland, Thomas Mitchell, Hattie McDaniel. Distributor: Films Inc.
When all is said and done, there's no place like home for Scarlett O'Hara. His-Dra

1748   GOODBYE, COLUMBUS
105 min., color, 1969.
Director: Larry Peerce. Cast: Ali MacGraw, Richard Benjamin, Jack Klugman, Nan Martin, Michael Meyers. Distributor: Paramount Pictures Corp.
Poor boy falls for rich Jewish princess from Westchester. Dra

1749   THE GOODBYE GIRL
110 min. , color, 1977.
Director: Herbert Ross.   Cast: Richard Dreyfuss, Marsha
Mason, Quinn Cummings.   Distributor: Swank Motion Pictures.
Erstwhile New York chorus dancer and her young
daughter are deserted by the latest live-in boyfriend, and
must learn to adapt to a new, and initially unwanted, male
tenant. Com

1750   THE GRADUATE
105 min. , color, 1967.
Director: Mike Nichols. Cast: Dustin Hoffman, Anne
Bancroft, Katharine Ross, William Daniels. Distributors:
Audio Brandon Films; Twyman Films.
A mother and daughter battle it out for the same
young man. Com

1751   THE GRAPES OF WRATH
115 min. , b&w, 1940.
Director: John Ford. Cast: Henry Fonda, Jane Darwell,
John Carradine, Charley Grapewin, Russell Simpson. Distributor: Films Inc.
The migration of poor white farmers from the Midwestern dust bowl to the California fruit valleys in search
of work. See also THE OKIES--UPROOTED FARMERS
(1047). Dra

1752   THE GREAT GATSBY
146 min. , color, 1974.
Director: Jack Clayton. Cast: Mia Farrow, Robert Redford, Bruce Dern, Sam Waterston, Karen Black. Distributor: Paramount Pictures Corp.
The Jazz Age and a rich young man's obsession with
a married belle both end in tragedy. Dra

1753   THE GREAT LIE
107 min. , b&w, 1941.
Director: Edmund Goulding. Cast: Bette Davis, Mary
Astor, George Brent. Distributor: United Artists/16.
Two women love the same man, who is allegedly killed
in a plane crash. One woman has his baby, one has his
name. Dra

1754   THE GROUP
150 min. , color, 1966.
Director: Sidney Lumet. Cast: Joanna Pettet, Joan Hack-
ett, Elizabeth Hartman, Jessica Walter, Candice Bergen,
Kathleen Widdoes, Mary-Robin Redd, Shirley Knight, Larry
Hagman, Hal Holbrook, James Broderick. Distributor:
United Artists/16.
Lives of eight Vassar graduates, Class of 1933.
Dra

1755   GUESS WHO'S COMING TO DINNER?
108 min., color, 1967.
Director: Stanley Kramer.   Cast: Katharine Hepburn,
Spencer Tracy, Katharine Houghton, Sidney Poitier, Cecil
Kellaway, Beah Richards.   Distributors: Audio Brandon
Films; Twyman Films.
How a wealthy, liberal couple react to the news
that their daughter intends to marry a black man.   Also
covers his parents' reaction to the news that he intends to
marry a white woman.   Com-Dra

1756   A GUIDE FOR THE MARRIED MAN
91 min., color, 1967.
Director: Gene Kelly.   Cast: Walter Matthau, Inger Stevens, Robert Morse.   Distributor: Films Inc.
A philanderer teaches a friend how to cheat on his
wife.   Com

1757   GYPSY
142 min., color, 1962.
Director: Mervyn LeRoy.   Cast: Rosalind Russell, Natalie
Wood, Karl Malden.   Distributor: Twyman Films.
Childhood and early adulthood of vaudevillian and
stripper Gypsy Rose Lee, with special focus on her indomit-
able stage mother Rose.   Mus-Bio

1758   THE HAPPY ENDING
112 min., color, 1969.
Director: Richard Brooks.   Cast: Jean Simmons, John
Forsythe, Shirley Jones, Lloyd Bridges, Teresa Wright,
Dick Shawn.   Distributor: United Artists/16.
After 16 years of marriage, an unhappy wife turns
to pills and booze.   Dra

1759   THE HAPPY LAND
75 min., b&w, 1943.
Director: Irving Pichel.   Cast: Don Ameche, Frances Dee,
Harry Carey, Ann Rutherford.   Distributor: Films Inc.
Stricken father, grieving over the loss of his only
son in war, is given a new reason to live by his son's war
buddy.   Dra

1760   THE HARD WAY
109 min., b&w, 1942.
Director: Vincent Sherman.   Cast: Ida Lupino, Joan Les-
lie, Dennis Morgan, Jack Carson, Gladys George, Faye
Emerson.   Distributor: United Artists/16.
An ambitious, domineering woman wrecks her own
life, while trying to push her younger sister to stardom.
Dra

1761   HARRY AND TONTO
115 min., color, 1974.

Director: Paul Mazursky. Cast: Art Carney, Ellen Burstyn, Chief Dan George, Geraldine Fitzgerald, Larry Hagman. Distributor: Films Inc.
72-year-old retired gent and his cat travel across
America in search of personal liberation. Com

1762   HAS ANYBODY SEEN MY GAL?
89 min., color, 1952.
Director: Douglas Sirk. Cast: Charles Coburn, Piper
Laurie, Rock Hudson, Lynn Bari. Distributor: Univer-
sal/16.
A rich man gives a fortune to a family, moves in
with them in disguise, and watches the family fall apart.
Set in the Twenties. Com

1763   A HATFUL OF RAIN
107 min., b&w, 1957.
Director: Fred Zinnemann. Cast: Eva Marie Saint, Don
Murray, Anthony Franciosa, Lloyd Nolan, Henry Silva.
Distributor: Films Inc.
Effects of one man's drug addiction on his wife,
father, and brother. Set in New York City. Dra

1764   HAWAII
161 min., color, 1966.
Director: George Roy Hill. Cast: Julie Andrews, Max
von Sydow, Richard Harris. Distributor: United Artists/16.
1820--New England couple settle in Hawaii and try to
Christianize the natives. His-Dra

1765   THE HEART IS A LONELY HUNTER
124 min., color, 1968.
Director: Robert Ellis Miller. Cast: Alan Arkin, Chuck
McCann, Sondra Locke, Biff McGuire, Cicely Tyson, Stacy
Keach, Jr. Distributors: Audio Brandon Films; Twyman
Films.
The friendship between two special people--a deaf
mute and a retarded man--initiates a friendship of more
lasting consequence, that of the deaf mute and a lonely,
sensitive young girl. Dra

1766   THE HEARTBREAK KID
104 min., color, 1973.
Director: Elaine May. Cast: Jeannie Berlin, Charles
Grodin, Cybill Shepherd, Eddie Albert. Distributor: Films
Inc.
Two young Jewish newlyweds honeymoon in Miami
Beach, where the husband falls for a blond gentile. Com

1767   THE HEIRESS
115 min., b&w, 1949.
Director: William Wyler. Cast: Olivia de Havilland,
Ralph Richardson, Montgomery Clift, Miriam Hopkins. Distributors: Universal/16; Twyman Films.

A plain spinster with a tyrannical father is courted by a conniving man who's just interested in her money. See also WASHINGTON SQUARE (1460). Parents' Magazine Special Merit Award. Dra

1768   HERE COME THE NELSONS
76 min. , b&w, 1952.
Director: Frederick de Cordova. Cast: Ozzie, Harriet, David & Ricky Nelson; Rock Hudson, Ann Doran, Jim Backus, Gale Gordon. Distributor: Universal/16.
Hi Dave! Hi Rick! Hi Mom! Hi Dad! Com

1769   HERE COMES COOKIE
66 min. , b&w, 1935.
Director: Norman Z. McLeod. Cast: George Burns, Gracie Allen, Betty Furness. Distributor: Universal/16.
Afraid that one of his daughters will marry a fortune hunter, a millionaire gives all his money to his other daughter (Gracie Allen). Com

1770   HERE COMES THE GROOM
114 min. , b&w, 1951.
Director: Frank Capra. Cast: Bing Crosby, Jane Wyman, Franchot Tone, Alexis Smith. Distributor: Paramount Pictures Corp.
An American reporter in France brings two war orphans home when he returns to marry his fiancée, who intends to marry someone else. The reporter has to marry quickly or he'll lose custody of the kids. Mus-Com

1771   A HERO AIN'T NOTHIN' BUT A SANDWICH
105 min. , color, 1977.
Director: Ralph Nelson. Cast: Cicely Tyson, Paul Winfield, Larry B. Scott. Distributor: Films Inc.
Young Benjie has been abandoned by his father and has a hard time coping with his mother's boyfriend, as well as the pressures of ghetto life. He becomes a junkie, but his mother's boyfriend tries to turn the boy around. Dra

1772   HESTER STREET
91 min. , b&w, 1975.
Director: Joan Micklin Silver. Cast: Carol Kane, Steven Keats, Mel Howard. Distributor: Cinema 5--16mm.
A Russian Jew comes to America before his wife in the late 19th century. He settles on the Lower East Side of New York, quickly takes to life in America, and is attracted to a modern woman. When his wife arrives, he is embarrassed by her Old World ways. Dra

1773   HIGH SOCIETY
107 min. , color, 1956.

Director: Charles Walters. Cast: Bing Crosby, Grace
Kelly, Frank Sinatra, Celeste Holm. Distributor: Films
Inc.
   A reporter and photographer covering a posh Philadelphia wedding cause the bride to question her choice of
a second husband. Remake of THE PHILADELPHIA STORY
(1936). Mus-Com

1774   HILDA CRANE
       87 min. , color, 1956.
       Director: Philip Dunne. Cast: Jean Simmons, Jean-Pierre
       Aumont, Guy Madison, Peggy Knudsen. Distributor: Films
       Inc.
          After two bad marriages, a woman wonders if she
       can still find happiness in love. Dra

1775   HOLIDAY
       94 min. , b&w, 1938.
       Director: George Cukor. Cast: Katharine Hepburn, Cary
       Grant, Edward Everett Horton, Lew Ayres, Binnie Barnes.
       Distributors: Audio Brandon Films; Swank Motion Pictures.
          Set to marry a snobbish girl, a young man with
       dreams falls for her fun-loving sister. From the play by
       Philip Barry. Com

1776   HOT SPELL
       86 min. , b&w, 1958.
       Director: Daniel Mann. Cast: Shirley Booth, Anthony
       Quinn, Shirley MacLaine, Earl Holliman. Distributor:
       Paramount Pictures Corp.
          The patriarch of a Southern family wants to go to
       Florida with his young girlfriend. However, he's got to
       break with his wife and three kids first. Dra

1777   A HOUSE DIVIDED
       68 min. , b&w, 1932.
       Director: William Wyler. Cast: Walter Huston, Helen
       Chandler, Kent Douglass, Vivian Oakland. Distributor:
       Universal/16.
          A mail-order bride falls for the son instead. Dra

1778   HOUSE OF STRANGERS
       101 min. , b&w, 1949.
       Director: Joseph L. Mankiewicz. Cast: Edward G. Robin-
       son, Susan Hayward, Richard Conte, Luther Adler. Dis-
       tributor: Films Inc.
          Italian American crime-family drama. Dra

1779   THE HOUSE OF THE SEVEN GABLES
       88 min. , b&w, 1940.
       Director: Joe May. Cast: Vincent Price, Margaret Lind-
       say, George Sanders, Nan Grey, Alan Napier. Distributor:
       Universal/16.

Ill-fated New England family. See also the short
of the same name (668). Dra

1780   HOUSEBOAT
110 min., color, 1958.
Director: Melville Shavelson. Cast: Cary Grant, Sophia
Loren, Martha Hyer, Harry Guardino. Distributor: Paramount Pictures Corp.
A widower, with three small kids who dislike him,
hires a governess and asks her to marry him. Com

1781   HOW DO I LOVE THEE?
110 min., color, 1970.
Director: Michael Gordon. Cast: Jackie Gleason, Maureen O'Hara, Rick Lenz, Shelley Winters, Rosemary For-
syth. Distributor: Films Inc.
A talkative atheist, who moves furniture for a living,
clashes with his overly religious Bible-thumping wife. Com

1782   HOW THE WEST WAS WON
155 min., color, 1963.
Directors: John Ford, George Marshall, Henry Hathaway.
Narrator: Spencer Tracy. Cast: Carroll Baker, Lee J.
Cobb, Henry Fonda, Carolyn Jones, Karl Malden, Gregory
Peck, George Peppard, Robert Preston, Debbie Reynolds,
James Stewart, Eli Wallach, John Wayne, Richard Wid-
mark, Walter Brennan, Andy Devine, Raymond Massey,
Agnes Moorehead, Thelma Ritter. Distributor: Films Inc.
The story of several generations of a New England
farm family and their travels through the Erie Canal and
settlement in the West in the mid-to-late 1800s. Wes

1783   THE HOWARDS OF VIRGINIA
117 min., b&w, 1940.
Director: Frank Lloyd. Cast: Cary Grant, Martha Scott,
Sir Cedric Hardwicke. Distributor: Twyman Films.
The Howard family and the Peyton family, joined in
marriage, become separated by their opposing political
views. Set during the American Revolution. His-Dra

1784   HUD
112 min., b&w, 1963.
Director: Martin Ritt. Cast: Paul Newman, Melvyn
Douglas, Patricia Neal, Brandon de Wilde. Distributor:
Paramount Pictures Corp.
Hud vs. his father, tradition, and himself. A Texas
ranch family. See also THE AMERICAN WEST: A DYING
BREED (73). Dra

1785   THE HUMAN COMEDY
120 min., b&w, 1943.
Director: Clarence Brown. Cast: Mickey Rooney, Marsha
Hunt, James Craig, Frank Morgan, Van Johnson, Fay
Bainter, Donna Reed. Distributor: Films Inc.

Small-town California family is upset when their
eldest son goes off to WWII. Their young son becomes the
head of the family, goes to school, and works nights. Dra

1786 HUSBANDS
142 min., color, 1970.
Director: John Cassavetes. Cast: John Cassavetes, Peter
Falk, Ben Gazzara. Distributor: Swank Motion Pictures.
Three men share their mid-life crises. Dra

1787 HUSH, HUSH, SWEET CHARLOTTE
133 min., b&w, 1965.
Director: Robert Aldrich. Cast: Bette Davis, Olivia de
Havilland, Joseph Cotten, Agnes Moorehead, Cecil Kellaway.
Distributor: Films Inc.
A woman tries to drive her elderly cousin crazy to
get the family inheritance. Hor

1788 I LOVE MY WIFE
95 min., color, 1970.
Director: Mel Stuart. Cast: Elliott Gould, Brenda Vaccaro, Angel Tompkins. Distributor: Universal/16.
A young doctor is bored with his marriage. Com

1789 I LOVE YOU ... GOODBYE
74 min., color, 1974.
Director: Sam O'Steen. Cast: Earl Holliman, Hope Lange,
Patricia Smith, Michael Murphy. Distributor: Learning
Corp. of America.
At age 36, a wife and mother leaves home to dis-
cover her own identity. She gets a job and an apartment,
and her husband has a hard time taking it all seriously.
See also AM I WIFE, MOTHER ... OR ME? (60). Dra

1790 I MARRIED A WITCH
78 min., b&w, 1942.
Director: René Clair. Cast: Veronica Lake, Cecil Kellaway, Fredric March, Susan Hayward, Robert Benchley.
Distributors: Audio Brandon Films; Kit Parker Films.
A Salem witch puts a curse on the family of her
Puritan judge--each male member of his family will suffer
unhappiness in love. Centuries later, her spirit is released
and she materializes to wreak havoc in the life of the new-
est male member of the clan. Com

1791 I MARRIED A WOMAN
84 min., b&w, 1958.
Director: Hal Kanter. Cast: George Gobel, Diana Dors,
Adolphe Menjou. Distributor: Westcoast Films.
While trying to save his job and his marriage, an
ad executive gets caught in one mess after another. Com

1792   I NEVER SANG FOR MY FATHER
90 min. , color, 1970.
Director: Gilbert Cates.   Cast: Melvyn Douglas, Gene
Hackman, Dorothy Stickney, Estelle Parsons. Distributors:
Twyman Films; Kit Parker Films.
A difficult aging man's strained relationship with his
grown son and daughter reaches a crisis point when their
mother and the man's wife dies. See also WHEN PARENTS
GROW OLD (1504). Special Joint Award from the National
Council of Churches and the National Catholic Office for Mo-
tion Pictures. Dra

1793   I REMEMBER MAMA
135 min. , b&w, 1948.
Director: George Stevens.   Cast: Irene Dunne, Barbara
Bel Geddes, Oscar Homolka, Philip Dorn. Distributor:
Films Inc.
Teenage girl reminisces about her early home life
in San Francisco. Com-Dra

1794   I WAS A MALE WAR BRIDE
105 min. , b&w, 1949.
Director: Howard Hawks.   Cast: Cary Grant, Ann Sheridan, Marion Marshall, Randy Stuart, William Neff. Distributor: Films Inc.
A captain meets a WAC lieutenant in the American
zone of occupied Germany during WWII. After a stormy
courtship, they marry, only to find military complications
blocking their return to the U. S. Com

1795   I WILL FIGHT NO MORE FOREVER, THE STORY OF
CHIEF JOSEPH
106 min. , color, 1976.
Director: Richard T. Heffron.   Cast: Ned Romero, James
Whitmore. Distributor: Macmillan Films.
Nez Percé Chief Joseph, formerly a peace-loving man,
suffered intolerably under the white man and tried to fight
his way to freedom in Canada. He had his 300 braves,
women, and children with him; they fought 11 weeks and
1, 600 miles, and were 30 miles from the border when Chief
Joseph surrendered. His-Dra

1796   I WILL, I WILL ... FOR NOW
108 min. , color, 1976.
Director: Norman Panama.   Cast: Elliott Gould, Diane
Keaton, Paul Sorvino, Victoria Principal, Robert Alda.
Distributor: Films Inc.
A divorced New York couple continue their troubled
relationship and end up in a California sex clinic. Com

1797   I'D CLIMB THE HIGHEST MOUNTAIN
88 min. , color, 1951.
Director: Henry King.   Cast: Susan Hayward, William

Lundigan, Rory Calhoun, Alexander Knox. Distributor:
Films Inc.
At the turn of the century, a small southern town
gains a new minister and his big-city bride, who is stunned
by the conditions in the town. Dra

1798   IMITATION OF LIFE
106 min. , b&w, 1934.
Director: John M. Stahl. Cast: Claudette Colbert, Warren William, Ned Sparks, Louise Beavers, Rochelle Hudson, Alan Hale. Distributor: Universal/16.
A black cook and a white widow band together to
market the black woman's secret pancake batter. They are
a great financial success, but not without suffering some
severe family problems. Dra

1799   IMITATION OF LIFE
124 min. , color, 1959.
Director: Douglas Sirk. Cast: Lana Turner, John Gavin,
Sandra Dee, Juanita Moore, Susan Kohner, Dan O'Herlihy,
Robert Alda. Distributor: Universal/16.
In this remake, the white woman rises to success
as an actress. Focuses on her life with her daughter and
her black maid's problems with her own daughter. Dra

1800   THE IMPOSSIBLE YEARS
92 min. , color, 1968.
Director: Michael Gordon. Cast: David Niven, Lola Al-
bright, Chad Everett, Ozzie Nelson. Distributor: Films
Inc.
A psychology professor has his own problems raising
his two teenage daughters. Com

1801   IN THIS OUR LIFE
96 min. , b&w, 1942.
Director: John Huston. Cast: Bette Davis, Olivia de
Havilland, Dennis Morgan, George Brent, Billie Burke,
Charles Coburn, Lee Patrick. Distributor: United Art-
ists/16.
The spoiled daughter of a genteel but poor Virginia
family is used to getting her own way. She steals her sister's husband and her boyfriend, is shunned by her family,
and dies in a car crash. Dra

1802   INDEPENDENCE DAY
87 min. , color, 1976.
Director: Bobby Roth. Distributor: Tricontinental Film
Center.
A young black couple move to Los Angeles from the
South for a better life. They struggle for decent housing
and for better relations with each other. Dra

1803   INSIDE DAISY CLOVER
128 min., color, 1966.
Director: Robert Mulligan.   Cast: Natalie Wood, Ruth
Gordon, Robert Redford, Christopher Plummer, Roddy
McDowall.   Distributor: Audio Brandon Films.
A poor, street-smart girl is groomed into a film
star by a lecherous movie mogul.   In the process, she
loses her beloved mother, marries a homosexual film star,
and has a nervous breakdown.   Mus-Dra

1804   INTERIORS
99 min., color, 1978.
Director: Woody Allen.   Cast: Diane Keaton, Geraldine
Page, E. G. Marshall, Maureen Stapleton, Sam Waterston,
Marybeth Hurt, Richard Jordan, Kristin Griffith.   Distributor: United Artists/16.
Bergmanesque psychological drama centering on the
three grown daughters of a Long Island couple whose marriage is on the rocks.   Dra

1805   ISLANDS IN THE STREAM
110 min., color, 1977.
Director: Franklin J. Schaffner.   Cast: George C. Scott,
David Hemmings, Gilbert Roland, Claire Bloom, Susan
Tyrrell.   Distributor: Paramount Pictures Corp.
A divorced, American middle-aged artist lives on a
Caribbean island.   He tries to channel his visiting sons into
manhood, but his own demons hurt his chances.   Dra

1806   IT GROWS ON TREES
84 min., b&w, 1952.
Director: Arthur Lubin.   Cast: Irene Dunne, Dean Jagger,
Richard Crenna, Joan Evans, Les Tremayne.   Distributor:
Universal/16.
What happens to a family when their backyard tree
sprouts five- and ten-dollar bills?   Com

1807   IT HAPPENED TO JANE
98 min., color, 1959.
Director: Richard Quine.   Cast: Doris Day, Ernie Kovacs,
Jack Lemmon.   Distributor: Twyman Films.
A young widow, with two children, tries to make ends
meet by catching Maine lobsters and selling them to restau-
rants in New York.   Parents' Magazine Family Medal Award.
Com

1808   IT'S A BIG COUNTRY
88 min., b&w, 1952.
Directors: Richard Thorpe, John Sturges, Charles Vidor,
Don Weis, Clarence Brown, William A. Wellman, Don Hart-
man.   Cast: Ethel Barrymore, Gary Cooper, Van Johnson,
James Whitmore, Janet Leigh, Fredric March, Gene Kelly.
Distributor: Films Inc.

Eight vignettes profile people who represent various walks of American life: immigrant families, etc. Dra

1809 IT'S A GIFT
71 min., b&w, 1934.
Director: Norman Z. McLeod. Cast: W. C. Fields, Baby LeRoy, Kathleen Howard, Tommy Bupp, Tammany Young. Distributor: Universal/16.
Grocer Harold Bissonette sets out with his nagging family to claim his dream-come-true orange grove in California. Com

1810 IT'S A WONDERFUL LIFE
130 min., b&w, 1946.
Director: Frank Capra. Cast: James Stewart, Donna Reed, Ward Bond, Beulah Bondi, Lionel Barrymore, Henry Travers, Thomas Mitchell. Distributors: Audio Brandon Films; Twyman Films; Kit Parker Films; Images.
George Bailey grows up, marries, fathers three children in one small American town, all the while dreaming of traveling to exotic lands. One Christmas Eve, when he questions whether his life has been of any value, George learns how blessed he's been. Parents' Magazine Family Medal Award. Dra

1811 IT'S ONLY MONEY
84 min., b&w, 1962.
Director: Frank Tashlin. Cast: Jerry Lewis, Zachary Scott, Joan O'Brien, Jesse White, Jack Weston. Distributor: Paramount Pictures Corp.
Jerry learns that he's heir to a family fortune; but if greedy relatives have their way, he won't be around to collect it. Com

1812 THE JAZZ SINGER
89 min., b&w, sou. & sil., 1927.
Director: Alan Crosland. Cast: Al Jolson, May McAvoy, Warner Oland, Otto Lederer, Eugene Besserer. Distributor: United Artists/16.
A cantor's son is caught between his devotion to his family and his desire for a career on Broadway. He is disowned by his father, but reconciled at the old man's deathbed. Mus-Dra

1813 JENNY
88 min., color, 1970.
Director: George Bloomfield. Cast: Marlo Thomas, Alan Alda, Vincent Gardenia, Marian Hailey, Elizabeth Wilson. Distributor: Films Inc.
An unmarried, pregnant girl and a draft-evading filmmaker decide to marry for convenience's sake: she gets a father for her baby; he gets out of the draft. Com-Dra

1814　JESSE JAMES
106 min., color, 1939.
Director: Henry King.　Cast: Tyrone Power, Henry Fonda,
Randolph Scott, Brian Donlevy, John Carradine.　Distributor: Twyman Films.
　　In 1867, the James brothers are law-abiding Missouri
farmers who love their aging mom.　When railroad men
burn their home to the ground and their mother is killed,
the brothers vow revenge.　Wes

1815　JOE
107 min., color, 1970.
Director: John G. Avildsen.　Cast: Peter Boyle, Dennis
Patrick, Susan Sarandon, Pat McDermott, K. Callan.　Distributors: Swank Motion Pictures; Institutional Cinema.
　　A wealthy executive accidentally kills his daughter's
hippie boyfriend.　He and his wife are blackmailed into a
relationship with a blue-collar bigot and his wife.　Together,
the two men set out to infiltrate and destroy hippies and all
they stand for.　Dra

1816　THE JOLSON STORY
128 min., color, 1946.
Director: Alfred E. Green.　Cast: Larry Parks, Evelyn
Keyes, William Demarest.　Distributor: Audio Brandon
Films.
　　Al's Jewish homelife.　Mus-Bio

1817　JOY IN THE MORNING
103 min., color, 1965.
Director: Alex Segal.　Cast: Richard Chamberlain, Yvette
Mimieux, Arthur Kennedy, Oscar Homolka, Sidney Blackmer.　Distributor: Films Inc.
　　A law student marries, but the harsh realities of
married life almost wreck the couple's relationship.　Dra

1818　JUNE BRIDE
97 min., b&w, 1948.
Director: Bretaigne Windust.　Cast: Bette Davis, Robert
Montgomery, Fay Bainter, Tom Tully, Barbara Bates, Mary
Wickes, Jerome Cowan.　Distributor: United Artists/16.
　　Assigned to cover a typical wedding in Middle America, the editor of a slick women's magazine and her assist-
ants move into the bride's home and remake the house and
the family into something glossy to catch their readers' attention.　Com

1819　JUNIOR BONNER
100 min., color, 1972.
Director: Sam Peckinpah.　Cast: Steve McQueen, Robert
Preston, Ida Lupino, Joe Don Baker.　Distributor: Films
Inc.
　　Junior is a rodeo rider.　His brother is a real es-

tate developer. His father is an ex-rodeo champ, and his mom is Ida Lupino. Low-key contemporary western. Wes-Dra

1820 JUST FOR YOU
104 min., color, 1952.
Director: Elliott Nugent. Cast: Bing Crosby, Ethel Barrymore, Jane Wyman, Natalie Wood, Regis Toomey. Distributor: Paramount Pictures Corp.
A successful Broadway producer was obsessed with his career and neglected his children. Now a widower, he attempts to win them back with the new woman in his life. Mus

1821 KATHLEEN
85 min., b&w, 1941.
Director: Harold S. Bucquet. Cast: Shirley Temple, Herbert Marshall, Laraine Day. Distributor: Films Inc.
Problem daughter of a wealthy widower is helped by a female psychologist, and so is her dad. Dra

1822 THE KENTUCKIAN
104 min., color, 1955.
Director: Burt Lancaster. Cast: Burt Lancaster, Diana Lynn, Dianne Foster, Walter Matthau. Distributor: United Artists/16.
Big Eli and his son travel across the Kentucky frontier in the early 1800s, hoping for a new life in Texas. Wes

1823 THE KETTLES SERIES (9 Films)
72-82 min. each, b&w, 1949-57.
Directors: Charles Lamont, Edward Sedgwick, Lee Sholem, Virgil Vogel. Cast: Marjorie Main, Percy Kilbride. Distributor: Universal/16.
Comic adventures of Ma and Pa Kettle and their 13 kids, the hillbilly family introduced in THE EGG AND I (1703). Various titles are available. Com

1824 THE KISS BEFORE THE MIRROR
66 min., b&w, 1933.
Director: James Whale. Cast: Nancy Carroll, Frank Morgan, Paul Lukas, Walter Pidgeon, Gloria Stuart. Distributor: Universal/16.
Troubled relationship between a husband and wife, ending in murder and a courtroom. See also WIVES UNDER SUSPICION (2089). Dra

1825 KISSES FOR MY PRESIDENT
113 min., b&w, 1964.
Director: Curtis Bernhardt. Cast: Fred MacMurray, Polly Bergen, Arlene Dahl, Edward Andrews, Eli Wallach. Distributor: Audio Brandon Films.

A glamorous, intelligent woman is elected President of the United States, and her business-tycoon husband becomes the first male "First Lady" in American history. Com

1826   KNOCK ON ANY DOOR
99 min., b&w, 1949.
Director: Nicholas Ray.   Cast: Humphrey Bogart, John Derek, George Macready.   Distributor: Audio Brandon Films.
A sensitive Italian American boy ends up in the gutter. A family friend, who is also a defense attorney, tries to save him. Dra

1827   KOTCH
114 min., color, 1971.
Director: Jack Lemmon.   Cast: Walter Matthau, Felicia Farr, Deborah Winters, Charles Aidman.   Distributor: Films Inc.
A 72-year-old grandfather loves his little grandchild but drives his daughter-in-law nuts, so he leaves and sets out on his own. He befriends the family's pregnant babysitter and helps her straighten out her life. Com

1828   THE LAST ANGRY MAN
100 min., b&w, 1959.
Director: Daniel Mann.   Cast: Paul Muni, David Wayne, Betsy Palmer, Luther Adler, Claudia McNeil.   Distributors: Audio Brandon Films; Twyman Films.
Doctor Abelman has devoted his life to healing and aiding the families in his poor Brooklyn neighborhood. Dra

1829   LAST OF THE RED HOT LOVERS
98 min., color, 1972.
Director: Gene Saks.   Cast: Alan Arkin, Sally Kellerman, Renee Taylor, Paula Prentiss.   Distributor: Paramount Pictures Corp.
A middle-aged, happily married man tries to get some thrills by having an affair. From the play by Neil Simon. Com

1830   THE LEARNING TREE
107 min., color, 1969.
Director: Gordon Parks.   Cast: Kyle Johnson, Alex Clarke, Estelle Evans, Dana Elcar.   Distributors: Twyman Films; Swank Motion Pictures.
A teenage black boy grows up in rural Kansas. Based on Gordon Parks's autobiographical novel about growing up black in 1920s Kansas. Dra

1831   LEAVE HER TO HEAVEN
110 min., color, 1945.
Director: John M. Stahl.   Cast: Gene Tierney, Cornel

Wilde, Jeanne Crain, Vincent Price, Gene Lockhart, Darryl
Hickman, Chill Wills. Distributor: Films Inc.
A jealous wife stops at nothing--even murder--to
monopolize the attention and affection of her husband. Dra

1832 LIES MY FATHER TOLD ME
102 min. , color, 1975.
Director: Jan Kadar. Cast: Yossi Yadin, Len Birman,
Jeffrey Lynas, Marilyn Lightstone. Distributor: Swank Motion Pictures.
A child shares a special life with his wise old grandfather, a junkman in the Canadian Jewish ghetto in the early
part of this century. The child's father, a dandy and idle
dreamer, is no match for the grandfather. Dra

1833 LIFE WITH FATHER
118 min. , color, 1947.
Director: Michael Curtiz. Cast: William Powell, Irene
Dunne, Elizabeth Taylor, Edmund Gwenn, Zasu Pitts. Distributor: Twyman Films.
An authoritarian, Victorian father tries unsuccessfully
to control his submissive, but clever, wife and their sons,
who work through their mother to get what they want. Com

1834 THE LITTLE FOXES
116 min. , b&w, 1941.
Director: William Wyler. Cast: Bette Davis, Herbert
Marshall, Patricia Collinge, Ray Collins, Dan Duryea,
Teresa Wright, Charles Dingle. Distributors: Audio Bran-
don Films; Twyman Films.
The ruthless Hubbard family after the Civil War.
From the play by Lillian Hellman. See also ANOTHER
PART OF THE FOREST (1597). Dra

1835 LITTLE MURDERS
110 min. , color, 1971.
Director: Alan Arkin. Cast: Elliott Gould, Donald Sutherland, Alan Arkin, Vincent Gardenia. Distributor: Films
Inc.
Paranoia of a New York City family who barricade
themselves in their apartment for fear of being shot down
by snipers. Sat

1836 LITTLE NELLIE KELLY
98 min. , b&w, 1940.
Director: Norman Taurog. Cast: Judy Garland, George
Murphy, Charles Winninger. Distributor: Films Inc.
A girl tries to reconcile her Irish policeman father
and her stubborn grandfather during a St. Patrick's Day
Parade in New York City. From the play by George M.
Cohan. Mus

1837   LITTLE WOMEN
        116 min. , b&w, 1933.
        Director: George Cukor. Cast: Katharine Hepburn, Paul
        Lukas, Joan Bennett, Frances Dee, Edna May Oliver,
        Spring Byington. Distributor: Films Inc.
            A mother and her four daughters in rural America
        during the 1860s. From the book by Louisa May Alcott.
        Dra

1838   LITTLE WOMEN
        122 min. , color, 1949.
        Director: Mervyn LeRoy. Cast: June Allyson, Elizabeth
        Taylor, Margaret O'Brien, Janet Leigh, Peter Lawford,
        Mary Astor. Distributor: Films Inc.
            Remake. Dra

1839   LOLITA
        152 min. , b&w, 1962.
        Director: Stanley Kubrick. Cast: James Mason, Sue Lyon,
        Shelley Winters, Peter Sellers. Distributor: Films Inc.
            A mother lusts after a middle-aged professor who
        lusts after her nubile daughter. Dra

1840   THE LONELY MAN
        87 min. , b&w, 1957.
        Director: Henry Levin. Cast: Jack Palance, Anthony Per-
        kins, Neville Brand, Robert Middleton. Distributor: Para-
        mount Pictures Corp.
            An aging gunfighter tries to regain the love and re-
        spect of his family after deserting them for many years.
        Dra

1841   LONG DAY'S JOURNEY INTO NIGHT
        136 min. , b&w, 1962.
        Director: Sidney Lumet. Cast: Katharine Hepburn, Ralph
        Richardson, Jason Robards, Jr. , Dean Stockwell. Distri-
        butors: Twyman Films; Kit Parker Films; Audio Brandon
        Films (174 min. also); Films for the Humanities (54 min.
        only).
            The father is a has-been actor; the mother is a
        drug addict. One son is an alcoholic; the other son is con-
        sumptive. They rent a summer cottage and fight for their
        lives. From Eugene O'Neill's autobiographical play. Dra

1842   THE LONG, HOT SUMMER
        115 min. , color, 1958.
        Director: Martin Ritt. Cast: Paul Newman, Joanne Wood-
        ward, Anthony Franciosa, Orson Welles, Lee Remick, An-
        gela Lansbury, Mabel Albertson. Distributor: Films Inc.
            Turbulent relationship between a wealthy, aggressive
        father and his two grown children--one a frustrated, unmar-
        ried young woman; the other, a weakling married son. Dra

1843   THE LONG, LONG TRAILER
        96 min. , color, 1954.
        Director: Vincente Minnelli.   Cast: Desi Arnaz, Lucille
        Ball, Marjorie Main, Keenan Wynn.   Distributor: Films
        Inc.
              Lucy is the clumsy newlywed who can't cope with
        the honeymoon bungalow--a mobile home.   Com

1844   LOOK IN ANY WINDOW
        87 min. , b&w, 1961.
        Director: William Alland.   Cast: Paul Anka, Ruth Roman,
        Alex Nicol, Gigi Perreau, Jack Cassidy.   Distributor:
        Hurlock Cine World.
              Teenage son of an unhappy marriage turns to prowl-
        ing.   Dra

1845   LOVE CRAZY
        99 min. , b&w, 1941.
        Director: Jack Conway.   Cast: William Powell, Myrna Loy,
        Gail Patrick, Jack Carson.   Distributor: Films Inc.
              Marital disharmony and reconciliation.   Com

1846   LOVE STORY
        100 min. , color, 1970.
        Director: Arthur Hiller.   Cast: Ali MacGraw, Ryan O'Neal,
        John Marley, Ray Milland.   Distributor: Paramount Pic-
        tures Corp.
              Jenny, daughter of a poor Italian American, marries
        a rich preppie and then dies.   See also ... AND I WANT
        TIME (83).   Dra

1847   LOVERS AND OTHER STRANGERS
        106 min. , color, 1970.
        Director: Cy Howard.   Cast: Gig Young, Bea Arthur,
        Bonnie Bedelia, Anne Jackson, Harry Guardino, Michael
        Brandon, Richard Castellano, Diane Keaton, Cloris Leach-
        man.   Distributor: Films Inc.
              The traditional family wedding of a modern young
        couple who've secretly been roommates for some time.   Com

1848   LOVING
        88 min. , color, 1970.
        Director: Irvin Kershner.   Cast: George Segal, Eva Marie
        Saint, Sterling Hayden, Keenan Wynn.   Distributor: West-
        coast Films.
              A commercial artist faces a stressful point in his
        career, and his marriage is on the skids.   Dra

1849   LUV
        95 min. , color, 1967.
        Director: Clive Donner.   Cast: Jack Lemmon, Peter Falk,
        Elaine May.   Distributor: Audio Brandon Films.
              A schemer dumps his wife on an old college class-

mate in order to be free to marry someone else. From the play by Murray Schisgal. Sat

1850   MADAME X
100 min. , color, 1966.
Director: David Lowell Rich. Cast: Lana Turner, John Forsythe, Ricardo Montalban, Burgess Meredith, Constance Bennett, Keir Dullea. Distributor: Universal/16.
A woman, accused of murder, is defended by a young man who is really her son. She knows; he doesn't. Dra

1851   MADE FOR EACH OTHER
90 min. , b&w, 1939.
Director: John Cromwell. Cast: Carole Lombard, James Stewart, Charles Coburn, Ward Bond, Louise Beavers.
Distributor: Images.
A young couple meet, marry, move in with his mother, and have a child. The man doesn't get the promotion he expected, their child becomes seriously ill, and they can't afford the lifesaving medicine. Dra

1852   MADE FOR EACH OTHER
101 min. , color, 1971.
Director: Robert B. Bean. Cast: Renee Taylor, Joseph Bologna, Paul Sorvino, Olympia Dukakis. Distributor: Films Inc.
A Jewish girl from the Bronx meets an Italian guy from Brooklyn; they fall in love and their already-complicated lives are turned upside down. Definitely includes their neurotic parents. Com

1853   THE MAGNIFICENT AMBERSONS
88 min. , b&w, 1942.
Director: Orson Welles. Cast: Joseph Cotten, Dolores Costello, Tim Holt, Agnes Moorehead, Anne Baxter, Ray Collins. Narrator: Orson Welles. Distributor: Films Inc.
A family's fortune and frivolous life-style crumbles in the wake of new technology that renders them obsolete at the turn of the century. See also 1900: PASSING OF AN AGE (1023). Dra

1854   MAIL ORDER BRIDE
85 min. , color, 1964.
Director: Burt Kennedy. Cast: Buddy Ebsen, Keir Dullea, Lois Nettleton, Warren Oates. Distributor: Films Inc.
A man tries to marry off his friend's son, circa 1890, in Montana. Wes

1855   MAKE WAY FOR TOMORROW
92 min. , b&w, 1937.
Director: Leo McCarey. Cast: Victor Moore, Beulah Bondi, Barbara Read, Fay Bainter, Thomas Mitchell, Louise

Beavers. Distributors: Universal/16; Museum of Modern Art.
A homeless elderly couple with financial difficulties are unwanted by their children. Dra

1856   MAME
131 min., color, 1974.
Director: Gene Saks. Cast: Lucille Ball, Beatrice Arthur, Bruce Davison, Jane Connell, Robert Preston. Distributors: Twyman Films; Institutional Cinema.
Based on Broadway musical Mame--which was an adaptation of the play Auntie Mame--and the novel by Patrick Dennis. Mus

1857   MAN AND BOY
98 min., color, 1972.
Director: E. W. Swackhamer. Cast: Bill Cosby, Gloria Foster, George Spell, Yaphet Kotto. Distributor: Films Inc.
A black man struggles to maintain his dignity and raise his family in a hostile environment--the Arizona Territory of the late 1880s. Wes

1858   THE MAN ON THE FLYING TRAPEZE
68 min., b&w, 1935.
Director: Clyde Bruckman. Cast: W. C. Fields, Mary Brian, Kathleen Howard, Grady Sutton, Vera Lewis, Tammany Young, Walter Brennan, Carlotta Monti. Distributor: Universal/16.
Ambrose Wolfinger has everything: a shrewish wife, a mother-in-law, and a lazy brother-in-law. Com

1859   THE MAN WHO CAME TO DINNER
121 min., b&w, 1941.
Director: William Keighley. Cast: Monty Woolley, Bette Davis, Reginald Gardiner, Jimmy Durante, Billie Burke, Ann Sheridan, Mary Wickes. Distributor: United Artists/ 16.
An international raconteur on a cross-country lecture tour accepts a dinner invitation with a top Ohio family. He slips on some ice and ends up confined to the family's home, where he meddles in everyone's life. From the play by George S. Kaufman and Moss Hart. Com

1860   MANY RIVERS TO CROSS
92 min., color, 1955.
Director: Roy Rowland. Cast: Robert Taylor, Eleanor Parker, Victor McLaglen, Russ Tamblyn. Distributor: Films Inc.
A spoof on post-Revolutionary customs about a husband-hunting tomboy and a frontiersman. Com

1861   THE MARRIAGE-GO-ROUND
        98 min., color, 1961.
        Director: Walter Lang. Cast: Susan Hayward, James
        Mason, Julie Newmar. Distributor: Institutional Cinema.
        A professor struggles to remain faithful to his wife,
        while a Swedish bombshell wants him to father her baby.
        Com

1862   THE MARRIAGE OF A YOUNG STOCKBROKER
        95 min., color, 1971.
        Director: Lawrence Turman. Cast: Richard Benjamin,
        Joanna Shimkus, Adam West, Elizabeth Ashley. Distribu-
        tor: Films Inc.
        A husband gets more pleasure as a voyeur, so his
        marriage suffers. Com

1863   MARRIAGE ON THE ROCKS
        109 min., color, 1965.
        Director: Jack Donohue. Cast: Frank Sinatra, Deborah
        Kerr, Dean Martin, Cesar Romero, Tony Bill. Distribu-
        tor: Audio Brandon Films.
        An ad-agency executive has been happily married for
        19 years. His wife is bored with the marriage and wonders
        if she should've accepted the proposal of her husband's
        swinging bachelor friend. Com

1864   THE MARRYING KIND
        96 min., b&w, 1952.
        Director: George Cukor. Cast: Judy Holliday, Aldo Ray,
        Madge Kennedy, Sheila Bond. Distributors: Audio Brandon
        Films; Institutional Cinema.
        Opens in a divorce court. Flashback memories fill
        in the reasons for the dissolution of the couple's marriage.
        Dra

1865   MARTY
        91 min., b&w, 1955.
        Director: Delbert Mann. Cast: Ernest Borgnine, Betsy
        Blair, Karen Steele, Jerry Paris. Distributor: United
        Artists/16.
        An unmarried Bronx butcher lives at home with his
        mother. He falls for a plain, lonely girl he meets at a
        dance hall. Dra

1866   MARY, MARY
        126 min., color, 1963.
        Director: Mervyn LeRoy. Cast: Debbie Reynolds, Barry
        Nelson, Michael Rennie, Diane McBain. Distributor: In-
        stitutional Cinema.
        A man wants to remarry, but needs help from his
        ex-wife because he's in trouble with the Internal Revenue
        Service. Com

1867   MEET ME IN ST. LOUIS
        113 min., color, 1944.
        Director: Vincente Minnelli. Cast: Judy Garland, Margaret O'Brien, Tom Drake, Mary Astor, June Lockhart, Chill Wills, Marjorie Main, Leon Ames. Distributor: Films Inc.
        Problems arise in the idyllic life of the Smith family in St. Louis at the turn of the century. Mus

1868   THE MEMBER OF THE WEDDING
        91 min., b&w, 1952.
        Director: Fred Zinnemann. Cast: Julie Harris, Ethel Waters, Brandon de Wilde, Arthur Franz. Distributor: Audio Brandon Films.
        A young girl's growing pains, intensified by her brother's marriage, are shared with the housekeeper and her 6-year-old cousin. Dra

1869   MILDRED PIERCE
        111 min., b&w, 1945.
        Director: Michael Curtiz. Cast: Joan Crawford, Jack Carson, Ann Blyth, Eve Arden, Zachary Scott, Bruce Bennett. Distributor: United Artists/16.
        Housewife rises from waitress to self-made millionaire in the restaurant business. One daughter dies. The other daughter is spoiled rotten and bleeds her mother's bank account dry. Dra

1870   MILES TO GO BEFORE I SLEEP
        78 min., color, 1975.
        Director: Fielder Cook. Cast: Martin Balsam, Mackenzie Phillips. Distributors: Learning Corp. of America; Mass Media Ministries.
        A social worker in a home for wayward girls pushes her own lonely grandfather into a foster grandparents' program at the home. He haltingly becomes deeply involved in one adolescent girl's life and finds new reason to go on living. Dra

1871   THE MIRACLE OF MORGAN'S CREEK
        98 min., b&w, 1944.
        Director: Preston Sturges. Cast: Betty Hutton, Eddie Bracken, Diana Lynn, William Demarest. Distributor: Paramount Pictures Corp.
        Patriotic girl has a fling with departing soldiers, marries one of them and gets pregnant, without remembering anything about the guy. Her cloddish boyfriend comes to her rescue. Com

1872   THE MIRACLE WORKER
        107 min., b&w, 1962.
        Director: Arthur Penn. Cast: Anne Bancroft, Patty Duke, Victor Jory, Inga Swenson, Andrew Prine. Distributor: United Artists/16.

Anne Sullivan works with the deaf and blind child Helen Keller and her parents to make a human being out of the uncontrollable child. From the play by William Gibson. Bio

1873   MRS. WIGGS OF THE CABBAGE PATCH
80 min., b&w, 1934.
Director: Norman Taurog.   Cast: Pauline Lord, Zasu Pitts, W. C. Fields.   Distributor: Universal/16.
A shanty town mother's sacrifices for her five children. Dra

1874   MRS. WIGGS OF THE CABBAGE PATCH
80 min., b&w, 1943.
Director: Ralph Murphy.   Cast: Fay Bainter, Hugh Herbert.   Distributor: Universal/16.
Remake. Dra

1875   MR. AND MRS. SMITH
94 min., b&w, 1941.
Director: Alfred Hitchcock.   Cast: Carole Lombard, Robert Montgomery, Gene Raymond, Jack Carson.   Distributor: Films Inc.
After a three-day quarrel, a couple discover that their marriage isn't legal. Com

1876   MR. BLANDINGS BUILDS HIS DREAM HOUSE
94 min., b&w, 1948.
Director: H. C. Potter.   Cast: Cary Grant, Myrna Loy, Melvyn Douglas, Louise Beavers, Reginald Denny, Jason Robards, Sr.   Distributor: Films Inc.
Sick of Manhattan, a man decides to move his family to the suburbs of Connecticut. Com

1877   MR. HOBBS TAKES A VACATION
116 min., color, 1962.
Director: Henry Koster.   Cast: James Stewart, Maureen O'Hara, Fabian, John Saxon.   Distributor: Films Inc.
A banker takes his family on a vacation by the sea in a run-down house. They try to enjoy themselves despite the bad plumbing. Com

1878   MISTY
92 min., color, 1961.
Director: James B. Clark.   Cast: David Ladd, Pam Smith, Arthur O'Connell, Anne Seymour.   Distributor: Films Inc.
Two children live with their grandparents on a pony ranch on an island off Virginia. Dra

1879   MOLLY
83 min., b&w, 1951.
Director: Walter Hart.   Cast: Gertrude Berg, Philip Loeb, Eli Mintz, David Opatoshu, Barbara Rush.   Distributor: Paramount Pictures Corp.

The original Jewish mother: Molly Goldberg from the Bronx. Originally titled THE GOLDBERGS. Com

1880 MOTHER WORE TIGHTS
107 min., color, 1947.
Director: Walter Lang. Cast: Betty Grable, Dan Dailey.
Distributor: Films Inc.
A boy and girl form a vaudeville team and then marry. Covers their rise to fame and their children in flashback. Mus

1881 MOURNING BECOMES ELECTRA
121 min., b&w, 1947.
Director: Dudley Nichols. Cast: Rosalind Russell, Michael Redgrave, Raymond Massey, Katina Paxinou, Kirk Douglas.
Distributor: Films Inc.
New England man returns home from the Civil War and is murdered by his unfaithful wife. Their children seek revenge. From Eugene O'Neill's adaptation of Aeschylus' Oresteia. Dra

1882 MOVE OVER, DARLING
103 min., color, 1963.
Director: Michael Gordon. Cast: Doris Day, James Garner, Polly Bergen, Chuck Connors, Thelma Ritter. Distributor: Films Inc.
Wife Number 1, missing for seven years and declared legally dead, returns home on the same day her husband marries Wife Number 2. Remake of MY FAVORITE WIFE (1884). Com

1883 MY DARLING CLEMENTINE
97 min., b&w, 1946.
Director: John Ford. Cast: Henry Fonda, Linda Darnell, Victor Mature, Ward Bond. Distributor: Films Inc.
Wyatt Earp rides into Tombstone with his three brothers, as part of a cattle drive to California. When one of his brothers is killed, Wyatt stays on as the badly needed marshal to avenge his brother's death. Wes

1884 MY FAVORITE WIFE
88 min., b&w, 1940.
Director: Garson Kanin. Cast: Irene Dunne, Cary Grant, Randolph Scott, Gail Patrick. Distributor: Films Inc.
Missing wife, believed to be dead, returns to find her husband about to be remarried. She sets out to win him back. See also MOVE OVER, DARLING (1882). Com

1885 MY FRIEND FLICKA
90 min., color, 1943.
Director: Harold Schuster. Cast: Roddy McDowall, Preston Foster, Rita Johnson. Distributor: Films Inc.
A West Point soldier tries to instill discipline into his daydreaming son. Dra

1886   MY GIRL TISA
        95 min. , b&w, 1948.
        Director: Elliott Nugent. Cast: Lilli Palmer, Sam Wana-
        maker, Alan Hale, Stella Adler, Akim Tamiroff. Distri-
        butor: Corinth Films.
             In turn-of-the-century New York, an immigrant girl
        dreams of bringing her father to New York. Dra

1887   MY MAN GODFREY
        90 min. , b&w, 1936.
        Director: Gregory La Cava. Cast: William Powell, Carole
        Lombard, Gail Patrick, Eugene Pallette, Alice Brady. Dis-
        tributors: Universal/16;   Kit Parker Films; Images.
             Dizzy daughter of society family finds a man living in
        a dump and brings him home to be their butler. Com

1888   MY SISTER EILEEN
        108 min. , color, 1955.
        Director: Richard Quine. Cast: Betty Garrett, Janet
        Leigh, Jack Lemmon. Distributor: Institutional Cinema.
             Two Ohio sisters come to New York to make it big.
        Mus-Com

1889   MY SIX LOVES
        101 min. , color, 1963.
        Director: Gower Champion. Cast: Debbie Reynolds, Cliff
        Robertson, David Janssen, Hans Conried, Eileen Heckart.
        Distributor: Paramount Pictures Corp.
             A stage and movie star comes to her Connecticut
        farm for a long rest. She finds six young squatters on her
        property. The local parson suggests that he and she marry
        to give the kids a home. Com-Dra

1890   MY SON JOHN
        122 min. , b&w, 1952.
        Director: Leo McCarey. Cast: Helen Hayes, Robert
        Walker, Van Heflin, Dean Jagger. Distributor: Paramount
        Pictures Corp.
             How an American family meets a crisis when one son,
        his mom's favorite, is found to be a Communist party mem-
        ber. Dra

1891   NEVER SAY GOODBYE
        96 min. , color, 1956.
        Director: Jerry Hopper. Cast: Rock Hudson, George San-
        ders, David Janssen, Cornell Borchers. Distributor: Uni-
        versal/16.
             A doctor walks out on his wife and takes their daughter
        with him. The wife finds her husband years later, but the
        girl won't accept her as her mom. Dra

1892   NEVER TOO LATE
104 min., color, 1965.
Director: Bud Yorkin.   Cast: Paul Ford, Maureen O'Sullivan, Connie Stevens, Jim Hutton, Jane Wyatt, Henry Jones,
Lloyd Nolan.   Distributor: Audio Brandon Films.
    A middle-aged couple discover that they're expecting
a baby, to everyone's horror, especially their married
daughter who wants to be pregnant herself.   Com

1893   THE NEW LAND
161 min., color, 1973.
Director: Jan Troell.   Cast: Max von Sydow, Liv Ullmann.
Distributor: Swank Motion Pictures.
    A continuation of the Swedes' story begun in THE
EMIGRANTS (1707).   Karl Oskar and his wife settle in the
American Midwest in the mid-19th century.   His-Dra

1894   NEXT STOP, GREENWICH VILLAGE
111 min., color, 1976.
Director: Paul Mazursky.   Cast: Lenny Baker, Shelley
Winters, Ellen Greene, Lois Smith, Christopher Walken,
Dori Brenner, Antonio Fargas.   Distributor: Films Inc.
    A young man leaves his clinging Jewish mother for
his own apartment in Greenwich Village during the early
Fifties.   Com-Dra

1895   NIAGARA
89 min., color, 1953.
Director: Henry Hathaway.   Cast: Marilyn Monroe, Joseph
Cotten, Jean Peters, Casey Adams.   Distributor: Films Inc.
    Neurotic war veteran accidentally discovers his un-
faithful wife's plan to murder him (with her lover's help).
Dra

1896   NIGHT OF THE GRIZZLY
100 min., color, 1966.
Director: Joseph Pevney.   Cast: Clint Walker, Martha
Hyer, Keenan Wynn, Kevin Brodie.   Distributor: Paramount
Pictures Corp.
    A lawman gives up the dangerous life for that of a
rancher on Wyoming land he has inherited.   Just as he and
his family settle in, he, his wife, and kids must face a
grizzly bear, angry neighbors, and an outlaw he once sent
to prison.   Wes

1897   THE NIGHT OF THE HUNTER
91 min., b&w, 1955.
Director: Charles Laughton.   Cast: Robert Mitchum,
Shelley Winters, Billy Chapin, Sally Jane Bruce, Lillian
Gish, Peter Graves.   Distributor: United Artists/16.
    A ruthless killer terrorizes a widow and her two
children in an effort to find missing bank loot.   Dra

1898   NO DOWN PAYMENT
       105 min. , b&w, 1957.
       Director: Martin Ritt. Cast: Joanne Woodward, Sheree
       North, Tony Randall, Jeffrey Hunter, Cameron Mitchell,
       Patricia Owens, Barbara Rush, Pat Hingle. Distributor:
       Films Inc.
              Trials and tribulations of young marrieds in suburbia.
       Dra

1899   NOTHING BUT A MAN
       92 min. , b&w, 1964.
       Director: Michael Roemer. Cast: Ivan Dixon, Abbey
       Lincoln, Gloria Foster, Yaphet Kotto. Distributor: Mac-
       millan Films.
              A young black man settles down and marries a
       schoolteacher, the daughter of a preacher. He must then
       adjust to life as a family man, struggle to earn a living
       and not fall into a black stereotypic role. National Council
       of Churches Award. Dra

1900   NOW AND FOREVER
       82 min. , b&w, 1934.
       Director: Henry Hathaway. Cast: Gary Cooper, Carole
       Lombard, Shirley Temple, Sir Guy Standing. Distributor:
       Universal/16.
              A jewel thief tries to go straight for his little girl.
       Dra

1901   NOW, VOYAGER
       117 min. , b&w, 1942.
       Director: Irving Rapper. Cast: Bette Davis, Paul Hen-
       reid, Claude Rains, Gladys Cooper, Bonita Granville, Ilka
       Chase, Lee Patrick. Distributor: United Artists/16.
              A repressed, tyrannized spinster daughter of a so-
       cialite mother is treated successfully by a psychiatrist, who
       forces her to leave her mother's house. She takes a cruise
       and falls for a married man and his daughter. Dra

1902   OBSESSION
       98 min. , color, 1976.
       Director: Brian DePalma. Cast: Cliff Robertson, Gene-
       vieve Bujold, John Lithgow. Distributor: Swank Motion
       Pictures.
              The beautiful wife and small daughter of an up-and-
       coming land developer are kidnapped and lost to the man
       forever. He spends years mourning their loss, until he
       meets a young woman who resembles his deceased wife.
       Dra

1903   THE ODD COUPLE
       106 min. , color, 1968.
       Director: Gene Saks. Cast: Jack Lemmon, Walter Mat-
       thau, John Fiedler. Distributor: Paramount Pictures Corp.

Two previously married men set up housekeeping together. One is a fastidious neurotic; the other is a slovenly neurotic. From the play by Neil Simon. Com

1904 OH DAD, POOR DAD, MAMA'S HUNG YOU IN THE CLOSET AND I'M FEELING SO SAD
86 min., color, 1967.
Director: Richard Quine. Cast: Rosalind Russell, Robert Morse, Barbara Harris, Hugh Griffith, Jonathan Winters. Distributor: Paramount Pictures Corp.
Mom is an eccentric bully; Dad is a stuffed corpse in the closet; and baby is 25 years old. From the play by Arthur Kopit. Com

1905 OLD YELLER
83 min., color, 1957.
Director: Robert Stevenson. Cast: Tommy Kirk, Dorothy McGuire, Fess Parker, Kevin Corcoran, Jeff York, Chuck Connors. Distributor: Twyman Films.
A father must leave his family for a three-month-long cattle drive. His teenage son takes care of the family in his absence, which is complicated when the family dog contracts rabies when it saves the family from a rabid wolf. See also LOVE AND DUTY: WHICH COMES FIRST? (856). Dra

1906 ON THE WATERFRONT
108 min., b&w, 1954.
Director: Elia Kazan. Cast: Marlon Brando, Karl Malden, Rod Steiger, Eva Marie Saint, Lee J. Cobb. Distributors: Twyman Films; Swank Motion Pictures; Kit Parker Films.
An uneducated boxer, now a dock worker, falls for a well-educated, gentle young woman. He stands up to his corrupt brother, who works for the Syndicate. See also WHETHER TO TELL THE TRUTH (1511). Dra

1907 ONCE IS NOT ENOUGH
121 min., color, 1975.
Director: Guy Green. Cast: Kirk Douglas, Deborah Raffin, Alexis Smith, David Janssen, George Hamilton, Brenda Vaccaro. Distributor: Paramount Pictures Corp.
A fading movie producer marries a rich woman for her money. She's a lesbian. His beloved daughter falls for an aging writer. All suffer in the end. Dra

1908 THE ONE AND ONLY
98 min., color, 1977.
Director: Carl Reiner. Cast: Henry Winkler, Kim Darby, Gene Saks, Herve Villechaize. Distributor: Paramount Pictures Corp.
Brash young man dreams of stage stardom, but only achieves success as a flamboyant wrestler. His aspirations take their toll on his new bride. Com

1909   THE ONE AND ONLY GENUINE ORIGINAL FAMILY BAND
117 min., color, 1968.
Director: Michael O'Herlihy. Cast: Walter Brennan,
Buddy Ebsen, Lesley Ann Warren, John Davidson, Janet
Blair. Distributor: Twyman Films.
The story of the Bower family band, led by Grandpa
Bower, a staunch supporter of Presidential candidate Grover
Cleveland. Set in the Dakota Territory in the 1880s. Mus-
Com

1910   ONE-EYED JACKS
141 min., color, 1961.
Director: Marlon Brando. Cast: Marlon Brando, Karl
Malden, Katy Jurado. Distributor: Paramount Pictures
Corp.
Brando is betrayed by his best friend. He gets re-
venge through the man's family. Wes

1911   ONE FOOT IN HEAVEN
108 min., b&w, 1941.
Director: Irving Rapper. Cast: Fredric March, Martha
Scott, Beulah Bondi, Gene Lockhart, Harry Davenport,
Elisabeth Fraser, Frankie Thomas. Distributor: United
Artists/16.
The many difficulties courageously faced by a hard
working minister and his wife. Dra

1912   ONE IS A LONELY NUMBER
97 min., color, 1972.
Director: Mel Stuart. Cast: Trish Van Devere, Monte
Markham, Janet Leigh, Melvyn Douglas. Distributor: Films
Inc.
A young woman is unexpectedly abandoned by her
husband. She gets involved in an empty relationship with a
married man. Dra

1913   ONE POTATO, TWO POTATO
92 min., b&w, 1964.
Director: Larry Peerce. Cast: Barbara Barrie, Bernie
Hamilton, Richard Mulligan, Robert Earl Jones. Distributor: Swank Motion Pictures.
A white divorcée marries a black man and lives with
his parents. Her ex-husband fights for legal custody of
their daughter. Dra

1914   THE OTHER
100 min., color, 1972.
Director: Robert Mulligan. Cast: Chris Udvarnoky, Martin Udvarnoky, Uta Hagen, Diana Muldaur. Distributor:
Films Inc.
Rural family has young twin boys. One dies accidentally. The other, in the guise of the dead twin, commits
murder. Hor

1915   THE OTHER SIDE OF THE MOUNTAIN
103 min., color, 1975.
Director: Larry Peerce.   Cast: Marilyn Hassett, Beau
Bridges, Belinda J. Montgomery, Nan Martin, Dabney
Coleman.   Distributors: Universal/16; Twyman Films;
Swank Motion Pictures.
       Championship skier Jill Kinmont is crippled in an ac-
cident during a tournament.   She survives, thanks to the
love and devotion of her family and boyfriend and her
strength of character.   Bio

1916   THE OTHER SIDE OF THE MOUNTAIN, PART 2
99 min., color, 1978.
Director: Larry Peerce.   Cast: Marilyn Hassett, Timothy
Bottoms.   Distributor: Universal/16.
       Further story of Jill Kinmont, former skier, now
teacher.   Takes her up through her marriage.   Bio

1917   OUR DAILY BREAD
80 min., b&w, 1934.
Director: King Vidor.   Cast: Tom Keene, Karen Morley,
Barbara Pepper.   Distributors: Audio Brandon Films; Kit
Parker Films; Images.
       A group of people who are wiped out by the Depres-
sion set up a collective farm.   Dra

1918   OUR RELATIONS
74 min., b&w, 1936.
Director: Harry Lachman.   Cast: Laurel & Hardy, Sidney Toler, Daphne Pollard, Betty Healy, James Finlayson.
Distributor: Universal/16.
       Stan and Ollie take their wives out on the town and
bump into their twin brothers, who are the black sheep of
the family.   The wives mistake the twins for their husbands.
Com

1919   OUR TOWN
90 min., b&w, 1940.
Director: Sam Wood.   Cast: William Holden, Martha Scott,
Beulah Bondi, Fay Bainter, Thomas Mitchell.   Distributors:
Audio Brandon Films; Kit Parker Films; Images.
       In a small New England town at the early part of this
century, a doctor's son courts and marries the editor's
daughter.   She dies.   From the play by Thornton Wilder.
Dra

1920   OUR VINES HAVE TENDER GRAPES
105 min., b&w, 1945.
Director: Roy Rowland.   Cast: Margaret O'Brien, Edward
G. Robinson, James Craig, Agnes Moorehead.   Distributor:
Films Inc.
       Life in a Norwegian farming community in Wisconsin.
Dra

1921   THE OUT-OF-TOWNERS
        98 min., color, 1970.
        Director: Arthur Hiller. Cast: Jack Lemmon, Sandy
        Dennis. Distributor: Paramount Pictures Corp.
            A couple come to New York, where the husband has
        a job interview. They suffer every indignity Manhattan has
        to offer and return to their Midwestern home safe but not
        sorry. Com

1922   THE PAINTED DESERT
        75 min., b&w, 1931.
        Director: Howard Higgins. Cast: Bill Boyd, J. Farrell
        MacDonald, Helen Twelvetrees, William Farnum, Clark
        Gable. Distributor: Films Inc.
            Two men find an abandoned baby in the desert. They
        fight for the child; one wins; they swear never to speak to
        each other again. The baby grows up and falls for the
        daughter of the other friend. The young couple try to re-
        unite the estranged men. Wes

1923   PAPA'S DELICATE CONDITION
        98 min., color, 1963.
        Director: George Marshall. Cast: Jackie Gleason, Glynis
        Johns, Charlie Ruggles, Laurel Goodwin. Distributor: Para-
        mount Pictures Corp.
            In turn-of-the-century Texas, an impulsive father
        must buy the whole circus just to get the special pony and
        cart his daughter yearns for. Based on the life of actress
        Corinne Griffith. Com-Bio

1924   PAPER MOON
        102 min., b&w, 1973.
        Director: Peter Bogdanovich. Cast: Tatum O'Neal, Ryan
        O'Neal, Madeline Kahn, John Hillerman. Distributor:
        Paramount Pictures Corp.
            In the Thirties, a precocious little girl takes up with
        a con man whom she comes to regard as her father. Com-
        Dra

1925   THE PARENT TRAP
        124 min., color, 1961.
        Director: David Swift. Cast: Hayley Mills, Maureen O'-
        Hara, Brian Keith, Charlie Ruggles, Una Merkel. Distri-
        butor: Twyman Films.
            A pair of identical twins meet for the first time at
        summer camp. They manage to reinterest their divorced
        parents in a second marriage. Com

1926   PART 2, SOUNDER
        98 min., color, 1976.
        Director: William A. Graham. Cast: Harold Sylvester,
        Ebony Wright, Taj Mahal, Annazette Chase, Darryl Young.
        Distributor: Swank Motion Pictures.

A sequel to SOUNDER (2004). Here, the Depression-era black sharecroppers try to give their children a good education. Dra

1927   A PATCH OF BLUE
105 min., b&w, 1965.
Director: Guy Green. Cast: Sidney Poitier, Shelley Winters, Elizabeth Hartman, Wallace Ford. Distributor: Films Inc.
A blind teenager lives with her whoring mother and alcoholic grandfather in a tenement. She falls for a black man who befriends her in the park. Dra

1928   PENNY SERENADE
125 min., b&w, 1941.
Director: George Stevens. Cast: Cary Grant, Irene Dunne, Beulah Bondi, Edgar Buchanan, Ann Doran. Distributor: Kit Parker Films.
A couple adopt a child after their own baby dies. Dra

1929   THE PEOPLE NEXT DOOR
79 min., b&w, 1969.
Director: David Greene. Cast: Lloyd Bridges, Phyllis Newman, Kim Hunter, Fritz Weaver. Distributor: BFA Educational Media.
Two suburban families face ordeals involving their children, who, it turns out, are into heavy drugs. From TV. Dra

1930   THE PEOPLE NEXT DOOR
93 min., color, 1970.
Director: David Greene. Cast: Julie Harris, Eli Wallach, Deborah Winters, Hal Holbrook, Cloris Leachman. Distributor: Audio Brandon Films.
Same as above, but a theatrical release with a different cast. Dra

1931   PEOPLE WILL TALK
67 min., b&w, 1935.
Director: Alfred Santell. Cast: Charlie Ruggles, Mary Boland, Leila Hyams, Dean Jagger. Distributor: Films Inc.
Domestic trouble involving mom and dad and their honeymooning children. Com

1932   PERIOD OF ADJUSTMENT
112 min., b&w, 1962.
Director: George Roy Hill. Cast: Anthony Franciosa, Jane Fonda, Jim Hutton, Lois Nettleton, John McGiver. Distributor: Films Inc.
A disaster-prone honeymoon. From the play by Tennessee Williams. Com

1933   PETE 'N' TILLIE
       100 min. , color, 1972.
       Director: Martin Ritt.   Cast: Walter Matthau, Carol Bur-
       nett, Geraldine Page, Barry Nelson, Rene Auberjonois.
       Distributors: Universal/16; Twyman Films; Swank Motion
       Pictures.
            An unlikely couple meet and marry.   After nine
       years of marriage, they separate when they lose their only
       child.   Com-Dra

1934   PETULIA
       105 min. , color, 1968.
       Director: Richard Lester.   Cast: Richard Chamberlain,
       Julie Christie, George C. Scott, Shirley Knight, Joseph
       Cotten, Arthur Hill, Kathleen Widdoes.   Distributor: Twy-
       man Films.
            A romance between an aging, conservative doctor and
       a wacky young woman who is married to a rich, violent
       guy.   The doctor's wife and children also play a part.   Dra

1935   PEYTON PLACE
       157 min. , color, 1957.
       Director: Mark Robson.   Cast: Lana Turner, Diane Varsi,
       Hope Lange, Terry Moore, Lee Philips.   Distributor: Films
       Inc.
            Sexy soap opera about life in a small New England
       town.   Dra

1936   THE PHILADELPHIA STORY
       112 min. , b&w, 1940.
       Director: George Cukor.   Cast: Katharine Hepburn, Cary
       Grant, James Stewart, Ruth Hussey, Mary Nash.   Distri-
       butor: Films Inc.
            Wedding preparations for a wealthy socialite's second
       marriage are disrupted by a society reporter, who inadvert-
       ently falls in love with the bride, and the arrival of her
       ex-husband who wants her back.   Based on the play by Philip
       Barry.   Com

1937   PINKY
       102 min. , b&w, 1949.
       Director: Elia Kazan.   Cast: Jeanne Crain, Ethel Waters,
       Ethel Barrymore, William Lundigan, Nina Mae McKinney.
       Distributor: Films Inc.
            Light-skinned black nurse returns to her childhood
       home in the South.   Dra

1938   PLAY IT AGAIN, SAM
       85 min. , color, 1972.
       Director: Herb Ross.   Cast: Woody Allen, Diane Keaton,
       Tony Roberts, Susan Anspach, Jerry Lacy.   Distributor:
       Paramount Pictures Corp.
            When his wife walks out on him, a San Francisco

film critic suffers the humiliation of unsuccessful dating
and the pain of falling for the equally neurotic wife of his
best friend. From the play by Woody Allen. Com

1939   PLAZA SUITE
114 min., color, 1971.
Director: Arthur Hiller. Cast: Maureen Stapleton, Walter
Matthau, Barbara Harris, Lee Grant. Distributor: Paramount Pictures Corp.
A suite in New York City's Plaza Hotel provides the
setting for three vignettes. One involves a philandering
husband; another involves a shy bride who locks herself in
the bathroom and refuses to join her wedding downstairs.
From the play by Neil Simon. Com

1940   PLEASE DON'T EAT THE DAISIES
111 min., color, 1960.
Director: Charles Walters. Cast: Doris Day, David
Niven, Janis Paige. Distributor: Films Inc.
Obscure professor rises to fame as a top Broadway
critic. His troubles begin when he moves his family to
suburbia. From the play by Jean Kerr. Com

1941   THE PLEASURE OF HIS COMPANY
115 min., color, 1961.
Director: George Seaton. Cast: Fred Astaire, Debbie
Reynolds, Lilli Palmer, Tab Hunter, Gary Merrill, Charlie
Ruggles. Distributor: Films Inc.
A globe-trotting playboy returns home after 15 years
for his daughter's wedding. He also tries to break up his
ex-wife's marriage. From the play by Samuel Taylor &
Cornelia Otis Skinner. Com

1942   POLLYANNA
134 min., color, 1960.
Director: David Swift. Cast: Hayley Mills, Jane Wyman,
Richard Egan, Agnes Moorehead. Distributor: Twyman
Films.
Pollyanna is determined to see the good in everything
and does her best to melt the coldest of hearts. Parents'
Magazine Family Medal Award. Com

1943   POPI
113 min., color, 1969.
Director: Arthur Hiller. Cast: Alan Arkin, Rita Moreno,
Miguel Alejandro, Ruben Figueroa. Distributor: United
Artists/16.
Puerto Rican widower refuses to raise his two sons
in El Barrio. He sets them adrift in a boat, hoping they'll
be mistaken for Cuban refugees and adopted by a rich family.
Com-Dra

1944   THE POSSESSION OF JOEL DELANEY
       105 min., color, 1972.
       Director: Waris Hussein.   Cast: Shirley MacLaine, Perry
       King, Lovelady Powell.   Distributor: Paramount Pictures
       Corp.
            A divorced mother of two is called upon to help her
       younger brother, who is at first thought to be involved with
       drugs.   Hor

1945   PRETTY BABY
       109 min., color, 1978.
       Director: Louis Malle.   Cast: Keith Carradine, Brooke
       Shields, Susan Sarandon, Frances Faye, Antonio Fargas.
       Distributor: Paramount Pictures Corp.
            Set in the Red Light District of New Orleans in
       1917, the story of Violet, a young girl raised by her hooker
       mother in a brothel.   The child gets into the life at 12 and
       soon thereafter marries a photographer.   Dra

1946   THE PRIDE OF THE YANKEES
       128 min., b&w, 1948.
       Director: Sam Wood.   Cast: Gary Cooper, Teresa Wright,
       Walter Brennan.   Distributor: Audio Brandon Films.
            Life story of Lou Gehrig.   Bio

1947   THE PRISONER OF SECOND AVENUE
       98 min., color, 1975.
       Director: Melvin Frank.   Cast: Jack Lemmon, Anne Ban-
       croft, Gene Saks.   Distributor: Swank Motion Pictures.
            A couple living in New York crack under the strain
       of apartment living in Manhattan.   Their marriage is the
       first thing to go.   From the play by Neil Simon.   Com

1948   PROMISE HER ANYTHING
       97 min., color, 1966.
       Director: Arthur Hiller.   Cast: Warren Beatty, Leslie
       Caron, Bob Cummings, Keenan Wynn, Hermione Gingold.
       Distributor: Paramount Pictures Corp.
            A young widowed mother decides that her boss--a
       child psychologist who secretly hates kids--will be her
       next husband.   Com

1949   PSYCHO
       109 min., b&w, 1960.
       Director: Alfred Hitchcock.   Cast: Anthony Perkins, Janet
       Leigh, Vera Miles, John Gavin, Martin Balsam, John Mc-
       Intire.   Distributors: Universal/16; Twyman Films; Swank
       Motion Pictures.
            A secretary runs away with her boss's money and
       stops off at an out-of-the-way motel run by a shy young
       man and his unseen, castrating mother.   Hor

1950 PURSUED
101 min., b&w, 1947.
Director: Raoul Walsh. Cast: Teresa Wright, Robert
Mitchum, Judith Anderson, Dean Jagger, Alan Hale. Distributor: Corinth Films.
Jeb Rand is adopted by Ma Callum, who had an affair
with his father. Jeb is hated by other members of Ma's
family, for some mysterious reason. Wes

1951 QUEEN OF THE STARDUST BALLROOM
98 min., color, 1975.
Director: Sam O'Steen. Cast: Maureen Stapleton, Charles
Durning. Distributors: Learning Corp. of America; Mass
Media Ministries.
Bea Asher is suddenly widowed. A friend takes her
to the local dance hall, where she falls for a married mail-
man. Mus-Dra

1952 RABBIT, RUN
94 min., color, 1970.
Director: Jack Smight. Cast: James Caan, Anjanette
Comer, Jack Albertson, Henry Jones, Carrie Snodgress.
Distributor: Westcoast Films.
A former high-school basketball player finds his love-
less marriage to an alcoholic more than he can handle. Dra

1953 RACHEL, RACHEL
101 min., color, 1968.
Director: Paul Newman. Cast: Joanne Woodward, James
Olson, Kate Harrington, Estelle Parsons, Geraldine Fitzgerald, Donald Moffat. Distributor: Institutional Cinema.
A 35-year-old spinster still lives with her mother
and teaches school in her hometown. She yearns for a man
and child of her own. Dra

1954 THE RAINMAKER
121 min., color, 1956.
Director: Joseph Anthony. Cast: Katharine Hepburn, Burt
Lancaster, Lloyd Bridges, Wendell Corey, Earl Holliman.
Distributor: Paramount Pictures Corp.
Kansas spinster lives at home with her father and
two brothers. She is liberated by a charismatic con man.
From the play by N. Richard Nash. Dra

1955 A RAISIN IN THE SUN
128 min., b&w, 1961.
Director: Daniel Petrie. Cast: Sidney Poitier, Claudia
McNeil, Ruby Dee, Diana Sands, Ivan Dixon. Distributors:
Audio Brandon Films; Twyman Films; Swank Motion Pictures;
Kit Parker Films.
Dreams, ambitions, and frustrations of a poor black
family living on the South Side of Chicago. From the play
by Lorraine Hansberry. Parents' Magazine Special Merit
Award. Dra

1956   REBECCA OF SUNNYBROOK FARM
81 min. , b&w, 1938.
Director: Allan Dwan.   Cast: Shirley Temple, Randolph
Scott, Jack Haley, Bill Robinson, Gloria Stuart.   Distributor: Films Inc.
A talented moppet is sought by two rival cereal
manufacturers for a stint on their radio commercials.   Her
stepfather tries to exploit her talent.   Mus-Dra

1957   REBEL WITHOUT A CAUSE
111 min. , color, 1955.
Director: Nicholas Ray.   Cast: James Dean, Natalie Wood,
Sal Mineo, Jim Backus, Nick Adams, Ann Doran.   Distributors: Audio Brandon Films; Twyman Films; Swank Motion
Pictures.
James Dean's parents don't understand him.   Natalie
Wood's parents don't understand her.   Sal Mineo doesn't
have any parents, so he suffers, too.   Dra

1958   THE RECKLESS MOMENT
82 min. , b&w, 1949.
Director: Max Ophuls.   Cast: Joan Bennett, James Mason,
Geraldine Brooks, Henry O'Neill, Roy Roberts.   Distributor: Learning Corp. of America.
A California mother becomes involved with murder
and a blackmailer, all to protect her darling daughter.
Mys

1959   THE RED PONY
91 min. , color, 1949.
Director: Lewis Milestone.   Cast: Robert Mitchum, Myrna
Loy, Louis Calhern, Shepperd Strudwick, Peter Miles,
Margaret Hamilton.   Distributor: Kit Parker Films.
A central California ranch family, with focus on the
son and his first pony.   Dra

1960   THE RED PONY
101 min. , color, 1973.
Director: Robert Totten.   Cast: Henry Fonda, Maureen
O'Hara.   Distributor: Phoenix Films.
The story of a young boy and his family in rural
California and the boy's love for a pony.   TV version.   Dra

1961   THE REMARKABLE MR. PENNYPACKER
87 min. , color, 1959.
Director: Henry Levin.   Cast: Clifton Webb, Dorothy
McGuire, Charles Coburn.   Distributor: Films Inc.
An 1890s meat packer, with businesses in Harrisburg and Philadelphia, turns out to have wives and children
in both cities.   Com-Dra

1962   REMEMBER THE NIGHT
94 min. , b&w, 1940.

Director: Mitchell Leisen. Cast: Barbara Stanwyck, Fred MacMurray, Beulah Bondi, Elizabeth Patterson. Distributor: Universal/16.
A prosecuting attorney feels sorry for a shoplifter, so he bails her out of jail and lets her share the Christmas holidays with his Indiana family. Com-Dra

1963 RHAPSODY IN BLUE
139 min., b&w, 1945.
Director: Irving Rapper. Cast: Robert Alda, Joan Leslie, Alexis Smith, Charles Coburn, Oscar Levant. Distributor: United Artists/16.
Life story of George Gershwin. Mus-Bio

1964 RIVALS
101 min., color, 1972.
Director: Krishna Shah. Cast: Joan Hackett, Robert Klein, Scott Jacoby. Distributor: Audio Brandon Films.
A woman's second marriage upsets her son. Dra

1965 THE RIVER NIGER
105 min., color, 1976.
Director: Krishna Shah. Cast: Cicely Tyson, James Earl Jones, Lou Gossett, Jr. Distributor: Swank Motion Pictures.
The story of a black family trying to survive in the Watts ghetto in Los Angeles. From the play by Joseph A. Walker. Dra

1966 RIVERRUN
87 min., color, 1970.
Director: John Korty. Cast: Louise Ober, John McLiam, Mark Jenkins. Distributor: Swank Motion Pictures.
A young man and woman's idyllic life together on a San Marino County sheep farm is disrupted by the arrival of her father. He's upset to learn that his daughter is pregnant and not married. Dra

1967 ROCKY
121 min., color, 1976.
Director: John G. Avildsen. Cast: Sylvester Stallone, Talia Shire, Burt Young, Burgess Meredith. Distributor: United Artists/16.
Down-and-out fighter, his shy girlfriend, and her brutish brother, all rendered to perfection in this Academy Award-winning drama.

1968 ROOTS (Series of 11 Films)
approx. 50 min. each, color, 1977.
Producer: David L. Wolper. Cast: John Amos, Edward Asner, Lloyd Bridges, Georg Stanford Brown, LeVar Burton, Olivia Cole, Chuck Connors, Sandy Duncan, Lynda Day George, Louis Gossett, Jr., Lorne Greene, George Hamilton,

Burl Ives, Lawrence-Hilton Jacobs, Doug McClure, Vic
Morrow, Robert Reed, Richard Roundtree, Madge Sinclair,
O. J. Simpson, Cicely Tyson, Leslie Uggams, Ben Vereen,
Ralph Waite. Distributor: Films Inc.
Based on Alex Haley's Pulitzer Prize winner, this
made-for-TV miniseries traces Haley's family roots from
the birth of a baby called Kunta Kinte in the Mandinka village
of Juffure in the Gambia, West Africa, 1750, up through
his ancestors' freedom from slavery in post-Civil War South.
7 Emmy Awards. AECT Annual Achievement Award. Hu-
mitas Prize, Human Family Institute. His-Dra

1969   THE ROSE TATTOO
116 min., b&w, 1955.
Director: Daniel Mann. Cast: Anna Magnani, Burt Lancaster, Marisa Pavan, Jo Van Fleet, Virginia Grey. Distributor: Paramount Pictures Corp.
An Italian American widow lives in the past. She
takes great pride in her dead husband's love, until she is
shaken by gossip of his infidelity. From the play by Tennessee Williams. Dra

1970   ROSEANNA MCCOY
89 min., b&w, 1949.
Director: Irving Reis. Cast: Farley Granger, Joan Evans,
Charles Bickford, Raymond Massey. Distributor: Audio
Brandon Films.
Feuding Kentucky families. Dra

1971   ROSEMARY'S BABY
136 min., color, 1968.
Director: Roman Polanski. Cast: Mia Farrow, John Cassavetes, Ruth Gordon, Sidney Blackmer, Maurice Evans,
Ralph Bellamy, Patsy Kelly. Distributor: Paramount Pictures Corp.
A struggling Manhattan actor "sells" his wife to
some witches to beget the Devil's child. His price: an
acting job. Hor

1972   ROSIE!
98 min., color, 1967.
Director: David Lowell Rich. Cast: Rosalind Russell,
Sandra Dee, Brian Aherne, Audrey Meadows, James Faren-
tino, Margaret Hamilton. Distributor: Universal/16.
A zany millionairess outwits greedy relatives who
want to put her away and collect her money. Com

1973   ROUGHLY SPEAKING
117 min., b&w, 1945.
Director: Michael Curtiz. Cast: Rosalind Russell, Jack
Carson, Robert Hutton, Donald Woods, Alan Hale. Distributor: United Artists/16.
An ambitious wife struggles to raise her kids and help
her easy-going husband in his business. Dra

1974   THE ROYAL FAMILY OF BROADWAY
81 min., b&w, 1930.
Directors: George Cukor & Cyril Gardner.   Cast: Fredric March, Ina Claire, Mary Brian.   Distributor: Univer-
sal/16.
Antics of a theatrical family modeled after the Bar-
rymores.   From the play by George S. Kaufman & Edna
Ferber.   Com

1975   THE RUSSIANS ARE COMING, THE RUSSIANS ARE COMING
126 min., color, 1966.
Director: Norman Jewison.   Cast: Carl Reiner, Alan Ar-
kin, Eva Marie Saint, Brian Keith, Jonathan Winters, John
Phillip Law, Tessie O'Shea, Ben Blue.   Distributor: United
Artists/16.
When a Russian submarine gets stuck off the New
England coast, the whole town goes into a panic.   Com

1976   THE SAILOR TAKES A WIFE
92 min., b&w, 1946.
Director: Richard Whorf.   Cast: June Allyson, Robert
Walker, Hume Cronyn.   Distributor: Films Inc.
Hours after their meeting, a sailor and canteen girl
marry and live happily ever after--almost.   Com

1977   ST. LOUIS BLUES
93 min., b&w, 1958.
Director: Allen Reisner.   Cast: Nat King Cole, Eartha
Kitt, Pearl Bailey, Cab Calloway, Ella Fitzgerald, Ruby
Dee.   Distributor: Paramount Pictures Corp.
Bio of W. C. Handy, from childhood persecution at
the hand of his fundamentalist father, to his rise to fame.
Mus

1978   SALT OF THE EARTH
94 min., b&w, 1954.
Director: Herbert Biberman.   Writer: Michael Wilson.
Cast: Rosaura Revueltas, Juan Chacon, Will Geer.   Dis-
tributor: Macmillan Films.
Recreates events of a year-long strike of Mexican
American zinc miners in New Mexico.   From the point of
view of one of the wives, whose troubled marriage and
growing need for personal liberation are profiled as well.
Doc-Dra

1979   SAN DIEGO, I LOVE YOU
83 min., b&w, 1944.
Director: Reginald Le Borg.   Cast: Jon Hall, Louise Allbritton, Edward Everett Horton, Eric Blore, Buster Keaton.
Distributor: Universal/16.
An eccentric family comes to San Diego to promote
their father's inventions.   Com

1980   SARAH T ... PORTRAIT OF A TEENAGE ALCOHOLIC
       97 min., color, 1975.
       Director: Richard Donner. Cast: Linda Blair, Verna
       Bloom, William Daniels, Larry Hagman, Mark Hamill,
       Michael Lerner, Hilda Haynes. Distributor: Universal/16.
           A 15-year-old girl has a drinking problem. She's
       unable to cope with a new life in a new neighborhood and
       school, as well as her parents' divorce and mother's remar-
       riage. Dra

1981   THE SEARCHERS
       119 min., color, 1956.
       Director: John Ford. Cast: John Wayne, Vera Miles,
       Natalie Wood, Jeffrey Hunter, Ward Bond. Distributor:
       Swank Motion Pictures.
           A Texas Civil War veteran finds his brother and
       sister-in-law killed by Comanches and his two nieces cap-
       tured. He sets out with his brother's adopted son to find
       the girls and avenge his brother and sister-in-law's brutal
       murders. Wes

1982   THE SECRET LIFE OF AN AMERICAN WIFE
       92 min., color, 1968.
       Director: George Axelrod. Cast: Walter Matthau, Anne
       Jackson, Patrick O'Neal. Distributor: Films Inc.
           A neglected suburban housewife decides to test her
       sex appeal. Com

1983   SEND ME NO FLOWERS
       100 min., color, 1964.
       Director: Norman Jewison. Cast: Rock Hudson, Doris
       Day, Tony Randall, Clint Walker, Edward Andrews, Paul
       Lynde. Distributor: Universal/16.
           A hypochondriac makes plans for his funeral and
       looks for a replacement husband for his wife. Com

1984   SEVEN ALONE
       100 min., color, 1975.
       Director: Earl Bellamy. Cast: Dewey Martin, Aldo Ray,
       Dean Smith, Anne Collings. Distributor: Swank Motion
       Pictures.
           The story of the Sager family, who leave their Mis-
       souri home in 1843 to settle in Oregon. Wes

1985   SEVEN BRIDES FOR SEVEN BROTHERS
       103 min., color, 1954.
       Director: Stanley Donen. Cast: Howard Keel, Jane Powell,
       Jeff Richards, Russ Tamblyn. Distributor: Films Inc.
           When a woman marries a handsome stranger, she be-
       comes housekeeper to her husband's six sloppy brothers in
       a remote cabin. The brothers decide they want wives of
       their own. Mus

1986   THE SEVEN LITTLE FOYS
        95 min., color, 1955.
        Director: Melville Shavelson. Cast: Bob Hope, James
        Cagney, Milly Vitale. Distributor: Twyman Films.
        Eddie Foy, the famous vaudeville headliner, takes
        the country by storm with his seven kids and then is sent
        to court for violating the mores of his motherless kids.
        Parents' Magazine Family Medal Award. Mus-Bio

1987   THE SEVEN YEAR ITCH
        104 min., color, 1955.
        Director: Billy Wilder. Cast: Marilyn Monroe, Tom
        Ewell, Evelyn Keyes, Sonny Tufts, Oscar Homolka. Dis-
        tributor: Films Inc.
        A man, who is left alone in New York City one sum-
        mer by his vacationing family, is tempted by neighbor
        Monroe. From the play by George Axelrod. Com

1988   SHADOW OF A DOUBT
        108 min., b&w, 1943.
        Director: Alfred Hitchcock. Cast: Joseph Cotten, Teresa
        Wright, Macdonald Carey, Patricia Collinge, Henry Travers,
        Hume Cronyn, Wallace Ford. Distributors: Universal/16;
        Twyman Films.
        A young woman's almost psychic realization that her
        beloved uncle is actually the Merry Widow Murderer. Mys

1989   SHANE
        117 min., color, 1953.
        Director: George Stevens. Cast: Alan Ladd, Jean Arthur,
        Van Heflin, Brandon de Wilde, Jack Palance. Distributor:
        Paramount Pictures Corp.
        A retired gunfighter takes up the cause of a home-
        steading family terrorized by an aging cattleman and his
        hired gun. Wes

1990   SHENANDOAH
        105 min., color, 1965.
        Director: Andrew V. McLaglen. Cast: James Stewart,
        Doug McClure, Patrick Wayne, Katharine Ross, Rosemary
        Forsyth, Glenn Corbett, George Kennedy. Distributors:
        Universal/16; Twyman Films; Swank Motion Pictures.
        A widowed Virginia farmer stubbornly refuses to
        allow his family to take part in the Civil War. Parents'
        Magazine Family Medal Award. Bell-Ringer Award, Scho-
        lastic Magazine. His-Dra

1991   THE SHEPHERD OF THE HILLS
        98 min., color, 1941.
        Director: Henry Hathaway. Cast: John Wayne, Betty
        Field, Harry Carey, Beulah Bondi, Ward Bond. Distribu-
        tor: Universal/16.
        A mysterious man enters the household of a cursed
        Ozark family. Dra

1992   SHOW BOAT
110 min. , b&w, 1936.
Director: James Whale.   Cast: Irene Dunne, Allan Jones,
Helen Morgan, Paul Robeson, Charles Winninger. Distri-
butor: Films Inc.
Show boat entertainers--Magnolia and her husband
Gaylord--are tragically separated and reunited at a theater
years later to witness their daughter's first performance.
Mus

1993   SINCE YOU WENT AWAY
170 min. , b&w, 1944.
Director: John Cromwell. Cast: Claudette Colbert, Jennifer Jones, Monty Woolley, Shirley Temple, Joseph Cotten,
Lionel Barrymore, Agnes Moorehead, Robert Walker. Distributor: Audio Brandon Films.
A brave mother cares for her two growing daughters
and works for the war effort at home, while her husband is
away at war.   Dra

1994   SISTERS
92 min. , color, 1973.
Director: Brian DePalma. Cast: Margot Kidder, Jennifer
Salt. Distributor: New Line Cinema.
The story of Siamese twins--one died during the
operation to separate them; one lived and absorbed the identity of both.   Hor

1995   THE SISTERS
98 min. , b&w, 1938.
Director: Anatole Litvak. Cast: Errol Flynn, Bette Davis,
Anita Louise, Jane Bryan, Ian Hunter, Lee Patrick. Distributor: United Artists/16.
Lives and loves of the three Elliott sisters in turn-
of-the-century San Francisco.   Dra

1996   SLAUGHTERHOUSE FIVE
104 min. , color, 1972.
Director: George Roy Hill. Cast: Michael Sacks, Ron
Leibman, Valerie Perrine, Eugene Roche, Sharon Gans.
Distributors: Universal/16; Swank Motion Pictures.
Fantasy about a middle-class married man living in
suburbia who travels through a time warp.   He lives out
his dream future and relives his past.   Fan

1997   SMASH-UP: THE STORY OF A WOMAN
103 min. , b&w, 1947.
Director: Stuart Heisler. Cast: Susan Hayward, Eddie
Albert, Lee Bowman, Marsha Hunt. Distributor: Learning
Corp. of America.
A nightclub singer goes on the skids after she becomes an alcoholic.   Not until she suffers total degradation
and the near death of her child, does she dry out and shape
up.   Dra

1998   SNOWBALL EXPRESS
93 min., color, 1972.
Director: Norman Tokar.   Cast: Dean Jones, Harry Morgan, Keenan Wynn.   Distributor: Swank Motion Pictures.
The Baxter family inherits the estate of a distant Colorado uncle.   Com

1999   SO RED THE ROSE
83 min., b&w, 1935.
Director: King Vidor.   Cast: Margaret Sullavan, Randolph Scott, Walter Connolly, Robert Cummings.   Distributor: Universal/16.
During the Civil War, a Southern family awaits the return of a soldier.   Dra

2000   SOMETHING FOR THE BOYS
87 min., color, 1944.
Director: Lewis Seiler.   Cast: Carmen Miranda, Vivian Blaine, Phil Silvers, Perry Como.   Distributor: Films Inc.
Three cousins turn a rundown Southern plantation into a home for soldier's wives.   Mus

2001   SOMETIMES A GREAT NOTION
114 min., color, 1971.
Director: Paul Newman.   Cast: Henry Fonda, Paul Newman, Lee Remick, Richard Jaeckel, Michael Sarrazin.
Distributors: Universal/16; Swank Motion Pictures.
A Pacific Northwest lumberjack family refuses to join a statewide timber strike.   Problems within the family are also stressed.   Dra

2002   THE SONS OF KATIE ELDER
122 min., color, 1965.
Director: Henry Hathaway.   Cast: John Wayne, Dean Martin, Martha Hyer, Michael Anderson, Jr., Earl Holliman, Jeremy Slate.   Distributor: Paramount Pictures Corp.
Four brothers are reunited at their mother's funeral, and set out to avenge her death.   Wes

2003   THE SOUND AND THE FURY
115 min., color, 1959.
Director: Martin Ritt.   Cast: Yul Brynner, Joanne Woodward, Margaret Leighton, Stuart Whitman, Ethel Waters.
Distributor: Films Inc.
Degenerate Southern family.   Dra

2004   SOUNDER
106 min., color, 1972.
Director: Martin Ritt.   Cast: Cicely Tyson, Paul Winfield, Kevin Hooks, Carmen Mathews.   Distributor: Films Inc.
A black sharecropper family struggles to survive the Depression in the deep South.   See also   PART 2, SOUNDER (1926).   Dra

2005   THE SOUTHERNER
        91 min. , b&w, 1945.
        Director: Jean Renoir. Cast: Zachary Scott, Betty Field,
        Beulah Bondi, Percy Kilbride, Blanche Yurka. Distribu-
        tors: Audio Brandon Films; Kit Parker Films; Images.
        The plight of a poor white cotton farmer and his
        family. Dra

2006   SPENCER'S MOUNTAIN
        119 min. , color, 1963.
        Director: Delmer Daves. Cast: Henry Fonda, Maureen
        O'Hara, James MacArthur, Donald Crisp, Wally Cox,
        Mimsy Farmer. Distributor: Twyman Films.
        A Wyoming man and his nine children live at the
        base of a family mountain. The father promises to build
        a new house on the mountaintop, but poverty and other ob-
        stacles always prevent it. Dra

2007   A STAR IS BORN
        111 min. , color, 1937.
        Director: William A. Wellman. Cast: Janet Gaynor, Fred-
        ric March, Adolphe Menjou, Andy Devine, May Robson,
        Lionel Stander, Franklin Pangborn. Distributors: Audio
        Brandon Films; Kit Parker Films; Images.
        Woman rises to stardom, while her husband falls
        into the gutter. Dra

2008   A STAR IS BORN
        154 min. , color, 1954.
        Director: George Cukor. Cast: Judy Garland, James Ma-
        son, Jack Carson, Charles Bickford. Distributors: Audio
        Brandon Films; Twyman Films.
        Singer Esther Blodgett becomes star Vicki Lester,
        but her husband loses his grip. Remake. Parents' Maga-
        zine Special Merit Award. Mus-Dra

2009   STARS IN MY CROWN
        89 min. , b&w, 1950.
        Director: Jacques Tourneur. Cast: Joel McCrea, Ellen
        Drew, Alan Hale, Dean Stockwell, Amanda Blake. Distri-
        butor: Films Inc.
        Set in mid-19th-century backwoods America, where
        a new minister has to overcome great odds to get anybody
        to listen to his sermons. Dra

2010   STATE FAIR
        97 min. , b&w, 1933.
        Director: Henry King. Cast: Will Rogers, Janet Gaynor,
        Sally Eilers, Victor Jory, Louise Dresser, Lew Ayres,
        Norman Foster. Distributor: Films Inc.
        Members of a farm family anticipate an annual state
        fair for different reasons--prize hog, pickle and mincemeat
        contest, love, revenge. Dra

2011 STATE FAIR
100 min., color, 1945.
Director: Walter Lang. Cast: Jeanne Crain, Dana Andrews, Vivian Blaine, Dick Haymes. Distributor: Films Inc.
Musical remake.

2012 STATE FAIR
100 min., color, 1962.
Director: Jose Ferrer. Cast: Pat Boone, Bobby Darin, Pamela Tiffin, Ann-Margret, Tom Ewell, Alice Faye, Wally Cox. Distributor: Films Inc.
Remake of the musical.

2013 STELLA DALLAS
106 min., b&w, 1937.
Director: King Vidor. Cast: Barbara Stanwyck, John Boles, Anne Shirley, Alan Hale, Marjorie Main. Distributor: Audio Brandon Films.
After a woman loses her husband, she sacrifices everything for her daughter. Dra

2014 THE STEPFORD WIVES
114 min., color, 1975.
Director: Bryan Forbes. Cast: Patrick O'Neal, Katharine Ross, Paula Prentiss, Peter Masterson, Nanette Newman. Distributor: Swank Motion Pictures.
A city couple move with their children to a picturebook New England town where all the wives seem to turn into subservient robots. Hor

2015 A STOLEN LIFE
107 min., b&w, 1946.
Director: Curtis Bernhardt. Cast: Bette Davis, Glenn Ford, Dane Clark, Walter Brennan. Distributor: United Artists/16.
A pair of twins with different personalities--one a serious, sensitive artist; the other a seductive man-chaser-- lust after the same man. Dra

2016 THE STORY OF VERNON AND IRENE CASTLE
93 min., b&w, 1939.
Director: H. C. Potter. Cast: Ginger Rogers, Fred Astaire, Walter Brennan, Edna May Oliver. Distributor: Films Inc.
Bio of the couple who revolutionized ballroom dancing. Mus-Bio

2017 THE STRANGE LOVE OF MARTHA IVERS
116 min., b&w, 1946.
Director: Lewis Milestone. Cast: Barbara Stanwyck, Van Heflin, Kirk Douglas, Judith Anderson. Distributor: Paramount Pictures Corp.

The wealthy descendant of the founder of Iverstown is married to a weak, alcoholic public official. A childhood pal of both arrives and Martha Ivers is forced to reveal her secret. Mys

2018   STRANGERS ON A TRAIN
101 min. , b&w, 1951.
Director: Alfred Hitchcock. Cast: Farley Granger, Robert Walker, Ruth Roman, Leo G. Carroll, Marion Lorne. Distributor: Swank Motion Pictures.
Two men meet on a train and agree to a murder swap--a hated wife for a hated father. Mys

2019   STREET SCENE
82 min. , b&w, 1931.
Director: King Vidor. Cast: Sylvia Sidney, William Collier, Jr. , Estelle Taylor. Distributors: Audio Brandon Films; Kit Parker Films.
A New York City tenement block and a cross section of its inhabitants. From the play by Elmer Rice. Dra

2020   A STREETCAR NAMED DESIRE
122 min. , b&w, 1951.
Director: Elia Kazan. Cast: Marlon Brando, Karl Malden, Vivien Leigh, Kim Hunter. Distributor: United Artists/16.
Blanche comes to stay with her sister Stella and her brutish husband Stanley in the French Quarter of New Orleans. Stanley is immediately threatened by Blanche's air of Southern gentility; he calls her bluff and shatters her fragile psyche in the end. From the play by Tennessee Williams. Dra

2021   THE STRUGGLE
90 min. , b&w, 1931.
Director: D. W. Griffith. Cast: Hal Skelly, Zita Johann, Charlotte Wynters. Distributor: Audio Brandon Films.
A family tries to survive the Depression in New York City and deal with alcoholism. Dra

2022   THE SUBJECT WAS ROSES
107 min. , color, 1968.
Director: Ulu Grosbard. Cast: Patricia Neal, Jack Albertson, Martin Sheen. Distributor: Films Inc.
Life of a closely knit, middle-class Irish Catholic family in the mid-Forties. From the play by Frank D. Gilroy. Dra

2023   SUDDENLY, LAST SUMMER
114 min. , b&w, 1959.
Director: Joseph L. Mankiewicz. Cast: Elizabeth Taylor, Katharine Hepburn, Montgomery Clift, Mercedes McCambridge. Distributors: Audio Brandon Films; Twyman Films.
A young woman is traumatized after witnessing the

brutal murder of her homosexual cousin. Her aunt tries
to have her lobotomized so she won't reveal the truth about
her cousin. From the play by Tennessee Williams. Dra

2024 THE SUGARLAND EXPRESS
109 min., color, 1974.
Director: Steven Spielberg. Cast: Goldie Hawn, William
Atherton, Ben Johnson, Michael Sacks. Distributors: Uni-
versal/16; Twyman Films.
An escaped con and his dizzy wife kidnap a state
trooper in order to regain custody of their child. Com-
Dra

2025 SUMMER HOLIDAY
92 min., color, 1948.
Director: Rouben Mamoulian. Cast: Mickey Rooney, Walter Huston, Frank Morgan, Butch Jenkins, Gloria De Haven,
Agnes Moorehead. Distributor: Films Inc.
Musical version of AH, WILDERNESS! (1579) about
growing up in small-town America. From the play by Eugene O'Neill.

2026 SUMMER MAGIC
100 min., color, 1963.
Director: James Neilson. Cast: Hayley Mills, Burl Ives,
Dorothy McGuire, Deborah Walley, Eddie Hodges. Distributor: Twyman Films.
Recently widowed Mother Carey is forced to cut ex-
penses, so she and her children leave New York for a small
town in Maine. Parents' Magazine Family Medal Award.
Mus-Dra

2027 SUMMER OF MY GERMAN SOLDIER
93 min., color, 1978.
Director: Michael Tuchner. Cast: Kristy McNichol, Bruce
Davison, Esther Rolle, Michael Constantine, Barbara Barrie.
Distributor: Learning Corp. of America.
An abused, unwanted, teenage daughter of a Jewish
couple lives in small Southern town during World War II.
The lonely girl hides an escaped Nazi soldier and falls in
love with him. Dra

2028 SUMMER WISHES, WINTER DREAMS
95 min., color, 1973.
Director: Gilbert Cates. Cast: Joanne Woodward, Martin
Balsam, Sylvia Sidney. Distributor: Swank Motion Pictures.
A wife and mother with grown children suffers through
an emotional crisis. Dra

2029 SUMMERTREE
88 min., color, 1971.
Director: Anthony Newley. Cast: Michael Douglas, Brenda
Vaccaro, Jack Warden, Barbara Bel Geddes. Distributor:
Institutional Cinema.

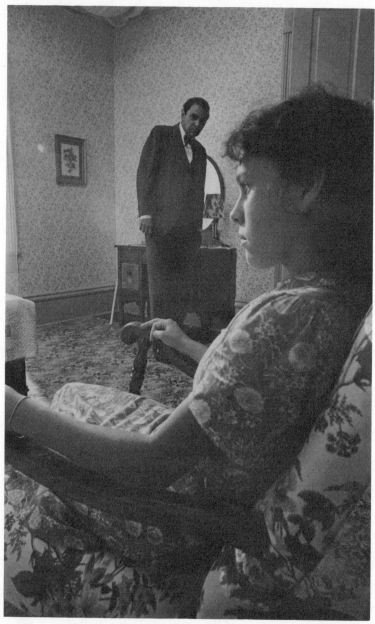

From <u>Summer of My German Soldier</u>. Courtesy Highgate
Pictures/Learning Corp. of America.

A young man decides to flee to Canada rather than be inducted into the U.S. Army. He clashes with his parents, goes to Vietnam, and is killed. From the play by Ron Cowen. See also MY COUNTRY, RIGHT OR WRONG? (980). Dra

2030 THE SUNSHINE BOYS
111 min., color, 1975.
Director: Herbert Ross. Cast: Walter Matthau, George Burns, Richard Benjamin, Lee Meredith. Distributor: Films Inc.
Two aged, feuding ex-vaudevillians cause lots of problems for each other and their families when they consent to reteam for a TV show. From the play by Neil Simon. Com

2031 SUPERDAD
95 min., color, 1974.
Director: Vincent McEveety. Cast: Bob Crane, Barbara Rush, Kurt Russell, Joe Flynn, Kathleen Cody. Distributors: Films Inc.; Twyman Films.
A father tries everything to control his daughter's life-style. Com

2032 THE SUSPECT
85 min., b&w, 1944.
Director: Robert Siodmak. Cast: Charles Laughton, Ella Raines, Dean Harens, Henry Daniell. Distributor: Universal/16.
A henpecked husband falls for a young woman and decides to kill his nagging wife. Dra

2033 SWEETHEARTS
114 min., color, 1938.
Director: W. S. Van Dyke II. Cast: Jeanette MacDonald, Nelson Eddy, Ray Bolger, Mischa Auer. Distributor: Films Inc.
The happy marriage of two Broadway musical stars is shaken. Mus

2034 TAKE HER, SHE'S MINE
98 min., color, 1963.
Director: Henry Koster. Cast: James Stewart, Sandra Dee, Robert Morley, Audrey Meadows. Distributor: Films Inc.
A father tries to protect his daughter from boys, etc. Com

2035 TAKING OFF
93 min., color, 1971.
Director: Milos Forman. Cast: Lynn Carlin, Buck Henry, Linnea Heacock, Georgia Engel. Distributor: Universal/16.
A teenage girl leaves home. Her parents go to the

SPFC (Society for Parents of Fugitive Children), where they realize if they can't beat the young, they might as well join them. Sat

2036   TELL ME WHERE IT HURTS
78 min., color, 1974.
Director: Paul Bogart. Cast: Maureen Stapleton, Paul Sorvino, Rose Gregorio, Doris Dowling, Louise Latham. Distributors: Learning Corp. of America; Mass Media Ministries.
A middle-aged housewife is in dire need of a change. First, her coffee-klatch group turns into a consciousness-raising group, and then she leaves home to find her first paying job. Her husband is totally disconcerted. See also DOES ANYBODY NEED ME ANYMORE? (385). Dra

2037   TENDER COMRADE
102 min., b&w, 1943.
Director: Edward Dmytryk. Cast: Ginger Rogers, Ruth Hussey, Robert Ryan, Kim Hunter. Distributor: Films Inc.
Young wives carry on when husbands go to war. Dra

2038   TENTH AVENUE ANGEL
74 min., b&w, 1948.
Director: Roy Rowland. Cast: Margaret O'Brien, Angela Lansbury, George Murphy, Phyllis Thaxter, Warner Anderson. Distributor: Films Inc.
A street urchin affects the lives of family and friends. Dra

2039   THERE'S ALWAYS TOMORROW
84 min., b&w, 1934.
Director: Edward Sloman. Cast: Frank Morgan, Binnie Barnes, Lois Wilson, Robert Taylor. Distributor: Universal/16.
A neglected married man is tempted to stray. Dra

2040   THERE'S ALWAYS TOMORROW
84 min., b&w, 1956.
Director: Douglas Sirk. Cast: Fred MacMurray, Barbara Stanwyck, Joan Bennett, Pat Crowley, Jane Darwell. Distributor: Universal/16.
Remake. A married man is tempted by a former sweetheart. Dra

2041   THERE'S NO BUSINESS LIKE SHOW BUSINESS
117 min., color, 1954.
Director: Walter Lang. Cast: Ethel Merman, Donald O'Connor, Marilyn Monroe, Dan Dailey, Johnnie Ray, Mitzi Gaynor. Distributor: Films Inc.
A family vaudeville team: the children grow up, fall in love, estrangement occurs. In the end, all are reunited in a big finale. Mus

2042   THIEVES
       103 min., color, 1977.
       Director: John Berry. Cast: Marlo Thomas, Charles
       Grodin, Irwin Corey, John McMartin. Distributor: Para-
       mount Pictures Corp.
           A couple grow up together, marry, become success-
       ful schoolteachers, but city life begins to wreck their mar-
       riage. Set in New York. From the play by Herb Gardner.
       Com

2043   THE THIN MAN SERIES (6 Films)
       86-112 min. each, b&w, 1934-47.
       Directors: W. S. Van Dyke II, Richard Thorpe, Edward
       Buzzell. Cast: William Powell, Myrna Loy. Distributor:
       Films Inc.
           Nick and Nora Charles solve murder mysteries with
       their pooch Asta. Titles available include: THE THIN
       MAN; AFTER THE THIN MAN; ANOTHER THIN MAN;
       SHADOW OF THE THIN MAN; THE THIN MAN GOES HOME;
       and SONG OF THE THIN MAN. Mys

2044   THINGS IN THEIR SEASON
       79 min., color, 1975.
       Director: James Goldstone. Cast: Patricia Neal, Ed
       Flanders, Meg Foster, Marc Singer. Distributor: Learning
       Corp. of America.
           The mother of a Wisconsin farm family is dying of
       leukemia. This catalyst forces the family to face up to
       problems they never had to face before. Dra

2045   THIS EARTH IS MINE
       125 min., color, 1959.
       Director: Henry King. Cast: Rock Hudson, Jean Simmons,
       Dorothy McGuire, Claude Rains. Distributor: Universal/16.
           Family saga set in a large California vineyard in the
       Thirties. Dra

2046   THIS PROPERTY IS CONDEMNED
       110 min., color, 1966.
       Director: Sydney Pollack. Cast: Natalie Wood, Robert
       Redford, Charles Bronson, Kate Reid, Mary Badham, Rob-
       ert Blake. Distributor: Paramount Pictures Corp.
           A woman runs a boarding house in a Southern rail-
       road town and rides herd over her restless daughter, who
       tries to escape with a handsome stranger. From the play
       by Tennessee Williams. Dra

2047   THOSE CALLOWAYS
       131 min., color, 1964.
       Director: Norman Tokar. Cast: Brian Keith, Vera Miles,
       Brandon de Wilde, Walter Brennan, Ed Wynn, Linda Evans.
       Distributor: Twyman Films.
           A man wants to create a bird sanctuary for wild

geese, but must face greedy hunters who would rather the
land be reserved for hunting. Set in the backwoods of Vermont. See also RESPONSIBILITY: WHAT ARE ITS LIM-
ITS? (1196). Dra

2048   A THOUSAND CLOWNS
118 min., b&w, 1965.
Director: Fred Coe. Cast: Jason Robards, Jr., Barbara
Harris, Barry Gordon, Martin Balsam, Gene Saks. Distributor: United Artists/16.
A nonconformist TV writer tries to raise his nephew
in his image--eccentric and idealistic. But he then has to
face social workers who want him to clean up his act and
set a better example for the boy. From the play by Herb
Gardner. Com

2049   THREE-CORNERED MOON
80 min., b&w, 1933.
Director: Elliott Nugent. Cast: Claudette Colbert, Richard
Arlen, Mary Boland, Wallace Ford. Distributor: Univer-
sal/16.
Zany members of a once-wealthy family try one crazy
scheme after another to make a living after their fortune is
lost in the stock-market crash. Com

2050   THREE DARING DAUGHTERS
115 min., color, 1948.
Director: Fred M. Wilcox. Cast: Jane Powell, Jeanette
MacDonald, Jose Iturbi, Edward Arnold, Ann E. Todd.
Distributor: Films Inc.
A woman takes her daughters on a cruise and tells
them she plans to remarry. They want her to remarry
Dad. Mus

2051   THE THREE FACES OF EVE
91 min., b&w, 1957.
Director: Nunnally Johnson. Cast: Joanne Woodward,
David Wayne, Lee J. Cobb. Distributor: Films Inc.
Psychological study of a woman with multiple per-
sonalities. Dra

2052   THREE SECRETS
98 min., b&w, 1950.
Director: Robert Wise. Cast: Eleanor Parker, Patricia
Neal, Ruth Roman, Frank Lovejoy, Leif Erickson. Distri-
butor: Corinth Films.
Three women each believe that the 5-year-old sur-
vivor of a plane crash is the child they gave up for adoption.
Dra

2053   THREE SMART GIRLS
84 min., b&w, 1937.
Director: Henry Koster. Cast: Deanna Durbin, Nan Grey,

Barbara Read, Binnie Barnes, Alice Brady, Ray Milland, Mischa Auer, Charles Winninger.   Distributor: Universal/16.
Three sisters try to break up their father's plans for remarriage and reunite him with their mother.   Mus-Com

2054   THREE SMART GIRLS GROW UP
73 min. , b&w, 1939.
Director: Henry Koster.   Cast: Deanna Durbin, Charles Winninger, Nan Grey, Helen Parrish, Robert Cummings.
Distributor: Universal/16.
Deanna meddles in her sisters' love lives.   Mus-Com

2055   THREE VIOLENT PEOPLE
100 min. , color, 1956.
Director: Rudolph Maté.   Cast: Charlton Heston, Anne Baxter, Tom Tryon, Gilbert Roland, Forrest Tucker.   Distributor: Paramount Pictures Corp.
Texas, 1866:   Two brothers and the wife of one become involved in conflict and a triangle.   Wes

2056   THE THRILL OF IT ALL
107 min. , color, 1963.
Director: Norman Jewison.   Cast: Doris Day, James Garner, Arlene Francis, Edward Andrews, Zasu Pitts.   Distributor: Universal/16.
A TV soap commercial star tries to convince her husband that her career won't interfere with her role as a wife.   Com

2057   A TICKLISH AFFAIR
89 min. , color, 1963.
Director: George Sidney.   Cast: Shirley Jones, Gig Young, Red Buttons, Carolyn Jones.   Distributor: Films Inc.
A navy widow takes her three kids to California to finally settle down.   Her young son has other plans.   Com

2058   TO EACH HIS OWN
122 min. , b&w, 1946.
Director: Mitchell Leisen.   Cast: Olivia de Havilland, John Lund, Mary Anderson, Philip Terry.   Distributor: Universal/16.
A woman has an illegitimate son, gives him up, meets him years later, and pretends to be his aunt.   Dra

2059   TO FIND A MAN
93 min. , color, 1972.
Director: Buzz Kulik.   Cast: Pamela Sue Martin, Lloyd Bridges, Phyllis Newman, Darren O'Connor, Tom Ewell, Tom Bosley.   Distributor: Swank Motion Pictures.
Two high-school kids try to find an abortionist.   Com-Dra

2060   TO KILL A MOCKINGBIRD
        129 min., b&w, 1963.
        Director: Robert Mulligan. Cast: Gregory Peck, Mary
        Badham, John Megna, Phillip Alford, Rosemary Murphy,
        Brock Peters. Distributors: Universal/16; Swank Motion
        Pictures; Twyman Films.
            Child's-eye-view of life in Depression-era South,
        with focus on the attorney father's defense of a black man
        wrongly accused of rape. Parents' Magazine Special Merit
        Award. Dra

2061   TOBACCO ROAD
        84 min., b&w, 1941.
        Director: John Ford. Cast: Charley Grapewin, Marjorie
        Rambeau, Elizabeth Patterson, William Tracy, Slim Summer-
        ville, Gene Tierney, Dana Andrews, Ward Bond. Distri-
        butors: Audio Brandon Films; Twyman Films.
            Decadent poor whites during the Depression. Dra

2062   TOMORROW IS FOREVER
        105 min., b&w, 1946.
        Director: Irving Pichel. Cast: Claudette Colbert, Orson
        Welles, Natalie Wood, Richard Long. Distributor: Budget
        Films.
            Believing her husband is killed in World War I, a
        woman remarries. Years later, her first husband returns
        incognito, but she recognizes him. Dra

2063   TOY TIGER
        88 min., color, 1956.
        Director: Jerry Hopper. Cast: Jeff Chandler, Laraine
        Day, Tim Hovey, Cecil Kellaway. Distributor: Univer-
        sal/16.
            A young boy invents a heroic, make-believe father.
        He lives with his widowed mother and must get someone to
        play the "father" role because his friends question his tales.
        Com

2064   TOYS IN THE ATTIC
        90 min., b&w, 1963.
        Director: George Roy Hill. Cast: Dean Martin, Geraldine
        Page, Yvette Mimieux, Wendy Hiller, Gene Tierney. Dis-
        tributor: United Artists/16.
            A ne'er-do-well and his weak wife return to New Or-
        leans to live with his two spinster sisters. From the play
        by Lillian Hellman. Dra

2065   THE TRAIL OF THE LONESOME PINE
        102 min., color, 1936.
        Director: Henry Hathaway. Cast: Sylvia Sidney, Henry
        Fonda, Fred MacMurray, Beulah Bondi, Nigel Bruce. Dis-
        tributor: Universal/16.
            An engineer sent to the Blue Ridge Mountains of Vir-
        ginia gets involved in a century-old family feud. Dra

2066   A TREE GROWS IN BROOKLYN
        128 min. , b&w, 1945.
        Director: Elia Kazan.   Cast: Peggy Ann Garner, Dorothy
        McGuire, James Dunn, Joan Blondell, Lloyd Nolan.   Dis-
        tributors: Films Inc. ; Audio Brandon Films; Twyman
        Films.
            A 12-year-old girl must cope with growing up in
        poverty, with her beloved but weak father and unsympathetic
        mother.   Parents' Magazine Special Merit Award.   Dra

2067   THE TRUE STORY OF JESSE JAMES
        93 min. , color, 1957.
        Director: Nicholas Ray.   Cast: Robert Wagner, Jeffrey
        Hunter, Hope Lange, Alan Hale, Agnes Moorehead.   Dis-
        tributor: Films Inc.
            Saga of the James brothers.   Wes

2068   THE TURNING POINT
        119 min. , color, 1977.
        Director: Herbert Ross.   Cast: Anne Bancroft, Shirley
        MacLaine, Mikhail Baryshnikov, Leslie Browne, Tom Sker-
        ritt.   Distributor: Films Inc.
            Examines choice in three women's lives: commit-
        ment to family or dance career.   Mus-Dra

2069   UNDERCURRENT
        116 min. , b&w, 1946.
        Director: Vincente Minnelli.   Cast: Katharine Hepburn,
        Robert Taylor, Robert Mitchum.   Distributor: Films Inc.
            A woman marries a rich young man and later sus-
        pects him of being a lunatic.   Dra

2070   AN UNMARRIED WOMAN
        112 min. , color, 1978.
        Director: Paul Mazursky.   Cast: Jill Clayburgh, Michael
        Murphy, Alan Bates.   Distributor: Films Inc.
            A woman believes she is lucky to be the only one
        in her crowd to have a successful marriage, until her hus-
        band leaves her for a younger woman.   She survives the
        pain and liberates her sex life.   Dra

2071   UP THE SANDBOX
        88 min. , color, 1972.
        Director: Irvin Kershner.   Cast: Barbra Streisand, David
        Selby, Jane Hoffman, Ariane Heller, John C. Becher.   Dis-
        tributor: Swank Motion Pictures.
            Neglected young housewife depends on her fantasy
        to pull her through.   Com

2072   THE WAR BETWEEN MEN AND WOMEN
        110 min. , color, 1972.
        Director: Melville Shavelson.   Cast: Jack Lemmon, Bar-
        bara Harris, Jason Robards, Jr. , Herb Edelman, Lisa Ger-
        ritsen.   Distributor: Westcoast Films.

A lovable but grumpy cartoonist dislikes women, kids and dogs, but he marries a divorcée with three kids and a pregnant dog. Com

2073   THE WAY WE WERE
118 min., color, 1973.
Director: Sydney Pollack. Cast: Barbra Streisand, Robert Redford, Bradford Dillman, Lois Chiles, Patrick O'Neal, Viveca Lindfors, Murray Hamilton. Distributor: Swank Motion Pictures.
An unlikely pair--a WASP, jock writer and a radical--fall in love and marry. Story moves from late Thirties into the blacklist period in Hollywood when their marriage and conflicting ideologies crack. Dra

2074   A WEDDING
124 min., color, 1978.
Director: Robert Altman. Cast: Lillian Gish, Desi Arnaz, Jr., Carol Burnett, Mia Farrow, Vittorio Gassman, Nina Van Pallandt, Dina Merrill, Pat McCormick, Geraldine Chaplin, Viveca Lindfors. Distributor: Films Inc.
Records the interactions of two families--old money and new money--on the wedding day that unites both families. Sat

2075   WE'RE NOT MARRIED
85 min., b&w, 1952.
Director: Edmund Goulding. Cast: Ginger Rogers, Marilyn Monroe, Fred Allen, Victor Moore, David Wayne, Eve Arden, Zsa Zsa Gabor, Paul Douglas, Eddie Bracken, Mitzi Gaynor, Louis Calhern, James Gleason. Distributor: Films Inc.
Five couples, all married by the same justice of the peace, discover that their marriages are not valid. Com

2076   WHAT EVER HAPPENED TO BABY JANE?
132 min., b&w, 1962.
Director: Robert Aldrich. Cast: Bette Davis, Joan Crawford, Victor Buono. Distributors: Audio Brandon Films; Swank Motion Pictures.
Sibling rivalry continues into old age, as two reclusive sisters--one, a former child vaudeville star; the other, a film star--battle their last battle for "top billing." Hor

2077   WHERE LOVE HAS GONE
114 min., color, 1964.
Director: Edward Dmytryk. Cast: Susan Hayward, Bette Davis, Michael Connors, Joey Heatherton. Distributor: Paramount Pictures Corp.
A teenager kills her mother's lover. Dra

2078   WHERE THE LILIES BLOOM
        97 min., color, 1974.
        Director: William A. Graham. Cast: Julie Gholson, Jan
        Smithers, Matthew Burril, Harry Dean Stanton, Helen Har-
        mon. Distributor: United Artists/16.
        Four children (ages 5-16) in the Blue Ridge Moun-
        tains of North Carolina struggle to keep their family to-
        gether when their father dies. Dra

2079   WHERE THE RED FERN GROWS
        100 min., color, 1975.
        Director: Norman Tokar. Cast: James Whitmore, Be-
        verly Garland, Jack Ging, Lonny Chapman, Stewart Peter-
        sen. Distributor: Swank Motion Pictures.
        A young boy, spurred on by his grandfather's values,
        works hard to save for two fine hunting dogs. Set in the
        Ozarks of Oklahoma during the Thirties. Dra

2080   WHERE'S POPPA?
        87 min., color, 1970.
        Director: Carl Reiner. Cast: Ruth Gordon, George Segal,
        Trish Van Devere, Ron Leibman, Vincent Gardenia. Dis-
        tributor: United Artists/16.
        New York lawyer tries to institutionalize his senile
        mother so he can have a healthy love life. Com

2081   WHO'S AFRAID OF VIRGINIA WOOLF?
        129 min., b&w, 1966.
        Director: Mike Nichols. Cast: Elizabeth Taylor, Richard
        Burton, George Segal, Sandy Dennis. Distributor: Swank
        Motion Pictures.
        An aging professor and his castrating wife get to-
        gether with a young professor and his neurotic wife for a
        night of drinks, revelations and recriminations. From the
        play by Edward Albee. Dra

2082   THE WIDOW
        99 min., color, 1976.
        Director: J. Lee Thompson. Cast: Michael Learned,
        Bradford Dillman. Distributor: Lucerne Films.
        Based on the book by Lynn Caine. The story of her
        trauma after the death of her young husband. Bio

2083   THE WILD COUNTRY
        100 min., color, 1971.
        Director: Robert Totten. Cast: Steve Forrest, Jack Elam,
        Vera Miles, Ron Howard. Distributor: Twyman Films.
        The Tanner family comes from the East to settle in
        the Grand Tetons in the 1880s. Wes

2084   WILD IS THE WIND
        114 min., b&w, 1957.
        Director: George Cukor. Cast: Anthony Quinn, Anna

Magnani, Anthony Franciosa. Distributor: Paramount Pictures Corp.

An immigrant Nevada rancher brings a woman over from Italy to be his second wife, but he still grieves for his deceased first wife, who was the sister of his new bride. Wes

2085 WINTERSET
80 min., b&w, 1936.
Director: Alfred Santell. Cast: Burgess Meredith, John Carradine, Margo, Eduardo Ciannelli, Mischa Auer. Distributors: Audio Brandon Films; Kit Parker Films.

Son seeks to clear his father's name; his father was electrocuted for a crime he didn't commit. From the play by Maxwell Anderson. Dra

2086 WITH SIX YOU GET EGGROLL
95 min., color, 1968.
Director: Howard Morris. Cast: Doris Day, Brian Keith, Pat Carroll, Barbara Hershey, George Carlin, Alice Ghostley. Distributor: Twyman Films.

A widow with three children meets a widower with a daughter of his own. They marry, over the objections of the kids. Com

2087 WITHOUT LOVE
111 min., b&w, 1945.
Director: Harold S. Bucquet. Cast: Katharine Hepburn, Spencer Tracy, Lucille Ball, Keenan Wynn, Gloria Grahame, Distributor: Films Inc.

A scientist marries his assistant for the sake of their work. Their platonic relationship turns into something more. Com

2088 WIVES AND LOVERS
106 min., b&w, 1963.
Director: John Rich. Cast: Janet Leigh, Van Johnson, Shelley Winters, Martha Hyer, Ray Walston. Distributor: Paramount Pictures Corp.

A young writer's novel is a success. His wife supported him all the years it took to write the book. Both are tempted by other people in their glamorous new lifestyle. Com

2089 WIVES UNDER SUSPICION
75 min., b&w, 1938.
Director: James Whale. Cast: Gail Patrick, Warren William, Constance Moore, William Lundigan. Distributor: Universal/16.

A District Attorney, prosecuting a love-related murder case, finds some discord in his own home. Remake of THE KISS BEFORE THE MIRROR (1824). Dra

2090   WOMAN OF THE YEAR
114 min., b&w, 1942.
Director: George Stevens. Cast: Katharine Hepburn,
Spencer Tracy, Fay Bainter, Reginald Owen, William Bendix. Distributor: Films Inc.
Hepburn is a political columnist. She's married to
a sports writer. Com

2091   A WOMAN UNDER THE INFLUENCE
155 min., color, 1974.
Director: John Cassavetes. Cast: Gena Rowlands, Peter
Falk, Katherine Cassavetes, Lady Rowlands. Distributor:
Faces International Films.
Mental crackup of the competent, but slightly child-
like, wife of a blue-collar worker. Shows the complex re-
actions of husband, kids, family, and friends. Dra

2092   WOMAN'S WORLD
94 min., color, 1954.
Director: Jean Negulesco. Cast: Clifton Webb, June
Allyson, Van Heflin, Lauren Bacall, Fred MacMurray, Arlene Dahl, Cornel Wilde. Distributor: Films Inc.
Three men and their wives are brought to New York
by their boss who is seeking a successor. Dra

2093   WRITTEN ON THE WIND
99 min., color, 1956.
Director: Douglas Sirk. Cast: Robert Stack, Dorothy
Malone, Rock Hudson, Lauren Bacall, Robert Keith. Dis-
tributor: Universal/16.
Last days of a second-generation oil family. Dra

2094   YANKEE DOODLE DANDY
126 min., b&w, 1942.
Director: Michael Curtiz. Cast: James Cagney, Joan
Leslie, Walter Huston, Irene Manning, Richard Whorf,
George Tobias. Distributor: United Artists/16.
Bio of George M. Cohan and family. Mus

2095   THE YEARLING
135 min., color, 1946.
Director: Clarence Brown. Cast: Gregory Peck, Jane
Wyman, Claude Jarman, Jr., Chill Wills. Distributor:
Films Inc.
A rural Florida family struggles to make ends meet.
Focuses on the son's relationships with his family, friends,
and his pet fawn. Dra

2096   YOU ONLY LIVE ONCE
85 min., b&w, 1937.
Director: Fritz Lang. Cast: Sylvia Sidney, Henry Fonda,
Ward Bond, Barton MacLane, Margaret Hamilton. Distributors: Audio Brandon Films; Kit Parker Films; Images.

A small-time crook marries and tries to go straight, but he is unjustly accused of murder and escapes prison, with the help of his wife, just before his pardon comes through. He kills a priest during his escape.   Dra

2097   YOU'LL LIKE MY MOTHER
93 min. , color, 1972.
Director: Lamont Johnson.   Cast: Patty Duke, Rosemary Murphy, Richard Thomas, Sian Barbara Allen.   Distributors: Universal/16; Twyman Films; Swank Motion Pictures.
A pregnant Vietnam War widow visits her mother-in-law for the first time and finds some surprises.   Hor

2098   YOUNG AT HEART
117 min. , color, 1954.
Director: Gordon Douglas.   Cast: Frank Sinatra, Doris Day, Gig Young, Ethel Barrymore, Dorothy Malone.   Distributor: Budget Films.
Musical remake of FOUR DAUGHTERS (1728).

2099   THE YOUNG STRANGER
89 min. , b&w, 1957.
Director: John Frankenheimer.   Cast: James MacArthur, Kim Hunter, James Daly, James Gregory.   Distributor: Kit Parker Films.
Lack of communication in a nouveau riche Beverly Hills family.   Dra

2100   YOUNG TOM EDISON
86 min. , b&w, 1940.
Director: Norman Taurog.   Cast: Mickey Rooney, Fay Bainter, Virginia Weidler, George Bancroft.   Distributor: Films Inc.
Boyhood of Edison.   Bio

2101   YOU'RE A BIG BOY NOW
96 min. , color, 1967.
Director: Francis Ford Coppola.   Cast: Peter Kastner, Elizabeth Hartman, Geraldine Page, Julie Harris, Tony Bill, Rip Torn, Karen Black, Michael Dunn.   Distributor: Audio Brandon Films.
A young man comes to the big city for sex and adventure.   His overbearing mother tries to stop him.   Com

2102   YOURS, MINE AND OURS
111 min. , color, 1968.
Director: Melville Shavelson.   Cast: Lucille Ball, Henry Fonda, Van Johnson, Tom Bosley.   Distributor: United Artists/16.
A widow with eight children marries a widower with ten.   Com

2103   ZANDY'S BRIDE
        97 min., color, 1974.
        Director: Jan Troell.   Cast: Gene Hackman, Liv Ullmann,
        Eileen Heckart, Joe Santos.   Distributor: Westcoast Films.
           A 19th-century California rancher tries to turn his
        mail-order bride into a submissive servant.   Wes

SELECTED RESOURCES

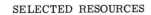

ARTICLES

Artel, Linda. "Ethnic America." Sightlines, Spring 1976, pp. 13-
14, 16-18, 20. Lengthy annotations of 33 shorts and features,
broken down by ethnic group.

Baldwin, James. "Growing Up with the Movies." American Film,
May 1976, pp. 8-18. The boyhood of the novelist, and his
thoughts about Hollywood features of the period (the Thirties) and
how they affected his lonely Harlem youth.

Barr, William R. "Brakhage: Artistic Development in Two Childbirth Films." Film Quarterly, Spring 1976, pp. 30-34. Films
considered are: WINDOW WATER BABY MOVING and THIGH
LINE LYRE TRIANGULAR.

Basinger, Jeanine. "When Women Wept." American Film, September 1977, pp. 52-57. On Hollywood's "women's films," which
have been known to involve much sacrifice and suffering in the
marital arena.

Betancourt, Jeanne. "Whatever Happened to ... Women in Film."
Media & Methods, October 1975, pp. 28-33, 76, 78. Themes,
stars, film critics, and filmmakers. With resources.

Biskind, Peter. "Rebel Without a Cause: Nicholas Ray in the Fifties." Film Quarterly, Fall 1974, pp. 32-38. Main focus--
REBEL WITHOUT A CAUSE.

Bobrow, Andrew. "The Adams Chronicles, A Production Profile."
Filmmakers Newsletter, March 1976, Vol. 9, No. 5, pp. 27-32,
34. Preproduction research, props, production problems, au-
thenticity, postproduction.

Byron, Stuart. "Television: Family Plot." Film Comment, March/
April 1977, p. 31. Criticism of the ROOTS' "defense of the
family unit" as the main reason for black survival.

Changas, Estelle. "Elia Kazan's America." Film Comment, Summer 1972, pp. 8-14. Touches on family interest in EAST OF EDEN, WILD RIVER, AMERICA AMERICA, and A STREETCAR NAMED DESIRE.

Chemasi, Antonio. "Comment: The Family Connection." American Film, June 1976, p. 2. Why family life is profitable on TV, yet rarely touched in feature films today.

Cicarelli, Paul M. "Making $$$ in Filmmaking: Filming Weddings? Yes!" Filmmakers Newsletter, November 1973, Vol. 7, No. 1, pp. 63-65. What production problems to expect if you want to film weddings for profit.

Cook, Bruce. "Public Television's Big Splash: The Adams Family Saga Is an Expensive but Worthy Bicentennial Gift to the Nation." American Film, December 1975, pp. 6-13. Production info.

De Witt, Karen. "A Memory of Harlem." American Film, November 1978, pp. 18-27. William (MEN OF BRONZE) Miles as he works on his documentary on the history of Harlem. A black man, Miles returns to his old "home town" and contrasts his memories with Harlem today.

Divoky, Diane. "Children's Rights." Sightlines, Spring 1975, pp. 15-16. 16mm films on the subject, with critical annotations.

Durgnat, Raymond. "King Vidor: Part I." Film Comment, July/ August 1973, pp. 10-49. Commentaries on such Vidor family films as THE CROWD, HALLELUJAH!, THE CHAMP, OUR DAILY BREAD, THE WEDDING NIGHT.

Egan, Catherine. "From Kitchen to Camera: Feminism and the Family Film." Sightlines, Spring 1978, pp. 9-12, 31-34. Lengthy feminist discussion of 35 16mm family life films; many were made by women. With distribution info.

Egan, Catherine. "6 American Families." Film Library Quarterly, Vol. 11, Nos. 1 & 2, 1978, pp. 5-14. Analysis of the filmic treatment of each of the families profiled in the TV series SIX AMERICAN FAMILIES.

Epple, Ron. "Films By/About Men." Media & Methods, October 1975, pp. 36-37, 39-41. Handful of shorts--narratives, documentaries and animated films.

Farber, Stephen. "Film Noir: The Society, Violence and the Bitch Goddess." Film Comment, November/December 1974, pp. 8-11. They were usually deadly, double-crossing, or domineering wives, and sometimes daughters with sacrificing mothers (MILDRED PIERCE).

Farber, Stephen. "New American Gothic." Film Quarterly, Fall 1966, pp. 22-27. Applicable films include: INSIDE DAISY CLOVER and HUSH, HUSH, SWEET CHARLOTTE.

Fox, Terry Curtis. "Paul Mazursky Interviewed." Film Comment, March/April 1978, pp. 29-32. The writer/director of films that often highlight aspects of family life talks about AN UNMARRIED WOMAN.

Freyer, Ellen. "Nell Cox: Feminist Filmmaker." The Feminist Art Journal, Summer 1977, pp. 34-36. Profile of Cox, who is both a mother and a filmmaker. She discusses her TV production LIZA'S PIONEER DIARY; with mention of A TO B.

Gaffney, Maureen. "Tom Davenport Discusses His Breakthrough Fairy Tale Films." young viewers, Spring 1978, pp. 5-7. Special focus on Davenport's live-action dramatic version of fairy tales RAPUNZEL, RAPUNZEL and HANSEL AND GRETEL.

Gill, June M. "The Films of Gunvor Nelson." Film Quarterly, Spring 1977, pp. 28-36. Covers SCHMEERGUNTZ, FOG PUMAS, MY NAME IS OONA, KIRSA NICHOLINA, and her family-roots film TROLLSTENEN.

Gilliard, Bari Lynn, and Victoria Levitt. "The Quiet One. A Conversation with Helen Levitt, Janice Loeb and Bill Levitt." Film Culture, Nos. 63-64, 1977, pp. 127-139. The filmmakers on the production of THE QUIET ONE: inception, casting, development of the script, etc.

Halberstadt, Ira. "Hester Street." Filmmakers Newsletter, January 1976, Vol. 9, No. 3, pp. 26-30. Producing and marketing this independent feature.

Halberstadt, Ira. "Scenes from a Mind: Woody Allen Is Nobody's Fool." Take One, November 1978, pp. 16-20. Allen talks about angst and INTERIORS. A review of the film (by James Monaco) is included on pp. 19-20, 61.

Hays, Lora. "From the Frying Pan to the Trim-Bin." Film Library Quarterly, Winter 1971-72, pp. 22-25. Personal thoughts on being a wife, mother and filmmaker.

Horowitz, Karen. "Explorations: Elephants, Home Movies, Senior Citizens, and Yanomamo Anthropologists Go Bananas." American Film, September 1976, pp. 66-68. A report on the annual Conference on Visual Anthropology, held at Temple University. Covers "home movie" films, e.g., FAMILY PORTRAIT SITTINGS, and some other family life films screened at the '76 conference.

Howard, Steve. "The Making of Alice Doesn't Live Here Anymore." Filmmakers Newsletter, March 1975, Vol. 8, No. 5, pp. 21-26. An interview with the director, Martin Scorsese.

Jacobs, Diane. "Where Love Has Gone." American Film, December 1978-January 1979, pp. 54-59. Love, marriage, divorce, and coupling in the films of the last decade; a positive view.

Jeffries, Georgia. "The Problem with G." American Film, June 1978, pp. 50-57. Why MPAA "G" ratings keep audiences away from so-called "family films."

Kinder, Marsha. "The Return of the Outlaw Couple." Film Quarterly, Summer 1974, pp. 2-10. Family renegades, e.g., THE SUGARLAND EXPRESS.

Krueger, Eric. "An American Family: An American Film." Film Comment, November/December 1973, pp. 16-19. Discusses some questions raised by the controversial WNET series AN AMERICAN FAMILY.

Lamont, Austin, and William Sloan. "The Autobiographical Cinema of Miriam Weinstein." Film Library Quarterly, Vol. 8, No. 2, 1975, pp. 14-16. Weinstein has made films about her father, her boyfriend, their marriage, and a film on the marital breakup of another young couple.

Loveland, Kay, and Estelle Changas. "Eleanor Perry: One Woman in Film." Film Comment, Spring 1971, pp. 64-69. Interview with the screenwriter, with focus on women in and on film and her script for DIARY OF A MAD HOUSEWIFE.

Luciano, Dale. "Long Day's Journey into Night: An Interview with Sidney Lumet." Film Quarterly, Fall 1971, pp. 20-29. Fascinating discussion with the director of the film version of Eugene O'Neill's autobiographical play.

Mason, Edward A. "The Children of Separation and Divorce." Sightlines, Spring 1978, pp. 15-19. 37 16mm films on the subject; with distribution info. Author is a psychiatrist and a filmmaker.

McClure, William J. "Finding the 6 Families: An Interview with Paul Wilkes." Film Library Quarterly, Vol. 11, Nos. 1 & 2, 1978, pp. 15-18. The associate producer/reporter/host/writer of the TV series SIX AMERICAN FAMILIES.

McNally, Judith. "California Reich: A Study of the American Nazi Party." Filmmakers Newsletter, November 1976, Vol. 10, No. 1, pp. 28-32. Filming the controversial documentary; its subjects are "the family next door."

McNally, Judith. "A Woman Under the Influence: An Interview with John Cassavetes." Filmmakers Newsletter, January 1975, Vol. 8, No. 3, pp. 23-27. Making the independent feature, which deals with the crackup of an American housewife.

Mead, Margaret. "The American Family: An Endangered Species?"
TV Guide, December 30, 1978-January 5, 1979, pp. 12-14.
Written just prior to Mead's death in November 1978, this article
traces the evolution of the family to its present troubled state; it
promotes TV as a possible source of positive role models, to
help parents and children survive traumatic family life changes.

Michener, Charles. "Film Festival Preview: Grey Gardens."
Film Comment, September/October 1975, p. 38. A review of
the film about the mother/daughter Beales, made by the Maysles
brothers.

Michener, Charles. "Robert Altman Interviewed." Film Comment,
September-October 1978, pp. 15-18. He discusses his latest--A
WEDDING--the ultimate family opus.

Morris, George. "McCarey and McCarthy: My Son John." Film
Comment, January/February 1976, pp. 16-20. Lengthy discussion of MY SON JOHN.

Place, Janey. "A Family in a Ford." Film Comment, September/
October 1976, pp. 46-51. Family and image analysis in John
Ford's THE GRAPES OF WRATH.

Raymond, Alan, and Susan Raymond. "Filming An American Family."
Filmmakers Newsletter, March 1973, Vol. 6, No. 5, pp. 19-21.
The husband/wife production team responsible for the controver-
sial TV series discuss their experiences.

Richardson, Brenda. "Women, Wives, Film-Makers: An Interview
with Gunvor Nelson and Dorothy Wiley." Film Quarterly, Fall
1971, pp. 34-40. The makers of SCHMEERGUNTZ and FOG
PUMAS; MY NAME IS OONA (Nelson); and KIRSA NICHOLINA
(Nelson).

Rosen, Marjorie. "Movies, Mommies, and the American Dream."
American Film, January-February 1976, pp. 10-15. Overview
of Hollywood's glorification of motherhood.

Rosenthal, Alan. "Arthur Barron of 'Sixteen on Webster Groves'
and 'The Berkeley Rebels.'" Film Library Quarterly, Winter
1970-71, pp. 21-31, 56. Interview with filmmaker Barron on
the production of his CBS-TV documentary SIXTEEN IN WEB-
STER GROVES, and the reaction to it.

Rothman, William. "Alfred Guzzetti's Family Portrait Sittings."
Quarterly Review of Film Studies, February 1977, pp. 96-113.
Focuses on one of the most ambitious films in the family portrait
genre to date.

Sarris, Andrew. "Growing Up with Gloria Jean." American Film,
April 1978, pp. 26-31. Movie-going and family memories of the
fan who grew up to be a critic.

"Saving the Family." Newsweek, May 15, 1978, pp. 63-90. Special report on family life in America. Touches on TV families.

Silver, Joan Micklin, and Raphael Silver. "Explorations: On Hester Street." American Film, October 1975, pp. 78-80. The writer-director and her husband, the producer, write about independently producing HESTER STREET.

Sklar, Robert. "Electronic Americana." American Film, March 1977, pp. 60-64. The more sensational episodes of TV series, many of which are family-related and produced by Norman Lear.

Sklar, Robert. "Is Television Taking Blacks Seriously." American Film, September 1978, pp. 25-29. Two black producers, a director/writer, and an actress discuss the promise of ROOTS and its effect on black TV shows.

Small, Edward S. "The Diary-Folk Film." Film Library Quarterly, Vol. 9, No. 2, 1976, pp. 35-39. The diary films of such experimental filmmakers as Jonas Mekas and Stan Brakhage.

Starr, Cecile. "Paul Mazursky's An Unmarried Woman." Filmmakers Newsletter, April 1978, Vol. 11, No. 6, pp. 28-31, 34. Making the film.

Sternburg, Janet. "Revealing Herself." Film Library Quarterly, Winter 1971-72, pp. 7-12, 60-64. Extensive analysis of the classic short film GROWING UP FEMALE: AS SIX BECOME ONE, with related books.

Taylor, Judith. "Movie Channel: Did She or Didn't She? Mystifying Women's Oppression." Women & Film, Vol. 2, No. 7, pp. 106-109. Feminist perspective of the TV drama special THE LEGEND OF LIZZIE BORDEN (ABC-1975).

Terry, John. "Filming An American Family in Super-8." Filmmakers Newsletter, March 1973, Vol. 6, No. 5, pp. 22-23. Super-8 was used to film one of the Loud son's summer trips.

Trojan, Judith. "The DeBolts--Who They Are Is Just the Beginning." Media & Methods, October 1978, p. 53. Lengthy review of the award-winning film WHO ARE THE DEBOLTS, AND WHERE DID THEY GET 19 KIDS?

Trojan, Judith. "Guilty by Reason of Race." Film Library Quarterly, Spring 1973, pp. 20-22, 27. Lengthy review of the film, which includes several generations of Japanese Americans.

Trojan, Judith. "An Interview with Martha Coolidge." The Feminist Art Journal, Summer 1976, pp. 14-18. The maker of notable autobiographical and family shorts talks about her first feature film, NOT A PRETTY PICTURE.

Trojan, Judith. "Who's Who in Filmmaking: Albert Maysles."
Sightlines, Spring 1978, pp. 26-30. Interview with one-half of
the Maysles brothers filmmaking team, focusing on their two
"family films"--GREY GARDENS and THE BURKS OF GEORGIA--
as well as on the Maysles' early family life.

Trojan, Judith. "Who's Who in Filmmaking: Beginnings ... Martha
Coolidge." Sightlines, May/June 1973, pp. 11-12. Profile of
the filmmaker and coverage of her first award-winning film,
DAVID: OFF AND ON (about her brother).

Varlejs, Jana. "Cine-Opsis." Wilson Library Bulletin, September
1976, pp. 80-81. 16mm films for library programs on non-sexist
roles, especially masculine sex-role stereotypes and alternative
role models.

Varlejs, Jana. "Cine-Opsis." Wilson Library Bulletin, March
1977, pp. 596-597. Films on parenting that are suitable for
library programming.

Walter, Richard. "David Hartman ... Birth and Babies." Filmmakers Newsletter, March 1974, Vol. 7, No. 5, pp. 62-65.
Charles Braverman's first video effort--a 90-minute ABC documentary on childbirth.

Ward, Melinda. "The Making of An American Family: Susan Raymond, Alan Raymond and John Terry." Film Comment, Novem-
ber/December 1973, pp. 24-31. The filmmakers lived with the
Loud family for much of seven months to produce this TV series.

Ward, Melinda. "Pat Loud: An Interview." Film Comment, No-
vember/December 1973, pp. 20-23. Interview with the wife/
mother of AN AMERICAN FAMILY--the 12-hour cinema-vérité
documentary series.

Waters, Harry F. "The TV Fun House." Newsweek, May 15,
1978, pp. 85-87. "Sitcom" or "domcom" and dramatic treatment
of the family on TV today vs. TV's early days vs. real-life.

Weis, Elisabeth. "Family Portraits." American Film, November
1975, pp. 54-59. Handful of some quality 16mm films on the
family.

Witus, Barbara. "Making a TV Special: Getting Married." Filmmakers Newsletter, June 1976, Vol. 9, No. 8, pp. 18-21.
Charles Braverman's film on American marriage rituals.

Wood, Robin. "Ideology, Genre, Auteur." Film Comment, Janu-
ary/February 1977, pp. 46-51. Theoretical analysis of family
films, in particular--Capra's IT'S A WONDERFUL LIFE and
Hitchcock's SHADOW OF A DOUBT.

Zito, Stephen. "Out of Africa: Alex Haley's Roots." American
Film, October 1976, pp. 8-17. The making of the TV miniseries.

Zito, Stephen. "Prime-Time Soap Opera." American Film, February 1977, pp. 22-27. Family life sagas on TV, e.g., Rhoda;
Family; Rich Man, Poor Man; One Day at a Time.

BOOKS & PAMPHLETS

Allyn, Mildred V., comp. About Aging: A Catalog of Films, 3rd
edition. Los Angeles: The Ethel Percy Andrus Gerontology Center, University of Southern California, 1977. Annotations pulled
from other sources (uncredited) lessen the credibility of this
project. Shorts and feature films; subject index; periodic revi-
sions.

American Issues Forum Film List. New York: The Educational
Film Library Association, 1975. Over 200 films dealing with
U.S. history, government, politics, culture, and life-styles. Includes films relating to family life. With title and distributor
index.

Artel, Linda, and Susan Wengraf. Positive Images: Non-Sexist
Films for Young People. San Francisco: Booklegger Press,
1976. Brief evaluative annotations on 16mm films, videotapes,
filmstrips, slides, and a few photo collections. With subject and
distributor indexes, and selected resources. Family life films
scattered throughout; most suitable for adult audiences.

Betancourt, Jeanne. Women in Focus. Dayton, Ohio: Pflaum Publishing, 1974. Women filmmakers and films on women. Useful
suggestions for programming, thematic index, filmmaker filmographies, short critiques of selected films, distribution info, and
annotated bibliography by Madeline Warren.

Boyle, Deirdre, and Stephen J. Calvert, eds. Children's Media
Market Place. Syracuse, N.Y.: Gaylord Professional Publications, with Neal-Schuman Publishers, Inc., 1978. Comprehensive
resource guide for parents, writers, filmmakers, and teachers
on all aspects of children's media. Entries include relevant
names, phones, addresses, and media info.

Burleson, Derek L., and Gary Barbash, eds. Film Resources for
Sex Education. New York: SIECUS/Human Sciences Press, 1976.
Approximately 200 films, strips, slides, cassettes, and trans-
parencies reviewed by SIECUS (Sex Information and Education
Council of the U.S.) editorial staff or Board of Directors. Materials listed alphabetically by title, with brief annotations that
are sometimes evaluative, although "inclusion ... does not con-
stitute endorsement by SIECUS." With combination subject/au-
dience-level index and distributor index.

Covert, Nadine, and Esmé J. Dick. Alternatives. New York: Educational Film Library Association, 1974. 12-page annotated filmography of 121 films on alternative life-styles. Some dated distribution info.

Cripps, Thomas. Black Film as Genre. Bloomington: Indiana University Press, 1978. The author devotes a chapter to NOTHING BUT A MAN. Lengthy blacks-in-film bibliography.

Dawson, Bonnie, comp. Women's Films in Print: An Annotated Guide to 800 16mm Films by Women. San Francisco: Bookleg-ger Press, 1975. Organized alphabetically by filmmaker's name, with a subject index to help you find films that relate to family life. International in scope. Distribution info.

Family Life Literature and Films: An Annotated Bibliography. Minneapolis: Minnesota Council on Family Relations, 1972. Multi-ringed 353-page softcover book divided into subject categories/ chapters with print and a smattering of AV materials (films and strips) in most areas. A fine resource for books and periodicals. Two supplements are available at this writing (1974 and 1976). Brief descriptive annotations.

Ferris, Bill, and Judy Peiser, eds. American Folklore Films & Videotapes: An Index. Memphis, Tennessee: Center for Southern Folklore, 1976. 338 pages of over 1,800 annotated films and videotapes covering a wide range of general Americana--folklife and culture. The subject index alone is 95 pages! With distributor address index and useful index of films from each distributor. Also, a "Special Collections" section that lists films and tapes not available for national distribution.

Foote, Horton. The Screenplay of To Kill a Mockingbird. New York: Harcourt, Brace & World, Inc., 1964. With cast and credits and a short intro by Harper Lee.

French, Brandon. On the Verge of Revolt: Women in American Films of the Fifties. New York: Frederick Ungar Publishing Co., 1978. Individual chapters on THE MARRYING KIND, SHANE, THE COUNTRY GIRL, MARTY, and others.

French, Warren. Filmguide to The Grapes of Wrath. Bloomington: Indiana University Press, 1973. Study guide includes complete credits, plot outline, chapter on director John Ford, preproduction info, lengthy analysis, Ford filmography, bibliography, and discussion of the novel-into-film.

Gaffney, Maureen, ed. More Films Kids Like. Chicago: American Library Association, 1977. Update of Susan Rice's Films Kids Like. A compendium of new, short 16mm films tested with 3-to-12-year-old audiences over a two-year period. The tests were conducted by the Children's Film Theater (N.Y.C.) in school settings in Manhattan, Brooklyn, and upstate N.Y. With follow-up activities, distribution info, and selected subject index.   Films listed alphabetically by title.

Garrett, George P. , O. B. Hardison, Jr. , and Jane R. Gelfman. Film Scripts One. New York: Appleton-Century-Crofts, 1971. Includes the final shooting script of A STREETCAR NAMED DE- SIRE. With credits, awards.

Gordon, Ruth, and Garson Kanin. Adam's Rib. New York: Viking Press, 1972. From the M-G-M Library of Film Scripts series. With credits.

Haskell, Molly. From Reverence to Rape: The Treatment of Women in the Movies. New York: Holt, Rinehart and Winston, 1973. Her chapters cover the decades, beginning with the Twenties. A feminist tract by a reliable and readable critic. No biblio.

Howard, Jane. Families. New York: Simon and Schuster, 1978. A tribute to the endurance of the American family, and the place to begin any contemporary research on American family life.

Johnson, Harry A. , ed. Ethnic American Minorities: A Guide to Media and Materials. New York: R. R. Bowker Company, 1976. Afro-Americans, Asian Americans, native Indian Americans, and Spanish-speaking Americans each have lengthy chapters. A last chapter covers "other ethnic minorities"--Eskimos, Jews, and immigrants and ethnics in general. Excellent, comprehensive re- source for teachers, community programmers, and social service professionals.

Katz, John Stuart, ed. Autobiography: Film/Video/Photography. Canada: Art Gallery of Ontario, 1978. Published in conjunction with a major conference on autobiographical media, this beauti- fully illustrated catalog contains short chapters (with selected filmographies and bibliographies) on many top film and video art- ists who have worked in the autobiographical/diary/family film genre. Valuable reference text.

Kreuger, Miles. Show Boat: The Story of a Classic American Musi- cal. New York: Oxford University Press, 1977. The novel, stage plays, radio broadcasts, and the films, researched by a buff. Profusely illustrated.

Lawhon, Del, and Beth Dankert. Parenting Materials. Charleston, W. Va. : Appalachia Educational Laboratory, 1977. Multi-ringed catalog of AV materials (16mm films, slides, tapes, Super-8, strips) on parenting. 154 entries are evaluated, one entry to a page. Evaluations and plot summaries are minimal, however, and age/grade levels are often not given in "target audience" sec- tion. With subject index, title index, and distributor address list, as well as sample evaluation forms.

The MHMC Guide to Recent Mental Health Films. New York: Mental Health Materials Center, 1976. Includes short evaluative descriptions of 230 mental-health films and other AV materials, reviewed and evaluated between 1974 and 1975 by the staff of the Mental Health Materials Center in N. Y. C. With "multiple asterisk" rating system and brief annotations that also contain evaluative comments. Needs an overall title index: materials are listed according to subject area.

Maynard, Richard A. , ed. Scholastic's Literature of the Screen: Men and Women. New York: Scholastic Book Services, 1974. Screenplays taken from three films dealing with the theme of men and women: SPLENDOR IN THE GRASS, THE FAMILY WAY, and NOTHING BUT A MAN. These are not original shooting scripts or screenplays.

Mellen, Joan. Big Bad Wolves: Masculinity in the American Film. New York: Pantheon Books, 1977. Mellen takes on the male mystique in film: historical (decade study) and feminist point of view.

Moral Choices in Contemporary Society: An Annotated List of Films. New York: Educational Film Library Association, 1977. Critically annotated list of 16mm films that correlate with 16 topics in a University of California Courses by Newspaper project. Includes many films that deal with family issues. Distributor index.

Naiman, Adeline, ed. Clorae and Albie: Resource Book. Newton, Mass. : Education Development Center, 1975. Teacher's guide for use with the film. Short bibliography, scene outline, key dialogue, projects. For use in EDC's film-based curriculum project entitled "The Role of Women in American Society. "

Naiman, Adeline, ed. Resource Guide: Sally Garcia and Family. Newton, Mass. : Education Development Center, 1978. Teacher's guide for use with the film. Includes a short, critically annotated filmography. Again, part of the EDC project "The Role of Women in American Society. "

Naiman, Adeline, ed. Teacher's Guide to Girls At 12 and Student Resource Book for Girls At 12. Newton, Mass. : Education Development Center, 1975. To key students and teachers into EDC's "The Role of Women in American Society" project and use of GIRLS AT 12, in particular. Student resource book includes an extensive filmography of related films, a bibliography, and various hands-on activities.

Naremore, James. Filmguide to Psycho. Bloomington: Indiana University Press, 1973. With plot outline, credits, chapter on Hitchcock, the production, shot and plot analysis, filmography, bibliography.

National Catalog of Films in Special Education. Columbus, Ohio:
National Center on Educational Media and Materials for the Handicapped, 1977. The first edition (others projected) of films dealing with all areas of special education--family life included.
With helpful special-ed vocabulary. Films listed alphabetically
by title, with brief descriptions and distributor info, subject index, and list of producers and distributors. Compiled by the
staff of the New York State Education Dept. (Area Learning Resource Center) and the National Center on Educational Media and
Materials for the Handicapped.

Planned Parenthood Federation of America, comp.   Film Directory.
New York: Planned Parenthood Federation of America, n. d.
Films from Planned Parenthood and a variety of other producers
are listed under special subject headings. Strips and slides are
briefly noted. Short annotations; some critical commentary and
notes on use. Title and distributor index.

Rice, Susan, ed. Films Kids Like. Chicago: American Library
Association, 1973. Original volume documenting child-tested
16mm films and the work of the Children's Film Theater. Brief
programming and activity suggestions.

Rosen, Marjorie. Popcorn Venus: Women, Movies & the American
Dream. New York: Coward, McCann & Geoghegan, 1973. Lively,
in-depth panoramic history of women, on and off-screen, from
silents through sound and sex.

Schultz-Writsel, Lynn, Project Director. A Comprehensive Resource
Guide to 16mm Mental Health Films. Springfield, Va. : The Mental Health Media Evaluation Project, 1977. Briefly annotated list-
ing of some 1, 300 16mm films relating to mental health--many
cover family life. Comprehensive subject index. Films listed
alphabetically by title; also a 4-p. feature film section and distributor list.

Schultz-Writsel, Lynn, Project Director. An Evaluative Guide to
16mm Mental Health Films. Springfield, Va. : The Mental Health
Media Evaluation Project, 1977. Some 360 mental health (broad
distinction) films are evaluated by Mental Health Association volunteers and staff, film specialists, mental-health professionals,
and educators. Titles listed alphabetically are given a brief content description, notes for age and subject use, and a one-line
evaluation. With distributor list and subject index. Lists only
those films rated "good or above" and recommended by the Mental Health Association.

Spoto, Donald. Camerado: Hollywood and the American Man. New
York: New American Library, 1978. Husbands and lovers, cow-
boys and cops; another addition to the new film-book genre--men
in the movies--this was, at least, written by a man.

Trojan, Judith. Aging: A Filmography. New York: Educational
Film Library Association, 1974. 130 critically annotated 16mm
shorts about and for the aged. Includes a "selected features"
section, subject index, and distributor address list.

Tuchman, Gaye, Arlene Kaplan Daniels, and James Benét, eds.
Hearth & Home: Images of Women in the Mass Media. New
York: Oxford University Press, 1978. Anthology of reports by
social scientists and professionals in the communications, psychology, and sociology fields on "the images of women in the
media." Specifically examines sex-role stereotyping. Much on
television and print media. With an annotated bibliography on
"The Image of Women in Television."

Weibel, Kathryn. Mirror Mirror: Images of Women Reflected in
Popular Culture. New York: Anchor Books, 1977. With a
chapter on "Women in Television" and another on "Women in
Movies."

White, David Manning, and Richard Averson. The Celluloid Weapon:
Social Comment in the American Film. Boston: Beacon Press,
1972. Various family features abound in this over-sized, super-
ficial book, but a broad overview of the history of the message
film is to be had here.

Wilkes, Paul. Six American Families. New York: The Seabury
Press, 1977. Subtitled "An Insider's Look into the Families
Seen on National Television." Wilkes was the writer/host/re-
porter and one of the associate producers of the SIX AMERICAN
FAMILIES series. He devotes a chapter to each family and a
final chapter on finding and filming the families. With production
credits.

Wilson, Michael, and Deborah Silverton Rosenfelt. Salt of the Earth.
Old Westbury, N.Y.: The Feminist Press, 1978. A reprint of
the screenplay by Michael Wilson and a new commentary by Deborah Silverton Rosenfelt, which covers the history and climate
in which SALT OF THE EARTH grew. Plus short articles originally published in 1953 on the making of the film and written by
those who were involved in some way.

Worth, Sol, and John Adair. Through Navajo Eyes: An Exploration in Film Communication and Anthropology. Bloomington:
Indiana University Press, 1972. Account of the authors' work
with a group of Navajo Indians living in the Southwest. The authors taught them filmmaking and editing so that they could film
their lifestyle/culture from their own point of view. Teaching
problems, methodology, and description and analysis of the films
are reported in the book.

Zornow, Edith, and Ruth M. Goldstein. Movies for Kids. New
York: Avon Books, 1973. Subtitled "A Guide for Parents and
Teachers on the Entertainment Film for Children 9 to 13." 300

From Who Are the DeBolts?　Courtesy Pyramid Films.

features and shorts suitable for family viewing, and advice on "how to look at a movie. "

MEDIA DISTRIBUTORS & PUBLISHERS

Children's Television Workshop
Community Educational Services Division
One Lincoln Plaza
New York, NY　10023
212-595-3456
Makes available to parents and teachers the following materials geared to CTW's Sesame Street:　SESAME STREET SCRIPT HIGHLIGHTS--a $5 annual subscription brings weekly bulletins containing the contents, special activities, and instructional goals of upcoming shows.　THE MUPPET GALLERY--is available for $1 each, in English or Spanish, and introduces parents and teachers to the muppet stars, to help them clarify to their kids the roles and goals of each character.　With activities and stories-to-read-aloud.　SHARING THE STREET:　ACTIVITIES FOR ALL CHILDREN--an activity book for those working with kids with special needs; $2 each.　SESAME STREET ACTIVITIES--an activity manual for parents and teachers working with kids; $2 each; in English or Spanish.

CRM/McGraw-Hill Films
110 15th Street
Del Mar, CA　92014
714-453-5000
A fine catalog of psychology and guidance-oriented films; many deal with family issues.

Family Communications, Inc.
4802 Fifth Avenue
Pittsburgh, PA　15213
412-687-2990
A non-profit corporation formed in 1971 by Fred Rogers.　Not

only produces Mister Rogers' Neighborhood for PBS, but also other kinds of AV materials (videotapes, records, etc.) for children in the area of preventive mental health.

Family Films
14622 Lanark Street
Panorama City, CA 91402
213-997-7500
Offers a collection of short and feature-length 16mm dramatic films for rental; all dealing with Christian themes, and many relating to family living.

Learning Corporation of America
1350 Avenue of the Americas
New York, NY 10019
212-397-9330
Many family life and values entertainment shorts and features, for sale and rental, for children and adults. Many made-for-TV award winners.

MTI Teleprograms Inc.
3710 Commercial Avenue
Northbrook, IL 60062
Impressive collection of public-awareness and professional-training films on the subjects of child abuse and family violence.

The Media Guild
P.O. Box 881
Solana Beach, CA 92075
714-755-9191
See Paulist Productions below.

New Day Films
P.O. Box 315
Franklin Lakes, NJ 07417
201-891-8240
Distribution cooperative founded in 1972 by independent feminist filmmakers to handle films about women's issues (and men's). Many films are now classics. The filmmakers are available to speak with their films.

New York University Film Library
26 Washington Place
New York, NY 10003
212-598-2250
Professional-level films on child development, psychology, special education.

Parents' Magazine Films, Inc.
52 Vanderbilt Avenue
New York, NY 10017
212-661-9080
Offers filmstrip catalog with materials on child development,

parent education, family relationships, and handicapped children.

Paulist Productions
P. O. Box 1057
Pacific Palisades, CA 90272
213-454-0688
Specializes in Christian values dramas (Catholic point of view), many of which deal with family issues and engage top actors and directors.   Some titles are distributed by The Media Guild (see address above).

Pennsylvania State University
PCR Films
University Park, PA 16802
814-865-6314
PCR Films (Psychological Cinema Register) is a "nonprofit agency of Pennsylvania State University. It serves as an educational resource for films in the general areas of psychology, psychiatry, animal behavior, anthropology, and related behavioral sciences." A rental source, some sales films.

Perennial Education, Inc.
477 Roger Williams
P. O. Box 855
Ravinia
Highland Park, IL 60035
312-433-1610
Specializes in quality sex-education, family-planning, and -living films, videotapes, and strips for all ages and handicapped and retarded audiences, as well.

Polymorph Films, Inc.
118 South Street
Boston, MA 02111
617-542-2004
Seasonal catalogs of documentary films about family living are a specialty.

Serious Business Company
1145 Mandana Boulevard
Oakland, CA 94610
415-832-5600
Woman-owned and operated, this innovative distributor of mostly short, independent animated and experimental films, offers, in addition, an extremely attractive and useful catalog for programming purposes.

Time-Life Video
Time & Life Building
1271 Avenue of the Americas
New York, NY 10020
212-841-4554

Many family life TV specials, e. g. , <u>ABC Afterschool Specials</u>
are handled by this company in film and video formats.

PERIODICALS

<u>Film Library Quarterly</u>, Vol. 5, No. 1, Winter 1971-72.
Entire issue devoted to women in/on film.   Subscription info:
Film Library Information Council, Box 348, Radio City Station,
New York, NY   10019.

<u>Mass Media Newsletter</u>
2116 N. Charles Street
Baltimore MD 21218
Published twice monthly, except June, July, August, December.
A quality newsletter that covers many new 16mm film, TV, and
print releases on family, guidance, and religious themes.

<u>Media Report to Women</u>
3306 Ross Place, N. W.
Washington, D. C.   20008
Published monthly, with notices of media relating to feminist issues, parenting, children, etc.

<u>Ms.</u> , Vol. VII, No. 2, August 1978.
This issue inaugurates a series of articles on "Who Is the Real American Family?" In general, <u>Ms.</u> is the place to look for reviews of films
and books relating in some way to feminist concerns. <u>Ms.</u> Subscription
Dept. , 123 Garden Street, Marion, OH 43302.

<u>Parents' Magazine</u>
52 Vanderbilt Avenue
New York, NY   10017
This monthly includes in every issue a "Family Movie Guide, "
which rates current feature films to help parents monitor their
children's viewing.

<u>Perspectives on Film</u>, No. 1, September 1978.
The first issue of this in-house periodical, published as a service
to customers of the film collection of the Pennsylvania State Uni-
versity, Audio Visual Services, focuses on "Religion and the
American Family. " Films listed in articles and filmographies
are available for rental from the Penn State University collection,
Audio Visual Services, Special Services Building, University Park,
PA   16802.

<u>Rehabfilm Newsletter</u>
20 West 40 Street
New York, NY   10018
Quarterly newsletter published by the International Rehabilitation
Film Review Library.   News of TV productions, AV materials,
and conferences relating to special education and rehabilitation of
the handicapped.

Sightlines, Vol. 11, No. 3, Spring 1978.
Entire issue of this quarterly devoted to Family Life films, with
12 p. pullout section entitled young viewers, which deals with
media for children. Subscription info: The Educational Film
Library Association, Inc. , 43 West 61 Street, New York, NY
10023.

DISTRIBUTOR ADDRESS LIST

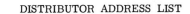

ABC Wide World of Learning
1330 Avenue of the Americas
New York, NY   10019

AIMS Instructional Media Services Inc.
626 Justin Avenue
Glendale, CA   91201

Agency for Instructional TV
Box A
Bloomington, IN   47401

American Cancer Society
777 Third Avenue
New York, NY   10017

American Educational Films
132 Lasky Drive
P. O. Box 5001
Beverly Hills, CA   90212

American Personnel and Guid-
ance Association
Film Department
Two Skyline Place, Suite 400
5203 Leesburg Pike
Falls Church, VA   22041

American Society for Psycho-
prophylaxis in Obstetrics,
Inc.
1411 K Street, NW, #200
Washington, DC   20005

Appalshop Films
Box 743
Whitesburg, KY   41858

Association Films, Inc.
866 Third Avenue
New York, NY   10022

Atlantis Productions, Inc.
1252 La Granada Drive
Thousand Oaks, CA   91360

Audio Brandon Films, Inc.
34 MacQuesten Parkway South
Mount Vernon, NY   10550

BFA Educational Media
2211 Michigan Avenue
P. O. Box 1795
Santa Monica, CA   90406

Balkan Arts Center
P. O. Box 315
Franklin Lakes, NJ   07417

Bandanna Media, Inc.
William R. Pace
36640 Howard
Farmington Hills, MI   48018

Barr Films
3490 E. Foothill Boulevard
P. O. Box 5667
Pasadena, CA   91107

Behavioral Images
302 Leland Street
Bloomington, IL   61701

Benchmark Films, Inc.
145 Scarborough Road
Briarcliff Manor, NY   10510

Penny Bernstein
55 Leroy Street
New York, NY   10014

Blackwood Productions Inc.
251 West 57 Street
New York, NY   10019

Brakhage Films
c/o Jane Brakhage
Box 170
Rollinsville, CO   80474

Brigham Young University
Media Marketing, W-STAD
Provo, UT   84602

William Brose Productions, Inc.
10850 Riverside Drive
North Hollywood, CA   91602

Billy Budd Films, Inc.
235 E. 57 Street, Rm. 8D
New York, NY   10022

Budget Films
4590 Santa Monica Boulevard
Los Angeles, CA 90029

Bullfrog Films, Inc.
Oley, PA 19547

CRM/McGraw-Hill Films
110 15th Street
Del Mar, CA 92014

California Newsreel
630 Natoma Street
San Francisco, CA 94103

Calvin Communications, Inc.
1105 Truman Road
P. O. Box 15607
Kansas City, MO 64106

Canyon Cinema Cooperative
2325 Third Street, Suite 338
San Francisco, CA 94107

Carousel Films, Inc.
1501 Broadway
New York, NY 10036

Case Western Reserve University
versity
Health Sciences Communications
Center
2119 Abington Road
Cleveland, OH 44106

Center for Southern Folklore
1216 Peabody Avenue
P. O. Box 4081
Memphis, TN 38104

Center for Urban Education
0245 S. W. Bancroft
Portland, OR 97201

Centron Films
1621 West Ninth Street
Box 687
Lawrence, KS 66044

Children's Home Society of California
fornia
Public Affairs Department
5429 McConnell Avenue
Los Angeles, CA 90066

Children's Rehabilitation Unit
University of Kansas Medical
Center
39th & Rainbow
Kansas City, KS 66103

Churchill Films
662 North Robertson Boulevard
vard
Los Angeles, CA 90069

Cinema 5--16mm
595 Madison Avenue
New York, NY 10022

Cinema Medica, Inc.
2335 W. Foster Avenue
Chicago, IL 60625

Maxi Cohen & Joel Gold
31 Greene Street
New York, NY 10013

Corinth Films
410 East 62 Street
New York, NY 10021

Coronet Films
65 E. South Water Street
Chicago, IL 60601

Counterpoint Films
14622 Lanark Street
Panorama City, CA 91402

Mai Cramer
61 Jackson Street
Cambridge, MA 02140, or
Mai Cramer
Salisbury Road
Sheffield, MA 01257

Creative Film Society
7237 Canby Avenue
Reseda, CA 91335

Crystal-Nonas Films
1221 Sunset Plaza Drive
Los Angeles, CA 90069

Tom Davenport Films
Delaplane, VA 22025

Davidson Films, Inc.
850 O'Neill Avenue
Belmont, CA 94002

Sid Davis Productions
c/o Davis Communications
Media--DACOM
626 Justin Avenue
Glendale, CA 91201

De Nonno Pix Inc.
7119 Shore Road
Brooklyn, NY 11209

Dennis Films, Inc.
161 E. Erie Street
Chicago, IL 60611

Diocese of Buffalo
Office of Communications
100 South Elmwood Avenue
Buffalo, NY 14202

Direct Cinema Limited
P. O. Box 69589
Los Angeles, CA 90069

Walt Disney Educational Media
Company
500 South Buena Vista Street
Burbank, CA 91521

Document Associates, Inc.
211 East 43 Street
New York, NY 10017

Documentaries for Learning
Harvard Mental Health Film
Program
Edward A. Mason, M. D., Director
58 Fenwood Road
Boston, MA 02115

Education Development Center
Distribution Center
39 Chapel Street
Newton, MA 02160

Educational Film Systems, Inc.
11466 San Vicente Boulevard
Los Angeles, CA 90049

Encyclopaedia Britannica Educational Corporation
425 North Michigan Avenue
Chicago, IL 60611

Mary Elaine Evans
P. O. Box 02046
Columbus, OH 43202

FMS Productions Inc.
1040 North Las Palmas Avenue
Los Angeles, CA 90038

Faces International Films Inc.
650 North Bronson Avenue
Los Angeles, CA 90004

Fenwick Productions
Box 277
West Hartford, CT 06107

Film & Video Service
P. O. Box 299
Wheaton, IL 60187

Film Communicators
11136 Weddington Street
No. Hollywood, CA 91601

Film Images
1034 Lake Street
Oak Park, IL 60301

Filmakers Library Inc.
133 East 58 Street, Suite 703A
New York, NY 10022

FilmFair Communications
10900 Ventura Boulevard
P. O. Box 1728
Studio City, CA 91604

Film-Makers' Cooperative
175 Lexington Avenue
New York, NY 10016

Films for the Humanities
P. O. Box 2053
Princeton, NJ 08540

Films Inc.
733 Green Bay Road
Wilmette, IL 60091

FilmWright
4530 18th Street
San Francisco, CA 94114

Focus International Inc.
1776 Broadway
New York, NY 10019

Joel Gold see Maxi Cohen

Allan Grant Productions
P.O. Box 49244
Los Angeles, CA 90049

Carol Greenfield
215-01 89th Avenue
Queens Village, NY 11427

Grove Press Film Division
196 West Houston Street
New York, NY 10014

Alfred Guzzetti
167 Babcock Street
Brookline, MA 02146

Harper & Row Media
10 East 53 Street
New York, NY 10022

Harvest Films, Inc.
309 Fifth Avenue
New York, NY 10016

Haymarket Films
1901 W. Wellington Avenue
Chicago, IL 60657

Alfred Higgins Productions, Inc.
9100 Sunset Boulevard
Los Angeles, CA 90069

Home Owners Warranty Corp.
National Housing Center
15th & M Streets, NW
Washington, DC 20005

Human Resources Development
Trust
B.C.P.O. Box 3006
East Orange, NJ 07019

Hurlock Cine World
13 Arcadia Road
Old Greenwich, CT 06870

Image Associates
P.O. Box 40106
352 Conejo Road
Santa Barbara, CA 93103

Image Resources
P.O. Box 315
Franklin Lakes, NJ 07417

Images
300 Phillips Park Road
Mamaroneck, NY 10543

Indiana University
Audio-Visual Center
Bloomington, IN 47401

Institute for Policy Studies
1901 Q Street, NW
Washington, DC 20006
Attn: Penny Bernstein

Institutional Cinema Inc.
10 First Street
Saugerties, NY 12477

International Film Bureau Inc.
332 South Michigan Avenue
Chicago, IL 60604

Iris Films
Box 5353
Berkeley, CA 94705

Ivy Film
165 West 46 Street
New York, NY 10036

Journal Films, Inc.
930 Pitner Avenue
Evanston, IL 60202

The Junior League of
Louisville
627 West Main Street
Louisville, KY 40202

Kinetic Film Enterprises Ltd.
781 Gerrard Street East
Toronto, Ontario Canada
M4M 1Y5

Lawren Productions, Inc.
P. O. Box 666
Mendocino, CA 95460

Learning Corp. of America
1350 Avenue of the Americas
New York, NY 10019

J. B. Lippincott Company
Audiovisual Department
East Washington Square
Philadelphia, PA 19105

The Little Red Filmhouse
666 No. Robertson Boulevard
Los Angeles, CA 90069

Lodon Films
c/o Lois Goodkind
52 Undercliff Terrace South
West Orange, NJ 07052

Ellen Lorbetske
1251 W. Thorndale Avenue # 1
Chicago, IL 60660

Lucerne Films Inc.
7 Bahama Road
Morris Plains, NJ 07950

MTI Teleprograms Inc.
3710 Commercial Avenue
Northbrook, IL 60062

Macmillan Films, Inc.
34 MacQuesten Parkway South
Mount Vernon, NY 10550

Mass Media Ministries
2116 North Charles Street
Baltimore, MD 21218

Maysles Films, Inc.
250 West 54 Street
New York, NY 10019

McGraw-Hill Films
110 15th Street
Del Mar, CA 92014

The Media Guild
118 South Acacia
P. O. Box 881
Solana Beach, CA 92075

Media Projects, Inc.
5215 Homer Street
Dallas, TX 75206

Meyer Children's Rehabilitation
   Institute
Media Resource Center
444 South 44 Street
Omaha, NB 68131

Miller Productions, Inc.
P. O. Box 5584
Austin, TX 78763

Modern Talking Picture Service,
   Inc.
5000 Park Street North
St. Petersburg, FL 33709

Motion, Inc.
4437 Klingle Street, NW
Washington, DC 20016

Mountain Moving Picture Co.
Box 1952
Evergreen, CO 80439

Multi Media Resource Center
1525 Franklin Street
San Francisco, CA 94109

Multimedia Program Productions
140 West Ninth Street
Cincinnati, OH 45202

Museum of Modern Art
Dept. of Film Circulation
11 West 53 Street
New York, NY 10019

National Audiovisual Center
General Services Administration
Washington, DC 20409

National Film Board of Canada
1251 Avenue of the Americas
16th Floor
New York, NY 10020

National Fire Protection Assoc.
Publications Sales Dept.
470 Atlantic Avenue
Boston, MA   02210

National Geographic Society
Educational Services
17th & M Streets, NW
Washington, DC   20036

National Society for the Prevention of Blindness
79 Madison Avenue
New York, NY   10016

New Day Films
P. O. Box 315
Franklin Lakes, NJ   07417

New Line Cinema Corp.
853 Broadway
New York, NY   10003

New York State Society for Autistic Children
169 Tampa Avenue
Albany, NY   12208
Attn: Ruth Dyer

New York University
Film Library
26 Washington Place
New York, NY   10003

New Yorker Films
16 West 61 Street
New York, NY   10023

Robert Newman
United Church Board for Homeland Ministries
287 Park Avenue South
New York, NY   10010

Eliot Noyes Productions
117 Prince Street
New York, NY   10012

Odeon Films
P. O. Box 315
Franklin Lakes, NJ   07417

Orlando Public Library
10 N. Rosalind
Orlando, FL   32801

PRP Productions
1765 P Street, NW
Washington, DC   20036

Pacific Street Film Collective
P. O. Box 315
Franklin Lakes, NJ   07417

Paramount Communications
5451 Marathon Street
Hollywood, CA   90038

Paramount Pictures Corp.
Non-Theatrical Division
5451 Marathon Street
Hollywood, CA   90038

Parenting Pictures
121 N. W. Crystal Street
Crystal River, FL   32629

Parents' Magazine Films, Inc.
52 Vanderbilt Avenue
New York, NY   10017

Kit Parker Films
Carmel Valley, CA   93924

Paulist Productions
P. O. Box 1057
Pacific Palisades, CA   90272

Pear Films Company
13041 10th Avenue South
Seattle, WA   98168

Pennsylvania State University
Audio Visual Services
Special Services Building
University Park, PA   16802

Perennial Education, Inc.
477 Roger Williams
P. O. Box 855
Ravinia
Highland Park, IL   60035

Perspective Films
369 West Erie Street
Chicago, IL   60610

Phoenix Films, Inc.
470 Park Avenue South
New York, NY   10016

Pictura Films
111 Eighth Avenue
New York, NY   10011

Polymorph Films, Inc.
118 South Street
Boston, MA   02111

Pyramid Films
Box 1048
Santa Monica, CA   90406

Radom Productions
477 Roger Williams
P.O. Box 855
Ravinia
Highland Park, IL   60035

Read Natural Childbirth Foundation
1300 South Eliseo Drive, Suite 102
Greenbrae, CA   94904

Research Press
2612 North Mattis
Champaign, IL   61820

Richfield Productions
8006 Takoma Avenue
Silver Spring, MD   20910

The Dick Roberts Film Co., Inc.
48 West 10 Street
New York, NY   10011

S-L Film Productions
P.O. Box 41108
Los Angeles, CA   90041

Gary Schlosser
8777 Skyline Drive
Los Angeles, CA   90046

Jerome L. Schulman, M.D.
Children's Memorial Hospital
2300 Children's Plaza
Chicago, IL   60614

Screen Education Enterprises, Inc.
P.O. Box C-19126
Seattle, WA   98109

Serious Business Company
1145 Mandana Boulevard
Oakland, CA   94610

Shadowstone Films
1402 Duke University Road
Durham, NC   27701

Silo Cinema, Inc.
P.O. Box 315
Franklin Lakes, NJ   07417

Smithsonian Institution
Folklife Programs
L'Enfant Plaza
Washington, DC   20024

Society for Nutrition Education
2140 Shattuck Avenue, Suite 1110
Berkeley, CA   94704

Southerby Productions Inc.
1709 E. 28 Street
Long Beach, CA   90806

Special Purpose Films, Inc.
26740 Latigo Shore Drive
Malibu, CA   90265

The Stanfield House
12381 Wilshire Boulevard
Los Angeles, CA   90025

Martha Stuart Communications, Inc.
P.O. Box 127
Hillsdale, NY   12529

Swank Motion Pictures, Inc.
201 South Jefferson Avenue
St. Louis, MO   63103

TeleKETICS
Franciscan Communications Center
1229 South Santee Street
Los Angeles, CA   90015

Temple University
Department of Radio-TV-Film
Annenberg 102
Philadelphia, PA   19122
Attn: Distribution Coordinator

Texture Films, Inc.
1600 Broadway
New York, NY   10019

Third Eye Films
12 Arrow Street
Cambridge, MA   02138

Third World Newsreel
160 Fifth Avenue, Rm. 911
New York, NY   10010

Time-Life Multimedia
c/o Time-Life Video
Time & Life Building
1271 Avenue of the Americas
New York, NY   10020

Trainex Corporation
12601 Industry Street
Garden Grove, CA   92641

Transactional Dynamics Institute
P. O. Box 414
Glenside, PA   19038

Tricontinental Film Center
c/o UNIFILM
419 Park Avenue South
19th Floor
New York, NY   10016

Tupperware Home Parties
Educational Services
P. O. Box 2353
Orlando, FL   32802

Twyman Films, Inc.
4700 Wadsworth Road
Box 605
Dayton, OH   45401

US Films
310 West 14 Street
New York, NY   10014

United Artists/16
729 Seventh Avenue
New York, NY   10019

United Films
1425 South Main
Tulsa, OK   74119

United Way of America
801 N. Fairfax Street
Alexandria, VA   22314
Attn: Archives

Universal/16
445 Park Avenue
New York, NY   10022

University of California
Extension Media Center
2223 Fulton Street
Berkeley, CA   94720

University of Michigan
Media Resources Center
400 Fourth Street
Ann Arbor, MI   48109

University of Minnesota
Audio Visual Library Service
3300 University Avenue South-
east
Minneapolis, MN   55414

University of Southern Califor-
nia
Film Distribution Center
Division of Cinema-Television
University Park
Los Angeles, CA   90007

Urbanimage Corporation
253 Summer Street
Boston, MA   02210

Victoria Films
Heron House, Suite 103
Reston, VA   22090

From Getting Married. Courtesy BFA Educational Media.

Viewfinders, Inc.
800 Custer Avenue
P. O. Box 1665
Evanston, IL 60204

WAVE-TV
P. O. Box 32970
Louisville, KY 40232

WGBH-TV Educational Foundation
125 Western Avenue
Boston, MA 02134

WNET/Thirteen
Media Services
356 West 58 Street
New York, NY 10019

Miriam Weinstein
36 Shepard Street
Cambridge, MA 02138

Westcoast Films
25 Lusk Street
San Francisco, CA 94107

Weston Woods
Weston, CT 06883

Woman's Eye
Multi-Media Productions
7909 Sycamore Drive
Falls Church, VA 22042

Wombat Productions, Inc.
Little Lake, Glendale Road
P. O. Box 70
Ossining, NY 10562

Women Make Movies, Inc.
257 West 19 Street
New York, NY 10011

Xerox Films
245 Long Hill Road
Middletown, CT 06457

Zipporah Films
54 Lewis Wharf
Boston, MA 02110

Numbers refer to entry, not to page.

Nine Months in Motion 1022
1900: Passing of an Age 1023
Nixon's Checkers Speech 1024
No Down Payment 1898
No Hiding Place 1025
No Place Like Home Series 1026
No Tears for Kelsey 1027
No Trespassing 1028
Nobody Important 1029
The North American Indian--Part
   III Series 1030
North American Indians Today
   Series 1031
Northeast Farm Community 1032
Not by Chance 1033
Not Me Alone 1034
Not Together Now: End of a Mar-
   riage 1035
Notable Contributors to the Psy-
   chology of Personality Series
   1036
Notes on an Appalachia County:
   Visiting with Darlene 1037
Nothing but a Man 1899
Now and Forever 1900
Now, Voyager 1901
Now We Live on Clifton 1038
Nueva: An Alternative 1039
Nursery School Child-Mother In-
   teraction: Three Head Start
   Children and Their Mothers
   1040
Nursing Series 1041
Nurturing 1042
Nutrition and Dental Care in
   Pregnancy 1043
Nutrition Education Series 1044
Nutrition: The Consumer and the
   Supermarket 1045

Obsession 1902
The Odd Couple 1903
Of Sugar Cane and Syrup 1046
Oh Dad, Poor Dad, Mama's Hung
   You in the Closet and I'm
   Feeling so Sad 1904
The Okies--Uprooted Farmers
   1047
Old Enough to Know 1048
Old-Fashioned Woman 1049
Old Yeller 1905
Olivia: Mexican or American--

Differences in the Family
   1050
Omowale--The Child Returns
   Home 1051
On Being an Effective Parent
   (Thomas Gordon) 1052
On Being Sexual 1053
On Death and Dying 1054
On the Run 1055
On the Seventh Day 1056
On the Waterfront 1906
Once Is Not Enough 1907
The One and Only 1908
The One and Only Genuine
   Original Family Band 1909
One and the Same 1057
One-Eyed Jacks 1910
One Foot in Heaven 1911
One Generation Is Not Enough
   1058
One Hour a Week 1059
One Is a Lonely Number 1912
One More Time 1060
One More Year on the Family
   Farm? 1061
One of a Kind 1062
One Potato, Two Potato 1913
One Special Dog 1063
One to Grow On Series 1064
Ordinary People 1065
The Oregon Trail 1066
The Originals: Women in Art
   Series 1067
Oscar at Home 1068
The Other 1914
The Other Side of the Moun-
   tain 1915
The Other Side of the Moun-
   tain, Part 2 1916
Our Daily Bread 1917
Our Family Album/Nuestro Al-
   bum de la Familia! 1069
Our Family Works Together
   (2nd Edition) 1070
Our Little Munchkin Here 1071
Our Own Two Hands 1072
Our Relations 1918
Our Totem Is the Raven 1073
Our Town 1919
Our Vines Have Tender Grapes
   1920
Ourstory Series 1074
The Out-of-Towners 1921

Sweethearts   2033
Sylvia, Fran and Joy   1343

Take Her, She's Mine   2034
Taking Care of Business   1344
Taking Measure   1345
Taking Off   2035
A Tale of Today   1346
Talent for Tony   1347
Talking About Breastfeeding   1348
Talking Together   1349
The Tap Dance Kid   1350
Tapestry of Faith   1351
Teachers, Parents and Children
   1352
The Teaching Triad   1353
Teenage Father   1354
Teenage Mother: A Broken Dream
   1355
The Teenage Years Series   1356
Telespots Series   1357
Tell Me My Name   1358
Tell Me Where It Hurts   2036
Tender Comrade   2037
The Tenement   1359
Tennis Mothers   1360
Tenth Avenue Angel   2038
Testament   1361
That Great Feeling   1362
That's Our Baby   1363
The Theft   1364
Their Special Needs   1365
There's Always Tomorrow   2039
There's Always Tomorrow   2040
There's No Business Like Show
   Business   2041
They're Attacking My Tree Fort
   1366
Thieves   2042
Thigh Line Lyre Triangular   1367
The Thin Edge Series   1368
The Thin Man Series   2043
Things Are Different Now   1369
Things, Ideas, People   1370
Things in Their Season   2044
Third Generation   1371
Thirdstring   1372
The 30-Second Dream   1373
This Child Is Rated X   1374
This Earth Is Mine   2045
This Is It   1375
This Is the Home of Mrs. Levant
   Graham   1376

This One for Dad   1377
This Property Is Condemned
   2046
The Thorne Family Film   1378
Thornton Wilder   1379
Those Calloways   2047
Those Mail Order Millions
   1380
Those Who Mourn   1381
Those Who Stay Behind   1382
Though I Walk Through the
   Valley   1383
A Thousand Clowns   2048
Three-Cornered Moon   2049
Three Daring Daughters   2050
The Three Faces of Eve   2051
Three Films   1384
Three Secrets   2052
Three Smart Girls   2053
Three Smart Girls Grow Up
   2054
Three Styles of Marital Con-
   flict   1385
Three Violent People   2055
Three's a Crowd   1386
The Thrill of It All   2056
A Ticklish Affair   2057
Tillie's Philodendron   1387
A Time for Decision   1388
The Time Has Come   1389
Time Structures   1390
A Time to Be Born   1391
Time's Lost Children   1392
To a Babysitter (2nd Edition)
   1393
To All the World's Children
   1394
To Be a Family   1395
To Be a Man   1396
To Be a Parent   1397
To Be Growing Older   1398
To Be Married   1399
To Each His Own   2058
To Find a Man   2059
To Kill a Mockingbird   2060
To Life, with Love   1400
To Live Again Series   1401
To Live as Equals   1402
To Nourish a Child: Nutrition
   from Newborn Through Teens
   1403
Tobacco Road   2061
Todd--Growing Up in Appala-
   chia   1404